Science Education in Asia and the Pacific

INTERNATIONAL ENCYCLOPAEDIA OF SCIENCE AND TECHNOLOGY EDUCATION 4

SCIENCE EDUCATION IN ASIA AND THE PACIFIC

By

Dr. Digumarti Bhaskara Rao
M.Sc., M.A., M.A., M.Ed., Ph.D.
Dean, Faculty of Education
Member, Academic Senate
Ex-Chairman, Board of Studies in Education
Member, Research Advisory Committee
Acharya Nagarjuna University
D-43, S.V.N. Colony
Guntur-522 006 (India)

DISCOVERY PUBLISHING HOUSE PVT. LTD.
NEW DELHI-110 002

Edition – 2016

ISBN: 978-81-7141-548-9 (Set)

International Encyclopaedia of Science and Technology Education

Published by:

DISCOVERY PUBLISHING HOUSE PVT. LTD.
4383/4B, Ansari Road Darya Ganj
New Delhi - 110 002 (India)
Phone: +91-11-23279245, 43596064-65
Fax: +91-11-23253475
E-mail: discoverypublishinghouse@gmail.com
sales@discoverypublishinggroup.com
web: www.discoverypublishinggroup.com

Printed at:
Infinity Imaging Systems
Delhi

Preface

Science and Technology have occupied almost all spheres of human life. The wonderful achievements of science and technology have glorified the modern world and transformed the modern civilization into a scientific and technological civilization. Considering the importance of science and technology, they have been incorporated in every stage of education.

This International Encyclopaedia of Science and Technology Education is developed covering a wide range of aspects related to science and technology education for the benefit of all those who are associated with science and technology education. This Encyclopaedia is consisting of eleven volumes, namely:

1. Science and Technology Education,
2. Science Education in Developing Countries,
3. Organisational Structure of Science,
4. Science Education in Asia and the Pacific,
5. Science and Technology Education for All,
6. Values, Ethics, Talent and Girls in Science and Technology Education,
7. Popularisation of Science and Technology Education,
8. Science, Power and Society
9. Information Technology,
10. Teacher Training in Science and Technology Education and
11. Science, Technology and Society—A Curriculum Framework.

I convey my cordial thanks to UNESCO-PROAP, Bangkok, Thailand; UNESCO-ROSTE, Venice, Italy; UNESCO Paris, France; IIEP, Paris, France; Commonwealth Secretariat, London, UK; UNCTAD, Geneva, Switzerland, Queen's University, Kingston, Canada; and Alberta Education, Edmonton, Canada for their kind co-operation in preparing this Encyclopaedia.

DR. DIGUMARTI BHASKARA RAO
Secretary
Academy of Communication Culture Education
Science and Service
GUNTUR (A.P.)

Contents

An Introduction to Science and Technology Education in Asia and The Pecific

What is Science?

The world in which we live is, in some ways, still much the same as it has always been science Man first began to try to understand it. It is the world of light and darkness, of earth, sun and the universe; the world of time and motion, of seasons and climates, of forces and energy and matter. It is a world of land and sea, of plants, animals and of ourselves; a world of growing and developing, of procreation, of aging and dying. It is a world of winds and clouds, of rains, typhoons and monsoons, of rocks and soils and of thousands of other things and events. It is also a world of Man's inventiveness form the simplest of tools to the most sophisticated of satellites.

Man has learned how to live in this world, to conquer it, not by force but by understanding. And understanding is the quest of science. Superstition and magic have often taken the place of understanding. But slowly an organized and ordered way of looking at the physical world, and learning from it. Has emerged and this we call the process of science. Science is thus a special interaction between the searching human mind and the physical biological world in which we live.

Science is a process of diligence, refined over the years, by which we observe things as they are and events as they happen. It strives to be precise and accurate. It is a process of ordering and classifying and so of establishing relationships; of formulations, explanations and hypotheses, through experiments. And so of understanding our world.

The aim of science is the understanding of laws of nature which are independent of the human mind, but the human mind itself is a function of brain cells well as its spiritual nature.

Asking questions and solving problems, following the processes of science, is an intellectual strategy which every learning human being should adopt. It is one of the most powerful tools in man's quest for understanding, for sharpening his power of reasoning, for developing the world in which he lives and for enhancing the quality of life.

What is Technology?

Technology is the applications of science, and like science it self, can be traced back to be earliest days when Man first began to adapt to living in the world.

At the personal and national levels the applications of science—that is, technology—have developed in various forms over the centuries, from the earliest crude tools of stone age men to the sophisticated personal technology of today and to the even more sophisticated technology of nations. Technology is manifest in the applications of science to health, nutrition, medicine, sanitation, agriculture, engineering and in the general creative response of Man to the problems of his life and his environment.

On course the applications of science through technology and industrialization can lead to pollution, depletion of resources and other environmental damage. This is the area where values and ethics impinge on science and technology, where personal and social attitudes are all important and where the proper and responsible use of science and technology is an argent need for all nations and for all individuals.

Science and Technology Education

The need for all citizens—in school or in the community in general—to have some understanding of science and technology and their role in society, is the message of this publication. The motto 'Science for All' reflects the recognition of science and technology as being of value for the individual, for the community and for society as a whole. It also reflects the need to demoratize science, to make science available for all as part of culture and society. A scientifically informed populace can more easily take part in and support national and local decision-making which involves technological change and relate such changes to their won moral and cultural values. In addition, it provides a wide talent base from whom technical and scientific specialists may arise. But, above all, science and technology education means the provision to all individuals, through national programmes and in other ways, of scientific competencies, knowledge and skills which will improve their quality of life and contribute to community national and economic development.

General Education Problems, Issues and Trends

Population. About 60 per cent of the world's population—2.8 billion—live have in the Asia and Pecific region. By the end of the century the population of the region will be about 3.5 billion. At present 40 per cent of the population is under the age of 15 years and the annual rate of increase of the school-going age group is five times more than that of the total population. Furthermore, the majority of people live in rural areas (60-70 per cent).

The implications of all this for the educational systems of the region are considerable and the problems enormous.

Recent History of Educational Development in the Region. In most countries the concept of education was—and still is in some cases—the preparation of trained manpower with priority given to secondary and higher levels of education and to formal education rather than adult or non-formal education.

The consequences have been an increase in the number of illiterates, despite the expansion of the formal system; an increase in the number of unemployed or underemployed; and a general support for, in some cases, a small industrial sector based on Western methodology, rather than on the much larger traditional craft economy.

Thus, the educational system as a whole has continued to support or serve the interests of socially and intellectually privileged groups rather than society in general.

Recent Trends and New Directions. Among the major trends in the region are:

(a) The move to make primary education universally available in those countries where, at present, primary education is not enjoyed by the whole of the primary age group;

(b) The emphasis on adult literacy;

(c) The change in secondary education from an academic education for the elite to a general education for all with greater flexibility in curricula and with more relevance to local society, including job-oriented curricula and links between education and work; and

(d) Development of non-formal education, based on community needs, as complementary to the formal education system—with links between the two.

Science and Technology Education within the Formal Educational Systems

National Science Policies. Most countries in Asia and Pecific have national science policies, usually linking scientific and industrial research and development with economic development and national goals. In a few countries—Bangladesh, China, India, Japan, Malaysia and Sri Lanka—the importance of science education is specifically mentioned in the national science policy. The Republic of Korea and Japan have a 'Science education promotion law', Pakistan has a National Education Policy specifically concerned with science education, and the Philippines is adopting a 'Science education development plan'. In the other countries, the growing recognition of the importance of science education at all levels is implicit.

Science Education at Primary Level. All countries in the region have improved their primary education—both qualitatively and quantitatively. Science is taught as a core subject in all countries, but not necessarily form the first grade.

In some countries science is presented as part of 'Environmental studies' or as 'General science' from from grade I; in other it is introduced for the first time from grade III.

However, the time available for science varies considerably from country to country.

In every country the objectives of teaching science at this level are carefully prescribed. Many such objectives emphasized the need for primary school children to understand nature, to appreciate the environment and to develop enquiring minds and process skills. The content of primary science course invariably includes topics such as earth, soil, rocks, the universe, air, water, human body, health and nutrition, living creatures and natural resources.

This emphasis on the local environment and nature and on learning by doing is not always reflected in the time available for practical activities. In some countries the practical aspects are left entirely in the hands of the teachers to organize as demand appropriate. In others (e.g. Japan, Malaysia, New Zealand, the Philippines, the Republic of Korea, Singapore, the Socialist Republic of Viet Nam, Thailand), a high proportion of time (about 50 per cent or more) is prescribed for practical science learning activities. Such activities—in all countries—are usually conducted in the primary school classroom and not in a laboratory; with locally available materials or with specially-designed kits of apparatus, locally-made with low-cost equipment. In some cases use of the local environment such as the school compound, school garden and village environment is part of the practical work.

There are, however, severe constraints operating in almost all the countries in the region which make the full value of practical work difficult to achieve. These constraints include shortage of materials, kits and equipment, large classes, and most serious of all, untrained or unqualified teachers.

Science Education at the Secondary level. The changes in secondary education, in general, have been less spectacular than at the primary level; and in science education the approach at this level, in most countries is still academic, elitist and subject-oriented.

At lower secondary level—grades VI to VIII—science is usually now a compulsory core subject and is often taught as an integrated or general science. In some, however, separate sciences of biology, chemistry and physics, are offered even at this level (e.g. in India, the Lao People's Democratic Republic, Maldives, Mongolia, Socialist Republic of Viet Nam and the Union of Soviet Socialist Republics). The time available for science at junior secondary level varies between 15 per cent and 25-30 per cent.

At the upper secondary level science education is mostly in the form of separate sciences and in many countries is an optional or elective course. However, in China, the Lao People's Democratic Republic, Mongolia, the Philippines, the Republic of Korea, Thailand, Socialist Republic of Viet Nam and the Union of Soviet Socialist Republics, science is compulsory for all students right up to the end of the secondary stage. Where science is offered as an elective subject, the time available varies from about 35 per cent to as much as 60 per cent and, in many cases, practical activities can occupy nearly half the time.

With a few notable exceptions (the Union of Soviet Socialist Republics and Socialist Republic of Viet Nam for example) where emphasis is given to work experience, and to the polytechnic approach within schools, the majority of students still receive secondary science as a traditional orientation for universities and other forms of higher education. The curricula are not, generally speaking, relevant to the world of work and to the learner's social and physical environment. Technology education is not given sufficient emphasis.

These problems, which exist in the majority of the countries are recognized by the authorities but so far have not yet been overcome. This is due in large measures, to the problems of teacher retraining, as well as in some countries, to the undue influence of national examinations and of tertiary institutions. The attitudes of parents and of the students themselves, who traditionally believe that an 'academic' education is the 'best' route for successes in life, is another dominant factor in many countries.

School Science Equipment and Educational Technology. The design, development, production and financial provision of science equipment countries to be a major constraint in a large number of countries. Some countries (e.g. Banglades, China, India, Lao People's Democratic Republic, Nepal, Pakistan, and the Philippines) report that more than 80 per cent of school are poorly equipped or have no equipment at all. These countries, and many others, have established equipment centres to help in the design and development to production stage of locally made equipment. Other countries, of course, are already .able to manufacture most of their school equipment requirements within the state or private enterprises of the individual country.

Many countries report instances of equipment not being properly used by the teachers and not properly stored or maintained. Indeed, repair and maintenance of equipment—and the financial support that this demands is just not possible in many systems. This is where kits of apparatus have been generously supplied by international or bilateral aid agencies.

The situation regarding educational technology is probably much worse. Even the simplest of audio-visual aids are lacking in many countries and provision of the basic 'software' is the greatest problem. With the availability of computer-assisted learning as an aid to science education many countries are just not able, yet, to provide the hardware; and, furthermore, the lack of suitable software and the necessary expertise to develop software is a greater constraint.

Nevertheless, there is a general recognition among the education authorities, in all countries, of the importance and relevance of modern educational technology and a desire to make full use of such aids for science education as and when circumstances permit. Australia, China, Japan, Malaysia, New Zealand, the Philippines, the Republic of Korea, Sri Lanka, Singapore and the Union of soviet Socialist Republics have reported pilot projects on computer education or computer-assisted learning at the secondary level in support of science education. Micro-computers are available, at least in some schools in these countries.

Teacher Training

There is a unanimous opinion in all countries, that the science teacher occupies a key role in the development of science education in schools. Equally, it is unanimously agreed that the training, re-training and continuing education of science teachers are fundamental for the success of science education programmes.

The qualifications prescribed for science teachers differ from country to country. In Bangladesh, India, Lao People's Democratic Republic, Nepal, Pakistan, Papua New Guinea and Singapore the science teacher at primary level—invariably a teacher who teachers all subjects—requires a secondary school certificate plus one or two year of professional training. In Japan and the Philippines, the requirement is for graduates of universities or teacher training colleges. In the remaining countries the requirements are somewhere between the two extremes. But in many countries there are many teachers in primary schools who do not even have the minimum level of qualification or training.

For secondary science teachers most countries prescribed a university degree with professional training; some prescribe a Master's degree for teaching grades XI and XII. But again the proportion of those teaching science who actually have such prescribed qualifications and training varies from country to country. In some (e.g. Afghanistan, the Lao People's Democratic Republic, Nepal, Pakistan and the Philippines) only 25 per cent have the required qualifications; in others this rises to 75 per cent or more (India, Indonesia, Iran, Japan, Malaysia, Maldives, Papua New Guinea, the Republic of Korea, Singapore and Sri Lanka); whilst in the remaining countries the proportion of qualified science teachers is nearer to 100 per cent. The nature and structure of pre-service training programmes in many colleges and universities have not changed much over the years. There is considerable scope for improvement in this direction; to make the training more relevant and more up-to-date.

However, even where the teaching force is largely qualified for science education the need for in-service or refresher training is very great, especially as new curricula and new methodologies of teaching science are introduced.

Almost all countries have, in fact, undertaken in-service teacher training—through a variety of programmes—but the problem of reaching and retraining the large number of teachers involved is an enormous one. The variety of programmes in use range from special in-service centres, both national and local or regional, offering short-and long-term courses, to the use of radio, TV and Open Universities for distance education. Some experimental work has been carried out (for example in the Philippines and Thailand) with in-service re-training making use of school-college complexes with the retraining being carried out largely in the individual schools. Radio and TV can be used in this way also.

Non-formal Education Programmes and the Popularization of Science*

Most countries have programmes or projects for out-of-school science and technology education but most of these are designed to support the existing school science programme through enrichment activities, rather than being aimed at the population in general.

Those programmes supporting school science include, in many countries, science clubs, science fairs, science exhibitions, science talent searches and olympiad competitions, as well as community schools based on local crafts and technologies. Community schools, in countries such as Papua New Guinea and Bangladesh, provide course on agriculture, housing, elementary mechanics, food preparation, knitting and embroidery and also offer extension courses out-of-school for the local community.

Countries such as China and India, with large populations and limited resources for formal education have established a larger number of non-formal education centres to provide education, including science education, for out-of-school youths. Field centres have been established in Sri Lanka.

For the popularization of science and the development of science education programmes for adults the position within the Asia and the Pecific region is not well defined and, in many countries, not well organized, structure, or financed.

---

* ROEAP. Bulleting of the Unesco Regional Office for Education in Asia and Pacific. *Out-of-school education in Asia and the Pacific*, special Issue, December, 1982.

The radio, T.V, films and the press are of course, used to report scientific events and in most countries these mass media carry science education programmes or articles, but their availability is limited.

In some countries, with vast areas, the mass media are used to research students who are unable to participate in formal schooling—in Australia, India, Japan and New Zealand for instance. However, the extent and coverage varies considerably on the public availability of radio and TV receivers and on the distribution of papers and journals.

Shortage of qualified personal or specialists to prepare and present programmes on radio and TV and to write articles in newspapers and magazines is another constraint.

Another trend for popularization of science is establishment of Science Museums or Science Centres. Such centres are often located only in major cities and are thus only available to those who have access to such cities. However, in India, example, travelling or mobile science museums are available for specific regions. In China, Children's Places have been established in many centres to provide resource units for children to visit and participate in activities. Indeed the trend for the more recently established science centres is for 'hands-on' types of exhibits which capture the imagination of young and old alike and stimulate a sense of curiosity. Australia, India, Japan, New Zealand, the Republic of Korea, Singapore and Thailand report encouraging results in this direction.

Innovations

The next section, which makes up the major part of this publication, gives a country-by-country account of the state of science education and its development. Most of these accounts also contain references to current research in science education and innovation.

However, the following notes comprise special highlights—not necessarily recent innovations—which have been extracted as being of special interests.

Afghanistan. Massive investment in science and technology for industrial growth. Also investment in in-service training of teachers to provide for one year of retraining every five years for all teachers.

Australia. School-based curriculum development—not centrally determined. No practical examinations but practical activity is given emphasis in the science curricula.

Bangladesh. Establishment of community schools as part of the secondary school system. These schools to be controlled by the government, whereas the majority of secondary schools are in the non-government sector, although receiving government subsidies.

China. Emphasis on out-of-school science with the establishment of Childrens' Palaces and the National Group for Youngsters' Scientific Activities as part of the China Association of Science and Technology.

India. Wide variety of out-of-school science activities organized by individual states and by central Government.

Indonesia. Science education related to life, but mainly at the elementary levels.

Iran. Students in high schools are expected to devote six hours per week working in the labour market.

Japan. Legislation for science education is provided in a Science Education Law. Emphasis on the love of living things.

Lao People's Democratic Republic. Emphasis on providing qualified science teachers through programmes to attract youth into teaching. Also relationship between education and work is emphasized throughout the curriculum.

Malaysia. Well structured curriculum development centre with ongoing programmes of revision and backed up by well organized research projects in science education.

Maldives. External influence of the London GCE examinations still prevails and thus determines the teaching at lower and upper secondary levels.

Mongolia. A five years retraining course provides for salary increase of 10-15 per cent.

Nepal. The process of curriculum development has been enunciated clearly in a policy statement. Major new initiatives through a national science education centre are being developed.

New Zealand. Stability of syllabuses—over 20-25 years—and little interest in social concerns.

Pakistan. Proposals for the establishment of a national science education centre.

Papua New Guinea. The new system and syllabuses place much emphasis on local social and environmental conditions and on child-centred activities.

Philippines. The social implications of science are given due prominence in the secondary school syllabuses, (e.g. colloids in chemistry are related to paints, mayonnaise, milk, soap, cheese, fruit jellies).

Republic of Korea. Emphasis on practical work and on links between school and industry.

Singapore. Specialization, streaming and express streams are introduction as part of the New Education System. Science is now an examinable subject in the primary school leaving examination.

Microcomputers have been made available to all schools.

In-service training is now school-based (on-service) as well as institution based.

The Annual Youth Science Fortnight attracts 100,000 students.

Socialist Republic of Viet Nam. Teachers of science are encouraged and expected to make their own teaching aids and equipment. The curricula emphasize the theoretical bases of science.

Sri Lanka. The process and organization of curriculum development are well established and effective. A system of 'master teachers' is used for in-service training at the district level.

Field Studies Centres have been established to assist with out-of-school science education.

Thailand. The comitment by Government to science education has been strengthened—financially and organizationally—by the success of the Institute for the Promotion of Teaching Science and Technology (IPST) and its 36 regional centres, recently established.

Turkey. The centralized science education equipment centre with manufacturing capacity has provided all schools with science apparatus in kits or individual items for many years. More than 700 persons are employed in this Educational Instrument Production Centre.

Union of Soviet Socialist Republics. Polytechnic education is the main feature of this system, which provides science education and technical/vocational training related to work experience, within the school system.

Comparative Tables and Figures

The following tables and figures provide a summary in visual form of some comparisons among the countries of the Asia and Pecific region regarding the organization of the science curricula, the qualifications of science teachers, the allocation of time for practical activities, the availability of science equipment and the availability of mass media.

Table 1. Organization of Science Teaching

Country	Class													Science enrolment when optional or elective
	1	2	3	4	5	6	7	8	9	10	11	12	13	
Afghanistan (AFG)			C	NS			C	SS						Comp
Australia (AUS)		C	GS/ES								E	SS		
Bangladesh (BGD)			C	ES			C	SS			E	SS		33%
China (CPR)			C	IS					C	SS				Comp
India (IND)		C	ES/	GS			C-SS		C	SS	E	SS		no data
Indonesia (INS)	C	ES			C-GS		C	GS		E	SS			no data
Iran (IRA)			C	IS			C-CS			E	SS			40%
Japan (JPN)			C		GS		C	GS			E	SS		30%
Lao (LAO)				C	IS		C	SS	C	SS				Comp
Malaysia (MAL)			C	ES			C	IS		C-GS/SS		E	SS	45%
Maldives (MDV)	C	ES		C	CS			C-SS	E	IS/SS				60%
Mongolia (MON)						C	SS							Comp
Nepal (NEP)					C	GS	Health		E	SS				no data
New Zealand (NZE)				C	GS				C	IS	E	IS/SS		60%
Pakistan (PAK)			C	GS		C	GS			E	SS			40%
Papua New Guinea (PNG)			C	GS				C	IS		O-GS/SS			no data
Philippines (PHI)			C	IS	Health		C-GS		C	SS				Comp
Rep. of Korea (ROK)			C	IS			C	CS		C	SS			Comp
Singapore (SIN)				G	GS		C	GS	O	GS/SS		E-SS		4.8%
Soc. Rep. of Viet Nam (VIE)					GS		C	SS			C	SS		Comp
Sri Lanka (SRL)			C	ES				C	GS		E	SS		25%
Thailand (THA)			C	IS			C	IS		O	IS/SS			no data
Turkey (TUR)		C	ES	C	GS	C	GS		C	CS/SS				Comp
USSR (USR)				C	IS			C-SS						Comp

GS – General Science
ES – Environmental Studies
IS – Integrated Science
SS – Separate Subjects: physics, chemistry, biology, etc.
CS – Combined Science
NS – Nature Study
C – Compulsory
E – Elective
O – Optional

Table 2. Percentage of science teachers possessing required qualifications

Level	Countries (arranged from left to right along the 0–25–50–75–100 scale)
Upper Secondary Level	PAK, NEP, PHI, LAO; TUR; CPR / NZE; VIE; IND; PNG; IRA / JPN / MAL / MDV / ROK / SIN / SRL (at 100)
Lower Secondary Level	CPR / PAK; NEP; LAO; VIE / SRL; TUR; IRA; BGD / NZE / SIN; IND / PNG; ROK; JPN / MAL / MDV / PHI (at 100)
Primary Level	PAK; NEP; LAO; VIE; SRL; CPR / TUR; ROK; SIN; IND; BGD; IRA / JPN / MAL / NZE / PHI (at 100)
	0 · 25 · 50 · 75 · 100

Table 3. Time allocation for science activities, practical/laboratory works as per cent of total time allotment for science

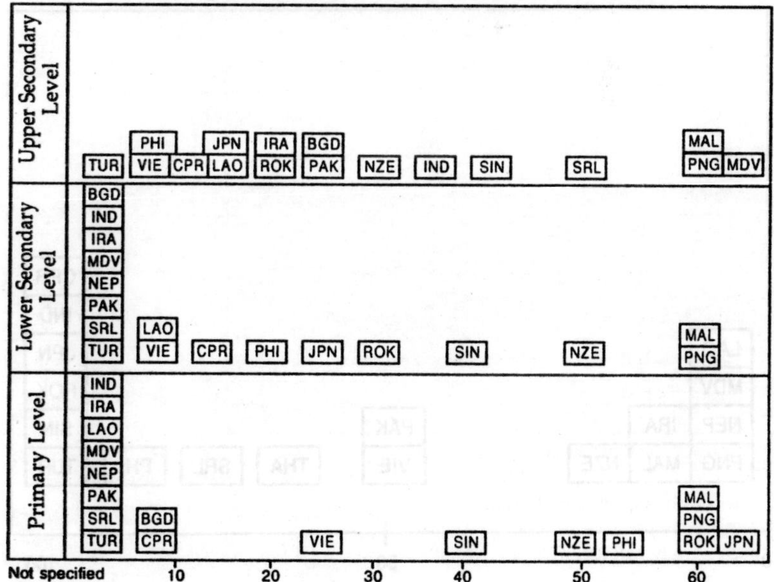

Table 4. General situation with science equipment/teaching aids

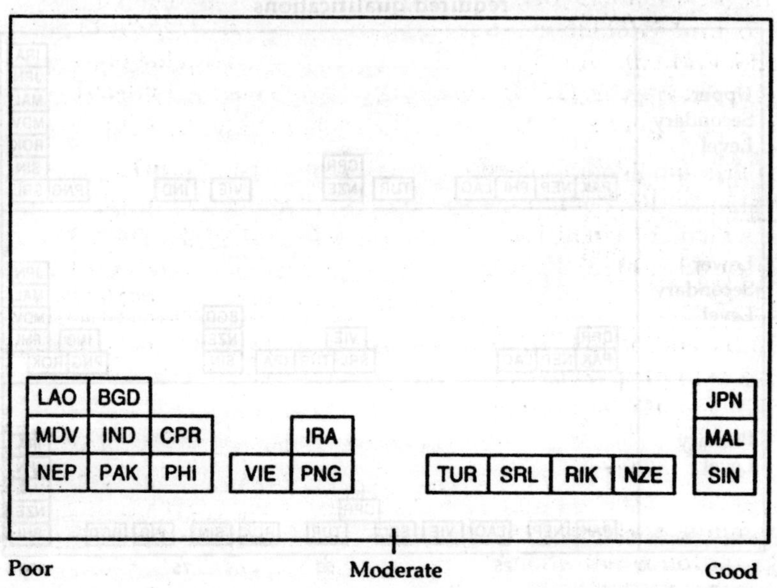

Table 5. Science equipment produced locally (%)

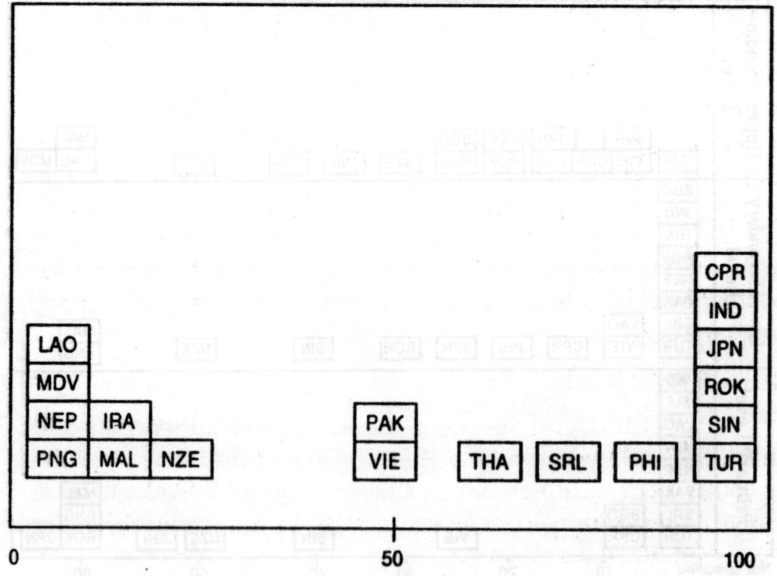

1

Afghanistan

The Democratic Republic of Afghanistan lies in the heart of Asia, occupying an area of approximately 647,500 square kilometres. The country is, in the main, a highland mass lying mostly at an altitude of 1,200 metres or more, and is divided into two geographical areas comprising the valleys of the north which are fertile and the rocky southern section, partly frosted and rich in timber.

For administrative reasons, the country is divided into 29 provinces, each with an appointed provincial centre. Kabul, as the capital, is by far the largest cultural, social and commercial centre with a population of about one million. The population of the country is estimated at 15.2 million (1979). Of the total population, 90 per cent live in rural areas. The average birth rate is 50.5 per thousand and the death rate is 26.5 per thousand, and the annual growth rate is estimated at 2.3 per cent. There are several languages spoken in the country but Pashto and Dari are the most widely used, both stemming from Indo-European languages.

General Education

All educational institutions are organized, supervised and directed by the government. The Ministry of Education has the responsibility for implementing the strategies of the government related to educational development within the overall plan for social-economic development.

Formal education is promoted by 3,370 primary and village schools, 140 intermediate schools, 200 lycees (high schools) and 25 vocational schools. There are also two universities, one polytechnic and several other institutes of higher learning. Compulsory and free primary education for all school-age children and expansion of free intermediate, higher and vocational education are priority developments.

Attempts have been made since the Saur Revolution (27 April 1978) to rise the quality of education for which purpose the Ministry of Education has begun the renewal and systematic review of curricula and instructional materials. Efforts have been intensified to train teachers to meet the needs of the country, particularly in the elimination of illiteracy.

Attempts have also been made to improve the manpower situation particularly in science and technology and the integration of science and technology into national plans for social and economic developments of the country.

The period of schooling for primary and secondary education has been reduced from 12 to 10 years as follows:

(a) Primary school (grades I-IV);

(b) Incomplete middle school (grades V-VIII); and

(c) Complete middle school (grades IX-X).

The last classes of secondary education (complete middle school, grades IX-X) are divided into social and natural science streams. Graduates from the secondary level attend vocational and higher education institutions for further training.

The informal education programme is conducted by nursery schools, the adult education programme, religious education, literacy education, home education, and private education.

Government Educational Organizations

1. The Compilation and Translation Department

The Compilation and Translation Department of the Ministry of Education is concerned with the curricula of all subjects for the whole country and with the provision of textbooks and teachers' guides for all schools in Afghanistan. It has section for biology, chemistry, physics and mathematics, language arts, research arts and practical work, theology, editors geography, history, and sociology.

2. Institute for Specialization of Teachers

The Institute for Specialization of Teachers is an academic and training organization for upgrading the professional level of teachers. It is also responsible for innovation in the area of planning, programming and curriculum development, and in providing new and progressive methods of teaching and the preparation of textbooks.

The Institute organizes seminars and workshops and provides lectures and field trips. It is intended that these in-service training courses will be available on such a scale that teachers and other educational personnel can attend on the basis of one year in every five years.

3. The Science Centre

The Science Centre, which has recently been merged with the Institute for Specialization of Teachers, was established in 1970 within the organizational structure of the Ministry of Education. The main function of this centre is to strengthen natural science and mathematics éducation in the school system. Experienced teachers are appointed as supervisors and simple kits for natural sciences experiments developed from local, inexpensive material. Supervisors help teachers in various disciplines on the theoretical and pedagogical value of the new experimental facilities.

The centre produced teaching aids from local, inexpensive material, maintains existing laboratories in educational institutions, gives on-the-job training to centre staff through international expertise and trough scholarships and fellowships, and co-operates with the educational programmes for radio and television.

Structure of Science Education

Since 1978 the science curriculum has been restructured by national and foreign experts working in the Compilation Department of the Ministry of Education. In the new syllabuses every effort has been made to meet the goals and functions of the Revolutionary Government, the broad aims of science educations, the needs of the pupils, and the society.

Science is not taught in grades I and II as specific subject, but part of science is combined with health and environment and is taught along with other subjects. In grades III and IV science is taught as a specific subject. After grade IV the science syllabuses are presented as separate disciplines. The following table shows the different science disciplines with the number of periods per week and per year.

Time allocation for each science discipline

Subject	*Grade level*	*No. of periods per weak*	*No. of periods per school year*
Nature study	III-IV	2	24
Biology	V-X	2	64
Physics	VI-X	3 average	96 average
Chemistry	VII-X	2 average (3 in grade X)	64 average (96 in grade X)

Objectives

The general objectives of science education in Afghanistan are the acquisition of knowledge, intellectual skills and values in the following areas:

1. Conservation and development of natural resources;
2. Science and technology and their effect on the economic system and the quality of life;
3. Safety and protection procedures in school, the home, the community and the nation;
4. Interpersonal relations;
5. Health, body-care and physical development of individuals; and
6. Physical and biological environment.

Science Education Programmes

The newly structured curricula are replacing general science at grades IV-VI, and chemistry, physics and biology at grades VII-XII.

The science curriculum materials are developed by: (a) studying the old curricula and instructional materials; (b) developing new curricula for different science subjects; (c) developing textbooks and teachers' guides; (d) trail testing in pilot schools; (e) evaluating the materials; (f) collecting feedback; (g) revising and reviewing; (h) approval by the professional committee members; (i) final approval of the Ministry; and (j) printing and distribution.

In addition to covering a much wider range of subject than hitherto, the new curricula for science subjects attempt to change the rote-memory method presently employed to one involving children in their won learning experience of science subjects. Consequently, there are many activities and experiments suggested for children and for teachers and many questions asked of students to stimulate their thinking. In addition, kits for nature study, chemistry, biology and physics are being devised through collaboration between the curriculum teams and staff of the National Science Centre and the Audio-Visual Institute.

The materials have so far been enthusiastically received, specially by the children. The nature study texts for grades III and IV and the biology text and teacher's guide for grade V were printed and distributed first. The remaining materials for biology, chemistry and physics are being progressively developed for grades VI to IX. Trails, revision and writing are continuing.

The new curriculum and instructional materials are prepared on the basis of the child's environment, because it is obvious that many of the more interesting aspects of a child's environment are scientific in nature. This is a particular true in this modern technological world. It is expected that with the effective implementation of these new science curriculum and instructional materials the future generation of young people will develop desirable talents, skills and values which will be conducive to the further development of the country.

Students science textbooks. The students' textbook have been prepared in such a way that each lesson requires the students to perform at least one experiment related to their environment.

The experiment cannot be well performed until the teacher has read the related part of teacher's guide carefully. The teacher is first required to master the lesson and related experiments, then to offer the material to the pupils, making use of environmental material and equipment and teaching in a cognitive way.

In each lesson the students are expected to solve questions or perform activities. These compromise activities that the teacher can explain to the students; question that the teacher will discuss with the students; and questions or experiments that the teacher gives as homework for the students.

The creative teacher is encouraged to go beyond the textbook and enrich the pupils' experiences by clarifying the lesson, developing extra questions and preparing similar experiments for the students to perform and further develop their creativity and under standing. Thus, opportunities are provided for the student under the leadership of the teacher to discuss daily life problems and to find solutions for these problems.

Teachers' guides. Each lesson in the teachers' guide is set out in the following manner:

(a) *Additional information.* Teachers are provided with additional information, alternative methods of teaching and useful experiments. Teachers are asked to read this section carefully before teaching the lesson.

(b) *Aim of the lesson.* The purpose of the of the lesson is clearly stated.

(c) *Materials needed.* The use of locally available materials and their relation to the environment are described.

(d) *Rehearsal.* In order that the teacher teaches the concepts of a particular lesson properly to the students, the need to rehearse the lesson is emphasized.

(e) *Working procedure.* Under this title, activities and experiments which are considered suitable for teaching the lesson are explained step by step.

(f) *Evaluation.* This section suggests how to determine the success of each lesson by discussing the questions at the end of each topic or lesson with the students.

(g) *Homework.* This part suggests the homework assignment to be given to the students.

Implementation. During the implementation of the new textbooks and programmes, it is recognized that all schools throughout the country will not be able to implement the revised curriculum and the accompanying instructional materials at the same pace. It is expected, however, that the schools will move as rapidly as circumstances and conditions permit toward this implementation.

Teacher Training

Pre-service teacher training. Institutions concerned with training teachers are the Pedagogical Academy which trains teachers at the levels of Bachelors and Masters Degrees and is also responsible for training teachers for: (a) institutes of teacher training, (b) primary schools, and (c) kindergartens; institutes of teacher training in the capital and provinces; universities which train teachers for high schools; and the national campaign against illiteracy which trains grade XII school-leavers through special programmes.

In-service teacher training. Teacher training institute graduates and unqualified teachers are assisted to upgrade and update their science knowledge and skills through workshops and seminars organized by the Ministry of Education, with the help of experts and other professionals. These workshop and seminars, some of which are sponsored by UNICEF, are supervised by the Departments of Compilation and Translation and the Institute for Specialization of Teachers in the capital and provinces. During the seminar, in-service training is given on textbooks, different methods of teaching, use of locally-available materials and the evaluation of pupils.

Problems

In Introducing and implementing the science programmes, the Ministry of Education is facing the following difficulties:

1. *Few school buildings.* According to the 1977 statistics from the Planning Department of the Ministry of Education, almost half of the schools in the country do not have buildings.

2. *Shortage of furniture and materials*. Most of the primary and secondary schools are facing shortages of desks, chairs, textbooks, libraries, laboratories and sports fields.
3. *Delay in the preparation of texts and teachers' guides*. Textbooks and teachers guides constitute the main teaching aids in education. For the preparation of textbooks and teachers' guides the following problems arise:
   (a) Lack of adequately trained personnel to compile textbooks and teachers' guides for the science subjects;
   (b) Lack of proper dictionaries for scientific terminology in the National languages;
   (c) Shortage of reference materials;
   (d) Shortage of laboratory equipment for curriculum developers;
   (e) Financial difficulties; and
   (f) Shortage of means and materials for printing.
4. *Lacks of suitably qualified trained teachers.*
5. *Lack of trained science supervisors* and a proper supervision system.

2
Australia

The settlements of modern Australia commenced in the late 1700s as a series of colonies of England, located at various parts on the coast. The colonies gradually developed into six separate States, which combined in 1901 as a federation called the Commonwealth of Australia. Today, Australia consists of six States and two Territories, with a total population of about 15 million.

Education in Australia is the responsibility of these eight 'States' (that is, six States and two Territories). There is also a Department of Education and Youth Affairs at the national level, and national statutory authorities such as the Schools Commission.

Although education is the constitutional responsibility of the States, the constitution also permits the Commonwealth to make special grants to the States, and to determine the uses to which the grants may be applied. This has enabled the Government to enter the field of education in special areas. The special grant of greatest relevance to science education was a programme to build science laboratories at secondary schools. From 1964 to 1975 at total of about $A 120 million* was spent on this programme.

As a result of the federal structure of Australian education, there is no official national policy for science education, nor at

* Approximately 1.05 Australian dollars ($A) = One US dollar.

this stage, is there any official statement derived from a consensus of the views of the separate State Education Departments. The only current statement which reflects an Australia-wide consensus is that developed by the Australian Science Teachers Association. This provides:

(a) a statement about the basic premises and assumptions concerning the place of science in the school curriculum;

(b) statement of the aims of science education; and

(c) a set of recommendations for the design of science courses at the primary, lower secondary and upper secondary levels.

Although there is no national policy statement on the role of education in achieving national goals, there has been considerable debate about what constitutes a core curriculum for Australian schools. The Curriculum Development Centre (CDC) has produced a document, *Core curriculum for Australian schools*, which ascribes a unique role to science within the total school curriculum in terms of understanding the environment and problems-solving in practical situations in the everyday life of individuals and society. The CDC document also contains implications for science education in the areas of 'environmental studies' and 'health education'.

There are no national policies dealing with science education for out-of-school youth or adults, or for the popularization of science and technology issues.

Each State has a system of government primary and secondary schools which cater for about 75 per cent of the students in the State. There are also parallel non-government systems, usually affiliated with religious denominations. About 20 per cent of the students attend catholic schools, and about 5 per cent attend other non-government non-catholic schools.

Attendance at school is compulsory for persons between the ages of 6 years and 15 years. The primary school system covers year levels (grade levels) up to Year 7 or Year 8. The secondary system goes to Year 12.

External examinations exist at Year 12 in all States except Queensland and the Australian Capital Territory. In Queensland

and the Australian Capital territory, school assessments are moderated against an aptitude test which is not bases on a prescribed syllabus. The other States have adopted a system of increasing the amount of teacher assessment in the final year. This teacher assessment is moderated against a State External examination for each subject. The teacher assessment usually contributes about 30 per cent to the final scored at the end of Year 12.

At levels below Year 12, external examinations have been eliminated. In the majority of States this has resulted in the schools and teachers being responsible for curriculum development and the assessment of student performance.

Students generally proceed from a primary school to a secondary school within their own locality. Primary schools and secondary schools are usually separate institutions. In Tasmania and the Australian Capital Territory the final two years of secondary schooling in the government system are provided at separate collages.

The majority of government schools are co-educational. In the non-government sector, most of the students are in single-sex schools but since 1970 there has been a move towards co-education.

Science Education in Schools

Science has usually been taught (as general or integrated science) from Year 1 to Year 10, inclusive to all students. However, many of the State systems have moved towards school-based curriculum development. This allows schools to define the core or compulsory subjects, and the class-time allocated to these subjects. Some schools make science an 'elective' subject, while other schools make the study of science compulsory for all students up to Year 10.

At the Year 11 and Year 12 levels the separate science subjects of biology, chemistry and physics are taught by specialist science teachers. Geology, human physiology, environmental science, human biology and physical science (chemistry plus physics) are also offered in various States.

The relative extent to which separate science subjects are studied at Year 12 is shown in Table 1.

Table 1. Approximate percentage of Year 12 enrolment taking science (1980)

States	*Biology* %	*Chemistry* %	*Physics* %	*Geology/ Earth Science* %
New South Wales	49	30	28	4
Victoria	6	31	25	
Queensland	61	36	29	4
South Australia	58	29	30	17
Western Australia	60	38	34	2
Tasmania	70	38	34	18

The general pattern is that biology is studied by most students, with chemistry and physics each studied by about one-third of the Year 12 students. Most of the students in the latter group would study both chemistry and physics. A small percentage of students study geology.

The percentage of students studying the physical sciences has decreased since 1970. In some States the absolute enrolment in chemistry and physics have declined. On the other hand, the participation rates for biology are much higher than in 1970.

A study of the enrolment statistics for males and females in science subjects indicates that almost three times as many males as females do physics and chemistry. However biology attracts almost twice as many females as males. At present there are various initiatives being taken, designed to increase the participation in science subjects of students at Year 11 and Year 12.

No clear picture is currently available across Australia of the amount of time spent on teaching science at each year level although the Second International Evaluation as Assessment (IEA) Science Study (for which data were collected in 1983) will provide information in this area. A Preliminary estimate would indicate:

(a) Primary level—about 1 hour per week;

(c) Lower secondary level—about 3 hours per week; and

(c) Upper secondary level—about 4 hours per week for each science subject.

As a function of the move toward school-based curriculum development at the primary and lower secondary levels, there is now considerable variability across schools and States in the mean classtime per week spent on the teaching of science.

Curriculum Development in Science

In order to provide an overall picture of the science curriculum, the following Table 2 is presented, which is an initial attempt to categorize the method of decision-making.

Table 2. Decision about science curriculum in Australian states

States	*Primary*	*Lower secondary*	*Upper secondary*
Australian Capital Territory	S	S	S
New South Wales	S	S	P
Victoria	S	S/T	P/S
Queensland	G	G	P/G
South Australia	G	S	P/S
Western Australia	G	P	P
Tasmania	G	S	P
Northern Territory	G	G	P

Key: G = course *guidelines* distributed by State Education Departments or statutory bodies.

P = course/syllabus *prescribed* by State Education Departments or statutory bodies

S = course prepared at the school level

T = course prepared by individual class *teachers* within the school

Primary Level. The earliest type of science introduced into primary schools was 'nature study' involving the identification and observation of the wide range of plants and animals indigenous to Australia. Over the last decade there have been numerous attempts to widen the scope of the science taught at the primary level.

Each State has a curriculum section attached to the Education Department. These sections prepare guidelines and suggestions for the primary science curriculum, but the decisions about the curriculum and the time allocation for science are made at the school level in most States. Individual teachers are responsible for the assessment of their students. The curriculum sections of the Education Department's may provide support services to assist primary teachers to development science curricula, but resources for these services are currently limited.

The curriculum statements in each State are prepared by staff of the curriculum sections of the Education Departments. These statements represent the considerable efforts by the States to improve science teaching in primary schools since 1970. However, there is still much work to be done to train teachers to teach the new science curricula.

Science in the primary school is usually taught by the students' normal class teacher. However, science is not a strong feature of primary school curriculum in Australia, and does not play a large part in the total school curriculum.

The present emphasis in the primary science curriculum is on the process of science rather than on knowledge of specific content areas and textbooks are rarely used.

Lower Secondary Level. During the last decade responsibility for curriculum development in science has tended to shift from the curriculum sections of the State Education Departments to the individual schools. This has enabled increased flexibility and diversity at the school level, but at the same time has greatly increased the demands on teachers.

The amount of science taught in secondary schools is about three hours per week, although there is much variation both within and between States. Integrated science is usually taught at this level, since it is not until 11 that students specialize in the separate science disciplines (biology, chemistry, physics, geology).

More than 95 per cent of students study science at the lower secondary level. The science curricula emphasize both content and process areas. Many schools are using materials produced by the Australian Science Education Project (ASEP). Teachers are also using a variety of textbooks for the selection of material required to cover their curriculum.

With secondary schools there is usually a separate science department organized by a head of department. This person is responsible for the following areas:

(a) providing assistance and training to less-experienced staff;

(b) supervising the development of curricula, the teaching of science, and assessment procedures;

(c) organizing the work of the laboratory assistants; and

(d) ordering the equipment and chemicals required for teaching science.

The materials prepared to ASEP are based on activity and enquiry. They are designed to cater for individual differences allowing for the students' developmental stages, based on three ability levels from Piaget's stages of intellectual development: the concrete, preformal and formal stages.

This national curriculum project was funded jointly by the Commonwealth and States of Australia, and the materials were designed for students in Years 7 to 10.

There are also many textbooks designed for science students at the lower secondary level. A comprehensive list of materials used at the lower secondary level has been produced by the Curriculum Development Centre.

Under the influence of ASEP, there has been a strong move, since 1970, from content-based lower secondary science to an approach based on student interest and on a social orientation to the study of science.

Upper secondary level. At the upper secondary level the universities and other tertiary institutions continue to influence both the curriculum and assessment procedures, although their power has considerably at the end of Year 12.

(a) *Upper secondary level biology*. During the 1970s there was strong growth in the teaching of biology. The main initiative was taken by the Australian Academy of Science which sponsored the preparation of the textbook, *The web of life*, and associated materials. The textbook was an adaptation of materials from the United States Biological Sciences Curriculum Study. The textbook has been adopted in several States.

(b) *Upper secondary level chemistry*. Chemistry teaching has been strongly influenced by curriculum developments in the United States. During the 1970s, the Chemical Education Materials Study (CHEM Study) was adopted in four States. The situation in Victoria is different in that the committee responsible for the curriculum has also undertaken the development of textbooks. The committee's recent publication. Chemistry-key to the earth, attempts to make chemistry more relevant to the future everyday needs of students.

The Australian Academy of Science has also been involved in the development of materials for senior chemistry courses. At this stage a recommended course of study has been produced, and the writing of textbooks for the course is underway.

(c) *Upper secondary level physics*. There have only been minor developments in the physics curricula over the last decade. Most Australian courses have been largely influenced by courses in the United States, especially PSSC Physics and Harvard Project Physics.

(d) *Upper secondary level geology*. Geology (or earth science) is offered at the Year 12 level in most States. In New Sough Wales, Queensland, and Western Australia, fewer than 5 per cent of the Year 12 population study this subject. The subject is more popular in Tasmania and South Australia.

The Australian Academy of Science has begun to produce materials for this subject at the Year 12 level.

Science Activities/Laboratory Work and Equipment

All statements about science curricula in Australia emphasize the important role of laboratory work and activities. However, no information is available about the amount of time actually devoted by teachers to this part of the curriculum. The Second IEA Science Study will provide data in this area.

Practical and laboratory work is generally not an examinable part of the curriculum, although students studying for external examinations at year 12 may need to provide evidence that they have carried out practical work.

Following the extensive funding by the Commonwealth Government for science laboratories and equipment during the period 1964-1975, most secondary schools are well equipped to enable students to undertake laboratory activities. However, few primary schools would have rooms equipped specially for science activities. Materials for school sciences are available from both Australian and overseas manufactures. Some States, such as Tasmania, have set up centres for the maintenance and production of science equipment.

Educational Technology

Most schools have an extensive range of educational technology èquipment, often managed through the school library-resource centre. Equipment would typically include overhead projectors, 35 mm slide projectors, 16mm movie projectors and video recording and production equipment. Science teachers would use this equipment where appropriate to the topics being taught.

Most secondary schools have at least one microcomputer or access, via terminals, to larger computers. The use of computers in science education is increasing rapidly, but it is probably too soon to make generalizations about patterns of usage. Some primary schools have microcomputers but little use is make of them in science, so far.

Teacher Training

1. The pre-service training of primary teachers is usually conducted in territory institutions set up for the sole purpose of training primary teachers. The usual course is of three years duration. Although there is no strong emphasis on science, some extra training in the teaching of science is available to those selecting this area as their speciality. Nevertheless, the science background of most primary teachers is week, especially in areas of physical science.

Each State conducts in-service activities to assist primary teachers to improve their ability to teach science, but this in-service training must compete for the time of teachers and the resources of the system with other subjects, especially language and mathematics.

Within each primary school there is usually one teacher with the special task of co-ordinating the teaching of science, and this may lead to some in-service training at the level of the individual school.

2. Science at the lower secondary school level is usually taught by a specialist science teacher. The pre-service training of these secondary science teachers usually involves an initial Bachelor of Science (B.Sc.) degree or similar course of three or four years followed by a Diploma of Education course of one year. There are also several institutions which integrate the science content and pedagogy components into a combined four-year course.

3. Teachers are usually trained to teach the specific science subjects (biology, chemistry, physics or geology) which are offered at the upper secondary school level. They may also elect to study the teaching of mathematics as an additional subject.

In addition to the pre-service training, science teachers are given the opportunity for in-service activities. These activities are usually organized by curriculum sections of the State Education Departments, by science teachers' associations or by tertiary institutions.

Most science teaching at the secondary school level takes place in rooms or laboratories designed specifically for the purpose. Most schools have laboratory assistants or technicians to assist in the preparation of equipment for lessons. In some schools, students use text books for science which cover the entire course for a year. In other schools the students use printed materials on a modular basis, where each module covers one topic. The materials for a given course may then be selected from several sources, including the ASEP modular materials. Other schools may make to use of printed materials. All schools have library facilities which include materials for science which can be used to supplement textbook materials.

Research

There is a strong emphasis on research in science and mathematics education. The Australian Science Education Research Association conducts an annual meeting, and the papers are produced in the annual volume, *Research in science education*.

Australia is participating in the Second IEA Science Study under the auspices of the International Association for the Evaluation of Educational Achievement (IEA). Data were collected in 1983 from Australia-wide samples of students at: (a) the ten-year old level: (b) the 14-year old level, and (c) the Year 12 level. Results, to be published from 1985 onwards, will give a current picture across Australia of science curricula, characteristics of students and their science teachers, and the achievement and attitudes of the Students.

The Second IEA Science Study is being conducted and co-ordinated in Australia by the Australian Council for Educational Research (ACER). Other institutions engaged in research on science education include the research and curriculum sections of the State Education Departments and territory institutions (such as Universities and Colleges of Advanced Education) involved in training teachers, including science teachers.

Out-of-school Programme

Formal education: For the school-age population, most States provide a range of science-related facilities. Many schools organize excursions for groups of students to visit and use these facilities. In most cases, the educational roles of the facilities are supported by the State Education Departments. This usually involves the secondment of a teacher to develop curriculum materials which will enhance the educational value of the visit made by groups of students. Most of the facilities are also available outside school hours, especially at week-ends, for use by the general public, including school students following their individual areas of interest.

However, it should be noted that most of the facilities are located in metropolitan areas, so that they are not accessible to the same extent to students from non-metropolitan areas.

The facilities include activity centres, with a wide range of 'hands-on' activities designed to stimulate interest, particular in the physical sciences, and environmental studies areas, specially designed to stimulate interest in geology. The 'Questacon' in Canbera and the CSIRO centre in Clayton, Victoria are the best known examples of activity centres.

Many States also support the activities of the Gould League, which is set up to encourage environmental education. When founded the emphasis of the Gould League was on the study of natural flora and fauna, but the current trend is to take a broader view of environmental education. The Gould League generally experts its influence by means of publications, and clubs at the primary school level.

Another area of out-of-school science education for school students is the Science Talent Search, conducted in most States by the Science Teachers Association. The Science Talent Search Talent Search usually culminates in an exhibition of projects associated with the presentation of awards to the prize-winning students.

During school hours, the Australian Broadcasting Corporation (ABC), and to a lesser extent the commercial (non-government) radio and television companies, present a range of programmes for students, including science programmes. Some programmes are specially linked to the curricula, while others are designed to stimulate students or provide a range of background information for which the broadcast media are especially suited.

Non-formal education. For those outside the formal education system, the best-known activities are the radio programmes produced by the ABC dealing with general scientific topics, health, and reviews of new scientific books and the science-related programmes of the government (ABC) and commercial (non-government) television channels.

A relatively high proportion of Australians purchase, and presumably read, newspapers, magazines and books. Matters of scientific interest are regularly reported in newspapers, and some newspapers have reporters or editors specializing in the science/

technology area. However, there are few articles designed primarily for instruction or information.

Among the wide range of magazines available, there are several dealing with science and technology, especially in electronics and computering. Most Australian towns suburbs have public lending libraries, and there is strong emphasis on building adequate stocks of non-fiction literature, including books and magazines on science and technology topics.

The States also have provision for 'adult education' in a general sense, with courses to cover a wide range of topics, including science and technology. The courses do not lead to the award of formal certificates and the system is very flexible, being strongly responsive to the perceived and expressed interests of the 'students'.

Current Innovations

Those involved in science education—in schools, in curriculum development, in teacher training institutions are constantly engaged in the assessment and development of their activities.

One innovation that should ultimately have a major effect on the teaching of science is the development, at the national level, under the auspices of the Schools Commission, of computer education in Australian primary and secondary schools. At present no detailed plans for the organization or funding of this innovation have been released, but attention will certainly be devoted to the development of high quality educational software and to the training of teachers.

3

Bangladesh

Education is acknowledged to play a vital role as an instrument for development and change. Bangladesh is in the process of recasting the system of education to link in it more with national development and the improvement of the quality of life.

In this age of science and technology there is an increasing demand for skilled manpower relevant to the development needs of the country. It is obvious that more and better education in science and technology has to be divided. Thus, there is a keen awareness of the need to improve the quality of science teaching and learning at all levels of school education; to expand the facilities of science education beyond the school; and to make it available to an increasing number of out-of-school youths and adults.

Structure of School Education

School education is divided in four stages:

(a) Primary stage from grade I to grade V (5+ to 10 years);

(b) Junior secondary stage from grades VI to VIII (10+ to 13 years).

(c) Secondary stage for grades IX and X (13+ to 15 years); and

(d) Higher secondary stage for grades XI and XII (15+ to 17 years).

Primary education, extending over five years, is free. There are about 42,000 primary schools in the country with an enrolment of about 8 million pupils. There are about 2,500 junior secondary schools, 6,500 secondary schools and 263 higher secondary schools, otherwise known as intermediate colleges. Altogether the enrolment is about 2 million students at the secondary stage.

The breakdown of enrolment into the four stages is shown in the table on the following page.

Structure of Science Education

Science is compulsory both at the primary and secondary level i.e., and to grade X. At the higher secondary level science is offered as an elective group of subjects. About 33 per cent of the higher secondary students choose the two year science elective.

Breakdown of enrolment from primary to higher secondary level

Stages	Grades	Enrolment	Remarks
Primary	I-V	8,285,807	1981 statistics
Junior Secondary	VI-VIII	223,984	1980 statistics
Secondary	IX-X	1,931,357	1980 statistics
Higher Secondary (science)	XI-XII	119,000	1978 statistics
Total		10,560,048	

Fifteen per cent of the total instructional time up to secondary level (grade X) is devoted to the teaching of science while 75 per cent of the total time is devoted to science teaching at the higher secondary level for those choosing science. This means that six periods per week for the science electives for grades XI and XII.

Curriculum Aim. The National Curriculum and Syllabus Committee, established in 1975, has produced new syllabuses and curricula up to grade X level. In science the aims are as follows :

Primary. Utilizing the natural inquisitiveness of children the main aims of this state are to help children develop their skills of observation properly, to express their observation correctly and to take decisions on the basis of their observation.

In grades I and II, pupils will be acquainted with the various components of their social as well as natural environment. On the basis of their experiences in these two grades pupils in grades, III, IV and V will learn about the different social institutions, natural problems and their solutions. They will also learn about the characteristics of the living and the non-living.

Junior secondary and secondary. At this level the main aims are to : (a) develop inquisitiveness about nature and environment; (b) develop skills of observation; (c) develop logical thinking; (d) develop attitudes free from superstitions; and (e) help learners solve their personal and social problems in their attempts to improve the standard of life.

Higher secondary. The main aim of teaching science at the higher secondary level is to help the learners prepare themselves for the different branches of science and for professions such as engineering, medicine and agriculture.

Curriculum Organization. In grades I and II, information, concepts and principles of both natural and social sciences have been integrated in a subject entitled 'Environmental Studies'. There are no prescribed textbooks for Environmental Studies at this level. In grades III, IV and V the subject Environmental Studies has been divided into two section—one dealing with the social environment; the other with the natural environment. Environmental Studies dealing with the social environment includes history, geography, civics, and population education. Environmental Studies dealing with the natural environment includes aspects of physics, chemistry, biology, health and nutrition, and population education. Textbooks for grades, III IV and V are available.

The science courses at the junior secondary stage contain aspects of physics, chemistry and biology as well as geography, hygiene, health the population education—all incorporated together in the subjected General Science. General Science at the secondary stage is divided into two sections. The first sections—physical science—contains physics and chemistry and the second section—the biological sciences—contains biology, agriculture, geography, health and population education.

At the higher secondary level the science curriculum is organized into separate subject disciplines such as physics, chemistry, biology and mathematics.

In the past, insufficient attention was given to linking the teaching and learning of science to the real-life situation of the learners. The content of each science course was full of information, facts and principles of science without any scope for their use in solving the problems of every day life. The curricula now in the effect have, however, attempted to overcome these shortcomings. The real life problems of the learners, such as population, malnutrition and conservation, have been incorporated into the science curricula, e.g., conservation of environment in grade III, environment for healthful living in grade IV.

Curriculum Evaluation and Renewal. The Government has recently set up a National Curriculum Development Centre (NCDC) for developing and evaluating the total curriculum of the country from the primary to pre-university stage. NCDC, in collaboration with other educational institutions of the Government, is devising evaluation procedures for science and other curricula.

It has been generally accepted by the NCDC that curricula should be revised and reviewed every five years. The present curricula for the primary level were implemented in 1978-1979. Accordingly, a committee has been constituted and begun to review the primary curricula. Curricula for the secondary level were introduced from 1981 to 1983. So a revision is soon to be commissioned. The new curricula for the higher secondary stage will be implemented in 1985.

Student Evaluation. At present, the system of evaluation at all stages of education is not objective-based. The majority of questions are of the essay type and based on the contents of the book, rather than the objectives set forth in the curricula. Most of the questions require recall of facts, information and principles of science. Questions to test the affective behaviour of the learners are rarely found in the question papers.

The Government has divided to introduce an objective-based evaluation system in the public examination at the secondary level (grade X). A task force especially appointed for this purpose has been constituted and begun work.

Science Activities/Laboratory Work and Equipment. At the primary level an attempt has been made to design the curriculum in such a way that the teaching/learning experiences and activities could be developed around the pupils environmental milieu with particular reference to the use of local resources available in the immediate neighbourhood of the school and the community. It has been suggested that the pupils' environment should be used as the laboratory for teaching/learning science at this level.

The Environmental Studies curriculum at the primary level emphasizes a knowledge of the pupils' immediate environment. There is no formal laboratory work at this stage. Instead, pupils are supposed to observe different phenomena of nature, collect, identify and preserve different living and non-living objects, perform simple experiments using indigenous materials, and describe or record their observations properly. It has been suggested in the curriculum that these science activities should be done along with the theory lessons. Hence there are no separate laboratory classes for the primary stage. This trend continues through the junior secondary stage. No formal laboratory period is suggested for these grades. The pupils are supposed to undertake different activities along with the theory lessons, during their leisure time or at home.

At the secondary stage however, there are prescribed practical experiments to be undertaken by the pupils. These practicals require about 25 per cent of the total time available for science teaching. At the higher secondary stage there are practical syllabuses for each of the science subjects with 33 per cent of the total time available for practical work.

Science Equipment. Science there is a no system of central purchases and no adequate financial provision for equipment and consumable, many schools have little or no science equipment. Some secondary schools have no science rooms or laboratories.

The Bangladesh Educational Equipment Board (BEEB) however has been set up to produce educational equipment of acceptable quality suited to curriculum requirements and ensure its prompt supply to the schools and colleges. The functions allocated to BEEB are as follows :

(a) Undertake overall responsibility for the design and development of prototype educational equipment for all schools (including technical/vocational schools);

(b) Make pre-production batches of new designs of educational equipment and arrange for these to be tested and evaluated in selected educational establishments;

(c) Receive from Government sources bulk orders of prescribed educational equipment items in order that BEEB can contract local workshops, on the most advantageous, to manufacture such items;

(d) Promote the production of educational equipment by offering contracts to all workshop to manufacturing such items and through the transfer of technology, stimulate production in local industry;

(e) Establish quality control facilities and organization for monitoring the quality of components and products produced by local workshops;

(f) Establish facilities for assembling and testing educational equipment and make arrangements for delivery of such equipment to the schools; and

(g) Make arrangements for the training of teachers and inspectors in the use, application and basic maintenance of such educational equipment.

Use of Educational Technology

The National Institute of Educational Media and Technology (NIEMT) and BEEB are the two national institutes engaged in producing and distributing audio-visual aids to reinforce and supplement science teaching.

NIEMT was established in 1956 as the Audio-Visual Education Centre. The main functions of this centre are to distribute educational films, film-strips, wall charts, and other audio-visual materials to educational institutions. Most of the films are in English and produced abroad. In recent years NIEMT has produced some films for science education with translation into Bengali. Among the 58 wall charts produced so far, 32 are specially for primary education and 26 for secondary level. More than, 880,000 prints of these charts have been distributed among the primary and secondary schools of the country. NIEMT has taken the initiative to broadcast school educational programmes through Radio Bangladesh since. 1981. Under the programme the Government of Japan has donated 1,100 sets of Audio-Control consoles and the majority have been distributed to different educational institutions through NIEMT. At present there are two programmes of 20 minutes each for secondary education each day. It is also telecasting a programme of 20 minutes per fortnight for primary education and three programmes of 20 minutes each per week through Bangladesh television.

There are no programmes where micro-computers are being used for science teaching.

Teacher Training

Qualifications. The minimum qualification required for a primary school teacher is Matriculation or Secondary School Certificate (SSC), but many teachers with Higher Secondary Certificate (HSC), Bachelor's Degree or even Master's Degree are teaching in primary schools. All these teachers are required to teach science subjects along with all other subjects at the primary level. Eighty-five per cent of primary teachers have the minimum qualifications; 15 per cent are unqualified.

Since the majority of junior and secondary schools are non-Governmental institutions, the minimum qualification for science teachers in these schools is not prescribed. It varies from school to school. In junior secondary schools no science teacher will have less than HSC in Science. In each of secondary schools there should be two science graduates (one mathematics and the other science) if the school is to be affiliated to the Board of Intermediate and Secondary Education for science subjects for examination purposes. About 20 per cent of science teachers in secondary schools have a pedagogical qualification (B. Ed. or M.Ed. degree) as well as an academic qualification.

At the higher secondary stage or the pre-university stage the science teacher should have at least a Master's Degree in any one of the science subjects. It is not necessary for such teachers to have a pedagogical qualification.

Pre-service Training of Primary Teachers. There are 48 Primary Training Institutes,* each with a capacity of 200 students. The duration of the course is one academic year but the Government is planing to introduce a two year training programme in the PTIs from the beginning of the 1984 academic year. The present one year course consists of educational theory (sociology, philosophy, psychology, history of education and child development studies), school subjects, students' teaching practice, and some co-curricular activities, each having both theoretical and practical aspects.

Pre-service Training of Secondary Science Teachers. There are ten Teachers' Training Colleges (TTCs) and the Institute of Education and Research (IER) at the University of Dhaka involved in training teachers for the secondary high schools. Among these institutions two are offering courses for Master's in Education Degree (in addition to B.Ed./Dip. Ed. degree). The duration of the B.Ed. course is one academic year. The course includes basic methodology, school administration theories, educational psychology, two elective school subjects, professional studies and practice teaching.

In-service training programme. The in-service training of science teachers, as well as other teachers, is carried out by the Academy for Fundamental Education (AFE) and by the National Institute for Educational Administration Extension and Research (NIEAER). The NIEAER is involved in training secondary school teachers—including science teachers—as an ongoing activity aimed at updating and upgrading the knowledge and competencies of the teachers. The duration of the in-service course is usually two weeks.

Research in Science Education

The type of research problems investigated in the area of science education are: curriculum development; curriculum evaluation; textbook evaluation; teaching facilities in the schools; effectiveness of science teaching methods; identification of skills for teaching science; module development in science especially in the area of educational measurement and environmental education; survey of science teaching methods; and development of achievement tests.

Most of the research in science education is carried out by the IER. University of Dhaka. Some TTCs also conduct research in science education but the total research effort is very limited.

Popularization of Science and Technology

Science Club Movement. The science and science club movement began in 1960. Now there are about 500 science clubs which: (a) study the nature of the local environment; (b) undertake research on local environmental problems; (c) study local plants, animals, insects; (d) prepare and design low-cost teaching aids and scientific instruments with locally available materials; (e) arrange popular science lectures for club members and also for outsiders; (f) undertake scientific projects; (g) collect and identify local medicinal plants; (h) design and prepare scientific toys; and (i) arrange field trips for members to places of scientific importance.

Some popular science magazines have played an important role in encouraging the science club movement. A few of the science clubs have their own little workshop and library and occasionally the publish scientific journals.

A National Science Week and the active interest of the National Museum of Science and Technology have increased the activities of the science club movement in the country.

Science Museum. In a developing country like Bangladesh the science museum plays a vital role in educating children, youths and adults about their environment and basic scientific knowledge. The National Museum of Science and Technology is situated in Dhaka. At present it has three main divisions, namely technology, physical science and biological science. In addition, there is a mini-planetarium attached to the museum. The museum was organized its galleries with suitable static and working exhibits, models, charts, and diagrams and animated posters.

The functions of the museum are to: (a) display and demonstrate the exhibits, working models, charts, diagrams and animated posters in the galleries; (b) display items prepared from low-cost materials; (c) display local industrial products; (d) co-operate with innovators; (e) arrange regular meetings and lectures on popular science in co-operation with science clubs, science teachers and people interested in science; (f) arrange film shows and video tape presentations on popular science topics; (g) prepare and display low-cost teaching aids for science teaching at the school level; (h) co-ordinate science club activities; (i) arrange on request, lectures on selected topics from school science curricula; (j) provide science library and workshop facilities; and (k) co-operate with the National Council for Science and Technology to arrange and popularize National Science Week.

The museum also has a regular programme for observing celestial bodies, lunar eclipse, solar spots and solar eclipse through the reflecting telescope.

In future it is hoped to establish regional science museums in Rajshahi, Khulna and Chittagong and to arrange a Mobile Science Exhibition for other places.

National Science Weeks, Science Fairs and Science Exhibitions. Science weeks, science fairs and science exhibitions are organized at different levels throughout the country by the National Council of Science and Technology. The aims are to:

(a) develop scientific literacy;

(b) familiarize and popularize science at all levels;

(c) encourage young people in creative work;

(d) encourage young people to prepare science projects and models with low-cost indigenous materials;

(e) search for young scientific talent form all walks of life;

(f) train young people in instrument making and carrying out observations with them;

(g) encourage the activities of the science clubs;

(h) encourage scientists to carry out their research activities according to the needs of the nation and to relate their work to the national problems;

(i) familiarize the public with the scientific activities of the professional experts and young science students;

(j) provide better public appreciation and understanding of science and technology, national resources and environment;

(k) make the public aware of the contribution of science to the benefit of society;

(l) develop scientific attitudes in the public; and

(m) develop rapport among students of different institutions, members of science clubs, and other innovators.

Mass Media. Radio Bangladesh broadcasts two or three regular programmes on science based on the formal school curricula at both primary and secondary level. In addition, there are radio also includes scientific topics useful for the general public in their other magazine programmes.

Television. Television is also a powerful medium at present covering 80 per cent of the land mass. Bangladesh television broadcasts two popular science programmes, one for children and young people and another for youths and adults, as well as programmes for primary and secondary science students.

Newspapers and Journals. There are about 25 daily newspapers, ten weekly papers and 200 periodicals. The newspapers publish current news on scientific topics and world scientific advancement but popular scientific articles are very rare in these dailies. Two or three of the renowned weeklies publish one or two pages of popular science articles in each of their issues.

Motion Pictures. The National Museum of Science and Technology arranges film shows on popular science for the general public and school students. The Audio-Visual Education Centre, Dhaka (now a component of NIEMT) arranges film shows for school students and teachers in the centre and sometimes in a particular school, on request. They have about 200 films on science and technology. In addition, the Science Cine Club, British Council, American Cultural Centre, Alliance Franchise and the German Culture Institute occasionally arrange film shows on science and technology.

Conclusion

Bangladesh is overwhelmed with educational problems and is desperately trying to solve them. The science policy of the country and the new curricula in science emphasize the development of science education. Steps have already been taken in this direction. But there is so far no reliable research evidence as to how far the system and the process have gained public acceptance.

Changes in the school curriculum should also bring about changes in the teacher education programme. How far this has been the case is unclear. Unless timely and proper steps are taken without regard to teacher education there is always a danger of reverting to the old traditional approaches to science education. Whatever suggestions may be given to the teacher for using the appropriate strategies for science teaching, he will be reluctant to sue them unless and until there is a change in this attitude towards doing so. Such attitude changes can be best brought at the teacher education level.

4

China

Since the founding of the People's Republic of China, much attention has been devoted to science education. The 'Joint Programme' adopted by the Chinese people's Political Consultative Conference in 1949 advocated, 'as common morality of all the citizens in the People's Republic of China, feelings for the motherland, for the people, for labour, for science and for public property', and advised them 'to strive to develop natural science in the service of industrial and agricultural production and the construction of national defence', and 'to encourage and award scientific findings and invasions, to popularize science knowledge'. These directives have been regarded as a foundation for the formulation of science education policies ever since.

Science education has developed through school education for young people, and through spare-time adult education for workers and peasants. In addition, as the media of science education for the entire people, the State has set up museums of natural history, planetariums, science and technology houses, botanical gardens and zoos; developed broadcast, film and television undertakings; and published various science and technology newspapers and magazines.

Since a National Science Congress in 1978, science education development has quickened in pace and is now one of the strategic priorities.

Science Education in Schools

Structure. Education from primary school level to pre-university level is divided into elementary and secondary. Elementary education comprises full-time primary schools, half-study and half-farming primary schools, adult elementary classes and literacy classes. Secondary education includes full-time secondary schools, secondary professional schools, vocational schools, technical schools and adult secondary schools.

Full-time primary schools are now in the process of transition from a five-year system to a six-year system; full-time secondary schools (or general secondary schools) are divided into lower secondary and upper secondary. At present, most of the general secondary schools are gradually changing to a system of three years in both lower and upper stages.

There are two types of secondary professional schools; those enrolling lower secondary leaves generally offer four year courses; those enrolling upper secondary leavers usually offer two year courses. Vocational schools and technical schools conduct a three year course for lower secondary leavers.

Table 1. Enrolment in primary and secondary schools, 1982

Type of school	*Number of students (millions)*
Secondary schools	47.36
Secondary professional schools	1.04
Secondary technical schools	0.63
Secondary teachers schools	0.41
General secondary schools	45.28
Upper grades	6.40
Lower grades	38.87
Agricultural schools (primary)	0.70
Agricultural schools (secondary)	0.35
Vocational schools	0.36
Primary schools	139.72

Science Curricula. Curricula, teaching hours and instructional objectives for each course are determined by the

Ministry of Education (MOE). The Ministry formulates basic instructional documents such as teaching plans and syllabuses and exercises leadership over the compilation of textbooks for the whole country. The Peoples's Educational Press attached to the MOE is responsible for compiling and publishing teaching materials.

The teaching programmes devised by the MOE in 1981 explicitly indicate that science courses are to be offered in all primary and secondary schools. For example, nature study is to be offered in primary schools from grades III to VI; and geography is to be offered in grade II to upper grade III; biology in lower grades I and II, and in upper grade III; physiological hygiene in lower grade III. Science course offered in primary and secondary schools are compulsory for all pupils.

Table 2. Teaching hours per week for science course in primary schools, 1981

Grade / Course	I	II	III	IV	V	
Nature study			2	2	2	
Geography			2			
Scientific activities	2	2	2	2	2	

Table 3. Teaching hours per week for science courses in secondary schools, 1981

Grade / Course	Lower secondary			Upper secondary				
	I	II	III	I	II	III		
Physics		2	3	4	3	4		
Chemistry		3	3		3	3		
Geography	3	2			2			
Biology	2	2			2			
Physiological hygiene		2						

In addition to the 26 periods per weak of compulsory courses, there are four periods of elective course in upper secondary grades II and III, with the purpose of developing the strengths of individual students and preparing them for employment or higher education.

Content and Renewal of Science Course. Six different sets of textbooks for primary and secondary schools have been edited and published by the People's Educational Press with a view to meeting the needs of political and economic development. Generally, revision and renewal of textbooks is undertaken every two to four years. At present, the press is preparing for the completion of a new set of textbooks for key secondary schools.

The content of the present courses is based on the following broad aims:

(a) *Nature study at primary level.* To guide the child in recognizing the world of nature and understanding the exploration, exploitation, transformation and preservation of it by man; to help him grasp essential knowledge of nature; to develop his love for science and his desire as well as ability to learn and use science; to inculcate in him a correct outlook of nature, scientific attitude and love for his native place and the country; and to promote his wholesome growth in body and mind;

(b) *Geography at primary level.* To guide the child in a knowledge of his hometown, motherland and the world and in the exploration, transformation and preservation of nature by man;

(c) *Chemisty at secondary level.* To enable the student to grasp solidly and systematically the rudiments of chemistry, to acquire some basic chemical skills and to understand their usage in practice; and to train and develop his ability in chemistry;

(d) *Biology at secondary level.* To train the student to grasp the rudiments of biology and basic skills and a competence to observe and analyse biological phenomena; to lay the foundation needed for his further study of science and culture;

(e) *Physiological hygiene at secondary level.* To enable the student of obtain a rudimentary knowledge of the structure, function, hygiene and protection of the human body; to urge him to render him sound in body and mind; to enable him to acquire skills for doing experiments of simple dissection;

(f) *Geography at secondary level.* For lower grades, to enable the student, on the basic of geographical education carried out in primary school to understand more rudiments of the geography of China and the world and to acquire a knowledge of physical geography; and to help him obtain initial skills for using maps. At upper secondary grades, to have a systematic command of the basic theories concerning the relationship between man and geographical conditions, and to understand how to exploit and transform nature rationally, to develop production and to protect the environment; and

(g) *Physics at secondary level.* To enable the student to obtain systematic and basic knowledge of physics indispensable to his further study of modern science and technology, and to understand its application in practice; to help him acquire experimental skills, the ability to think and to use mathematics in solving problems in physics.

Science Textbooks—an Evaluation. An evaluation of the new textbooks in current use has shown that at primary level the books have replaced traditional cramming methods with a more stimulating approach based on question, observation, experiments and stories; The texts are also more succinct and interesting and are designed to encourage pupils to undertake activities such as growing plants, raising animals, collecting specimens, and making observations.

At the secondary level the new books cover a wider range and are much appreciated by teachers. In biology, for example sections on physiology, reproduction, evolution and ecology have been added. The main reservations seem to be the inability of some traditional teachers to use the books in the required manner.

Experimental Work. Problems exist in the quantitative and qualitative nature of practical work in school science education. More attention has been given in recent years to the importance of activity work by pupils and provision is made at all levels, within the syllabuses, for experiments and practical work by teachers and students. The number of hours prescribed for such work has increased, as a percentage of the total time, to about 14 per cent at junior secondary level and 12.5 per cent at upper secondary level.

The supply of equipment is a major problem. Lists of apparatus have been compiled and a production system established. Priority has been given to the national key secondary schools and training of staff undertaking.

A 1981 investigation in the provinces showed that 2.8 per cent of all primary schools are equipped with all the items in the list of equipment; 6.8 per cent with half the items and about 90 per cent in urgent need. Most of the latter are in the rural areas. At the secondary level the same investigation revealed that 80.7 per cent of the schools in need of apparatus.

The industrial system for producting equipment, set up before 1966, consist of factors directly under the MOE, as well as some provincial instrument plants and a large number of workshops, most of which are run by different schools, with factories under the MOE as their centre. The output of this system is increasing rapidly. During the last five years, the whole country has been provided with equipment and apparatus for primary and secondary schools to the value of more than five billion yuan;* one billion each year. Twenty-one per cent of the listed items have undergone redesign or have been newly designed. Today, the system is specializing in producing more than 370 prototypes.

The Science and Technology Section and Laboratory Management Section of the MOE are responsible for revising the list, and organizing and co-ordinating all the factories concerned in the design, production and evaluation experimental equipment and apparatus. The MOE decided recently to

* Approximately 1.98 China yuan = One US dollar.

establish an Institute for Teaching Instrument and Facility Research to develop the range of equipment needed and to design apparatus.

In addition to state investment, local investment and self-help are two important sources of experimental instruments and facilities. For example in 1981 in Human province, the state invested 400,000 yuan, the province raised 600,000 yuan, and money gathered for instruments from different towns, villages and schools amounted to 2,900,000 yuan in all.

Educational Technology

There are more than 100,000 epidiascopes and 60,000 slide projectors used for teaching purposes in all the key primary and secondary schools in cities and towns. Due to the low rate of lantern slide production, the supply falls short of demand, and slide projectors are more often used.

More than 100,000 audio tape-recorders are available for instructional purposes all over the country which are mainly used in language teaching and music learning.

Over 17,000 film projectors have been provided for secondary schools in various municipalities and towns, but the rate of utilization is very low because few instructional films are available.

North-east China, Guangdong Province and Beijing are taking the lead in using video recorders. More than 400 video recorders are being used for teaching purposes, most of which are in the teacher training institutions.

Many districts have begun to offer course in computer and software programming. In Shanghai, for example, no less than 20 computer groups are equipped with 50 micro computers at instructional stations for youngsters' science activities, children's palaces and schools in different district and countries.

In November 1982, a 'Contest of Shanghai Youngsters on Computer Programming' was launched. It was jointly sponsored by 13 organizations including the Shanghai Electronic Society and the Institute for Modern Education Research of the Huadong Normal University. This contest promotes programming in

BASIC. The mathematics models and design programmes that are devised will, it is hoped, stimulate the students' desire for knowledge, widen their horizon of scientific culture, and develop their logical thinking.

Teacher Training

Qualifications. At the National Forum on Primary and Secondary Teacher Training held in 1977, the MOE put forward standards for the in-service training of primary and secondary teachers. Primary teachers must raise their qualifications to the level of regular secondary normal school graduates; lower secondary teachers must reach that of regular special normal college graduates; and upper secondary teachers must reach regular undergraduate level.

Statistics in 1980 showed the most teachers have not yet reached these educational standards set by the State. Teacher qualifications are lower now than at any time New China came into being, and inevitably, the improvement of education is being seriously retarded. The position with aspects to secondary science teachers is given in the following tables.

Table 4. Number of secondary science teachers, 1981-1982

(in thousand)

Subject	*Total*	*Lower secondary*	*Upper secondary*
Physics	278.7	212.8	65.9
Chemistry	181.9	122.4	57.4
Biology	67.2	49.4	17.7
Geography	82.8	69.2	13.6
Physiological hygine	12.6	11.9	0.7

Table 5. The academic background of upper secondary science teachers, 1980-1981

(in thousands)

Subject	*Total number*	*Under-graduate*	*College or university leaver*	*Secondary school leaver and below*
Physics	78.2	29.8	23.0	25.4
Chemistry	66.4	24.8	20.0	21.4
Biology	15.1	7.0	4.6	3.5
Geography	13.1	4.5	3.5	5.1

Table 6. The academic background of lower secondary science teachers, 1980-1981

(in thousands)

Subject	*Total number*	*Under graduate*	*College or univer leaver*	*Secondary school leaver*	*Other*
Physics	224.3	9.5	21.6	173.4	19.8
Chemistry	123.2	6.9	14.4	92.5	9.4
Biology	41.0	5.0	6.2	23.1	6.6
Geography	64.9	4.3	6.3	41.5	12.8
Physiological hygiene	9.6	0.7	1.0	5.8	2.1

Institutions for Teacher Training

(a) *Education colleges.* Education colleges and teachers' colleges are responsible for training teachers for upper secondary schools at provincial level and lower secondary school teachers at district level. Teacher training schools at country or municipal district level are responsible for training primary school teachers.

(b) *Correspondence departments of normal colleges or schools.* These are responsible for in-service training of primary and secondary teachers on a regional basis.

Other Types of Teacher Training

(a) *Self-help.* Teachers are encouraged to improve their own educational standards by private study leading to recognized examinations.

(b) ***On-the-job training.*** Individual schools are encouraged to offer on-the-job training for inexperienced teachers using older and more experienced teachers as tutors.

(c) ***Short course.*** Education colleges and teachers' colleges offer short-term course on aspects of teaching methods and materials. These are specifically aimed at unqualified teacher and those who have difficulty in teaching the new materials.

Out-of-school Science Education for Young People

Activities in out-of-school science education for young people have played an important role in the all-round improvement of education, in the development of young people's scientific competence, and in the earliest possible identification and training of science talent. Out of school science education has developed vigorously in the last few years and great efforts have been made at the central and local levels, mainly under the following categories.

Leadership. To strengthen leadership, various organizations have been set up both at the central and local levels. In June 1981, the National Leading Group for Youngsters' Scientific Activities (NLGYSA) was formed through the joint action of five organizations—the China Association for Science and Technology (CAST), the Ministry of Education, the State Commission for Physical Culture and Sports, the Communist Youth League, and All-China Women's Federation. The main task of the group is to :

(a) co-ordinate efforts made by various departments to develop out-of-school science activities for young people;

(b) identify and study problems existing in out-of-school science activities, involving tactics and policies;

(c) organize activities and to share experience; and

(d) promote international exchanges in this field.

Leading groups of offices have been set up accordingly at the provincial, municipal and autonomous region levels for such activities.

CAST, science its restoration in 1978, has regarded the development of science education for young people as one of its main tasks. In CAST, there is a department for young people where the acting organ of NLGYSA is located. CAST has brought its advantages as a mass body into full play and stimulated various associations, societies and pop-science institutions to develop their work on science activities for young people.

Some primary and secondary schools in the country have set up leading groups for out-of-school science activities consisting of principals and science teachers.

In other places, institutions for developing young people's science activities are located in educational administrative departments. In Shanghai, for example, an 'Institute for Promoting Pop-Science Activities among Youngsters' has been set up jointly by five organizations—Shanghai Committee for the Communist Youth League, Shanghai Association for Science and Technology, Shanghai Education Department, Shanghai Commission for Physical Culture and Sports, and Shanghai Women's Federation. Its task is to exercise leadership and co-ordinate science activities for young people in the whole city. In addition, there is a children's palace (founded by the China Welfare Institute) in Shanghai, and each district and country has its own children's palace under the leadership of an educational department at the same level. These are important places for out-of-school science activities.

A leading group for science activities had been set up in about one-third of the 3,328 primary and 916 secondary schools in Shanghai. Preliminary statistics indicate that there are 3,131 science amateur groups with 114,228 members in schools all over the city. Thus, a net work of out-of-school science education has taken shape, enabling such activities to achieve remarkable results in the whole area.

One of the key links in developing science activities for young people is the provision of instructors. An association of instructors for young people's science activities has been set up in most of the provinces, municipalities and autonomous regions of the country. In June, 1983, the China Association of Instructors for Youngsters' Science Activities was established to give guidance to local branches in organizing activities; develop various activities for members, and thus help to raise their professional levels; pass on suggestions and opinions to the Government; organize research work, and to compile and publish a journal of the association and develop communication and exchange with foreign organizations of a similar nature. There are, at present, some 400,000 instructors in associations throughout the country.

Associations of young amateurs are the young people's own organizations; they develop various activities under the guidance of academic societies. Associations for astronomy, geology, biology, radio and mathematics have been set up in some districts, municipalities and autonomous regions. In Shanghai for example, seven different associations have been created—associations for chemistry, astronomy, electronics, mathematics, aviation, navigation and geology; and preparation is being made for the founding of associations for biology and photography. These associations are often located in the municipal children's palace.

Activities. The main types of activities organized in recent years include lectures on pop-science, talks on science and technology, and various kinds of training classes; visits to science research institutions, zoological and botanical gardens and museums; meeting scientists, technicians and engineers; experiments and projects; film shows, lantern slide shows, pre-recorded television programmes, reading pop-science books and magazines; writing short scientific papers, dairies, and investigation reports; summary and winter science camps and science parties; and exhibitions of projects and artifacts and science contests.

There have also been several national level activities :

(a) A National Exhibition of Scientific Artifacts by Young people was held in Beijing, in 1979, where more than 8,000 artifacts of excellence made by young people throughout 29 provinces, municipalities, and autonomous regions were displayed. During this two month show, 280,000 people visited the exhibition.

(b) A national summer aviation camp was held in 1979 with 3,000 young aviation amateurs of all nationalities. The young campers, who were made aware of the principles of aeronautics and aviation history, watched demonstration flights, and enjoyed themselves by flying planes and developing their perceptual understanding of their interest in and their feelings for aviation.

(c) In 1981, 3,100 young students took part in decentralized geology summer camp activities, and in 1982, nearly 10,000 students from the country at large participated in such activities.

(d) The First National Contest on Creations and Inventions by Young People and Symposium for Young People was held in August, 1982, attended by 290 primary and secondary students of ten nationalities, the youngest being only 7 years old.

(e) 'Love for Science Month' is a designated month each year, when primary and secondary students are requested to read a book on science, to come to know that story of a scientist, to see a science film, to undertake a scientific experiment or to write a short paper.

Science education for adults Adults constitute the majority of the national population of 1,000 million. Most of them are workers and peasants, who are directly engaged in industrial and agricultural production. In this group, persons aged between 18 and 50 years are greatest in number. Accordingly, it is assumed that science education for adults is intended mainly for workers and peasants of this age range.

Science this kind of education is intended for huge masses of people, whose studying conditions are different, the principle of integrating teaching with production offers education of varied forms according to the local conditions.

Relevant statistics for 1982 show that the total enrolment of adults studying in higher institutions was 1,172,600 comprising :

(a) Workers and peasants at universities : 143,500;

(b) Radio and TV universities : 347,200;

(c) Normal schools of higher education and colleges for middle school teachers' training : 474,100; and

(d) Correspondence departments run by regular colleges and universities, evening universities and independent correspondence colleges : 207,800.

The total enrolment of adults attending secondary schools was 10,804,100 comprising :

(a) Technical secondary schools : 3,263,900

(b) Spare-time secondary schools : 6,349,900 and

(c) Schools for primary school teacher training : 1,190,300

This constituted an increase of 31.6 per cent over 1981.

Training Programmes. Training programmes have been established for technical and managerial staff, workers and peasants. These programmes include science education related to the local environment and local employment such as agriculture. The scale of the operations is enormous. For example, it is planned to reach more than 100 million peasants during the Sixth and Seventh Five-Year Plans so that, by 1990, 20 per cent of peasants will be educated up to agricultural primary or secondary vocational school level. This training will take place in technical schools for peasants run by production brigades and people's communes, some full-time, some part-time.

Statistics in 1982 show that nearly 14 million peasants were studying in educational institutions of all kinds and 70 per cent were studying agricultural science and techniques. Such adult education is leading to improved grain production and improved average incomes.

Activities. There are more than 400 museums in China including a number of museums of natural science, and 20 botanical gardens. The biggest museums of natural science are located in Shanghai, Beijing, Tianjin, and Dalian. The Shanghai Nature Museum is a comprehensive museum which comprises multiple nature sciences such as palaeontology, botany, zoology, anthropology, astronomy and geology. There is a plan to complete before 1985 six branch museums of zoology, botany, palaeontology, anthropology, geology and astronomy. Today, the museum of zoology has been built and the preparations for the construction of other have begun. This museum has eight exhibition halls for palaeozoological history, human evolution and modern animals. The annual average number of visitors is 550,000; mostly teenagers. Several temporary exhibition halls have been opened with exhibitions entitled 'Ancient Dead bodies in China', 'Total Solars Eclipse in 1980 in Yunnan Province', 'Ramer Animals' and so on. Sometimes, exhibitions are improvised to spread scientific knowledge to the masses. In 1981, the exhibitions, including mobile ones, attracted a total of 850,000 visitors. Near the museum, there is a cinema screening science films, open to the public, and specializing in popularizing scientific knowledge. In 1983, it gave 527 shows to 68,000 spectators, many of whom were teenage students.

Apart from comprehensive museums of natural science, there are many specialized museums such as museums of geology, anthropology, medical history, science and technology, and industrial agricultural and aeronautical exhibitions. For example, Beijing Planetarium contributes to the popularization of astronomical knowledge, where various kinds of exhibitions on special topics are held and ancient astronomical instruments, ancient methods for astronomical observation and an ancient calendar of China are on display.

Films, TV, broadcasting, pictures, charts, slide shows, galleries, picture posters and propaganda cars represent important other ways to popularize science among the masses. Most of the provinces and municipalities all over the country have scientific and technical film studios, which have produced many films of this type to popularize science and technology. Local science associations and departments concerned in different places take charge of the distribution and projection of these kinds of films. For example, under the guidance of the Municipal Science Association of Shanghai, the science and educational film administration centre of the municipality was set up with correspondent organizations in districts and countries to do the job. Incomplete statistics in 1982 show that the institutions of the municipal science association system gave

2,434 shows of science and educational films with a total of 1,012,402 spectators.

TV and broadcasting can be used as effective instruments for popularizing science. In addition, video, slide shows, pictures, picture-story books, and galleries on streets are other ways of spreading popular science. In 1980, the Science Association of China, the Publishing House for Popular Science and the Institute for Energy Resources of the Academy of Sciences of China jointly published pictures about energy resources with an impression of 53,000 copies.

Recreation places an clubs of popular science have been established in recent year as a means of popularizing science. The advantage is the integration of science education with entertainment. It has become one of the new entertainments loved by teenagers. For instance, the recreation place of popular science which was built with funds of the Municipal Science Association of Shanghai, has fluorescent material, electronic sound control, electronic music, meteorological observation, laser and other topics and attracted 200,000 visitors in January, 1983 alone.

Popular science publications are admired by teenagers and the masses generally. In the whole country, there are 17 publishing houses of popular science books, 130 different popular science magazines and 50 science newspapers with a impression of 4 million copies each issues. To satisfy the mass demand for scientific and technical knowledge, certain districts began to publish newspapers specifically for this purpose. For example, in Human province, 96 counties and towns have their own newspapers of agricultural science and techniques with an impression of 2,540,000 copies, an average of four copies per peasant family. This is development without precedent in the history of China.

In recent years, more and more popular science books have been published. According to statistics, 1,427 popular science books were published in 1980, 2,100 in 1981, and in 1982 the Agricultural Publishing House alone published 120 books on agricultural science and techniques. The total print of popular science books exceeds 5 million copies.

Research in Science Education

The Central Institute of Educational Research was re-established, in 1978. In 1979, the Ministry of Education and the Academy of Social Science of China jointly convened a first conference for planing the national programme for educational research at which the 'Plan and Programme for Developing Educational Science from 1978 to 1985' was discussed and approved. This conference played a major role in encouraging, motivating and organizing educational research. In the past four years research work in science education has progressed considerably. By the end of 1982, research staff in the Central Institute of Educational Research numbered 120. There are 16 provinces and municipalities, and 36 institutions of higher education (mainly normal colleges and schools, and a small number of comprehensive universities) where institutes of educational research have been set up with 1,200 professional personnel; there are 28 provinces, municipalities and autonomous regions where societies of education have been founded with 12,000 members. Research on science education is underway in all normal colleges and schools as well as institutes for educational research attached to some of the comprehensive universities. Yet, generally speaking, this kind of work had only just begun. The Central Institute of Educational Research is now preparing for a second national conference on programmes for educational research so that such research may help to contribute more to the development of education policies identified in the Sixth Five-year Plan. Research on science education will be include in the national programmes for educational research, and it will thus contribute to the development of science activities.

5

India

India is a land of incident civilizations having a rich heritage of science. The study of science such as astronomy, chemistry, mathematics, medicine and surgery dates back a very long time. The ancient literature in science education through the media of India languages in modern India.

First exposures to modern science education began with the advent of western foreign powers. Even before independence in 1947, India produced a Noble Laureate, several Fellows of the Royal Society and many eminent scientists.

India is a vast country with 23 states and nine union territories having a diverse social and cultural heritage. Recognizing the varying levels of economic and social conditions and the numerous languages, education has been retained as a state responsibility. The Central Government, of course, provides leadership and acts as a catalyst and co-ordinator of progressive changes. But it would be a mistake to consider any single statement of state or government policy on science education. The Scientific Policy, Resolution (1985) and the National Policy on Education (1968 and 1986), both passed by Parliament; the Report of the UNESCO Planning Mission (1964); the Report of the Education Commission (1964-66); and the successive Five-Year Plan documents accepted by the government are all important indicators of the educational policy of the country.

Science Policy

The Science Policy Resolution, piloted by Jawaharlal Nehru, at the first Prime Minister, was adopted by Parliament in 1958. It recognizes technology as a key factor for economic development, emphasizes the importance of the study of science and its application not only as a means of providing material and cultural amenities and services to every member of the community but as a method of influencing basic human values.

Although the Science Policy Resolution does not specifically mention school education or out-of-school education as such, it impact on both have been tremendous.

In pursuance of the Science Policy Resolution, the government took several steps to establish institutions for education and research, founded institutions for governmental guidance and created conditions which three Conferences of Scientists and Educationists in 1958, 1963, and 1970 and a round table conference of scientists and technologist in 1966 to assess the follo-up action on the Resolution. Some of the recommendations of these conferences that have a direct bearing on school science education and the popularization of science for out-of-school youths and adults through formal and non-formal means are :

(a) Efforts should be made to disseminate and popularize science using media such as documentary films, radio television, popular science journals and magazines;

(b) The search for scientific talent should be started at the higher secondary school level;

(c) Efforts should be made to provide facilities for the manufacture of instruments and scientific apparatus required by schools and colleges; and

(d) Scientists in universities and laboratories should take part in school science education. They should establish contacts with local educational authorities in advisory capacities.

The National Council of Educational Research and Training (NCERT) was established (1961) as an autonomous body to assist and advise in implementing the education policies of the government and to work for all-round improvement of school education in close collaboration with the states and union territories.

In 1986, Parliament adopted a resolution: 'National Policy on Education' which states that science and mathematics should be an integral part of general education throughout the school stage (*i.e.* first ten years of education).

The National Policy Resolution of 1968 laid great emphasis on non-formal and adult education for overcoming mass illiteracy, which is necessary for national development in general.

Successive Five-Year Plans from the Second Plan to the Sixth Plan (1980-85) review the progress and projections of various aspects of education, including science education, and determine the priority of financial allocation and operational emphases for the various states and agencies which are concerned with the actual implementation of policies. The Sixth Five-Year Plan, for example, seeks to strengthen science teaching through provision of laboratory equipment both for class experiment and demonstration; through the supply of science kits at primary and middle level; and by the design, production and supply of an appropriate kit for secondary and higher secondary stages.

The Structure of School Education

Shortly after independence the 'Secondary Education Commission' was set up in 1952, to make suggestions for improving education at the secondary level.

Bases on the recommendations of the Commission, a decision was taken to develop a national pattern of education with 11 years of school education followed by three year first degree course. The last three years of the school stage, called the higher secondary stage, were to comprise diversified streams such as science, humanities and commerce. The three year first degree course was introduced in almost every state, but not many states were quick to implement the decision on the pattern of higher secondary education.

Another 'Education Commission' was set up in 1964 to consider the educational structure in general and recommended that school education should extend over 12 years with some flexibility in its sub-stages, such as :

(a) Primary stage of seven years followed by a lower secondary stage of three years or a primary stage of eight years followed by a lower secondary stage of two years for general education courses;

(b) Higher secondary stage of two years; and

(c) A higher education stage having a course of three years or more for the first degree, followed by courses of varying duration for the second or research degrees.

The National Government adopted a resolution—'The National Policy on Education' (1968) which stated : 'It will be advantageous to have a broadly uniform educational structure in all parts of the country. The ultimate objectives should be to adopt the 10+2+3 pattern'.

Subsequently, the Ministry of Education and Social Welfare established an expert group in 1973 to develop the curriculum for the 10+2 pattern and a document entitled *The Curriculum for the Ten-year School—A Framework was published in 1975.*

A large number of states have accepted and implemented the 10+2 pattern of school education although there is variety in the substages of primary, middle, secondary and senior (higher) secondary.

Science Education in Schools

Structure. Teaching of science in some form or other begins right from Class I in all the states and union territories. In Classes I to V, it is taught under different names *e.g.* elementary science, nature study, general science, environmental studies. In Classes VI to VIII, it was mostly taught as a general science up to 1967. Teaching of science as separate disciplines (physics, chemistry and biology) was then introduced in a phased manner in Classes VI to VIII under a UNESCO/UNICEF-Assisted Science Education Project. Science gradually became a compulsory subject for all students up to Class VIII.

Under the 10+2 pattern of schooling, after the first ten years the students are expected either to enter the world of work, or to continue studying in the two year (+2) stage. In the case of the latter, a student may either study in the academic stream preparing for higher education or he may enter the vocational stream which would prepare him for a trade or technical skill.

A student who chooses the academic stream and studies science offers physics, chemistry and biology as separate disciplines. Students who plan to move to engineering colleges after completing the +2stage must also study mathematics whereas those planning to enter medical course must offer biology.

Time Allocation. There is a prescribed minimum of 240 working school days in a year—220 days for instruction and 20 days for school camps and community services.

The 'Report of the Review Committee on the Curriculum for the Ten-year School' made recommendations for time allocations for different subjects. The time allocation recommend for science and mathematics is given in *Table 3*.

Aims and Objectives of Teaching Science

(a) *Primary Stage.* The primary stage of education covers, roughly, the children aged 6 to 11 years studying in Classes I to V. Before the child enters school, he has developed spontaneity, curiosity, creativity an activity. The content and methods of teaching science at the primary stage are geared to the promotion and substainment of these qualities.

Table 1. Time allocation recommended for science and mathematics

Stage/ classes	*Total No. of periods per week*	*Time allocation per week as percentage*	
		Science	*Mathematics*
Primary Classes I-V	24 to 30 periods	(As Environmental Studies it includes social studies, nature study and health education)	20
Middle Classes V/VI to VII/VIII	32 periods	(As Science—an integrated course)	12.5
Secondary Classes IX to X	32 periods	15.6	12.5

In Classes I and II science is taught as Environmental Studies. Environmental Studies is continued in Classes III to V, with the following objectives based on the suggestions of the Review Committee :

(i) To enable children to observe their environment and enrich their experience, thereby developing skills in the process of science, such as observing, communicating, measuring, making a guess, experimenting to test the guess;

(ii) To gain knowledge of scientific facts and principles, and have a better understanding of the phenomena taking place in the environment around them;

(iii) To develop scientific attitudes in life, which may include a rational outlook, open-mindness, a positive inclination for democratic, secular and socialist outlook to situations in life, opposition to prejudices based on sex, caste, religion, language or region; and

(iv) To develop creative faculties, imagination and independent thinking for locating problems, suggesting solutions and trying out ideas.

(b) ***Middle Stage.*** The middle school years (11-14 years) sees adolescent development and this period can be difficult for many children. Problems of adjustment in the family, the school and the society begin to appear. The child, however, becomes a boy or a girl with greater intellectual, emotional, physical and social maturity than the primary school child. Social demands and responsibilities begin to appear. For many children this stage is terminal. They should, therefore, be prepared adequately to face life and develop capabilities and attitudes for productive work in which they have to participate. Accordingly the general objectives of teaching science at this stage are to :

(i) emphasize the relevance of science to daily life;

(ii) develop scientific attitudes;

(iii) create an environment conducive to greater reliance on the use of principles and practices of science;

(iv) acquaint the pupils with varirous natural phenomena;

(v) emphasize the experimental nature of science; and

(vi) emphasize the unity of methods of different disciplines of science.

(c) ***Secondary Stage.*** The ninth and tenth years comprising the secondary stage are the final years of general education. After this the student may either enter the world of work or take up vocational or academic courses. All the objectives of teaching science at the middle school stage are extended and intensified with aims and objectives to :

(i) enable the students to recognize the role of science in day-to-day life;

(ii) promote interest in students for science and to enable them to use science as an important tool for developing industries, agriculture and medicine; and

(iii) develop some basic concepts in science which provide a background for learning science at the senior level.

(d) ***Higher (senior secondary) stage.*** At the senior secondary stage there are certain major objectives which are common for all the disciplines, namely, physics, chemistry and biology. These are to :

(i) strengthen the concepts developed at the secondary level and further develop new concepts to provide a sound background for higher studies;

(ii) develop competence in students to pursue professional course, such as engineering, medicine or agriculture as their future carrier;

(iii) acquaint the students with different aspects of science used in daily life and to enable them to recognize that science plays an important role in the service of man;

(iv) expose students to different processes used in industry and other areas of production and to acquaint them with the technology involved; and

(v) provide relevant content materials useful for vocational courses at the senior secondary stage.

Organization and Content of Science Course

(a) *Primary stage.* In Classes I and II, the study is centred around the immediate environment of the child, and the two aspects of the environment, social and physical, are not segregated. Different units include family, home, school neighbourhood, the earth, sky and man's life.

In Classes III to V, the social and physical aspects of the environment are dealt with separately as Environmental Studies Parts I and II, respectively. The content of Environmental Studies Part II, is organized spirally, centred around living things, the human body, nutrition, health and hygiene, soil erosion, natural resources air, water and weather, properties of matter and materials, housing and clothing, force, work and energy, the earth and the sky.

(b) *Middle Stage.* In accordance with the recommendations of the UNESCO Planning Mission (1964), and the subsequent development of the UNESCO Experimental Project and its implementation under the UNICEF-Assisted 'Science Education Project' (SEP), the teaching of science as separate disciplines was introduced in a large number of schools at the middle stage (Classes VI-VIII). Some states are continuing with the separate disciplines approach, whilst other states are following the physical sciences (physics and chemistry) and life sciences (botany, zoology and human physiology) approach.

After the '12 year schooling' was accepted in principle, work started on the development of an alternative integrated science course up to Class VIII, which avoids compartmentalization of science into different disciplines. In order to have a smooth transition from the disciplinary to the integrated approach, integration only at an elementary level was attempted and the environment was used as one of the factors for developing the teaching/learning activities.

(c) *Secondary Stage.* Physics, chemistry and life sciences are aspects of sciences at the secondary level. In some states, science is taught as physical sciences and biological sciences at this level, in others as physics, chemistry and biology. At present the Central board of Secondary Education (CBSE) prescribes two course for the secondary level, science course, A, under which a student has to study science as separate disciplines, physics, chemistry and biology, and course B which is an integrated course. A student can opt for either one of these courses.

Recently, however, the CBSE has decided to offer only a single interdisciplinary course.

(d) ***Higher (senior secondary) stage.*** The science course at the senior secondary stage consist of physics, chemistry and biology.

The course in chemistry at the senior secondary level (+2 stage) as developed by the NCERT, is major change from previous courses, The following aspects are worth mentioning :

— Chemistry is presented as a unified subject. There is no traditional classification as physical, inorganic or organic chemistry. Basic concepts are developed in the beginning and applied to the study of elements and their compounds in subsequent units.

— Development of the concepts in the textbooks is through the spiral approach.

— The course provides sufficient background for professional courses like medicine or engineering, which students may offer after this stage.

— Students offering professional and vocational courses may not be interested in abstract theory, but instead would like to know how the principles of chemistry can be applied. With this in mind, in many cases, derivation of mathematical formulae and equations has been avoided but these formulae and equations have been applied in explaining physico-chemical principles. Equal emphasis has been given to chemical principles and descriptive chemistry in the text and correlating the two.

— Similar to secondary education, senior secondary education is also linked with National Development Goals.

— Areas of an inter-disciplinary nature are given adequate emphasis (chemistry occupies a rather central and unique position among the science).

— SI Units are used throughout the textbooks.

— The laboratory part of the course in chemistry includes some traditional, some open-ended and some environmental investigations.

Like chemistry, the teaching of physics at the senior secondary level (+2 stage) shows a major change from the past. The following aspects are worth mentioning.

— It has an integrated approach *e.g.* in the chapter on 'Waves' the concepts in mechanics, light and sound have been developed.

— The approach is similar to PSSC of the USA: mathematical derivation of equations has not been given so much importance as the use of the final form of equation to develop concepts in physics.

— There are a number of new topics introduced for the first time in the physics course such as, theory of relativity and astro-physics.

— Only very elementary knowledge of calculus has been used in deriving equations.

— For the first time, projects in physics practical work have been introduced.

Some of the special features of the biology course developed by NCERT are :

— Students will be able to proceed for higher education in ecology, botany, physiology, microbiology, agriculture, anthropology and medicine.

— They will also be prepared for vocations such as controlling pests, vegetative propagation in horticulture, apiculture, seri-culture, pisciculture and poultry farming.

— A number of skills (both for productive work and higher studies) are expected to be developed e.g. ability to identify local plants and animals, ability to identify important discuses of cultivated plants and diseases of domestic animals. They will be able to undertake small individual projects and open-ended experiments and prepare charts and models.

— Students will be able to understand the various biological aspects of social problems such as that of environment, population, and individual and community health resources.

Curriculum Development in Science

The National Council of Educational Research and Training (NCERT), is the key body at the national level for curriculum development and improvement of school education. NCERT is responsible for developing syllabuses, textbooks, teacher's guides, test items, science kits and various teaching aids for improving science education throughout the school stage.

Under the UNICEF-Assisted 'Science Education Project' science curricula materials were developed within NCERT by the academic staff of the Department of Education in Science and Mathematics, in collaboration with UNESCO experts.

Simultaneously 20 study groups were set up in physics, chemistry, biology and mathematics at various universities and research centres throughout the country under the chairmanship of eminent professors and scientists. They developed alternative versions of curricula and textbooks for use in elementary and secondary schools.

Yet another method adopted by NCERT has been the development of text materials through Editorial Boards, consisting of eminent professors and with books prepared by authors commissioned for the purpose. This mechanism was used in the wake of the adoption of the 10+2 pattern of school education when curriculum materials were required speedily. Materials produced by NCERT have been freely made available for adoption or adaptation by the states.

At the state level, every state has a board of secondary/high school education which prescribes the syllabus and textbooks for the secondary and senior secondary stage of education and conducts public examinations at the end of these stages. Curriculum development at the elementary stage (I—VIII is the responsibility of the State Department of Education through State

Institutes of Education, State Institutes of science Education, and the State Council of Educational Research and Training.

At the national level, the Central Board of Secondary Education with about 1,200 affiliated schools all over the country conducts All-India and Delhi Senior Secondary and Secondary examinations. Eminent educationists, university professors, school principals and practising teachers are members of the subject committees of the CBSE.

The Board prescribes textbooks for its various courses by: (a) adopting textbooks developed by NCERT if they cover the syllabus of the Board; (b) inviting manuscripts from private publishers; and (c) undertaking a book development programme under which it commissions authors or a team of authors to write a book for subsequent publication by the Board.

In many states, organizations such as Textbook Bureau/Text book Corporations also exist. Preparation, production and publication of textbooks is undertaken by these organizations in collaborations with different state educational agencies and experts.

As the states began to use new science materials, a need was felt to set up an institution in each state which could undertake in-service training of teachers and handle field problems. Institutes designated as State Institutes of Education were set up at the initiative of the National Government and began training teachers and supervisors and collaborating with NCERT in all aspects of curriculum development.

Some states also established State Institutes of Science Education solely to look after the improvement of science education; other expanded the State Institutes of Education to create or strengthen a science unite in the institution. There were other states that set up a State Council of Educational Research and Training on the model of NCERT and undertook similar functions at the state level.

For a vast country like India, it is difficult to follow a uniform pattern and cycle for curriculum revision. However, the states and union territories are advised not to revise the syllabus and change the textbooks more frequently than every five years.

At the national leave, the last revision took place from 1975 to 1978 when the 10+2 pattern of school education was adopted. Another revision of curricular materials is now planned during the period 1984-1986.

Evaluation. An historical perspective in Indian education would reveal that examinations continue to dominate the education system. The Report of the Secondary Education Commission (1952-53) commented :

> The examinations determine not only the content of education but also the methods of teaching, in fact the entire approach to education. They have so pervaded the entire atmosphere of school life that they have become the main motivating force of all effort on the part of pupil as well as teacher.

After reviewing the defects of evaluation at the secondary education stage, the Commission recommended a new approach to evaluation at school stage and made a number of concrete proposals for the improvement of the external examinations and the methods of internal assessment. As a result of these proposals, a movement was started for examination reform which gathered momentum with the establishment by the Government of the Central Examination Unit with its trained evaluation officers, in 1958. This unit later merged into NCERT's Department of Measurement and Evaluation.

The outstanding feature of the new reform movement is the emphasis laid on : (a) format of questions such as, short answer, multiple choice; (b) coverage of syllabus; (c) difficulty level of questions; (d) provision of parallel internal options if required; (e) proper weighted distribution on testing of various skills and abilities such as knowledge, comprehension, application, skills; and (f) fulfilment of various stated objectives of the course.

This has found increasing acceptance in recent years. Under the examination reform movement, NCERT, in collaboration with various state educational agencies mounted a multi-pronged drive for the popularization of new techniques of evaluation. It introduced thousands of teachers and training college lecturer to new techniques of evaluation, set up a large pool of test items and trained paper-setters. It resulted in the setting up of an evaluation unit in each board. Through this movement the written external examinations conducted by the boards have improved considerably. However, it left untouched the testing of applications and problem solving abilities.

On external public examination is held at the secondary or matriculation stage and another at the senior/higher secondary/ intermediate stage. In most of the states science students are examined only on theory at the secondary stage but on both theory and practical at the senior/higher secondary stage through external examinations. Certain well-defined trends have emerge in this area. The chief among these are : the evaluation of both the process as well as the product of performance, wide coverage of skills instead of limited coverage, and more objective scoring instead of arbitrary and subjective scoring.

There is also an annual internal examination conducted by individual schools at the end of each academic session and periodic assessment. On the basis of their achievement in annual and periodic tests, students are promoted from one class to the next.

Laboratory Work and Equipment

Time Allocation for Practical Work. At primary level, the curricula developed and implemented both at the national and state levels, laid special emphasis on the performance of activities by pupils for learning science. Most of these activities are, however, related to the child's own environment. All learning of science at this stage flows from the concrete experiences gathered from the activities in the environment. Thus, the child's activities are fully integrated with the learning of science. As such there is no separate allocation of periods for practical work and theory at this stage and the teacher is free to organize practical activities for children according to the requirements of the topic.

For the middle level, the 'Curriculum for the ten year school—a framework' advocates :

> For the teaching of science, there should be a gradual introduction of contrived situations. The students should handle scientific appartus and perform experiments. Demonstrations by the teacher interspersed with questions and answers could help to establish the properties of substances or cause-effect relationships. Concrete

experiences gained through demonstrations or thorough experimentation by the pupils will help the understanding of theory.

In keeping with these guidelines, NCERT has developed an integrated science curriculum for which textbooks entitled *Learning Science: Parts I, II, III* have been developed. An integrated science kit has been developed to enable the teacher to demonstrate. In some cases the pupils also perform experiments.

At the secondary level about 30 per cent to 35 per cent of total time devoted to teaching science should be available for practical work. A single textbook containing course in physics, chemistry and biology, entitled *Science Part I (for Class IX) and Science Part II* (for Class X) has been so developed that teaching and learning in science is not dependent on the availability of a formal laboratory and sophisticated equipment.

At the senior secondary level, practical work is no longer confined to verification of laws such as Boyle's law. Open-ended experiments have been introduced. Project-work has been added in physics. Some environmental investigations in chemistry have been introduced. Process skills are being given importance in practical work.

The approach of teaching at the +2 stage is based on experiment and enquiry. However, laboratory facilities being limited in schools, it has not been possible to organize adequate laboratory work and to link practical work with theory.

Examination in Practical Work. Practical work is an examinable subject at the end of secondary and senior secondary stages for schools affiliated to the Central Board of Secondary Education, Delhi. The position in the states differs from Board to Board. In some, it is examinable only at the senior secondary stage, whereas in others practical work is not examinable at all.

At the senior secondary examination of the Central Board, 30 per cent marks are reserved for practical work and 70 per cent for the theory paper in physics, chemistry and biology. The position is more or less the same at the secondary level and in other state Boards where practical work is examinable.

Availability of Science Equipment. Although science is a compulsory subject in the first ten years of schooling, some schools do not have provision for teaching science through practical activities.

Even where such provision exists, science is not necessarily taught using apparatus. Even if science equipment is available in schools, it may not be adequate for teaching the subject. Under the UNICEF-Assisted Science Education Project science kits have been supplied to some schools.

School science equipment is available from indigenous sources and some apparatus is exported to neighbouring countries. The Indian Standards Institution has prescribed specifications for many items of school science equipment.

The workshop department of NCERT is involved in designing and producing kits of apparatus required for the primary and middle stage of education. There are also private manufacturers who manufacture science equipment for all stages of education.

Some aspects of work relating to the production of equipment undertaken in the Workshop Department of NCERT are :

(i) *Planning and development*

- Designing a kit/piece of equipment;
- Developing a prototype;
- Try-out in actual classroom conditions;
- Modifications in the light of feedback reviewed.

(ii) *Production and dissemination*

- Preparation of blueprints;
- Limited production of science kits/equipment;
- Preparation of a kit manual and film on the use of kit;
- Training key personnel from states in the use of science kits and in the inspection for quality control;

— Supply of kits to states on request;
— Supply of blueprints to states and private manufacturers.

Educational Technology

Realizing the importance of the use of audio-visual techniques in education, the Government set up a unit for the production of visual aids in the Ministry of Education. In 1951, a Conference on Audio-Visual Education was organized. It recommended the establishment of a National Board of Audio-Visual Education to lay down policies for the development of audio-visual education in the country and to periodically assess the progress achieved in this field in the states and at the centre.

The importance of audio-visual education was accepted by the Government of India by inclusion of audio-visual programmes in the various five-year plans and also by setting up the National Institute of Audio-Visual Education in 1959. The Institute was housed in specially built premises, with an excellent auditorium in New Delhi. It organized training for leaders at the state level, produced inexpensive AV materials including films and film-strips, and provided extension services, through the circulation of films, film-strips and distribution of audio-visual literature. In 1961 the National Institute of Audio-Visual Education became a constituent department of the National Institute of Education of NCERT and in 1969 it was renamed the Department of Teaching Aids (DTA) of NCERT.

In the early 1970s a Centre for Educational Technology (CET) was established within NCERT, with technical assistance from UNESCO. This centre, working at the national level, was given the main responsibility of preparing suitable programmes for school level to be used under a distance project: CET has been closely associated with the planning of school broadcasts and the school programme for the Indian Satellite INSAT, (1980). Using two-hour school programmes through INSAT, viewed in thousand of elementary schools, the science syllabus was fully covered through well planned ETV lessons prepared in advance. Use was made of special teaching aids including educational films, tape/slides, film-strips and graphic aids, already prepared for the purpose, by the DTA.

Besides curricular topics, several other themes related to science and of vital importance for national development such as 'Health and Nutrition', 'Population Education', 'Environmental Education' have been covered through INSAT. With increase local production of TV sets, more and more schools and communities have benefited from such programmes.

During the 1970s, production of cassette tape-recorders increased considerably and they became available to teacher training institutes and even some schools. However, not every school benefited science good quality cassette tapes were still imported and expensive.

Transistorized radio sets operation on dry cells or mains electricity came within the reach of the majority of schools because of easy availability and low cost.

Hundreds of training college teachers, key persons of AV units in states, school-teachers and other interested in the field of educational technology and in science education have been trained during the last three decades. Today all states and union territories have educational technology units. These units are well equipped with hardware such as 16 mm sound projectors, overhead projectors and 35 mm film-strip/slide projectors.

In some states, 10-25 per cent of secondary schools have a reasonably good collection of AV aids managed either by a science teacher or a teacher specially trained for the purpose.

Teacher Training

Qualifications of Teachers. The non-availability of qualified, trained teachers to work in schools is one of the crucial problems experience in the context of educational development in the country in the post-independence period. This problem is more acute in the case of science teachers because of qualitative expansion of educational facilities; the introduction of science as a compulsory subject up to Class X; and the rate of the knowledge explosion and consequent updating of science syllabuses.

For a primary school teacher, the minimum qualification is matriculation or secondary certificate followed by an Elementary Teachers Training Certificate after a course of two years duration.

For the middle school stage the minimum qualification is the senior (higher) secondary certificate followed by the Elementary Teachers Training (two-year) certificate. In the Union Territory of Delhi and in some other states, graduation with a teacher training degree is required for this level.

For secondary school teachers, the minimum qualification required is a Bachellor's degree followed by one-year professional training in a secondary teachers' training college.

The minimum qualification for the senior/higher secondary stage is a post-graduate degree in the relevant subject followed by one-year professional training in a secondary teachers' training college.

It can be seen from the table that a high proportion of teachers are still inadequately qualified. Efforts have been made both at the national and state levels to overcome this deficiency through the organization of summer institutes for in-service teachers (1964-1977); a crash programme for teacher training (early 1970s); the UNICEF-Assisted Science Education Project (SEP) for primary and middle teachers (1967-1978); post-graduate diploma courses for teachers of secondary and higher secondary levels in various states (1970s); distance learning (SITE, Open School-mid 1970s); and the establishment of centres of continuing education (late 1970s).

Table 2. Distribution of teachers working in recognized institutions

(Figures in thousands)

Stage	*Total No. of working teachers*	*No. of teachers teaching science*	*No. of science teachers competent to teach science*	*No. of science teachers not competent to teach science*
Primary	1,500	1,230	1,080	150 (12.2%)
Middle	580	260	240	20 (7.7%)
Secondary	380	95	79	16 (16.8%)
Higher/Senior Secondary	120	30	9	21 (70%)

Pre-service Training. The weak points of the prevailing system of teacher education have been highlighted from time to time by the 'University Education Commission' (1949), the 'Secondary Education Commission' (1953), the 'International Team on Teachers and Curricula in Secondary Schools' (1954) and by the 'Education Commission' (1964-1966). According to these reports training institutions for primary and secondary teachers, by the large, have remained isolated from the main stream of the academic life of the university as well as from the daily problems of the schools. Competent staff are not attracted to these institutions. Vitality and realism are lacking in the curriculum, and the programme of work continues to be largely traditional. Set patterns and rigid techniques are followed in the practice teaching.

To provide a structural base for facilitating desired changes in the existing system of teacher education, the Government of India established the National Council of Teacher Education (NCTE) in 1973. The Department of Teacher Education of NCERT acts as the secretariat to the NCTE. This is now the key body planning programmes of teacher preparation both at the pre-service and the in-service level. The document *Teacher education curriculum—a framework* (1978) prepared by NCTE provides guidelines on the various aspects of teacher education and incorporates many suggestions for improving the quality of teacher education in the country.

The traditional curricula were loaded more with topics such as philosophy of education, educational psychology, sociology of education; content and methodology being almost non-existent. In the suggested course structure, the components of : pedagogical theory, working with the community, content and methodology, including practice teaching and related work, have been modified at all stages of teacher education. The respective weightage distributed among these areas is 20 per cent, and 60 per cent respectively.

It should be noted, however, that a large number of teacher training institutions are under the administrative control of the different state governments. Therefore the suggestions of the NCTE have still to be implemented in most of the states.

The total number of primary and secondary teacher training institutions in India is 1,059 and 494 respectively.

In-service Training. To sustain the quality of teacher education it is essential to provide refresher courses in content and methodology. In-service education programmes for teachers are organized by the extension departments of teacher training colleges. The former Directorate of Extension Programmes for Secondary Education, Government of India and later the Department of Extension and Field Services (NCERT) also organize seminars, workshops and orientation courses for the teachers. Thousands of science teachers and teacher educators involved in the Science Education Project for improving science teaching were also specially refrained by the Department of Science Education (NCERT).

The University Grants Commission (UGC) in collaboration with NCERT and USAID organized summer institutes in science and intermediate colleges between 1963 to 1977. NCERT took over the responsibility for organizing summer science institutes at school level from the UGC from the summer of 1972. With the introduction of the 10+2 pattern of school education, there arose an urgent need for intensive in-service education for science and mathematics teachers to handle the new curricula effectively. Accordingly, each year for three years (1975 to 1977), about 100 summer science institutes, each for 50 teachers, were organized to cover all the teachers at secondary and senior secondary stage using the new curricula.

In spite of the above efforts the need for a permanent infrastructure for in-service education on a continuing basis was strongly felt. This resulted in the setting up of State Institutes of Education and State Institutes of Science Education in states and union territories. While the State Institute of Education looks after the in-service training of elementary teachers the State Institute of Science Education is responsible for secondary and senior secondary science teachers. More recently, the State Councils of Educational Research and Training (SCERT), a counterpart of NCERT at state level, are being gradually established in the states by merging all such in-service teacher education institutions.

In 1977 at the national level, NCERT launched a scheme of 'Centres of Continuing Education' for secondary teachers and primary teacher educators to provide an infrastructure for in-service teacher education on a continuing basis. These centres conduct short-duration courses (about 30-40 hours) not only for science teachers but for other subject teachers also. After the launching of this scheme, the summer science institute programme (NCERT) ceased. Initially about 100 centres have been set up, each catering to the needs of the teachers in two or three adjoining districts.

Yet another project for providing training to science teachers and teacher educators in improved methods of science teaching is the 'All-India Science Education Project' undertaken in 1980-1981. It is a collaborative project between the National Government and the British Council and is being implemented by NCERT on behalf of the Government.

Under this project a number of science teachers teaching physics, chemistry or biology at the +2 stage and teacher educators preparing teachers for the +2 stage are awarded fellowships at the Centre for Science Education, Chelsea College, London, for a period of nine months. The teachers who return after training are used as resource persons for conducting post-training workshops in the states to which they belong. Through these workshops, they train more teachers in advanced methods of science education.

Research in Science Education

Research is almost restricted only to the development of instructional materials, methodology of teaching and the resources and facilities available in schools for teaching science. Moreover research conducted on these problems in university departments of education, teacher training colleges or the NCERT is not disseminated properly. A wide communications gap exists not only between research centres but also within individual centres. No journal of standing, devoted exclusively to research in science education, exists. Some investigations are published in national or international educational journals but most workers and consumers in India are unaware of their findings.

Science education as a separate department does not exist in any of the universities. Most research work in science education at Ph.D. level is accepted under the faculty of education. Perhaps the non-existence of a separate department of science education is one of the main reasons of such poor quality of research related to science education.

Programmes for Out-of-school Youth and Adults and Popularization of Science and Technology

The need for a universal scientific literacy had been felt by many eminent Indian scientists and educationists long before independence. The 'Indian Association for Cultivation of Science' established in 1876, the 'Prasharan Movement' in Mysore and the 'Nav Jeevan Samaj' in Gujarat carried out non-formal science teaching for the out-of-school populace, the latter undertaking non-formal teaching of agriculture and its practical application.

After independence, the first model science club, 'Science for Children', was set up in Calcutta during the late 1950's with a view to stimulating, an interest in science. The Vikaram A. Sarabhai Community Science Centre, was founded by local initiatives in Ahmedabad in 1963. In addition to the science programmes for children, this Centre runs several community-oriented programmes in science and technology for the ordinary citizen. It also brings out periodically, a wall science newspaper and publishes mini-books on science for everyone.

The 'Indian Association for Extra-curricular Scientific Activities (IAESA)' was founded in 1968. Besides other activities, IAESA organized the first All-India student fair in 1970 in collaboration with the Indian Science Congress Association. In co-operation with NCERT, IAESA organized a UNESCO regional seminar for leaders of youth science activities in Asia. The World Wild Life Fund (India) helped in developing wild-life clubs in schools. This has helped to create awareness for the preservation of wild-life.

Science Museums. The Council of Scientific and Industrial Research, New Delhi, set up the first science museum in 1959 in Calcutta known as 'Birla Industrial and Technological Museum' (BITM) and established similar museums in Bangalore (1965); Bombay (1977) and Patna (1978). These museums were transferred later to the National Council of Science Museums under the Ministry of Education. Besides the exhibits in the museums, they have mobile science vans to bring science and technology to the rural areas. There are also two 'District Science Centres' attached to Bangalore museum, and two to BITM, Calcutta. These centres cater for the needs of the people of the respective districts. Exhibits in these museums cover the subject area of travel and also show the contemporary technological developments of the country. Recently a 'National Museum of Natural History' has been set up in New Delhi to provide an historical perspective of the progressive use of science and technology by mankind.

Another prominent science museum for creative activity is the Birla Institute of Technology and Science at Pilani, Rajasthan. This is not only an excellent museum, it also trains science teachers in the setting up of science clubs and science museums in schools.

In Calcutta and Bombay, there are planetaria for the public. The Jawahar Lal Nehru Memorial Fund is establishing a large planetarium in Delhi. Besides these, there are small planetaria for the public in a few other cities.

Bal Bhawans and Science Clubs. Today it is generally accepted that the teaching and learning exercise cannot be confined to a school classroom. Therefore, institutions have been set up to provide children with the experiences and opportunities that are beyond the scope of the usual academically-oriented curricula, and yet are vitally important to the physical, mental and emotional growth of the child. Jawahar Bal Bhawans are such institutions in India, named after the late Pandit Jawahar Lal Nehru, the first Prime Minister after independence. There are 12 such institutions. Facilities exist in these Bal Bhawans for science activities such as animal clubs, including care of live animals, plant clubs including gardening, weather clubs, radio clubs and the like. In addition, Bal Bhawans have facilities for the creative development of arts, music, dance and drama.

In addition, there are a number of government aided science clubs which organize symposia and seminars on science topics, essay competitions, debates and lectures by eminent scientists. Children can also take up project work in science, develop models and collect insects and flowers in these science clubs.

Science Fairs and Exhibitions. Inspiration for round-the - year activities is provided by science fairs which are periodically held at district, zonal and state levels and culminate in the national level.exhibition which is held annually. Also, the science exhibition in individual schools has become a regular feature.

The first National Science Exhibition in the country was organized by IAESA in 1970. In the following year the National Science Exhibition was organized by the University Grants Commission (UGC) and NCERT. Subsequent national exhibitions have been organized by NCERT in collaboration with Jawahar Lal Nehru Memorial Fund (JNMF). The exhibition is called the 'National Science Exhibition for Children', and involves almost all States and the Union Territories. Scientific films are shown by the organizers and eminent scientists are invited to deliver lectures during the exhibition. Some universities, public sector organizations and selected science clubs and museums are also invited to bring their exhibits. This has resulted in interaction between the schools and professional organizations.

Selection of exhibits for the national level is made from among the best district level science exhibits displayed in the state exhibitions. Exhibits based on rural technology are given prominence.

Talent Search. An important part of the total programme undertaken by NCERT with direct relevance to the country-wide spread of scientific culture, is identifying and developing scientific talent at various stages of the secondary and senior secondary schools. Since its inception in 1964 and until 1976, NCERT operated what was known as a National Science Talent Search Scheme to identify pupils with a marked aptitude for scientific studies. Up to 1976 the search test was conducted annually in all states the union territories for those students who were at the eleventh year of their schooling. With effect from 1977, NCERT enlarged the scope of the scheme. In addition to basic sciences, the scheme, now known as the 'National Talent Search Scheme; includes social sciences and professional courses, such as medicine and engineering. The test is held at one stage, namely Classes X. Seven hundred and fifty students are selected through a competitive process every year. Students are selected through a general mental ability test, an aptitude test and finally through an interview.

A science talent search programme is also carried out by non-governmental organizations. The Jagdish Bose Science Talent Search Scheme (Calcutta) offers 20 awards for science and technology students in the State of West Bengal. The Union Territory of Delhi and the State of Rajasthan conduct Junior Science Talent Search Examinations for students in Class IX and award scholarships to selected students for two years.

Science Magazines, Journals, Newsletters and Newspapers. Leading national daily newspapers have a weekly children's forum through which scientists communicate with children. In addition, local newsletters of limited circulation are published by hundreds of voluntary organization which are actively engaged in out-of-school scientific activities.

There are also some very effective and widely circulated journals which are enjoyed by students in schools. There are a number of science magazines published in regional languages in various states.

The NCERT, National Book Trust, Children's Book Trust, and the Publications Divisions of the Government of India have also developed several supplementary reading materials in science for children.

Non-formal Education. Many children in the age group 6-14 cannot afford to attend formal school for five or six hours during the school day as they are either helping in productive work on the family farm or are compelled to undertake domestic work.. To help such children, there are 17,000 non-formal education centres for primary level and about 3,000 centres for middle level throughout the country. Some of these centres are using the same syllabuses and textbooks as used in the formal schooling; some use different types of instructional material which are more relevant to the environment. The simple aim to improve functional literacy and to provide guidance on basic aspects of science such as health and hygiene.

Science and Technology for Women. The application of science and technology for the improvement of the life and status of women depends on the development of home technology, suitable agriculture technologies and technology for improvement of productivity. In the Sixth Five-Year Plan considerable importance has been given to these areas for women. There are at present 11 agencies throughout India working for women's education and about 300 at the local or state level. They are concerned mainly with the development of crafts and functional literacy.

Science information and educational programmes on Indian television. There are 20 centres and 21 low-power transmitters for television. Indian television includes a regular fortnightly series on science which is telecast from all centres. Some centres also produce and broadcast, periodically, special science programmes of their own. Through the national network the programmes are transmitted in English and Hindi at prime viewing time.

Programmes related to environment, health, nutrition and various aspects of agriculture are independently transmitted in regional languages from various centres. Science related topics also figure in special audience programmes like programmes for children, youth programmes and programmes for housewives. There are also special programmes on the problems, duties and rights of citizens and these sometimes include information on subjects related to science and technology such as electricity and water supply and sewage disposal. There are, in addition, several programmes from foreign TV companies on science subjects such as wild-life, evolution of human society, under-sea exploration, geology and mountain vegetation.

A project, the 'Satellite Instructional Television Experiment' (SITE) was carried out by the Government of India during 1975-1976 in collaboration with the United States Government. Under the project 48,000 primary school teachers were trained in one year both in the content of science and the approach to teaching science. This proved to be a very effective method of training teachers and the evaluation report of the project proved favourable.

Current Innovations

Innovations in Curriculum Development. Since 1975 a number of innovations have been introduced in curriculum development in science education.

Using the environment and local resources for science education at the primary level. An innovative project was started in 1975 with the specific aim of helping states develop a 'Teacher's handbook' for using the environment and local resources for teaching science at primary level. Four zonal workshops were held in which the majority of states and union territories participated. As a result of these workshops, guidelines were prepared for states to develop a teacher's handbook based on their own syllabus and environment. The hand-book was tried out in a limited number of schools by the States concerned and revised.

Environmental studies for Classes I—V. This innovative project began as a follow-up of the recommendations contained in the document 'The Curriculum for the Ten-Year School—A Framework'. Under the project, a teacher's guide for Classes I and II was developed. There are no textbooks for Classes I and II. For Classes III to V, a textbook and a teacher's guide has been prepared for each class. The approach to the content is very flexible varying from one local environment to another, and there is no emphasis on coverage of specific content.

Pilot project on nutrition and health education and environmental sanitation at primary level. About 50 per cent of total deaths of India occur within the age group 0-14 years. The major causes of this high infant and child mortality rate are malnutrition and infection. This is largely due to ignorance of nutritional facts and to undesired practices and beliefs. The importance of nutrition and health education in this context cannot be overstressed.

With UNICEF assistance a scheme was launched to develop a functional nutrition, health education and environmental sanitation programme for the primary school. To implement the scheme five Regional Centres were established. A package of instructional materials in the regional language was developed by each centre through basic experiments and teaching guides on food and health habits.

The instructional package developed in each centre includes a syllabus, reading materials for pupils of Classes III—V, a teachers's guide, a teacher training school syllabus and reference manual.

Hoshangabad Project for science teaching through discovery approach. Under the guidance of an eminent scientist Prof. Anil Sadgopal, a project from the grass-roots level began in 1972 in Hoshangabad (Madhya Pradesh). Its main aim was to conduct a field survey and develop strategies and instructional material for teaching science through the discovery approach in rural schools. In the first phase, 16 schools in the 'Development Blocks' of Hoshangabad and Bankhedi were taken up. This project was run in a collaboration with Delhi University and the Tata Institute of Fundamental Research, Bombay. It was funded by various sources, including the UGC.

In 1978, the project was expanded to cover 208 schools. At this stage, NCERT provided funds for the supply of science kits to the schools. For this, a unit was set up at the Regional College of Education, Bhopal to procure and supply equipment. After expansion, the total responsibility of the project is now with the Directorate of Education, Madhya Pradesh.

Innovations in Teacher's Training

(a) *Satellite Instructional Television Experiment.* The Satellite Instructional Television Experiment trained 48,000 primary teachers in science content and methodology during the course of one year. Normally it would have taken the country ten years to carry out the same training task.

(b) *Centres for continuing education.* About 100 centres have been opened throughout the country for conducting short-duration courses not only for science teachers but other teachers as well.

(c) *Orientation of in-service teacher education personnel in environmental studies.* For the successful implementation of environmental studies at primary level a need was felt for in-service training of practising teachers. Key-persons from states who were expected to organize in-service teacher training programmes, were oriented under this programme. The innovative aspect of the programme was the absence of formal lectures and orientation through activities.

(d) *All-India Science Education Project*. This project, in collaboration with the British Council, selects small group of teachers in science subjects from different states to train annually at the centre for Science Education, Chelsea College, Chelsea (London).

Programmes for Locating and Nurturing Science Talent. The National Talent Search is a well established programme of NCERT for selection of about 500 students at three different levels in the area of science as well as humanities. Scholarships are available up to Ph.D. level as well as for professional studies such as engineering and medicine. Summer institutes are organized where those awarded scholarship meet eminent scientists.

The Vikram A. Sarabhai community science centre, Ahmedabad, undertakes teacher training programmes and runs community programmes. Students are given facilities to carry out experiments and try out new ideas. The open laboratory on Sundays and the 'Science Playground' are big attractions.

6

Indonesia

Indonesia is located between two continents, Asia and Australia, and between two oceans, the Pacific and the Indian Oceans. The land area is 5,000,000 square kilometres consisting of 6,000 inhabited islands. Approximately two thirds of its region are inland seas.

According to the 1980 census, Indonesia has 147.3 million people. There are 25.5 million primary school age children (7—12 years), and 21.8 million secondary school age children (13-18 years). Almost all types of education are administered and supervised by the Ministry of Education and Culture; but about 10.7 per cent of the 7-12 year olds are under the supervision of other ministries, especially the Ministry of Religion. Many schools are administered by private social bodies but technically they are supervised by the government and they have the same curricula as the public schools. In 1983, 93.9 per cent of the 7—12 years old were in primary schools, 37.9 per cent of the 13—15 years old in junior secondary schools and 22.1 per cent of the 16—18 years old in senior secondary schools.

Efforts of the government and private bodies to increase school enrolments are continuously made, so that within a short time it is hoped that all 7—12 years old can be accommodated in primary schools. Secondary school and university enrolments will be increased by establishing new schools and universities. For example, in 1983, the government was building 1,000 new junior secondary schools throughout the country.

At present, the government places a high priority on education. In the 1982-1983 annual budget, the educational and cultural sector has the highest expenditure compared with other sectors. Science and technology for national development are also given high priority in the decrees of the People's Consultative Assembly.

In-school Education

The School Structure. There are five levels of school :

(a) *Pre-school or kindergarten.* This level of education is for children 5 or 6 years of age and lasts two years. Pre-school education is not a prerequisite for entering primary school;

(b) *Primary school.* This level is for children 6 years of older. Children older than 7 years are given priority. Primary school extends for six years. For those who are over-age for primary school, non-formal education is an alternative.

(c) *Junior secondary school.* Schools of this level are divided into general and vocational consisting of technical schools and home economics junior secondary schools. The number of vocational schools is very small (only 4 per cent) compared with the general junior secondary schools 96 per cent. The duration of schooling in each type is three years.

(d) *Senior secondary schools.* The senior secondary schools are also of two types: general and vocational consisting of technical senior secondary schools, economics senior secondary schools, home economics senior secondary schools, normal schools, and the sports normal schools. The ratio between general schools and vocational schools is almost balanced (55 : 45). Generally this level of schooling lasts three years.

(e) *Higher education.* Higher education comprises universities, institutes, academies, and polytechnics. It lasts between 3 and 11 years.

Table 1. The school system

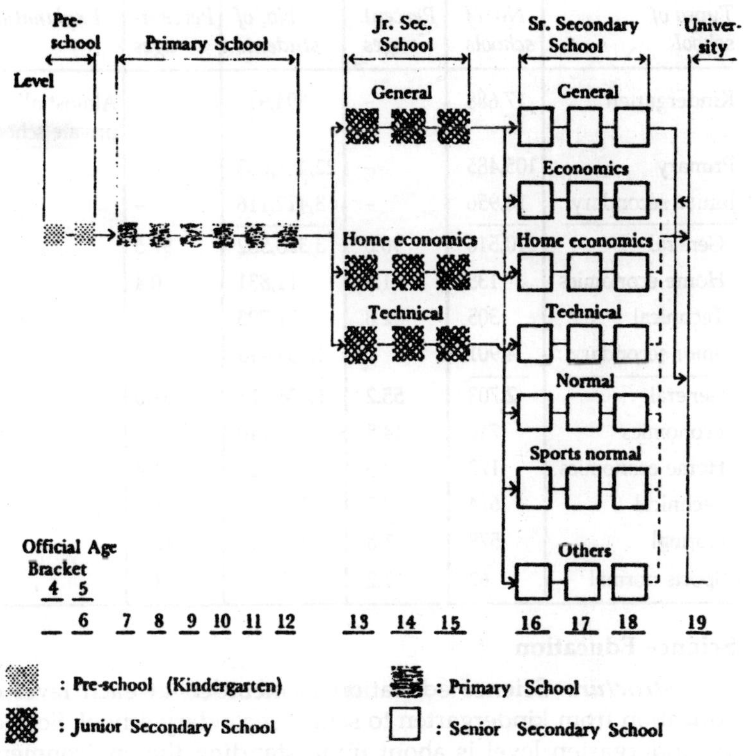

Enrolments Per Level of School. Although compulsory education has not yet been implemented in Indonesia, the government, even since the First Five-Year Development Plan, has tried to accommodate as many primary school age children as possible.

It is planned that compulsory education will be implemented in the Fourth Five-Year Development Plan which starts in 1984-1985. With efforts to increase school capacities annually, the number of students in schools also increases.

Table 2. Types of school, number of schools, number of students and their percentages for 1980-1981

Types of school	*No. of schools*	*Percent ages*	*No. of students*	*Percent-ages*	*Explanation*
Kindergarten	17,688	–	894,915	–	Almost all are private schools
Primary	105,485	–	22,487,053	–	
Junior secondary :	10,956	–	3,412,116	–	
General	10,516	96.0	3,328,582	97.5	
Home economics	135	1.2	11,831	0.4	
Technical	305	2.8	71,703	2.1	
Senior secondary :	4,901	-	1,754,495	-	
General	2,703	55.2	1,036,016	59.0	
Economics	710	14.5	229,140	13.0	
Home economics	173	3.5	23,640	1.4	
Technical	674	13.2	233,675	13.3	
Normal	579	11.8	213,155	12.2	
Sports normal	62	1.2	18,869	1.1	

Science Education

Structure. Science education is included at each level of education from kindergarten to senior secondary school. Science at kindergarten level is about understanding the environment. The scope broadens through grades I to III of primary school. From grades IV to VI, general science is introduced which includes the atmosphere, soil and rocks, plants and animals, various kinds of power, heat, light, sound, electricity, magnets, the human body, the solar system, communication, vehicles, and matter and its nature.

At junior secondary school, particularly in the general secondary school, science is taught from grades I to III to expand and deepen what has been learned in primary school and new topics such as radio-activity are added. General science is taught for the first semester at senior secondary school but streaming is introduced after that. The three streams in general senior secondary schools are science, social science and language. The science stream is sub-divided into physics, chemistry, biology, and earth and space sciences. In the social science stream, the science subject matter is a minor elective programme along with drawing and foreign languages, whereas the language stream does not include any science in its curriculum.

Of the three streams, the science stream has the highest number of students. The language stream is least popular, and, therefore, most general senior secondary schools have only the science and the social science streams. Both parents and students, generally, favour the science stream because its graduates have more opportunities in the choice of work or school for further studies as compared with social science or language graduates.

At the vocational senior secondary school, science is offered in accordance with the nature of the skills being taught.

Time Allocation. The total average of class periods for science per week is given in the following table for each level of school. The average percentage hours of science is also included.

In the general senior secondary school, there is also skill training as an elective supporting subject. If this subject is selected to support the science stream, the number of science periods per week becomes 14 class hours or 37.8 per cent. At the general junior secondary school if skill training periods are used to support science, then the total science periods become seven class hours per week or 19.0 per cent.

Curriculum Aspects

The implementation of the present curricula have been carried out during the past five years. The primary and secondary school curricula were completed in 1975, and science then, all primary and secondary schools have used these curricula. The vocational curricula were completed the following year.

Objectives of Science Teaching. The objectives of science teaching for each type and level of education are as follows :

Pre-school or kindergarten. The pupils are : (a) to know about nature; (b) to maintain and utilize the environment and to avoid its dangers; (c) to appreciate the cleanliness of their

Table 3. Average number and percentage of science class periods per week.

Types of school	*Average science class periods week*	*Average percentage of science class periods*	*Remarks*
Kindergarten	5	12.5	
Primary	3	9.4	
General	4	10.8	
Home economics	–	–	
Technical	–	–	
General	9	24.3	Specially for science stream
Economics	n.a.	0.0	
Home economics	2	5.0	Up to grade II only
Technical	3	7.5	Depends on the stream and is up to grade II only
Normal	2	5.0	Primary school stream for non-science major
	4	9.2	Primary school stream for science major
	2	5.0	Kindergarten stream
Sports	–	–	

bodies and personal objects; (d) to love animals and plants; (e) not to be afraid of animals, plants and natural phenomena; and (f) to believe in the Creator.

Primary school. The pupils are to : (a) know, understand and be able to apply some useful basic concepts of science; (b) know and understand mutual relationship among various kinds of living beings and concrete things as related to human life; (c) acquire skills through employing scientific methods to solve simple problems faced in daily life; (d) develop scientific attitudes; (e) be aware of the importance of science for the country and national development; and (f) appreciate nature and glorify the Creator.

General junior secondary school. The students are to : (a) understand basic science concepts which are useful for everyday life; (b) master science as an asset for further study and to utilize progress in technology; (c) be skilful in applying scientific methods to understand natural phenomena based on their laws and their inter-relationships; (d) develop scientific attitudes; (e) be responsible for maintaining their environment; and (f) love nature and glorify the Creator.

General senior secondary school. The students are to : (a) have scientific knowledge in physics, biology and chemistry, as a means of continuing their studies and living in society; (b) know the existence of relationships between science (including physics, biology and chemistry) and other disciplines; (c) be skilful in applying scientific methods to solve problems; (d) develop scientific attitudes; (e) be aware that science (including physics, biology, chemistry, earth and space science) influences the way of life and thinking of society; and (f) love and glorify and Creator.

Teacher training. Student teachers are to : (a) know and understand the concepts of science which are closely related to human life and the needs of teaching in primary school and kindergarten; (b) have knowledge about human effort in using the environment to meet the requirements of life with healthy surroundings; (c) have knowledge about interactions between living beings and their surroundings; (d) have skills in conducting experiments in science and in applying scientific methods to solve simple problems in science; (e) have skills in methods of teaching science at the primary school level; (f) develop scientific attitudes; and (g) love fellow human beings, the universe and glorify the Creator.

Organization of Science Curriculum. At the primary school and kindergarten levels, the science content is general in nature; the stress is on environmental science. At the junior secondary school level, science is divided into physical science, life science, and earth and space sciences. Physical science covers physics and chemistry; life science covers biology; and earth and space sciences comprise astronomy, geology, geophysics and meteorology. At the senior secondary school level, in the general senior secondary school for instance, science is taught as physics, chemistry, biology, and earth and space sciences for the science stream, whereas for the social science stream it is not presented as separate subject matter but as several selected topics which may help students to understand those natural phenomena most closely related to daily life.

Mechanism of Curriculum Development. Educational activities in Indonesia are still very much decided by the Ministry of Education and Culture in Jakarta. The development, monitoring, and evaluation of curriculum implementation are handled by the relevant Directorate Generals in the Ministry of Education. In particular the development and evaluation of the school curricula from kindergarten of senior secondary school are the responsibilities of the Curriculum Centre of the Office of Educational and Cultural Research and Development. Various parties are involved in the development of curricula, including experts in curriculum development, educationists, subject matter specialists, experienced teachers, employers of graduates from industry, and agriculture and university teachers.

These experts make use of results of educational researches implemented in previous years (National Assessment of Education Project in the First Five-Year Development Plan), and are guided by the 1945 Constitution to develop the curriculum for each level and for each type of school. The curriculum development is thus based on 'expert judgment' not through a 'pilot study'. Therefore, there is only one kind of curriculum for each type of school; no alternatives have been prepared.

Improvement of Curriculum and Development of New Curricula. The government has observed the present curricula in use for more than five years and noted its strong and weak points. At the same time opinions have been received from various users of the curricula, expressed in meetings, seminars and articles in newspapers.

As a result, the Curriculum Centre of the Office of Educational and Cultural Research and Development has implemented a phase I evaluation of all curricula used in each type of school. This evaluation covers evaluation of objectives and content of curricula, processes of curriculum implementation and the observed results. It will be used as a base for short-term curriculum revision during the Fourth Five-Year Development Plan. A phase II evaluation will be implemented as a follow-up and this is intended for long-term curriculum revision and to provide new conceptual and operational bases.

Simultaneously with the implementation of the phase II evaluation, the government will refine the work of the National Commission for Educational Reform. It is hoped that the two results can be completed in the Fourth Five-Year Development Plan so that before beginning the Fifth Five-Year Development Plan, the schools will have already implemented the new curricula.

Examinations

To determine how for students have achieved the desired objectives for each level and type of school, every teacher has to conduct formative and summative tests. Furthermore, at the end of each level of education final examinations are administered for certification purposes. For those who wish to continue their studies to the next higher level, there are entrance tests, because the number of applicants is always larger than the places available.

The tests administered by teachers and those set at the end of each level basically measure cognitive skills. Tests to measure the affective domain in science education have not yet been developed. Some schools, however, have included psychomotor skills in the science tests.

Science Activities, Laboratory Work and Equipment

While all schools use the national curricula, the teaching is done in the vernacular of each particular region.

As theory and practical work are designed to be integrated, laboratory facilities, such as equipment and materials have been available for all schools, both public and private since 1979. The science equipment is supplied as multi-purpose kits for primary schools grades I to VI.

There are no science laboratories in primary schools, but almost all public general junior high schools, have standardized science laboratories and equipment provided by the Curriculum Centre. This has the advantage of quality control.

Although equipment and material are sent by the centre, the use of simple apparatus made of local material is always encouraged, and the Curriculum Centre of the Office of Educational and Cultural Research and Development is developing a guidbook on this aspect. This centre also lays down some principles to be applied in the development of equipment, namely, the apparatus should be in the form of kits suitable for multipurpose experiments, and made of cheap, local material. It should be made for the use of groups consisting of three to eight students; and the working mechanism of the apparatus (e.g., the way a galvanometer works) should as far as possible be large enough to be seen by the students.

Only a limited range of equipment is imported, including microscopes and electronic equipment. For the secondary level approximately 15 per cent of materials and equipment are imported.

Kits for the primary and general junior secondary schools are designed by the Curriculum Centre in co-operation with the Bandung Teacher Training Institute and a foreign consultant. From time to time, consultative assistance is also received from the Indonesian Institute of Sciences and the Bandung Metal Industrial Research Workshop. Chemicals and equipment, which are not part of the kit, are designed by a team consisting of representatives of the Directorate General for Primary and Secondary Education, the Bandung Teacher Training Institutes and the Bandung Institute of Technology. After the kits are designed, a model is developed, tried out and evaluated. Then the model is offered to a private company for production according to needs. The successful bidder is then responsible for the procurement, packing and distribution of the materials and equipment to the schools.

After the kits of science equipment and materials reach the schools, the Curriculum Centre is responsible for monitoring their use, followed by an evaluation, to determine any shortcomings. The result is used to improve or modify the kits in the future. A Directorate General for Primary and Secondary Education team also monitors and evaluates the use of chemicals and equipment in schools, especially those items which are not part of the kits.

Use of Educational Technology

The use of audio-visual aids in the teaching/learning process, such as pictures, charts and graphics is generally widespread in schools. These are either made or bought by the school, or provided by the government.

The use of films as a teaching aid is, however, very limited. Films about science are still very scarce, be they locally produced or imported. In the big cities, science films can be borrowed from the libraries of embassies or consulates, though in limited numbers and types. Schools wishing to make use of this opportunity are still very few. More sophisticated aids such as micro-computers are not yet used in teaching in Indonesian schools.

Science Teacher Training

Generally, primary school teachers are classroom teachers who have to teach all subjects for the class (except for religion and sports). In secondary schools, teachers are subject teachers who generally teach one subject only.

The minimum qualification for science teacher's is a teacher training graduate certificate or a teaching certificate. In the case of primary school teachers, the normal school provides six years training after primary school. At the normal school students may choose science as their major subject.

The minimum qualification for science teachers in general junior secondary schools is Diploma I which is a four year training course after general junior secondary school, and they must have specialized in science for one year.

The minimum qualification for science teachers in general senior secondary schools is a three year course after general senior secondary school and, during these three years, they must have specialized in one subject area, such as physics, chemistry or biology.

With the availability of the teacher training course, which is equivalent to the normal school course, almost all primary school teachers have currently reached the minimum qualification.

According to the school statistics issued by the Office of Educational and Cultural Research and Development in 1983, and based on the 1981-1982 teacher data, the percentage of science and mathematics teachers who taught according to their educational training are 87 per cent for the general junior secondary schools and 85 per cent for the general senior secondary schools. It is expected that within a short time science teachers with inadequate educational background will be upgraded through various government programmes. For example, there is a diploma programme for the supply of secondary school teachers using a special development budget.

Apart from increasing the number of science teachers through pre-service training, an intensive in-service training programme is being conducted for both primary and secondary science teachers to improve their competence and skills. This in-service training is conducted separately for each type and level of school. Primary teacher in-service training is conducted by the Directorate for Primary Education; vocational teacher in-service training by the Directorate for Vocational Secondary Education; and in-service training for General Secondary Education teachers is conducted by the Directorate for General Secondary Education. Currently, particularly in the regions, a number of teachers with non-science educational backgrounds are being trained in this way. In the Third Five-Year Development Plan, distance learning using modules has been developed for the in-service training of teachers.

In the conventional in-service training programme for science teachers, the teachers attend training centres for two weeks. During this period, they develop a science programme which is then tried out in schools for about six weeks. Discussions are held every Saturday under the guidance of tutors to improve the implementation of the programmes. Then these same teachers get together again for two weeks to discuss their experiences before returning to schools for another four weeks. After this, the participants convene again at the training centre for a week. During this time they improve the programme developed in the light of experience in the field. Then the participants return to their schools for another eight weeks and finally gather again at the centre for a week. During this last week of in-service training they evaluate the activities and further refine the programme.

Research

Research has been carried out on various aspects of science teaching in Indonesia related to primary school and the general junior and senior secondary schools. Research on teaching equipment is especially focused on science equipment for practical work; for example, the development of science kits for the primary school and the general junior secondary school. Research on improving methods of teaching science is also conducted, particularly on science teaching methodology through process skills. This research and development of science kits, simple apparatus and process skills is administered by the Curriculum Centre of the Office of Educational and Cultural Research and Development, assisted by science educators from the Teacher Training Institute and the Directorate General for Primary and Secondary Education.

At the same time, the teacher training institutes emphasize research at the junior and senior secondary schools covering facilities and the teaching/learning process. Research on facilities includes science textbooks. Science lecturers at the Faculty for the Teaching of Science and Mathematics scrutinize science books used at the general junior and senior secondary schools and the results are used to suggest improvements, which may sometimes take the form of supplementary books. The results are also used as discussion material by the students of the faculty, who are being trained to teach at the secondary school.

Another activity at the teacher training institutes is research on the implementation of the teaching/learning process. In this research, lecturers, assisted by students, discuss their findings in seminars.

Programme for Out-of-school Education, Youth and Adults to Popularize Science and Technology Education

Activities intended to popularize science for both students and youth and adults outside formal education have been conducted through various media and cover several branches of science. There are various science activities, especially at the senior secondary school level which have been carried out through extra curricular programmes. These include science clubs at schools, such as the Club of Nature Lovers; and the Amateur Radio Broadcasting Club. Occasionally, these clubs arrange exhibitions which usually attract attention from the students of other schools, parents, and the community.

Science education has been presented continuously through television. The aim of this programme is to increase the science knowledge of in-school as well as out-of-school youth. The programme is arranged by the Indonesian Institute of Science. Since 1969 this Institute has enriched the science education broadcasts by conducting contests for youth on scientific achievements and creativity. To date, there have been nine fields of study contested every year. They include electronics, remodelling, biology, physics, chemistry, mathematics, environmental studies, applied technology and social sciences. Each year the Indonesian Institute of Science announces the contest titles which are open to all interested students. In 1982, there were 1,400 participants.

When the total eclipse occurred in several regions in Indonesia, the Indonesian Institute of Science co-ordinated the activities of young people coming from provinces in Java, to conduct research on the behavioural changes of living beings during the total eclipse and also to observe social changes of human beings. The Indonesian Institute of Science also arranged mobile scientific exhibitions to provide information to the general public. As Indonesia consists of thousands of islands, the Indonesian Institute of Sciences also conducted marine camping activities with the purpose of making the Indonesian youth love and like their country.

For the past six years, the Ministry of Education and Culture has conducted science achievement contests for 12 to 21 year olds, irrespective of their educational background and social status. Although the implementation looks similar to that conducted by the Indonesian Institute of Sciences, it has an entirely different philosophical background. The difference is in the free choice of their own scientific research topics. This freedom elicits spontaneous efforts from each participant free of any ties. Besides, based on the papers submitted to the committee, scientists in Indonesia obtain a picture of the scientific competence of the society. Selected young inventors, 5 to 20 in number, are invited to Jakarta for interviews to determine the best. These are not only given certification of merit and prizes, but are also given a chance to visit Europe to attend the Annual European Young Scientist Contest sponsored by Philips.

Current Reforms

Of the many activities currently underway, three are emphasized as being of special significance. These are the development of science teaching methods which are based on process skills; the implementation of science teacher in-service and on-service training; and the Science Achievement Contest.

Efforts to improve the teaching/learning process is directed towards changing the role of teachers so that they may lead students to really understand the processes which occur in science. In this teaching/learning process, the students are encouraged to ask many questions, to conduct observations, to design and conduct research, and to interpret and communicate the findings.

The in- and on-service training programme has a great impact on changes in science teaching in secondary schools. For one semester (16—17 weeks), a science teacher continuously obtains guidance and directives from fellow teachers in other schools, from regional subject supervisors and instructors. Such training motivates teachers continuously to use methods which encourage students to learn actively and to stimulate students in other classes to apply the same methods of teaching.

The third activity which has brought changes in science teaching is the effort to spread science more widely, particularly through contests which are conducted by either the Ministry of Education and Culture or the Indonesian Institutes of Sciences. Both organizations give an opportunity to interested individuals who are in school or out of school. The contest activity is really preparing youths to become prospective scientists and experts in technology; fields which are greatly needed in a developing country like Indonesia. To guide the hundreds of science clubs, the Institute, in collaboration with the local authorities and the

Regional Office of the Ministry of Education and Culture, has taken the initiative to organize scientific leadership training for senior secondary school teachers. It is anticipated that these senior secondary school teachers will become advisers of youth scientific associations in their respective regions. The involvement of teachers is considered urgent as there are no private professional associations yet available to extend their services and guidance towards these youth activities.

7

Islamic Republic of Iran

In the constitution of the Islamic Republic of Iran, there are various aspects which directly or indirectly relate to the teaching of science. The major points are: (a) utilizing advanced science and arts, human skills and experiences; (b) enforcing the spirit of survey, research and innovation in different scientific, technical, cultural and Islamic fields by establishing research centres and encouraging researchers; (c) gaining self-sufficiency in science, industry and agriculture; (d) training experts who would help to develop the economy of the country; (e) emphasizing the increase of the agricultural and industrial products to meet the needs of the people and enable the country to be self-sufficient; and (f) protecting the environment for the present and the future generations.

There are two institutions which are concerned with science and science education. One is the Centre of Scientific and Educational Policies, affiliated to the Ministry of Education; the other is the Institute of Scientific and Industrial Research.

The Structure of the Education System

The present system of education is divided into three phases: primary, guidance and secondary education which together occupy 12 years of schooling prior to university or higher education.

General or elementary education begins at the age of six. It is an eight-year programme in two stages. The first stage of primary education, extends over five years. The second stage, called the guidance cycle, occupies another three years.

In the initial planning of the curriculum these two stages were considered as general education for all; but in launching the plan it turned out otherwise. The guidance cycle can not be made compulsory until such time that provision for educating all the children in the primary age-group (6—10 years) both in rural and urban areas, throughout the country, is possible and maintained. Nevertheless, in all those areas where the Ministry of Education has been able to establish schools and provide facilities, formal education for the two stages of eight years is available and free.

Secondary education is four years formal schooling for students between the ages 13 and 17 years. After having successfully passed the requirements of the guidance cycle, students continue their studies in one of several areas of secondary education, provided they meet certain prerequisites demanded for that particular area.

High school education is mainly divided into theoretical (academic), and technical or vocational areas. The theoretical programme of the high school is divided into the major areas of sciences and humanities as electives from the first year. In the second year, science is divided into: (a) mathematics—physics; and (b) experimental science.

Humanities is also divided into: (a) literature-culture; and (b) socio-economics.

These divisions continue during the remaining years. Hence, in the present system of education those who take the theoretical programmes will receive a diploma in one of these four areas after four years of high school.

The technical/vocational education programme also takes four years. It is divided into industry, agriculture-rural vocations and services.

The industrial education branch comprises one of the following areas: building construction, electricity (which includes electro-technics and electronics), general mechanics, wood industry, auto-mechanics, moulding, metalwork, tools, machinery, mine machinery, ventilation and cooling, graphics and cartography, dyeing and weaving, chemical industry, mining and petroleum industry, and ceramics.

The rural vocational and agricultural programme covers the following disciplines : agriculture, cultivation, horticulture, irrigation, food industry and nutrition, rural administration, and farm machinery. Some of these subjects are offered by the Rural Vocational Schools of the Ministry of Education but others are conducted by the Agricultural Education Institutes affiliated to the Ministry of Agriculture and Rural Development.

The services programme includes commerce, office practice, technical, art, and health service.

In the present system of education, students are offered certificates at the successful completion of : (a) the requirements of the five-year primary; (b) the three year guidance cycle; and (c) the four year high school. These certificates are offered at provincial level (for primary school-leavers) and national level (for those completing 12 years).

The system of education also requires students to take three school examinations during each academic year and to pass them satisfactorily in order to be promoted to the next grade.

Students can continue their studies in different branches of secondary education according to the grades they have reached in the final examinations of the guidance course. For experimental science in high school, for example, the minimum grade for this subject in the guidance course should be 60 per cent.

A diagrammatic representation of the system is shown below.

Table - 1. Present school system in Iran

Employment | Higher Education

Employment

Services | Agriculture | Industries

Employment

Technical Voc. Section | Academic Section

Secondary Education

Employment

Primary Voc. Education

Guidance cycle
(Three years)
Second stage of General Education

Primary Education
(Five years)
First stage of General Education

Kindergarten

Grade	Age
	18
12	
11	
10	
9	14
8	
7	11
6	
5	
4	
3	6
2	
1	
	5

Number of Students. The number of students in different schools and levels of education are given in the following tables:

Table 2. Total number of students throughout the country 1982-1983

Course	*No. of students*
Primary	5,605,982
Guidance	1,794,804
Secondary Education (Academic)	933,103
Secondary Education (Technical)	80,472
Secondary Education (Services)	43,485
Secondary Education (Agricultural)	3,489

Curricula. The curricula of primary and secondary education are determined by pre-established patterns and students have to follow certain identical prescribed programmes for each subject and at each grade. The uniformity of the programmes makes it possible to compare progress at each stage, by grade and by subject.

Science Education

The Research and Curriculum Development Centre (RCDC) of the Ministry of Education is responsible for science programmes and for allocating appropriate time in the curriculum. However, the offices of Teaching Aids, Examinations, Teacher Training, and Printing and Distributing of Textbooks all work in close collaboration with the RCDC.

The RCDC consists of research, planning, evaluation and text-book preparation departments. Its activities include the review and revision of textbooks in primary, guidance and secondary education; holding regular meetings with experts to as to make fundamental changes at different levels; evaluation of textbooks to see how closely they follow the aims of the curricula; and bridging the gap between life and science by sending students to the work place so that they can observe and become familiar with the reality and practice of what they are being taught at school.*

This project is called KAD (knowledge and work) and occupies a school day each week.

Science in Primary Education. Science at this level is integrated. The basic concepts of science have been simplified and presented in five books. It is taught for three hours a week during the school year. The objectives are :

(a) Developing research and study habits;

(b) Training in scientific attitudes and applications;

(c) Forming correct habits based on appropriate trends;

(d) Teaching theoretical and practical aspects of some scientific concepts;

* This project is called KAD (knowledge and work) and occupies a school day each week.

(e) Bringing up students in a way that they do not only appreciate science but also approve of the fact that the origin of every value in science is from Allah; and

(f) Training students to study the relationship of cause and effect in order to realize that the Creation is goal centred.

The experimental science syllabus for primary school includes the main units on living things (plants and animals); human body and hygiene; the earth and its resources (soil, water, rocks); the earth in space; atmosphere; forces and motion; sound and communication; and magnetism and electricity.

These unit titles of the syllabus are repeated in each of the grades of primary education, but the content and the concepts are gradually expand in order to match the students' ability in comprehension as they develop.

Science in Guidance School. In guidance school, science changes its form from integrated to combined. The subject matter of this course is arranged in such a way that students first learn the general concepts of science in case they fail to pursue the study throughout the course.

The total content of the three science textbooks in this course comprises physics and biology each 35 per cent and chemistry and geology each 15 per cent. Five periods per week are available for science at this level. After completing this course, students should know the natural surroundings in which they live and discover the inter-relationships of living things, materials and phenomena; learn how to use their talent (how to reason) personally and explore concepts; observe accurately and express this observation through scientific hypothesis rather than by superstitious interpretation; and become accustomed to group work and co-operation with others.

Guidance School Science Syllabus

First year	*Second year*	*Third year*
Orientation–scientific method and procedures	Energy—origin and function	Simple machines and their functions
Matter–structure and states	Earth—structure, the changing crust; natural resources	Sources of energy (fuel, wind, atom)
Effect of heat on matter	Heat—control, use and production	Using electricity in the house; light and heat
Chemical changes	Weather changes and forecasts	Energy of light—laws (of light) in physics; eye structure and light transmission
Fire–functions, control and protection	Electricity—production and use	Producing necessary materials, chemical changes, mining, future of our natural resources
Common characteristics of living things; chemistry and structure of the cell	Human body—brief anatomy and physiology of different body systems	Fighting against diseases, body defence
Photosynthesis–interrelationship between producers and consumers	Man and his environment	Reproduction and growth in animals and plants Principles of heredity and evolution

Science in Secondary School. The grades obtained by students in science and mathematics in the guidance course form the basis of applying for academic or technical and vocational courses in general, and mathematics-physics and experimental science courses in particular.

A student with grades below 60 per cent in mathematics and science is not admitted to these two branches.

Teaching science in high schools is through separate subject disciplines with the time allocation as shown on the following page.

Science is also taught in technical and vocational branches but the objectives and contents differ from branch to branch.

	Hours per week			
	Ist year	2nd year	3rd year	4th year
Mathematics–physics option:				
Biology	2	–	–	–
Chemistry	3	3	4	5
Physics	3	3	4	7
Mathematics	7	9	10	11
Experimental sciences option:				
Biology	2	5	5	7
Chemistry	3	3	3	5
Physics	3	3	4	5
Mathematics	7	4	4	4
Earth science	–	–	2	2

Despite the variety of options available in technical and vocational courses the percentage of the students attracted is not high compared with the academic branches.

The objectives of science education at secondary school are to :

(a) Develop a scientific attitude (observation, collecting data, making hypotheses, . . .);

(b) Persuade students to solve problems using scientific methods;

(c) Introduce the practical and technological applications of science;

(d) Develop knowledge and understanding of scientific laws and phenomena; and

(e) Train in methods of manipulating laboratory equipment and observing safety rules in carrying out experiments.

The specific objectives in physics are to attract students to physics; acquaint students with concepts of physics; make students able to design simple experiments; and train students to use scientific methods.

The specific objectives in chemistry are to recognize chemical materials, and their relation to human life; learn basic concepts of principles and theories in chemistry; learn the principles of laboratory work; develop scientific attitudes; and become acquainted with the importance of chemistry and its effect upon the economy and human civilization.

The specific objectives in biology are to ear scientific concepts expressions, principles and laws of biological phenomena related to everybody life; become acquainted with scientific methods; comprehend the interrelationship of biology with other sciences; learn the practical applications of biology; show interest in collecting data and information about biology; preserve the environment and natural resources; obey different aspects of principles of health; and acquire the necessary skills in laboratory work.

The specific objectives in the earth sciences are to become acquainted with the basic concepts of geology, its value and its applications in daily life, and methods of studying and collecting information about geology; show interest in environmental preservation; and motivate curiosity to seek, search and find the facts of our surroundings.

Activities, Laboratory Work and Equipment.

Primary and guidance school level. No definite time is allocated to experimental and laboratory work in primary and guidance courses. In most cases experiments are by demonstration to interest and attract students and rarely to prove concepts.

According to a report only 0.5 per cent of the experiments are carried out by the students themselves. The following table shows that experiments are mostly carried out by the teachers often in collaboration with the students.

Secondary school science syllabus

Period	Physics	Chemistry	Biology	Geology
			(All branches)	
First year	Length, mass, time and their measurements, SI units	Scientific method and its uses in chemistry	*Ecology* Web of life	
	Rectilinear motion, velocity, acceleration and vector quantity	Some simple tools and equipment and their applications in the chemistry laboratory	Autotrophism and heterotrophism	Hydrosphere; composition
	Forces and the structure of matter; kinds of forces and their measurements	Basic problem of today's life (pollution, food deficiency, energy crisis . . .)	Ecosystem (structure and function)	
	Composition of forces; force as a vector quantity	Matter and its properties (molecular theory)	Populations as units of ecosystems	
	Centre of gravity and equilibrium	Basic concepts of chemistry (molecules and atoms, physical and chemical changes, chemical formula)	Interrelationship among populations	
	Newton's laws of motion	Air, oxygen	Bioms of the world	
	Work and energy; work and its measurement, simple machines	Hydrogen, water, solutions	Man and the ecosystem	

Secondary school science syllabus

Period	Physics	Chemistry	Biology	Geology
First year (cont'd)	Pressure in liquids and gasses		Hygiene Your appearance Infectious diseases Non-infectious diseases First aid Your behaviour	
Second year	Heat energy and temperature	Periodicity and periodic table	(Experimental science branch only) Chemical basis of life (living matter)	
	Wave motion	Electronic structure of the atom (ionization energy approach)	Cellular basis of life (cell structure of organelles)	
	The nature of light, reflection of light, mirrors	Electrons and the periodic table	Tissues and organs (plants and animals)	
	Refraction	Chemical bonding	Nutrition in organisms (digestive systems, food)	
	Lenses	Intermolecular attractions	Gas exchange (respiration in organisms)	
	Optical instruments	Thermochemistry (chemical reactions)		

Secondary school science syllabus

Period	*Physics*	*Chemistry*	Biology	Geology
	Analysis of light-colour	Rate of reactions Chemical equilibria		
Third year	Static electricity	Solution and ionic equilibria	Internal transport (plants, animals)	Experimental science branch only) How a geologist works
	Electric fields, potential and capacitance	Acids, bases and neutralization; pH	Regulation of body fluids (homeostasis)	Atmosphere: composition and structure; heating of the atmosphere, pressure and winds; evaporation and precipitation; climate, air pollution
	Electric current	Hydrolysis	Chemical control (hormones)	Hydrosphere; composition and temperature of sea water; water on land; freshwater problems
	Electrolysis	Solubility of salts and solubility product	Nervous control and sense organs	Minerals: identifying, classification
	Electric energy and power	Oxidation and reduction; electro chemistry	Behaviour	Magnetism and igneous rocks; volcanism

Secondary school science syllabus

Period	*Physics*	*Chemistry*	*Biology*	*Geology*
Third year (cont'd)	Magnets	Metals (Group I, II and III, general survey of the first row of transitional elements)	Locomotion (skeleton and muscles)	Metamorphism and metamorphic rocks
	Magnetic effect of an electric current	Iron, aluminum and magnesium industry		Weathering; mechanical and chemical; soils
	Electromagnetic induction			Sedimentation and sedimentary rocks
	The nature of matter:			Erosion by running water, ground water, waves, glaciers, wind
	Atomic structure: radioactivity			
Fourth year	Rectilinear motion, velocity, acceleration	*Part 1:* Hybridization and the shape of molecules	Reproduction	Earthquake and internal structure of the earth
	Dynamics; Newton's laws of motion	Non-metals (Groups VII, VI, V and IV)	Growth and development	Foldings and faultings

Secondary school science syllabus

Period	*Physics*	*Chemistry*	*Biology*	*Geology*
Fourth year (contd)	Vector and composition of vectors	Part 2: Organic chemistry Hydrocarbons (alkanes, alkenes, alkynes and aromatics	Genetics	Continental drift and plate tectonics
	Friction and streamlining	Alcohols, aldehydes and ketones	Evolution	Earth history; fossils, eras and periods of earth's history
	Projectiles	Carboxylic acids; fats, soaps and detergents	Origin of life	Topographic maps
	Circular motion, Kepler's laws, gravitational fields	Carbohydrates	Diversity of living things	Earth in space, stars, solar system; earth's motion
	Work-energy	Amines and amides		
	Rotation			
	Vibration and waves			
	Interference			
	Sound			
	Alternating currents			
	Light			
	The polarization of light			
	Electromagnetic waves			
	The solid state and semi-conductors			
	The models of the atom: nuclear physics			

Table - 2. How experiments are carried out in guidance schools

Mode of experimental work	*Per cent*
Experiments carried out by the teacher alone	25.8
Experiments carried out by the students alone	0.5
Experiments carried out by both teachers and students	62.0
No answer	11.7
Total	100.0

The reasons for lack of experiments was the subject of another study. This study showed that 38 per cent of science teachers present science both theoretically and through practical work but the percentage of experimental work is not clear. The table on the following page shows the reasons why science is not taught through practical work in guidance schools.

Table - 3. Major causes which prevent science teaching through experiment

Causes	*Per cent*
Crowded classes and overloaded books	20
Insufficient laboratory space and equipment	18
Teachers inability to use laboratory	15
Lack of co-operation of principals	9

Secondary School Level. Two hours per week (20 per cent of total time of teaching science) is allocated to laboratory activities in high school during each year. This is divided among teachers of physics, chemistry and biology. There is no doubt that teachers use demonstration methods but in most cases the experiments are not used to demonstrate concepts. In a study concerning the obstacles to practical work in chemistry at high schools the following conclusions were obtained:

Table - 4. Obstacles to practical work in chemistry

Obstacles	*High concern*	*Less concern*	*Low concern*	*Indifferent*
	Percent			
Lack of laboratory	62.86	33.57	3.57	0
Lack of interest by the teachers	80.42	17.48	2.10	0
Crowded classes	73.24	22.54	4.23	0
Teachers overworking (day or week)	63.83	29.74	4.26	2.13

Although the textbook in chemistry at high school are written in such a way that students could rediscover the concepts through experimentation themselves, the teachers fail to even demonstrate them.

No grades in the primary and guidance schools are registered in the records of the students for practical and laboratory work, but there is such a requirement in the record of the students in high school. However, in no cases do the grades reflect the true mark. Teachers generally base their grades in this regard on the theory and written examinations of the students. There are a few exceptions.

Equipment Manufacturers. In 1975, owing to the great sum of money spent on buying laboratory equipment from private companies a corporation entitled Education Industries Corporation (EIC) was formed to purchase and possibly manufacture materials and equipment.

The EIC founded four affiliated companies to manufacture and import glassware, audio-visual aids, wooden furniture (even school desks and benches) and software such as maps. In addition to equipping the school laboratories and workshops, EIC made several attempts to survey textbooks in order to list the necessary equipment for experimentation, to compile- laboratory manuals on how to carry out experiments and a guidebook on how to use laboratory equipment. It also held several in-service classes for teachers and those in charge of the laboratories. The affiliated companies have been closed but EIC has expanded and now includes some workshops for metalwork, carpentry and printing. EIC now produces transparencies, films, slides, charts, collections of rocks, minerals and fossils, microscopic slides and major items of laboratory equipment for different levels.

Research

Details of research on education and other studies in higher education by the Ministry of Culture and Higher Education have been published in a pamphlet (in Persian) entitled 'Cultural research and higher education planning book'.

The institute for Research and Planning in Science and Education is one of the institutes concerned with research, especially in science planning but this Institute has not been very active recently. Another institute is the Educational Research Institute (ERI) of the Teacher Training University, but this is also inactive now and its work has been taken over by the Research Department of that University. There is nothing to report in the field of science education.

In the School of Education of Tehran University some research has been undertaken as part of the dissertations of post-graduate students. This has been mostly on curriculum analysis, aims and objectives, planning and implementation and textbook content.

The Research and Curriculum Centre of the Ministry of Education is another institute which carries out research in the form of sending questionnaires to teachers and thus collecting views on, for example, textbooks. Here again no research has been undertaken specifically related to teaching science.

Educational Technology

A few years ago the government bought a number of television sets to be used in schools as teaching aids. At that time there was a broadcasting station specifically concerned with educational television. Owing to limited range, it was impossible to cover the whole country. Therefore, the main nationwide network broadcast educational films during the school day (usually in the mornings). However, it was not successful because of the inconsistency between broadcasting time of the television and the individual school time-tables. These programmes have ceased and the school television sets remain unused.

Meanwhile, the Open University was founded and set up a series of translations and productions of educational films broadcast in the afternoon before the main programmes of the country's network. The university is now closed and the broadcasts have ceased.

At the present time, two offices within the Ministry of Education are involved in developing educational media. The office of Teaching Aids Affairs is responsible for publishing magazines and complimentary books, designing and producing educational software, studying laboratory equipment and so on. This office has collected and translated books on simple science experiments and educational games, including puzzles and riddles; and designed and produced laboratory kits for the guidance course and kits and guides for making simple apparatus for high school physics.

The Office of Teaching Aids Affairs plans to take of the following steps in order to improve teaching science at schools :

(a) Identify the concrete and abstract concepts in textbooks from the point of teaching and learning and produce samples of materials and teaching aids;

(b) Produce both scientific and educational films to enhance the student's knowledge and lead them to a better understanding of nature; and

(c) Establish an information centre for teaching aid materials and samples.

The Office of Art Research produces educational and scientific short films commissioned by the Office of Teaching Aids Affairs. The Office of Art Research possesses about 100 film-strips on simple science and approximately 700 science films which can be borrowed by schools.

Teacher Training

Primary level. Except for physical education and religious teaching, which have separate teachers, all the other subjects in the primary course are taught by one teacher. Primary teachers should by graduates of Teachers Training Centres or high school graduates who have attended a special course.

Statistics from the Ministry of Education (1981—1982) show that of the total 189,285 primary school teachers 23,967 were teacher of physical education and religious education only and that 97 per cent of the rest (165,318) were high school graduates with a Diploma and 1.8 per cent with a post-Diploma degree. Thus, nearly all teachers in primary schools have attained the minimum standards required.

The Teacher Training Centres offer a two-year course for training primary and guidance level teachers. For primary teachers the structure of the course is given in the following tables.

Table—5. Subjects for two year training course for primary and guidance school teachers

Subject	*First year*		*Second year*	
	Ist semester	*2nd semester*	*Ist semester*	*2nd semester*
General subjects				
Basic Islamic education and ethics	–	–	2	2
Teaching skill	4	4	2	2
Evaluation methods	2	2	–	–
Educational aids	2	2	–	–
Health and nourishment	–	–	2	2
Total periods per week	8	8	6	6

Guidance Level. Teachers in the guidance course are required to attend a two-year post-Diploma course in a special training centre.

There were 19,119 teachers (in 1981—1982) teaching science at this level of whom 57.3 per cent held a post-Diploma qualification, 2.5 per cent had a Bachelor Degree in different fields, 39.4 per cent held a Diploma (*i.e.* high school graduate plus course) and 8 per cent held qualifications at a lower level. Thus, about three quarters of the teachers of science at this level had reached the minimum requirements.

Table—6. Subjects for two year training course for primary and guidance school teachers (cont'd)

Subject	*First year*		*Second year*	
	Ist semester	*2nd semester*	*Ist semester*	*2nd semester*
Main subjects:				
Teaching methods of Koran and religious education	2	2	2	2
Teaching methods of experimental science	4	2	2	2
Teaching methods of mathematics	2	4	2	2
Teaching methods of Persian language	4	4	2	2
Teaching methods of physical education	2	–	2	–
Teaching methods of art and handicrafts	–	2	–	2
Children's literature and the role of revolution in it	–	2	2	2
Agriculture	–	–	2	4
Teaching methods of social science	2	–	2	–
Total periods per week	16	16	16	16

The structure of the training course–in Teacher Training Centres—provides for general subjects (eight periods per week in the first year and two periods per week in the second year) as for primary teacher training. The main subjects for those choosing science (entitled 'Experimental science' in the structure) provide for 16 periods per week as shown in the following table.

Table 7. Main subjects for science teachers for guidance schools

Subject	First year		Second year	
	Ist semester	*2nd semester*	*Ist semester*	*2nd semester*
Chemistry	2	2	2	2
Teaching chemistry	2	2	2	2
Biology	2	2	2	2
Teaching biology	2	2	2	2
Geology and teaching geology	2	2	2	2
Physics	2	2	2	2
Teaching physics	4	4	4	4
Total periods per week	16	16	16	16

The content of the main experimental science subjects comprises surveying the related sections in the books of the guidance course; making simple equipment and performing experiments; and performing and practising teaching methods in related subjects.

High school level. The requirement to teach at this level is a degree from one of the Teacher Training Universities or a degree from any other University, plus One Year Post-graduate Course in education. There were 7,949 science teachers in high schools in 1981-1982 of whom 933 held post-Diploma qualifications only and the remainder held B.Sc. degrees.

The Teacher Training Universities provide a four year course and students graduate with B.A. or B.Sc. and qualification to teach. The Teacher Training University is located in Teheran and has four branches in the provinces. There are about 2,000 students in each university (500 students in each year).

The student take 120 hours for credit in science (100 in main subjects and 20 in other science subjects), 20-30 hours credit for education subjects and 30 hours credit in other subjects such as Persian and foreign languages and religion.

In-service Training. The Office of In-service Training (IST) was established in the Ministry of Education to serve and promote the teaching and administrative ability of the staff by holding short courses throughout the year. Training courses are specially held when there are changes and modification in curricula and textbooks.

In-service training for primary teachers is mostly held in local centres because there are qualified teachers with B.A. or B.Sc. degrees who can provide the necessary tuition. For teachers at the guidance level the courses are usually held in provincial centres rather than in small towns.

Courses for high school teachers are generally held in Teheran, or in one of the centres of the IST, or sometimes in the universities under the Board of Science.

Teaching Science Out-of-school

Television. Teaching by television is carried out through the second television network. There are special and general programmes. The special programmes are designed for students and are divided into four age groups : 3-6, 6-11; 11-14; and 14-18 years old. The general educational programmes are aimed at the general public.

These general programmes are divided into programmes in which teaching is presented in the form of entertainment; programmes in which information is given along with suitable films; and programmes in which science or a technique is directly taught.

Magazines. There are four or five monthly magazines publishing information on various aspects of science and three or four magazines on electronics.

Museums. Museums are mainly related to universities, educational institutions and government offices and they are established mainly for specialists rather than the general public.

They include Rocks, Fossils and Minerals Museum of the Geological Survey of Iran; Botanical Gardens affiliated to the Ministry of Agriculture; Zoological Museum affiliated to the Environmental Protection Organization; and Zoological Museum of the School of Science (Teheran University).

Innovations

In the area of curriculum development a council entitled the 'Experimental Science Teaching Council' has been established in the Research and Curriculum Organization of the Ministry of Education and includes experts in different levels from university to school. It will survey, analyse and recommend fundamental changes in science teaching in the primary and guidance courses. At the present time the Council is studying the objectives and goals of teaching science.

A Co-ordinating Centre of Laboratory Equipment has been established within the Educational Affairs Section of the Ministry of Education. Its functions are to list present teaching aids and equipment in schools; suggest the proper use of teaching aids; co-ordinate the activities of the Office of Education and those of curriculum and planning centres regarding teaching equipment; and establish similar centres in the provinces.

The Centre has so far prepared laboratory instructions for high school physics, chemistry and biology; adjusted the supply of equipment and materials so that all schools have the same basic range; made central laboratories for groups of nearby schools and produced items of laboratory equipment.

KAD Project. In 1982-1983 the Ministry of Education decided to delete six hours (out of 36 hours) from the school time-table of the high schools so that students could visit the labour market and local industries. A further two hours, outside the school time-table, were made available to be spent on the study of the reports, health and safety regulations, first aid, and ethical problems in work places.

This KAD project was introduced to motivate interest within the high school toward labour and services; acquaint students with the labour atmosphere and social inter-relationships; acquaint students with the application of industries, agriculture, science and services; and increase production to the level of self-sufficiency.

The project was introduced for the first year students of high schools and it is planned to gradually extend it to all four years of high school.

TAM Project. This project, recommended by the Higher Council of Education, is concerned with change in the present system of education in guidance schools. It was introduced on an experimental basis in 1982-1983. The project is being tested in selected schools in nine provinces and at the same time a team of experts from the Research and Curriculum Development Centre is evaluating its effectiveness.

8

Japan

The Japanese population of 120 million, with a density of 500 kilometre to the square, lives in a thin strand of islands, representing a mere 0.28 per cent of the world's land area, with no major natural resource, and it constitutes one of the most integrated nation families in the world. During the 1960s, following the rebuilding of the nation after the Second World War, Japan was able to double the gross national product in five years. This phenomenal economic growth also produced problems, such as serious industrial pollution, and these have caused Japan to search for a better cultural-economic balance. This searching has its implications for school curricula, particularly in science, since the utilization of science and the development of technology are both essentially social processes.

The General Education System

Structure of school education from primary to pre-university stage. The figure on the following page shows the structural organization of the present system of public education and indicates the normal age of admission of promotion to each grade of the educational system.

Table 1 shows the types of schools and courses, main types of establishing bodies, qualifications for admission (normal admission age), length of course, and requirements for graduation.

Kindergartens admit children aged 3, 4 or 5 and provide them with one-to-three year courses. General and special education through the elementary and lower secondary school level is compulsory; thereafter, and in other types of schools, it is voluntary. In principle, success in an entrance examination is one of the prerequisites to enter any school beyond the compulsory school level.

Organization of educational system

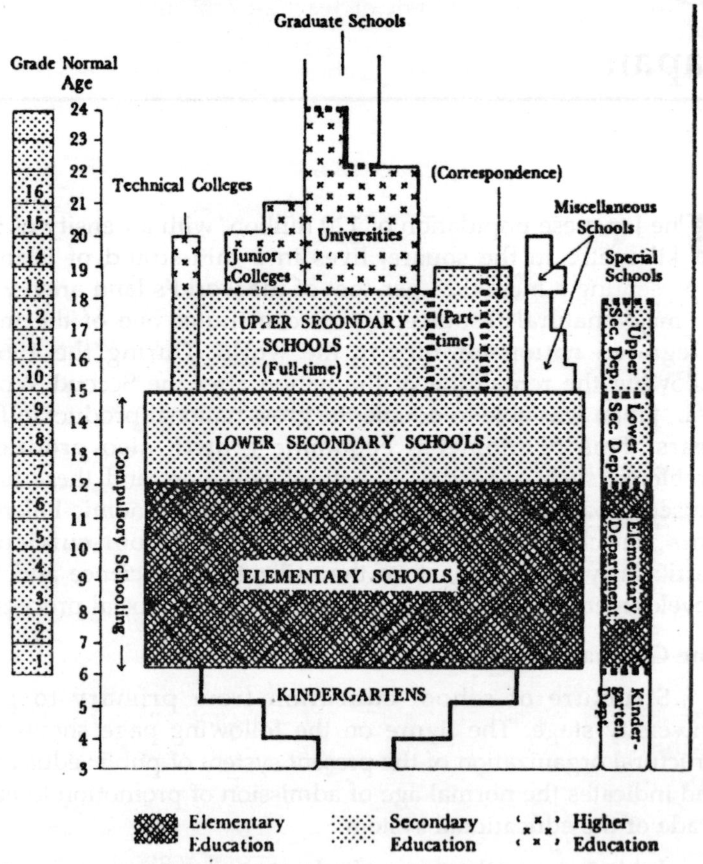

There are three types of upper secondary school courses : full-time, part-time and correspondence. The full-time course lasts three years, while both the part-time and the correspondence courses are four years or more. Part-time courses are of two types : day course and evening course, with the majority attending evening courses. Both the part-time and the correspondence courses lead to a diploma equivalent to that available to students in the full-time course.

In terms of the content of teaching, the upper secondary school course may also be classified into two categories : the general and the specialized vocational. General courses provide general education adapted to the needs of both those who wish to advance to higher education and those who are going into employment but have chosen no specific vocational area. Almost 70 per cent of the students in upper secondary schools are enrolled in general courses.

Specialized vocational courses are intended to provide vocational or other specialized education for those students who have chosen a particular vocational area as their future career. These courses are further classified into several categories: technical, commercial, agricultural, fishery, home economics, fine arts, science, mathematics, and so on.

Special education schools aim at giving physically or mentally handicapped children an education adapted to their individual needs. There are schools for the blind, for the deaf, and for those handicapped in other ways.

Universities require for admission the completion of upper secondary schooling or its equivalent, and offer at least 4-year courses leading to a bachelor's degree. They are divided into faculties such as law, literature, economics, education, science, technology and agriculture, and then subdivided into departments.

There are also a number of 'special training school' and 'miscellaneous school' other than the regular schools mentioned above. Special training schools are designed to offer systematic programmes of education aimed at developing each student's ability required for their working life or daily life, or at raising their level of general education.

Table-1. Types of schools and courses, establishing bodies, qualifications for admission, length of course and graduation requirement

Type of school	*Type of course*	*Main type of establishing body*	*Qualification for admission*	*Length of course (in years)*	*Requirement for graduation*
Kindergarten	One-year course Two-year course Three-year course	 Private Municipal	Age 5 Age 4 Age 3	1 2 3	
Elementary		Municipal	Age 6	6	Completion of six-year course
Lower secondary		Municipal	Completion of elementary school course, Age 12	3	Completion of three-year course
Upper secondary	Full-time course Part-time course Correspondence course	Prefectural Private Municipal	Graduation from lower secondary school, Age 15+	3 4 or more 4 or more	Acquisition of 80 credits
Special education	Kindergarten, elementary, lower secondary and upper secondary departments	Prefectural Municipal	Same as in kindergarten, elementary, lower secondary and upper secondary schools, respectively		

Miscellaneous schools provide students, mainly young, with vocational and practical courses in dressmaking, cooking, book-keeping, typing, automobile driving and repairing, computer techniques, and so on. Most courses in miscellaneous schools require for admission the completion of lower secondary schooling, whilst some require the completion of an upper secondary school course. The length of course varies from three months, to one year or more.

Enrolment at Each State of Education. *Table 2* gives the enrolment rate by school level, as percentages of the respective total population at the relevant levels. These figures show that:

(a) The diffusion of pre-school education is increasing; more than 60 per cent of the new entrants to elementary schools have attended kindergartens for at least one year.

(b) The enrolment rate in compulsory education is almost 100 per cent.

(c) Post-compulsory secondary education is almost universalized as shown by a more than 90 per cent enrolment rate.

(d) Though higher education also shows a higher enrolment rate (33.3 per cent in 1980), there is a significant difference in the rates for males and females; 42.7 per cent for males, and 23.6 per cent for females.

Table 2. Enrolment rate by the school level, 1980

School level	*Age*	*Male and female*	*Male*	*Female*
		Per cent		
Pre-school education (kindergarten)	3-5	42.4	42.3	42.6
Elementary education	6-11	99.98	99.98	99.99
Lower secondary education	12-14	99.98	99.98	99.99
Upper secondary education	15-17	92.9	91.7	94.3
Higher education	18-21	33.3	42.7	23.6

Science Education in Schools

The aims of science education are stated in the recently revised curricula: 'Course of study for elementary schools' 1980 and 'Course of study for lower secondary schools' 1981.

Aims of Elementary School Science. To develop the ability in and attitude toward making inquiries about nature through observations and experiments as well as to enhance the understanding of natural things and phenomena, thereby, nurturing a rich sensitivity to love nature.

Aims of Lower Secondary School Science. To develop students' ability in and positive attitudes towards making enquiries about nature through observations and experiments as well as to enhance the understanding of matter and phenomena in nature. Thus to encourage students to realize the relationship between nature and human beings.

Aims of Upper Secondary School Science. To develop students' ability and positive attitudes; to inquire into nature through observations and experiments; to enhance their understanding of fundamental concepts of matter and phenomena in nature; and to develop a scientific view of nature.

The Place of Science in the School Curricula

Kindergarten. Science, as such, is not part of the curricula in kindergartens, but would appear in a very elementary way within the areas of health and nature.

The minimum number of school days for kindergarten education is 220 days a year, and the standard number of classroom hours per day is four hours.

Each kindergarten compiles its curriculum on the basis of the kindergarten principles, covering 137 sections in six areas as follows:

Prescribed content of kindergarten education

Areas	*Section*
Health	24
Social life	27
Nature	21
Language	22
Music and rhythm	26
Art and craft	17

Elementary and Lower Secondary Schools. Science is taught from the first grade in elementary schools. It is a compulsory subject for all the students throughout the elementary and lower secondary school stage.

The standards for lower secondary schools allow several hours for elective subjects and individual school decide what to teach in these hours. Most lower secondary schools include several hours per week of English language instruction.

Upper Secondary Schools. *Table 3* shows the subject areas, subjects and the standard number of credits to be provided in upper secondary schools, according to the revised Course of Study. The curricula of individual schools must be organized so as to comply with these standards.

According to the Course of Study, local school curricula both for students in the general course and in the specialized vocational course must provide instruction in the following subjects :

Table—3. Subject areas, subject and standard number of credits of upper secondary schools

Subject area	*Subject*	*Standard No. of credits*
	Japanese language I	4
	Japanese language II	4
Japanese language	Japanese expression	2
	Modern Japanese	3
	Classics	4
	Modern society	4
	Japanese history	4
Social studies	World history	4
	Geography	4
	Ethics	2
	Political science and economics	2
	Mathematics I	4
	Mathematics II	3
	Algebra and geometry	3
Mathematics	Basic analysis	3
	Differentation and integration	3
	Probability and statistics	3

Subject area	*Subject*	*Standard No. of credits*
Science	Science I	4
	Science II	2
	Physics	4
	Chemistry	4
	Biology	4
	Earth science	4
Health and Physical education	Physical Education	3
	Health	2
Arts	Music I	2
	Music II	2
	Music III	2
	Fine Arts I	2
	Fine Arts II	2
	Fine Arts III	2
	Handicarft I	2
	Handicraft II	2
	Handicraft III	2
	Calligraphy I	2
	Calligraphy II	2
	Calligraphy III	2
Foreign languae	English I	4
	English II	5
	English II-A	3
	English II-B	3
	English II-C	3
Home-making	General home-making	4

Note:

1. Thirty-five units of school hours, each of which represents 50 minutes teaching, yield one credit.
2. Credit allocation to other subjects is prescribed by each establishing body of relevant upper secondary school.
3. A minimum of 80 credits is required for graduation from upper secondary schools.

The Proportion of Students Taking Science

At the elementary and lower secondary levels science is compulsory for all students. At grade X level in upper secondary school, Science I is also compulsory. For elective science in upper secondary schools a typical breakdown of study at grade XI level would be: physics 26 per cent; chemistry 42 per cent; biology 21 per cent; and earth science 11 per cent.

The Time Allocation for Science

The amount of time allocated to science in elementary and lower secondary schools is shown in the following table.

Per year	Elementary schools						Lower secondary		
	1st	2nd	3rd	4th	5th	6th	1st	2nd	3rd
Teaching hours of science	68	70	105	105	105	105	105	105	105
Total teaching	850	910	980	1,015	1,015	1,015	1,015	1,015	1,015
Percentage	8.0	7.7	10.7	10.3	10.3	10.3	10.3	10.3	13.8
Periods per week	2	2	3	3	3	3	3	3	4

In Upper secondary schools the time is variable, but a typical school would have five hours per week (out of 33 hours total)—15.2 per cent—in the first year (grade X) and perhaps 4-6 hours per week in the second and third years (grades XI, XII) where science is elective.

SCIENCE CURRICULUM OBJECTIVES

Primary School

Grade I. To recognize conspicuous features of living things in their surroundings through such activities as searching for and taking care of them, and experience the pleasure of intimacy with them.

To familiarize pupils with the surrounding things in nature, recognize conspicuous features about them through observations and experiments, and experience and pleasure of contact with them.

Grade II. To notice the ways of living and growth of living things, and experience the pleasure of intimacy with them while searching for and raising living things found in the surroundings.

To become familiar with natural things and phenomena in the surroundings, notice their features and how they change by observing them, and experience the pleasure of association with nature.

Grade III. To investigate the growth and activity of living things, understand the relationship between the growth and activities of living things and the climate of the seasons, and foster the attitude of loving and protecting living things while searching for and raising living things found in the surroundings.

To examine phenomena caused by air, sunlight, magnets; to understand the properties and functions of these, and to develop an interest in finding out the rules governing these phenomena.

To examine the weather and changes in the temperature of soil, water and air, to understand the features of these changes, and develop an interest in these natural phenomena occurring in the surroundings.

Grade IV. To understand that there are various stages in growth, that life is a continuous process, and that the growth of living things has close connection with nutrition and sunlight; to foster and attitude of loving and protecting living things while continuously observing the process of growth by raising living things.

To understand the properties and functions of the following, and develop an interest in finding out rules governing these phenomena : the solution of solids, the weight of objects, changes of state due to heat, and phenomena caused by electric current.

To understand the functions of running water, and the shape and movement of the sun and the moon, and to develop an interest in these natural phenomena.

Grade V. To understand that living things grow under the influence of their environment, and develop an attitude of respecting life, while examining the process of the growth and body structure of living things.

To understand the properties of substances and the regularity in changes, and foster an attitude to study them actively, while examination how a substance dissolves, how it burns, how the light moves, and how sound is transmitted.

To observe the movement of the stars, to understand the regularity of the universe, and to foster an attitude of observing astronomical phenomena in terms of the lapse of time and the expanse of space.

Grade VI. To examine the growth and reproduction of plants and the human body, to understand that living things grow and are reproduced; to study the structure and functions of the human body, and develop an interest in the interrelationship between living things and their environment.

To examine the properties of solutions in water, how substances are heated or burned, the function of a lever and an electromagnet; to understand the properties of substances and regularity in their change, and to foster an attitude to actively investigate the unknown by applying such knowledge to the natural phenomena.

To examine strata in rocks, the movement of the sun and the change of temperature on the surface of the ground, and to understand of water and sunlight.

Lower Secondary School

First section. To find problems among matter and phenomena which are related to substances and energy.

To understand, through observations and experiments, that substances are classified into elements and compounds and that a substance consists of particles of atoms, molecules, and ions, thereby developing scientific ways of viewing and thinking about substances.

To understand, through observations and experiments, the features and function of force and electric current, motions of bodies, and work caused by light, heat and electric current, thereby developing scientific ways of viewing and thinking about natural phenomena in connection with energy.

To understand the function of familiar substances and energy, and to develop a positive attitude towards effective utilization of substances and energy relevant to human life.

Second section. To find problems among living things and their surroundings, natural matters and phenomena, and to learn in the process of inquiring into nature how to discover regularities in nature and how to interpret natural phenomena.

To observe and experiment on the diversity and unity found in living things and surrounding natural matter and phenomena, to analyse causes and mechanism of generation of matter and phenomena, and to develop comprehensive ways of viewing and thinking about the natural world.

To consider the relationships between matter and phenomena in the natural world as well as harmony among them, and to realize the influence of the natural environment on the existence of human beings, thereby heightening interest in preservation of the natural environment; to understand biological phenomena and to develop a positive attitude towards the appreciation of life.

Upper Secondary School

Science I. To understand principles and laws as well as to realize the relationship between nature and human life, to observe and experiment on movement of bodies, changes of substances, and evolution and balance found in the natural world.

Science II. To develop the scientific method by inquiring into matter and phenomena in the natural world and to develop ability to solve scientific problems.

Physics. To understand principles and laws of physics by carrying out observations and experiments, on force and motion, wave motion, electricity and magnetism, selected from among natural matter and phenomena, and to develop an ability and positive attitude to consider phenomena from basis of physics.

Chemistry. To study principles and laws of chemistry by carrying out observations and experiments on chemical properties of substances, and chemical reactions selected from among natural matter and phenomena, and to develop ability and positive attitude to consider phenomena from the basis of chemistry.

Biology. To understand principles and laws of biology by carrying out observations and experiments on the formation of a bio-organism, living bodies and energy, homeostasis and regulation, and biotic communities selected from natural matter and phenomena, and to develop an ability and positive attitude to consider phenomena from the basis of biology.

Earth science. To understand principles and laws of earth science by carrying out observations and experiments on the structure of the earth, history of the earth, and the structure of the universe, selected from among natural matter and phenomena, and to develop the ability and positive attitude to consider phenomena from the basis of earth science.

Curriculum Revision

Since 1947-1948 the curricula at each of the three levels of education have been revised at least four times. The implementation of the most recent revisions following the timetable below.

Classification	1977	1978	1979	1980	1981	1982
Elementary school	Notification	Transitional measures		Full implementation		
Lower secondary school	Notification	Transitional measures			Full implementation	
Upper secondary school		Notication	Transitional measures			Grade by grade implementation

Evaluation

A model for evaluation of curricula and educational processes in general is based on the following sequences :

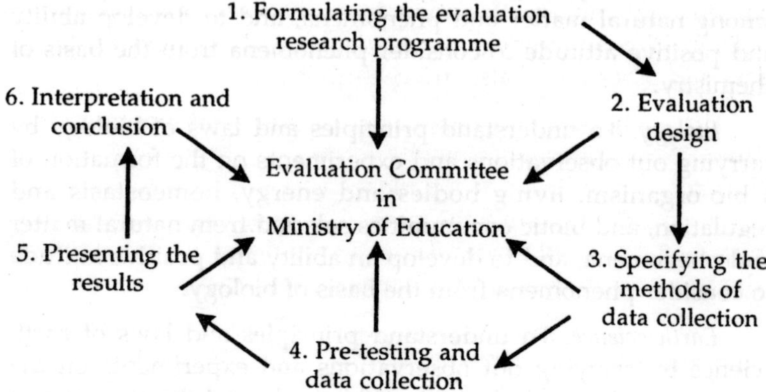

There are 40 evaluation pilot schools in Japan. These schools evaluate various aspects of the school curriculum: objectives, scope, the quality of teachers, the extent to which objectives in various subjects are implemented, equipment and materials, the abilities of students on intelligence and aptitude tests, achievement tests, personality measures, attitude and value scales, and so on.

National achievement tests. National achievement tests are designed from time to time to measure various specifications within the curriculum and to evaluate student performance in specific subjects. For example, in 1982 the following tests were applied:

	Elementary school	Junior secondary school
Subject area	Social studies, science, national language, mathematics	
Educational level	grade V grade VI	Ist grade (grade VII) 2nd grade (grade VIII) 3rd grade (grade IX)
Number involved	16,000 each	16,000 each
Total number	32,000	48,000

Science Equipment and Laboratory Work

A large variety of equipment, materials and tools is necessary for science education. This includes : scales, experimental implements and tools, field observation and survey tools, specimens, models, audio-visual teaching devices, tools, glass and other materials, and chemicals.

Under the terms of the Science Education Promotion Law, a national Government subsidy is provided for some science education equipment. The individual items and quantities which may be purchased with the national Government subsidy are specified under the Standards of Equipment for Science Education, which were introduced in 1954.

The actual Science Education Promotion Law, dated 1953, comprises the following articles:

Article 1

In view of the fact that science education has a role of special importance as the foundation on which to build a cultural state, the purpose of this law shall be to promote science education, in order that pupils may, through science education, acquire scientific knowledge, skills and attitudes, and develop ingenious creative abilities, and thereby be able to lead a scientific daily life; and may, in accordance with the purpose stipulated in Fundamental Law of Education (Law No. 25 of 1947) and the School Education Law (Law No. 26 of 1947), be brought up into useful members of the nation who can contribute to the development of the country.

Article 2

'Science education' in this law shall mean the education in science in elementary schools (including elementary departments of schools for the blind, the deaf and the otherwise handicapped). The same applies to the lower secondary schools (including lower secondary department of schools for the blind, the deaf and the otherwise handicapped). The same also applies to upper secondary schools (including upper secondary departments of schools for the blind, the deaf and the otherwise handicapped).

Article 3

The state shall endeavour to promote science education in accordance with the provisions of this law and other laws and ordinances, and to encourage local public bodies to endeavour to promote science education by the following means:

(a) To draft over all programmes for the promotion of science education;

(b) To improve upon the content and methods in science education;

(c) To provide schools with equipment and facilities for science education;

(d) To plan and execute a pre-service and in-service education programme for teachers and leaders in science education.

Article 4

In cases where the facilities provided are below the standard stipulated by government ordinance, the state shall subsidize, within the fiscal budget, 50 per cent of the expenses required for the project.

Proportion of time for practical work. The recommended proportions are as follows :

Elementary stage

Grade	*Practical activities laboratory work hours per year*	*Total teaching hours per year*	*Percent-age*
I	55	68	81
II	53	70	75
III	74	105	70
IV	67	105	64
V	61	105	58
VI	65	105	62

Lower secondary stage

Grade	*Practical activities laboratory work hours per year*	*Total teaching hours per year*	*Percent-age*
I	31	105	30
II	28	105	27
III	30	140	21

Upper secondary stage

Subject 1	*Practical activities laboratory work hours per year*	*Total teaching hours per year*	*Percent-age*
Science 1	16—27	140	12—19
Biology	17—30	140	12—22
Chemistry	16—27	140	12—19
Physics	16—25	140	12—18
Earth science	12—20	140	8—14

Practical work is not an examinable subject in public examinations in science.

Actual facilities in the schools. The recommended list of items and materials for practical work in science is revised whenever new courses of study are introduced. The actual provision of equipment in the schools is shown in the following table :

Proportion of schools with adequate equipment for teaching science through practical work, 1981

Elementary schools	51.7 per cent
Lower secondary schools	44.8 per cent
Upper secondary schools	42.6 per cent

It is hoped that provision of facilities will reach 70 per cent over the next five years.

Low-cost kits and materials for science practical work are provided by manufacturers within the Japan Association of Science Materials Manufacturers. Most of the equipment required is manufactured in Japan although some manufacturers import low-cost components and materials from Taiwan, Hong Kong and the Republic of Korea.

Specification of quality control and modifications to the recommended list of equipment are made by the Science Education Council. Recommendations are made to the Minister of Education who then issues appropriate amendments to the 'Standards for equipment for Science Education Law'.

Educational Technology

In 1978, the Ministry of Education revised the 'Standards for Provision of Instructional Aids and Equipment' which had been in force since 1967. The new standards defined, as instructional aids and equipment, 367 items for elementary schools and 312 items for lower secondary schools. These included items such as overhead projectors and other audio-visual aids, maps and woodworking instruments. On the basis of this standard, the Ministry drew up the 'Second 10-year Plan for Provision of Instructional Aids and Equipment to Compulsory Education School', which was launched in 1978, with a budget of 230 billion yen,* as a subsidy by the National Government, which is half the total amount required.

The percentage of local public schools furnished with typical instructional aids in 1980 is given in the following table:

Instructional aids	*Elementary school*	*Lower secondary school*	*Upper secondary school*
	Per cent		
Slide projectors	97.1	98.1	98.8
8 mm sound motion picture projectors	77.1	78.7	84.7
16 mm sound motion picture projectors	55.7	57.6	96.9
Overhead projectors	99.5	99.1	98.9
Tape recorder (open reel)	54.4	61.4	83.3
Tape recorder (cassette)	97.4	98.0	97.1
T.V. set (black and white)	43.3	40.6	62.7
T.V. set (colour)	98.1	94.3	90.6

The use of computers in education–Computer-Assisted Instruction (CAI) and Computer-Managed Instruction (CMI) is also being developed in some schools.

Many audio-visual associations and manufactures produce science slides, films, OHP transparencies, cassette tapes, video

* Approximately 230 Japanese yen (¥) = One US dollar.

tapes, science charts, workbooks and experimental notes. The National Broadcasting Corporation (NHK) broadcasts science programmes to the elementary and secondary schools every day. These are used widely to reinforce or supplement science teaching.

Computer programmes in science teaching are now at the experimental stage in colleges and universities.

Teacher Training

Minimum Qualifications. Teachers at kindergarten, elementary and secondary schools in Japan must have a relevant teaching certificate as provided for by the Educational Personnel Certification Law.

Certification requirements vary with school level. Teacher certificates for kindergartens and elementary schools are available for all subjects, while those for lower and upper secondary schools are available for specified subject areas.

Teacher certificates are divided into regular certificates and temporary ones. Persons who hold regular certificates are qualified for full teaching posts. This type of certificate is subdivided into first and second class.

The basic qualifications for the second class certificate for kindergarten, elementary and lower secondary teachers are that they must have studied for two years in a university (or the equivalent) and acquired 62 credits. The basic qualifications for the first class certificate for elementary and lower secondary teachers and second class certificates for upper secondary teachers are that they must hold a bachelor's degree. First class certificates for upper secondary teachers are granted to those who hold a master's degree or who have done one year's post-graduate study and acquired 30 credits beyond the bachelor's degree.

Students in teacher training courses are required, in addition to the basic qualifications, to obtain a prescribed number of credits in two subject groups in courses approved by the Minister of Education, Science and Culture. These are general education subjects and teaching and specialized subjects.

Teachers seeking higher class certificates must earn additional credits and must have served for the prescribed number of years with a good record as school teachers. The required credits may be acquired through in-service training (e.g. correspondence and other off-campus courses approved by the Minister of Education, Science and Culture) or by attending regular university courses.

Those who have temporary certificates can only qualify as assistant teachers. Temporary certificates for kindergarten, elementary and lower secondary teachers are granted to upper secondary school graduates (or the equivalent) who have passed the educational personnel examination conducted by prefectural boards of education. Those for upper secondary teachers are granted to those who have studied for two years in a university (or the equivalent) and acquired 62 credits.

Teacher certificates are granted by prefectural boards of education. Regular certificates are valid in all prefectures and for life, while temporary certificates are honoured for three years only, and valid only in the prefecture issuing them.

The Percentage of Qualified Teachers. The number of applicants for teachers at the elementary school level exceeds the demand. The number of applicants at the lower and upper secondary school level also for exceeds the demand. The proportion of teachers without the competent certificate to each varies from one prefecture to another. In Aomori Prefecture, for example, the proportion of unlicensed science teachers at secondary school was 49 per cent. By contrast it was merely 0.4 per cent in 1968 in Tokyo.

In order to secure able people of high quality for the teaching profession and to maintain and improve standards of school education, the Law Governing Special Measures for Maintenance and Enhancement of School Education Standards was enacted in 1974. In compliance with this Law, special measures have been taken for the improvement of salaries and allowances of public school teachers.

Pre-service Training. The course of training is of four years duration and certification depends on obtaining prescribed numbers of credits in general education and in the teaching subject groups.

At all colleges and universities, tests are given at the end of each semester to measure the student mastery of specific content of the individual subject. There is no national test or standardized evaluation system for student teachers. Some professors use evaluation to assess progress toward the specific objectives and content of a given course, a unit and a lesson. Diagnostic data are used to locate the causes of weaknesses and strengths in the attainment of students. Informal means such as individual interview, open ended questions and discussions, project work, analysis of writing in notebooks, and records of observation of student performance and behaviour are all in use.

In-service Training. The Ministry of Education, Science and Culture, prefectural boards of education, and prefectural education centres provide opportunities for systematic in-service training for public school teachers, principals and supervisors. Some of the larger municipalities and educational study groups also hold workshops and study meetings for in-service training.

The Ministry also holds Central Workshops for intensive in-service training of principals, vice-principals and experienced teachers (*e.g.* curriculum co-ordinators, heads of teachers' groups teaching the same grade or the same subject in a school), who are selected and sent by every prefectural board of education.

The predominant aim of in-serve training is to improve the professional abilities of teachers. Participation in an in-service training programme is not normally rewarded with a salary increase.

Science Education Centres. There are about 50 Science Education Centres retraining science teachers and developing research in science education. The type of work undertaken in Science Education Centres may be illustrated by example from the Centre of the Hiroshima Prefecture which was established in 1962. It is a three storey, 1,580 square metres building. It has a Director, nine professional staff and four clerical staff. Its activities are to : (i) organize in-service training courses in science for teachers at elementary (including kindergarten) and secondary levels; (ii) conduct research on science and science education including development of teaching materials for science; (iii) collect information on science education in Japan and abroad and to disseminate the information among the teachers; and (iv) encourage children to make a study of science in extra-curricular activities.

Within the Science Education Centre, there are study rooms, laboratories and preparation rooms, for each of physics, chemistry, biology and earth science. Facilities such as an astronomical observatory (dome), planetarium, greenhouse, library for teaching materials are annexed.

Research

The types of problems. Within science education the following topics on elementary school science have been studied during the period 1967 to 1982.

Topics on elementary school science studied during the period 1967 to 1982*

	Number of projects					
	Grades					
Topic	*I*	*II*	*III*	*IV*	*V*	*VI*
Plants	33	35	45	32	28	40
Animals	35	21	7	18	14	21
Electromagnetism	44	24	43	29	20	29
Solutions	21	32	13	62	27	41
Air	21	29	58	—	29	38
Force	30	40	—	22	17	23
Heat	—	—	—	39	14	9
Light	31	—	23	8	22	6
Sound	—	12	2	—	14	—
Earth	22	10	22	20	18	18
Weather	4	10	2	10	7	14
Universe	—	7	11	11	13	11

**Source:* Japan Elementary School Science Teachers Association

The list on the following page gives the range of research topics undertaken by science educators in teacher training colleges and attached experimental schools, during 1980-1982.

Out-of-school Programmes

Various formal and non-formal science education programmes are being used to reach out-of-school youth and adults in the area of science and technology education. Items covered include extra-curricular activities in science such as science clubs, science fairs, science museums, science exhibitions, films, broadcasts, TV programmes, science news, and popular science reading.

The range of research topics undertaken by science educators during 1980-1982

Subject of the studies	*Number of studies*	*Percentage of total studies*
Pre-service training	32	6.9
Science education in foreign countries	62	13.3
Science learning psychology	37	7.9
Philosophy of science education	18	3.9
Materials and lesson	34	7.3
Teaching strategy and technique	111	23.8
Evaluation	29	6.2
Physics-chemistry education	26	5.6
Experiments for physics-chemistry teaching	32	6.9
Biology-earth science education	16	3.4
Observation and experiment for biology-earth science teaching	19	4.1
Environmental education	27	5.8
Science curriculum	11	2.3
Educational technology	12	2.6

* *Source:* Japan Science Teaching Society

Science Fairs. Each year the Gaken National Contest of Children's Talent in Science is held with the topic being 'Nature Study' for elementary school children. The number of applications each year has risen from 154,069 in 1979 to 162,733 in 1982. Each prefecture selects the best three nature study entries; the Intermediate Selection Committee selects ten entries for each grade from I to VI; and the Central Selection Committee decides the winning entries.

The Japan Youth Science Prize offers the topic 'Scientific Investigations' to junior and senior high school students annually. The yearly average of applications is 5,000. Each prefecture selects the best entries and the Central Selection Committee chooses the best winning entries.

Science Invention Prize. An exhibition of school children's inventions entered its 41st year in 1983. This exhibition stimulates the creative powers of students.

Science Museum. The Science Museum is the pre-eminent general science museum in Japan with the objective of diffusing and developing an awareness of science and technology among people, especially the rising generation. The results of various rapid developments in science and technology are exhibited using actual examples, models or experimental equipment. The exhibits explain in a simple way the underlying theory and are arranged so that visitors may operate the displays themselves.

The Museum, under the administration of the Ministry of Education, Science and Culture, consists of two sections, one for natural history, and one for physical sciences and technology. Various facilities belonging to the Museum are located in and around Tokyo, including the headquarters in Ueno Park, eastern Tokyo, the Natural History Institute at Shinjuku, western Tokyo, the Garden for Nature Study at Shirogane near Meguro, southern Tokyo, and the Tsukuba Botanical Garden in Tsukuba Academic Town, Ibaraki Prefecture, 60 kilometres northeast of Tokyo.

Current Innovations

Master's Course in Teachers' Colleges. Two colleges–in the prefectures of Hyogo and Niigata offer two-year master's degree courses for educational philosophy, cognitive development of children and professional subjects. This is an attempt to provide high-level updating of science teachers (and others) through in-service training.

Research Project : Scientists in School Programme. A grant-in-aid from the government has enabled a project at

Hiroshima University to be launched which permits scientists to visit individual schools to assist with pilot lessons. This project has also sponsored a Citizens Scientific Movement for the protection of plants an established an Invention Club.

Sony Foundation of Science Education. The Sony Foundation of Science Education was established in 1972, when a programme was established for encouraging science education in elementary and junior high schools in Japan. Sony supports students through the Foundation to develop human potential and ability, especially emphasizing the ability to think.

Schools showing outstanding programmes in science education and the development of human potential through science education have been awarded funds for the furtherance of their efforts.

The Sony foundation, since its inception, has donated 552.2 million yen in total. More than 5,000 schools have applied for grants and 1,682 schools have received awards. Schools apply to the Foundation by submitting papers on, for example, how they foster abilities in nature study.

The Foundation also has an international educational exchange programme whereby students spend time in other countries and also whereby science teachers undertake short overseas tours to the USA. Five students were involved in the exchange programme in 1982 and 19 teachers participated in the overseas tour.

9

Lao People's Democratic Republic

The first Five-Year Plan (1981-1985) emphasizes the use of modern machines in the filed of socio-economic development and the increase of scientific and technical research. Education is regarded as a major factor in the development of manpower and the economy. The new approach to education is based on equality of all nationalities and on the principles that learning must go hand in hand with work; education must be related to society; and political, cultural and scientific education are interrelated.

The implementation of the new education will be based on the following objectives :

(a) The eradication of illiteracy;

(b) The promotion of cultural and scientific standards particularly among workers and farmers;

(c) The development of leaders for the future; and

(d) The training of skilled workers and cadres of scientific-technical personnel.

Educational System

The system of education comprises mass education; pre-school education; general education; and vocational and university education. The general education provides the cultural basis of education for everyone and lays the foundation for national development in the future.

The Structure of General Schools. The general schools are divided into three levels namely: primary school which is a five year course (P1 – P5) for children aged 6 to 11 years; lower secondary school which is a three year course (M1 – M3) for children aged 11 to 14 years; and upper secondary school which is a three year course for children aged 14 to 17 years.

Enrolment at Each of the Above Stages. Education has developed rapidly since 1975 particularly in regard to quantity. The number of schools has nearly doubled, while and total enrolment of students has more than doubled. Enrolment at the lower secondary and upper levels has increased eight times and ten times respectively. The comparison with education before 1975 is given in the table below.

General Schools

	Pre-1975	*1981-1982*
Number of schools	3,373	6,791
The total number of students	255,727	560,711
Primary level	245,852	480,535
Lower secondary level	8,364	64,456
Upper secondary level	1,510	15,720

(Statistics from Ministry of Education : 1982)

Science Education

Science begins at the primary level and is compulsory for all through to grade XI.

Primary level. Children learn basic science through their reading and recitation lessons in grades I, II and III. Grades IV and V have 7.5 per cent of instructional time allocated to teaching. This amounts to two hours a week.

Lower secondary level. At lower secondary school, science is taught for three hours week in M.1 (grade VI), six hours a week in M.2 (grade VII), and eight hours a week in M.3 (grade VIII). Physics is taught as separate subject from grade VII while chemistry is taught in grade VIII.

Upper secondary level. Upper secondary school science is taught for ten hours a week in U.1 (grade IX), ten hours a week in U.2 (grade X), and 11 hours a week in U.3 (grade XI). Mathematics is not included in these figures.

Objectives of Science Education

The main objective of teaching science in general schools is to train children at an early age to realize the scientific concept of the world so as to cultivate a correct attitude toward the various forms of superstitions. Specifically it is to develop, objectively and logically, the concepts of the existence, movement and interrelationship of matter; hence gradually enabling children to understand and mastery of nature and to know how to transform nature for the service of mankind.

The objectives of science teaching and learning at each stage are :

Primary level. To make children basically understand living and non-living things, to distinguish what are the useful and useless things for human life; to know the changes of seasons in each year; to know how to find out the four cardinal points of the compass; to know geographically and politically where Laos is located and its rich natural resources.

To make children logically and objectively understand about natural phenomena, such as thunder, thunderbolts, thunderstorms, earthquakes, so as to counteract controversial concepts learned through superstitions. They should also realize what wind, water, fluids and liquids are and how to use them in the service of mankind.

To make children understand about the human body and related aspects of health, cleanliness and sanitation.

Lower secondary level. To give children a basic knowledge of systematic natural science, so as to develop their concepts and attitudes about nature, love of nature and the realization of natural phenomena.

To make children acknowledge the role and contribution of science of human daily life, and how basic scientific criteria such as wind, water, heat, light are used in the sphere of agricultural production and animal husbandry.

Upper secondary level. To systematically constitute a wider and deeper knowledge of science so that students will be able to realize the basic principles and theories of science and develop the ability to apply scientific knowledge in the transformation of nature to the benefit of mankind.

Organization of Science Education

At the primary level science is taught as a basic subject and is not taught as separate subjects. It provides children with basic information about nature, and the content is linked to daily life, including the simple phenomena of nature, culture, animal raising, hygiene and prophylaxis.

At lower and upper secondary levels science is taught as separate subjects: zoology, botany, physics, chemistry.

Development of Curricula

There is, so far, no particular institute for the development and evaluation of science curricula, but there is a bureau for collecting data and information concerning the curriculum in general.

The general responsibility for education, including implementation of curricula, is divided as follows :

(a) The *Taseng* or county level is responsible for primary education (County Education Board);

(b) The *Muang* or district level is responsible for lower secondary education (District Education Board);

(c) The *Kweng* or provincial level is responsible for upper secondary education (Provincial Education Board); and is also responsible for all education in the province being a direct agent of the Ministry of Education.

At the central level there is a Committee for Educational Science Research and Textbooks (CESRT) set up by the Ministry of Education in 1983 by combining the department of research and textbooks and the scientific and educational research committee. At present the CESRT is the only institution for curriculum development and textbooks.

The present curricula were introduced in 1975-1976 and have not yet been revised.

Content of Science Curricula

In accordance with the present political and economic policy, science teaching and learning is focused on agriculture, forestry and irrigation development.

The content at primary level is concerned with basic techniques of growing vegetables, cereal plants, and fruit. It also covers hygiene, disease and sanitation. At lower secondary level the content includes a practical approach to agriculture and animal raising with aspects of vegetable gardening, forestry and farming. The emphasis at upper secondary level is on improving living standards through such methods as the use of electric power, irrigation and the selective breeding of plants and animals.

Evaluation of Students

Students are tested through internal lesson tests, monthly tests and semester examinations. There is also a final examination at the end of each stage or level of education. The decision as to whether a student satisfies the requirements for promotion to the next grade is based on the average scores for all subjects plus assessment of social and moral activities.

Practical Work in Science Education

The following table gives the time available for practical activities within the science lessons.

Class	*Total time for science teaching*	*Time for practical activity or laboratory work*	*Percentage*
Primary	106 hours	(a)	–
Lower secondary	428 "	33 hours (b)	8
Upper secondary	683 "	51 " (b).	13.4

(a) At the primary level there is no laboratory work, instead children are guided through the practical activities of adults by observing agricultural and co-operatives activities. In addition they have a daily exercise in looking after co-operative gardens in accordance with their ages, for at least one hour a day.

(b) These are hours for laboratory work in biology, physics and chemistry only; other activities such as growing plants and animal raising are excluded.

Examinations

In general schools, practical activities are not assessed for final examination purposes.

Equipment and Apparatus

With the rapid development of general schools there are many problems concerning the supply of instructional materials and equipment. In some schools in the urban areas there is some apparatus; but in rural areas teachers have to try to make use of local materials, particularly for biological experiments.

Educational Technology

At present, sophisticated educational technology is not used because it is unsuitable for the economic condition of the country. Generally speaking, simple educational technology has been practised only in some schools in the main cities. This includes slides, films, charts and so on. There is no educational technology in the form of computers, television sets and other electronic equipment.

Teacher Training

Previously, primary school teachers must have completed the five year primary school course and taken a three year teacher training course. This was replaced in 1983 with entrants who had completed lower secondary school and who would take either a two or three year teacher training course.

Secondary teachers must have completed lower secondary school and take a three year teacher training course.

Upper secondary school teacher training is at university level and may be one of two systems, either the regular system of 15 years duration comprising upper secondary school graduation and four years teacher training, or the accelerated system of 13 years duration (11+2). In addition the Pedagogic University of Vientiane is responsible for training science teachers for vocational schools and other universities as well as research assistants for other educational activities.

In 1981-1982 there were 30 teacher training schools of education throughout the country. There are 19 primary teacher training schools of which two are for ethnic tribes; there are ten secondary teacher training schools and one pedagogic university, with 1,805 students.

With the rapid expansion of the educational system there is a shortage of qualified teachers of science, particularly at the lower and upper secondary school levels. In the 1981-1982 year there were 16,230 primary science teachers, 3,219 in lower secondary and 879 in upper secondary.

In-service Training

In order to overcome the problem of unqualified science teachers the Ministry of Education has introduced, through Teacher Training Boards at different levels, a programme of in-service training. Six hours per week are allowed for teachers to improve their knowledge and competence, through evening classes or by correspondence. The in-service training follows the same curriculum as the pre-service courses.

Educational Research

There is, at present, no indigenous educational research in science being undertaken. The results of educational research in other countries is adapted and applied to the teaching of science in Laos.

Plans for educational research programmes for the future have been developed with special reference to the methodology of science teaching and to the improvement of qualifications.

In 1983, in order to implement these plans, the Ministry of Education set up an organization called the Committee for Educational Science Research and Textbooks (CESRT).

Out-of-school Science and Popularization of Science and Technology

Although priority is given to the eradication of illiteracy, attention is given, albeit limited, to the popularization of science and technology and to other out-of-school activities for youth and adults.

Radio broadcasts, daily newspapers and magazines are important media in the popularization of science and technology. Science topics on the radio programmes concern agriculture, forestry and animal husbandry, which are regarded as main tasks for the country. In addition, radio broadcasts on health advise people how to prevent diseases. In the daily newspapers, at least one column is reserved for the popularization of science. Among the newspapers and magazines that popularise science are *Pasason* (The people), *Vientiane May* (New Vientiane), *Suksamay* (The new education), *Heying Lao* (The Lao women), and *Sathalanasuk* (The health service).

In addition the Ministry of Education arranges a scientific exhibition, once a year, on the occasion of the National Day celebrations.

Current Innovations

Since the Lao People's Democratic Republic was established in 1975, all aspects of national development have been subject to innovation. In education the following innovations should be mentioned :

(a) Developing the content areas of the curriculum to be correlated with real life;

(b) Designing instructional materials related to the raw materials available in localities and the real circumstances of the country;

(c) Developing science teacher training at the central level, so as to update the science teachers' knowledge and competencies, particularly on mathematics, physics, chemistry and biology.

10
Malaysia

In Malaysia, a developing nation, the national ideology known as *rukunegara* refers, among other things, to a national aspiration for a progressive society oriented to modern science and technology. Science education therefore has been given due recognition as contributing to the totality of the individual's general education. Education policies have been geared to meet the needs for economic and social development. The four Malaysia Plans (1965-1985) have been formulated to meet these needs for rapid development, industrialization and modernization. The realization of the role of science education in this process of development is apparent in the second and third Malaysia Plans which have emphasized an education oriented towards science and technology, and towards meeting the manpower needs of the nation.

However, the Fourth Malaysia Plan (1981-1985), which emphasizes that the recommendations of the Cabinet Committee Report on Education (1979) would form the basis of the education programmes, points to the need for a balanced education, in particular a balance between the Sciences and the Humanities. While still catering to the nation's manpower needs, due consideration needs to be given to developing an understanding of the usefulness of scientific knowledge and processes in its application to daily life and society. The role of science education in the context of a general education needs to be examined. It is in this light that the Curriculum Development

Centre of the Ministry of Education is currently engaged in conceptualizing such a science education programme for the school level.

Besides the efforts towards improving school science education to cater for the overall development of the individual and thus the nation's needs, efforts are also being made towards improving science education outside the school level. The Science University, the Agriculture University and the University of Technology have been established with this aim in mind. The Ministry of Science and Environment was established in 1975. An Advisory Council for the Promotion and Development of Science has been established. All these are indicative of efforts towards improving and providing science education for out-of-school youth and adults, and towards the popularization of science and technology.

Structure of School Education

The System. The school system consists of primary, lower secondary, upper secondary and post secondary levels, (see Figure 1). Primary level education consists of six years (grades I-VI) and begins on the average, at age 6 plus. The lower secondary level consists of three years (grades VII—IX), and upper secondary education is two further years (grades X and XI). In general, post-secondary education consists of two years.

Pupils from Chinese and Tamil primary schools will have to spend an extra year in remove classes before proceeding to grade VII in lower secondary. This is a transitional period provided to give intensive language lessons to pupils who would be experiencing a change in the medium of instruction from the primary to the secondary.

At the upper secondary level, there are three streams, namely, the vocational, technical and academic streams. The academic stream is subdivided into Arts and Science streams.

The post-secondary level consists of Arts, Science and Technical streams. This level also includes teacher education colleges, polytechnics and other institutions offering Diploma courses.

School Enrolment. The enrolment for the various levels of the school system in 1977 is summarized in the table below.

Level	*Enrolment*
Primary	1,609,335
Lower secondary	632,753
Upper secondary	197,282
Post-secondary	23,028

Source: Educational Planning and Research Division, Ministry of Education, Malaysia. 1977.

At the upper secondary, 61.8 per cent of the pupils entered the Arts stream, 31.3 per cent entered the Science stream, 2.5 per cent entered the Technical stream and 4.4 per cent entered the Vocational stream. At the post-secondary level 53.1 per cent entered the Arts stream and 46.9 per cent entered the Science stream.

The transition rate from primary to lower secondary level as 87.8 per cent, from lower secondary to upper secondary level was 65.0 per cent, and from upper secondary to post-secondary level was 15.7 per cent.

In 1983 the enrolment at the primary level was more than two million. The secondary level enrolment was 1.1 million and the enrolment in technical and vocational streams was 19,000.

Science Education in Schools

General. Science in the existing curriculum is taught from grade I. It is a compulsory subject at all levels of school education with the exception of the pre-university level where it is an option. At the primary level science is taught as a single subject throughout the six years. With the introduction of the new primary curriculum in 1983, with the emphasis on the basic skills in education, science is to be incorporated as part of the subject Man and his Environment. Science will thus in future be introduced at the upper primary level (grade IV) as compared to introduction at grade I level in the existing curriculum.

At the lower secondary level (grades VII-IX) integrated science is taught to all pupils. At the upper secondary level,

Figure 1. School system of Malaysia, 1979*

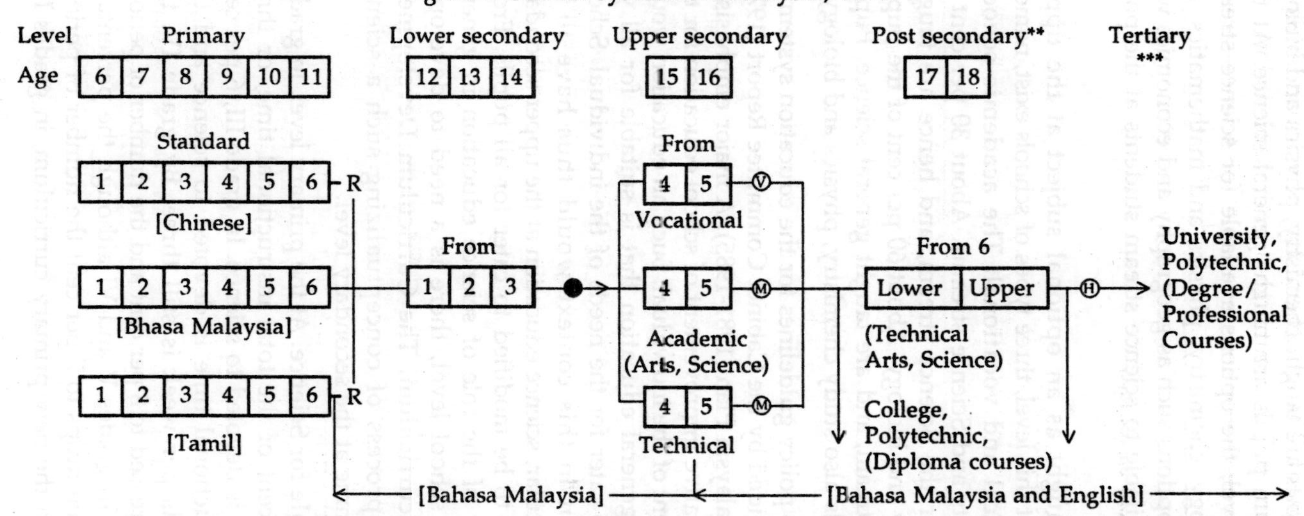

[ ] Indicates main medium of instruction.

Public examination

● Lower Certificate of Education (LCE)

Ⓥ Malaysian Vocational Certificate (MVC)

Ⓜ Malaysian Certificate of Education (MCE)

Ⓗ Higher School Certificate (HSC)

* Source : Asiah Abu Samah Curriculum Development in Malaysia

R : Remove classes are transitional classes of one year's duration provided to give intensive language lessons to pupils who have to change their medium of learning from Chinese or Tamil at the primary level to Bahasa Malaysia at the secondary level. An extra year must be added to the ages of pupils who proceed from the Remove classes.

** Sixth From classes, teacher training institutions, polytechnics and other institutions offering Diploma Coursess.

*** Universities and other institutions offering Professional Courses.

science stream pupils are taught chemistry, physics and biology and the arts stream pupils are taught general science. At the post-secondary level, the options available for science stream students are biology, chemistry, physics and mathematics. As from 1983, other options such as geography and economics will also be made available to science stream students at the post-secondary level.

Science is taught as an optional subject at the upper secondary level. At this level, three types of schools exist, namely academic, technical and vocational. The academic schools consists of the Arts and Science streams. About 30 per cent of the pupils opt for the Science stream, and hence are taught physics, chemistry and biology. About 60 per cent of the pupils opt for the Arts stream, and are taught general science. Pupils in technical schools also study chemistry, physics and biology.

Currently the policy guidelines for the education system in Malaysia are provided by the Cabinet Committee Report (1979) and the Fourth Malaysia Plan (1981-1985). A major emphasis is towards the qualitative improvement of school education for the overall development of the individual. Such an education would focus on a basic general education that is suitable for all yet flexible enough to cater for the needs of the individual. School science education in this context would thus have to be reviewed. In particular, science education at the upper secondary level would have to be modified to cater for all pupils. From the point of view of the role of science education in general education at the school level, there is a need to develop a 'Science for All' curriculum. The Curriculum Development Centre is in the process of conceptualizing such a science education programme at the secondary level.

Time Available for Science. At the primary level, in grades I and II, 6.5 per cent of the total instructional time, or three periods per week, is devoted to science. In grade III, 6 per cent of the total instructional time is devoted to science and the number of periods per week is still three. By grade IV, the percentage has increased to 8 per cent and the number of periods per week to four. In grades V and VI although the percentage of instructional time drops to 7 per cent the number of periods remains at four. In the new primary curriculum, in grades IV-

VI, 18.7 per cent of the total instructional time will be devoted to the subject Man and his Environment which incorporates science.

At the lower secondary level (grades VII-IX), 11 per cent of the total instructional time is devoted to science, with five periods of science per week.

At the upper secondary level (grades X-XI), for the Arts stream pupils who study general science, 11 per cent of the total instructional time is devoted to science which is equivalent to five periods of science per week. For the Science stream pupils who study chemistry, physics and biology, 34 per cent of the total instructional time is devoted to science, which is 15 periods per week.

At the pre-university level for the science stream, 72 per cent of the total instructional time is available for science, which is equivalent to 32 periods of science per week.

The Science Curricula Objectives. Science education at the primary level is aimed at learning skills of inquiry, fostering attitudes and developing basic concepts. Children are given the opportunity to acquire basic ideas that can lay the foundation for a gradually more sophisticated understanding of their environment. One of the main aims of teaching science at this level is to assist the pupils to learn how to live in their environment and to appreciate and intelligently use this scientific knowledge in dealing with problems in their environment.

At the lower secondary level, the objectives of science education are the acquisition of scientific knowledge, understanding basic principles, development of scientific practical skills and acquisition of a favourable attitude towards science. Due emphasis is given to conceptual understanding in science, scientific thinking and scientific processes.

At the upper secondary level science education is concerned with two categories of pupils namely the Arts and the Science stream pupils. Science education for the Arts stream is intended to encourage the students to adopt a scientific way of thinking, to develop certain basic manipulative as well as thinking skills, and to inculcate desirable attitudes towards science. Science education for the Science stream is aimed at the acquisition of a basic knowledge of biology, chemistry and physics and an understanding of their underlying principles. It emphasizes an understanding of the schemes of inquiry by defining a problem, stating a hypothesis, designing experimental investigations to test the hypothesis and making tentative valid educations. It also provides the foundation for further study of biology, chemistry and physics at a more advanced level.

Curricular Organization. The existing primary science curriculum is organized as an integrated science, emphasizing observation and study of the environment with the resulting development of concepts derived from them. It is divided into units, which include, among others, Animals and plants are living things; Land, water and air affect animals and plants; Adaptation to environment; and Life processes in plants and animals; to name but a few. Some units, which are touched on briefly in the lower grades, are given a deeper treatment in the upper grades, along with new units suitable to the interests and abilities of upper primary pupils.

The lower secondary level science curriculum is also organized as an integrated science in the following units: introducing science; observing living things; energy; matter as particles; some common gases; cells and reproduction; heat flow; electricity; hydrogen, acids and bases; detecting the environment; solutes and solvents; food and transport systems; more about electricity; support and movement; the earth.

These units are spread over a period of three years. The curriculum is activity-oriented and the teaching and learning activities come in the form of worksheets accompanied by teachers' guides.

The upper secondary science for the Arts stream is organized as integrated science. The content is selected and developed as integrated (interdisciplinary) themes. Integration of the various disciplines of science, where possible and relevant, is catered for in the curriculum. This is a functional science curriculum which emphasizes the applications of science to everybody living. Areas such as agriculture; industry; medicine; food; and health; among others, are included in the curriculum. Conceptual schemes are used to provide logical organization to the content. The curriculum is activity-oriented. Teachers' guides are provided, where additional information pertaining to the activities in the pupil's books, is included to assist the teacher, in the teaching/learning process. Topics covered in this science curriculum include: the world through our senses; light and colour; atoms and the structure of matter; energy conversions in our bodies; electricity and energy; chemicals and energy; the balance of nature; the world food problem and the chemist; production and transmission of electricity; cell division and inheritance; electricity and chemical reaction; motion; microbes and man; natural and synthetic carbon compounds; and communication (see Figure 2).

The upper secondary science for Science stream pupils is taught as separate subject disciplines of biology, chemistry and physics. These three curricula have been developed to provide a continuation from the integrated science curriculum at the lower secondary level. These curricula emphasize the understanding of basic concepts and principles in physics, chemistry and biology. The curricula are activity-oriented. Experimentation and inquiry emphasized in the curriculum seek to develop basic skills in science. Teachers' guides provide additional information pertaining to activities in the pupil's books, to assist teachers in the teaching/learning process.

Infrastructure for Curriculum Development. The Curriculum Development Centre of the Ministry of Education is responsible for developing and evaluating science curricula for the whole spectrum of school science education ranging from primary to lower secondary to upper secondary. The formation of the Central Curriculum Committee (CCC) in the late 1960s was an attempt to institutionalize curriculum development. This committee is a high-powered policy decision body responsible for the direction of curriculum development at the national level. The curriculum unit of the Educational Planning and Research Division of the Ministry of Education functioned as the secretariat to the CCC. Around this time, the Schools Division of the Ministry of Education had established a functional unit referred to as the Science Centre. This centre was responsible specifically for research, planning, organization and implementation of science curricula. The proposal for formalizing this centre as a science education centre resulted in the establishment of the Education Development centre which later became the Curriculum Development Centre in 1973. The infrastructure for curriculum development in Malaysia was thus established.

Figure 2. Conceptual relationship among topics

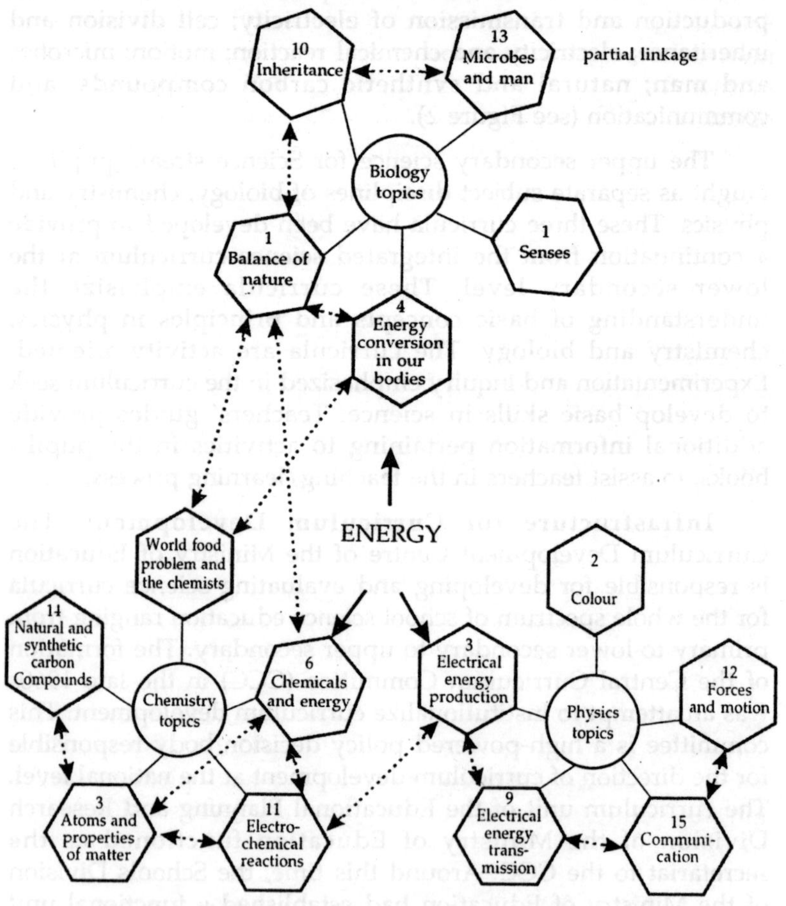

Source: General Science (Malaysian Syllabus) Teacher's Guide

The mechanisms used for developing and evaluation science curricula at the various levels of the school system are summarized in Figure 3 on the following page.

Curriculum Renewal. The primary science syllabus was introduced in 1965. Later, the concern for the poor performance of pupils in the rural primary schools, particularly in science and mathematics, and hence the need to remedy this situation, resulted in the establishment in 1968 of the special primary Science and Mathematics Project. This was a centrally controlled undertaking aimed at improving the quality of science and mathematics teaching at the elementary level. An important objective of this project was to provide sustained teacher support services, which included among others, teachers' guides introducing the inquiry-oriented approach to science teaching. Specifically the project attempted to prepare teachers' guides based on the existing syllabus, to train supervisors and key personnel, and to set up a number of Centres of Excellence that catered for teachers in the country. The project emphasized pupil-centred, activity oriented, inquiry-based teaching/learning of science. These curricular materials are currently used in the teaching of science at the elementary level.

Science curricular innovations at the secondary level were introduced in the late 1960s. The need to improve the quality of science education in Malaysia, besides the influence of world trends in science and science education in the post-sputnik era, resulted in the introduction of these innovations. Some modern science curricula that had been successfully implemented in other countries, were examined with the view to adapting them on the basis of their suitability. Thus the integrated science curriculum was introduced at the lower secondary level in Malaysian schools in 1969. This curriculum was based on the Scottish Integrated Science Curriculum. The Malaysian pure science curricula (biology, chemistry and physics) were introduced in 1972 for the upper secondary level science stream pupils. The Malaysian General Science Curriculum was introduced at the upper secondary level for the Arts stream pupils in 1974. These science curricula at the upper secondary level were adaptations from the Nuffield sciences of the United Kingdom. These science curricular innovations emphasized : i) updating

Figure 3. **Framework for science curriculum development.**

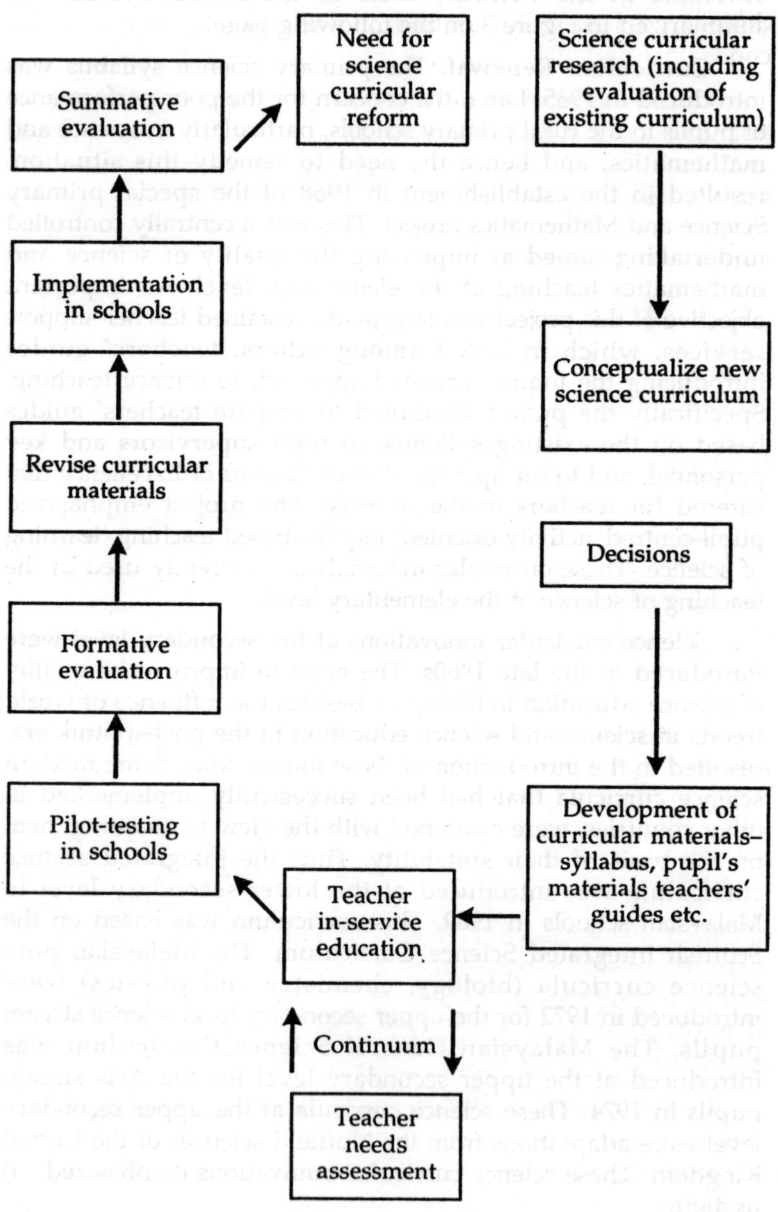

science content and the use of local materials where possible; ii) teaching/learning approaches which are inquiry and discovery based, pupil-centred and activity-oriented; and (iii) conceptual understanding and application to daily living.

Curricular relevance. The rationale for the introduction of science curricula innovations at the primary, lower secondary and upper secondary level was, among others, to make the science learned in schools applicable to real-life situations and to give due emphasis to social issues that are science-related, such as environmental pollution.

In the existing primary science curriculum, a section entitled 'Science in everyday life' is included. This section points out how science helps man to safeguard public health, provide better public services such as water purification plants, sewage disposal and electricity, improve agriculture and improve industrial production.

The application of science to everyday life is given due emphasis in the lower secondary integrated science curriculum. In the section on 'Energy' and 'Energy converters in action', common examples such as the electric fan, telephone, radio, and clock are used to emphasize the application of energy conversion in everyday life. In the section on 'Heart transfer' an explanation of natural phenomena such as radiation from the sun, and land and sea breezes, is given as applications to everyday life. In a section on 'The soil environment', there is a brief mention of man's interference and the need for conservation.

In the Malaysian general science curriculum for the upper secondary level, in a section on 'colour', reference is made to such aspects as application to colour printing and the importance of colour in everyday life. The curriculum includes a section on the effect of man on the balance of nature, where the different forms of pollution, their causes and control, and conservation of nature are dealt with social issues are thus given due emphasis.

In the section of 'Energy and chemical change' in the chemistry curriculum, reference is made to chemical changes in the production of energy for industrial purposes. In 'Rates of reaction', its application in manufacturing processes dealt with.

In the biology curriculum, the beneficial and harmful activities of microbes are discussed. Their applications to industry, sewage disposal and control of disease are treated. In the physics curriculum, the magnetic effect of a current, the electromagnet and its application in the making of the electric bell are included in the content.

As can be seen from the examples discussed above, there is a fair reflection of real-life situations and science-related social issues in the science curriculum. However, there is room for improvement in this area of science and social issues.

Assessment. New methods of assessing achievement in conjunction with the new science curricula, had to be introduced. Co-operation with the Examination Syndicate of the Ministry of Education was therefore necessary. Workshops were organized for selected teachers and other education personnel of the Ministry of Education for the purpose of test item construction. The resulting new mode of assessment covered areas of higher cognitive levels like application and synthesis, other than mere knowledge.

The assessment of pupil's achievement is carried out externally in the form of national public examinations. These examinations include the Standard 5 (grade V) assessment where test items are of the objective type. This includes multiple choice and multiple completion types of questions. The lower certificate examination for integrated science at the lower secondary level examines pupils' abilities to recall knowledge, comprehend scientific concepts and principles, and apply them. This is in keeping with the rationale, aims and objectives of the new curriculum. The test items are all of the objective type and include multiple choice and multiple completion types.

Examinations for general science and chemistry, physics and biology at the upper secondary level include questions of three types namely objective (multiple choice and multiple completion), structured and free response type. Structured type questions provide situations to assess the pupils' abilities to organize and present scientific ideas in a clear and logical manner. For chemistry, physics and biology, besides the theory papers, the pupils have to sit for a laboratory practical test which assesses the manipulative and observational skills, ability to record, present results and to make inferences from their results.

Science Activities Laboratory Work and Equipment. The new science curricula at the primary, lower secondary and upper secondary levels are all activity-oriented and inquiry based. As such, practical activities and laboratory work become an important component in the science teaching/learning situation. About 60 per cent of total curricular time available for science teaching is devoted to practical activities at all levels.

For the primary and lower secondary levels, practical work is not examinable in the public examinations. However, at the upper secondary level, practical work in chemistry, physics and biology for the science stream pupils is examinable in the Malaysian Certificate of Education examination. Students take a special practical examination consisting of a one and three-quarter hour paper, which represents 10 per cent of the marks in the examinations.

Generally, science equipment and apparatus available in schools is adequate to meet the needs of the new science curricula. The initial shortage of science equipment and apparatus experienced by schools through the introduction of new science curricula has largely been overcome. The Curriculum Development Centre of the Ministry of Education is currently engaged in the production of blueprints for prototype apparatus for commercial adoption or for use by teachers. Information to this effect is disseminated through the Science newsletter published by the Curriculum Development Centre. Some prototypes which have been developed for physics, include the pile driver, simple air-table, electronic circuit board, regulated power supply and longitudinal wave demonstration apparatus. These proto-types are currently being tried out in schools. With the help of the information disseminated through the newsletter, teachers are able to improvise some of the apparatus using locally available materials.

The infrastructure for prototype development of science apparatus and equipment and their quality control is well established with in the Ministry of Education. As such there is a gradual shift from importing science apparatus to one of reliance on local manufacture.

Currently a small percentage of the science apparatus used in schools is locally manufactured. A large percentage of the science apparatus is still imported.

The Science Centre set up in 1969 to plan develop implement and evaluate the school science curricula and which was later established as the Curriculum Development Centre in 1973 consisted of a prototype and quality control of apparatus unit beside the science and mathematics units. The functions of this prototype unit included among others, the development of prototype educational equipment for physics, chemistry, biology, general science, integrated science at the lower secondary level, and primary science. The prototype developed is based on the needs of science curriculum officers and science teachers who may wish to try out an apparatus they have designed. An important role of the prototype unit is to investigate and provide for the local production of such items, with the use of local materials as far as possible.

The Prototype Unit also provides technical know-how to local manufacturers. The unit has facilities for testing the quality of educational equipment manufactured. The samples supplied by manufactureres to the Central Tender Board are tested and their quality and suitability determined. This ensures the proper and economical use of school science funds.

Use of Educational Technology

Activity oriented, inquiry-based teaching/learning of science has created the need for the use of a greater range of resources. A wide range of audio-visual aids is used in schools for teaching science. Such audio-visual aids include slides, film-strips, wall charts, and three-dimensional models. The Audio-visual Aids section of the Ministry of Education has made available such resources and key personnel at the state level to enable maximum use of such aids in the teaching/learning process in most schools. Other sophisticated technologies used in schools include the overhead projector, audiotape cassette and video-tape cassette. Science teaching in schools is further supplemented by educational television programmes on science. However, programmes on using computers are not available. Efforts towards incorporating such strategies in science education are underway.

Teacher Education Qualifications

Primary. Science teachers at this level possess a minimum academic qualification of a certificate in the Malaysian Certificate of Education examination. In addition, they have undergone a three years teacher training programme to acquire professional qualifications. They are trained to teach all subjects including science at the primary level.

Lower Secondary. Science teachers at this level possess a minimum academic qualification of the Malaysian Certificate of Education. These teachers have to undergo a three-year teacher training programme in teacher training colleges specializing in science education. Beside the basic courses in education, science is an option at these colleges.

Upper Secondary. The minimum academic qualification of science teachers at this level is a science degree. To acquire their professional qualification, these teachers undergo a one year diploma in education course at university. In this diploma course, besides the core course in 'Principles of Educational Practice', two science methods courses are taken as options. (Science methods include chemistry, physics and biology).

Number of Teachers. The shortage of qualified and trained science teachers for various levels of the education system was a significant problem in the 1960s and the 1970s. However, this situation has improved to a large extent, with no severe shortage of science teachers at the various levels. This is shown by data from the Cabinet Committee Report on Education (1979).

Teachers	*Need*	*Available*	*Excess (+)/ Shortage (–)*
College trained	70,471	60,881	–9,590
Science graduates	2,711	1,590	–1, 121
Status in 1975			
College trained	84, 890	86, 965	+ 2, 075
Science graduates	7, 803	9, 570	+1, 767
status in 1975			

Pre-service Teacher Education Programme. Pre-service teacher education in Malaysia is organized at two levels, namely the Diploma in Education and the Certificate in Education. The Diploma in Education course is available in the Faculties of Education of universities, while the Certificate in Education course is offered by the Teacher Education Division of the Ministry of Education through its teachers' colleges.

Certificate in Education. The Teacher education programme for the Certificate in Education is aimed at producing qualified teachers for the elementary level and lower secondary level in schools. This is a new three-year programme, introduced in 1981, to replace the two-year Integrated Teacher Training Programme which has been in existence in all colleges since 1973. The introduction of this innovation in the teacher education programme at this level is in keeping with the recommendations of the Cabinet Committee Report on Education (1979).

Based on the entry requirements, selected candidates are sent to one of the 26 Teachers' Colleges in Malaysia to undergo a three-year full-time teacher education programme, leading either to the Primary School Teacher Certificate or the Secondary School Teacher Certificate. Provision is made for school subject specializations within each programme.

The teacher education curriculum at this level consists of : (i) Core courses : ii) School subject/Specialization courses; (iii) Self-enrichment courses; (iv) Teaching practice; and (v) Co-curricular activities.

Core courses are common to both the primary and lower secondary teacher programmes. The core courses consist of : (i) Education; (ii) Educational technology; (iii) National language (proficiency); (iv) English language (proficiency); (v) Physical and health education; (vi) Islamic civilization; and (vii) Islamic religious education (for Muslim students) or Moral education (for non-Muslim students).

The primary programme students would normally cover all subjects of the primary school curriculum with special emphasis given to their subject specialization. The secondary programme students would follow the courses of subject specialization, which in the case of science teachers would be science and mathematics. The school subject courses would cover pedagogical as well as academic aspects of the subject. The secondary programme students are also required to take specially designed enrichment courses on civics, music, art education and mathematics and science. These courses are intended to complement the training programme and to provide a balanced education for these prospective teachers.

The examination for this teacher education programme consists of two parts. Part I is taken at the end of term four of the nine terms and Part II is taken at the end of the three-year course. In the examination system, course work assessment and terminal examinations are of equal importance and are given equal weighted in the final results. The students undergo 18 weeks of teaching practice—6 weeks during Part I and 12 weeks during Part II.

Diploma in Education. This course is organized by the universities. A candidate for the course must be a graduate of a university. The programme of studies for the Diploma in Education at the University of Malaya extends over a period of one year of full-time study, and consists of theory and practical. The programme comprises 13 units of coursework, six units of practical teaching in the classroom, and one unit course in physical education and co-curricular activities. The 13 units of course work consist of :

(i) Three units of foundations of education, namely psychological studies in education, pedagogical studies in education and education in Malaysia;

(ii) *Six units of methodology of teaching.* A candidate must take two subject method courses. For science education, the subjects include physics, chemistry, biology, mathematics, agriculture, engineering technology and geology; and

(iii) Four units of educational electives courses to be chosen from a list of course offered by the faculty from time to time, including a one unit course in sociology.

The six units of Teaching Practice consist of ten weeks of teaching and guided observation in educational institutions and/ or micro-teaching laboratories.

The examination for the Diploma in Education consists of two parts. The Part I examination comprises, (i) a two-hour written paper in each of the prescribed courses in foundations of education; (ii) an examination and/or assignments in each of the four prescribed elective courses; and (iii) an examination and/or evaluation of physical education and co-curricular activities.

The Part II examination comprises, (i) an assessment of teaching practice; and (ii) such examinations and/or assignments as may be determined by the Faculty for the subject-method courses.

The programme described above is the end-on programme where the Diploma in Education course follows the completion of the basic science degree course. Another programme that is available now is the concurrent B.Sc.Ed. (Bachelor of Science with Education degree) course where the education competent is incorporated in the basic science degree programme. This is a four year programme.

In-service Education. With the introduction of the science curricula innovations in the various stages of school science education, there was a need to provide in-service education to science teachers at these various levels, in order to facilitate implementation. To begin with, in-service courses were conducted to familiarize science teachers with the content and teaching approaches implied in the new science curriculum. Participants in these initial in-service courses in turn became tutors for subsequent in-service courses. Thus the in-service courses held initially at the national level, were later held at the state levels. These courses were normally held during the school holidays. Such in-service courses for science teachers have been conducted for elementary science teachers, science teachers at the lower secondary level, general science teachers at the upper secondary level and chemistry, biology and physics teachers at the upper secondary level.

One the most crucial factors that determines the success of a curriculum innovation is the ability of the teacher to implement, as closely as possible, the philosophy and objectives of the innovation in the teaching/learning situation.

Undoubtedly, the one-shot type of in-service courses conducted initially following the introduction of curricula innovations is not sufficient. This points to the need to conceptualize in-service teacher education as a continuum to facilitate curriculum innovation and implementation. The introduction of a tutors' training programme in 1974 was a strategy to improve the effectiveness of the science teachers' in-service courses. Such a course was held again in 1975, and, in 1977 a five-year project (1977-1981) was formulated for key personnel in integrated science, general science and chemistry, physics and biology. The Curriculum Development Centre was responsible for organizing and conducting these in-service courses. The aims of these in-service courses were broadened from one of merely training tutors to that of enabling them to participate actively in curricular activities at the district, state and national levels, and in professional bodies like the Science Teachers Associations. The areas covered in these courses included :

(i) Philosophy and rationale of curricula;

(ii) Teaching/Learning approaches;

(iii) Laboratory management and improvisation;

(iv) Science terminologies in the national language;

(v) In-service education;

(vi) Curriculum evaluation;

(vii) Classroom testing techniques; and

(viii) Current science-related social issues such as environmental pollution and energy conservation.

Thus it can be seen that the science teacher in-service education provided is viewed as an on-going activity aimed at improving teacher competencies in various areas.

Research in Science Education

Problems Investigated and Remedial Actions. The science curriculum innovations, with their inquiry-based activity-oriented approaches to the teaching/learning of science, have given rise to some problems. One is the concern for the effective implementation of this inquiry-based teaching. Other problem areas include lack of apparatus, an important component in this activity mode of teaching/learning in science, and the concern for the effectiveness of in service education. Several studies have been carried out along the lones of these concerns in science education and steps have been taken, where possible, to remedy these situations.

In an evaluation of science and mathematics education in relation to the Mid-Term Review of the Second Malaysia Plan, Sim *et. al.*. (1973) pointed out that,

> [teachers] do not come to grips with the crucial issues, such as those pertaining to the careful differentiation of specific arrangements needed to ensure that every pupil, as well as the teacher, would be able to engage in meaningful inquiry.

In a study on the formative evaluation of the general science curriculum, carried out by the Curriculum Development Centre 1976, a systematic observation of the teaching/learning milieu was made at the classroom level. Information on the strengths and weaknesses in the teaching/learning processes of general science was thus obtained. Generally teachers did not raise pertinent questions during the period of pupil experimentation, which could enhance inquiry learning in science. Furthermore, effective consolidation in the teaching/learning of science, through discussions of results and inferences, was weak.

The summative evaluation of the integrated science curriculum is another study conducted by the Curriculum Development Centre in 1982. This study aimed to evaluate the extent of implementation of the teaching/learning of science, and its relationship to pupil achievement. A measure of pupil achievement was obtained through the administration of a pre- and post-test. A systematic observation of the teaching/learning situations in the classrooms of selected teachers was carried out. The instrument used for this purpose was a structured observation schedule. The teachers were categorized as high, medium or low implementors based on the extent to which they had implemented the intended teaching/learning behaviour. In general, the high implementing teachers obtained higher achievement in the pupils. High implementing teachers were more inquiry-oriented in their teaching/learning situations in the classroom. The strengths and weaknesses as revealed by this study have been used in the in-service education of science teachers.

A study on teacher perceptions of objectives for science teaching by Cheong and Wang (1977) revealed that teachers do not give due emphasis to objectives that are affect-oriented. This is inconsist with the explicit aims of the general science curriculum to promote the development of healthy attitudes and interests toward scientific activities. This study further revealed that graduate and non-graduate teachers possessed constrasting views as to which are the priority objectives of this curriculum. Graduate teachers were of the opinion that the general science curriculum aimed at developing certain higher level cognitive abilities, such as conceptual understanding and application of knowledge, while non-graduate teachers gave emphasis to lower level objectives such as observation and manipulative skills. One could infer that the in-service education has not been successful in communicating the intentions of the curriculum.

The science curriculum innovations, with emphasis on activity-oriented teaching, imply the need for effective laboratory management, maintenance of science apparatus and equipment and the need to improvise where necessary. A survey conducted by the Curriculum Development Centre in 1979 revealed the need for the improvisation of science apparatus, in particular for physics and to a certain extent in biology. This does not include common apparatus that can be purchased with the school science funds. It refers more to the high priced apparatus that can be improvised by using locally available materials. As a follow-up of this survey, workshops have been held to produce blueprints for such apparatus that can be improvised. Participants in these workshops include practising teachers, science curriculum officers and officers of the prototype Unit of the Curriculum Development Centre.

Institutions Responsible for Research in Science Education. Research in science education is conducted by the Ministry of Education and the Faculties of Education of the universities. The Regional Centre for Education in Science and Mathematics (RECSAM), situated in Penang, is a regional organization set up to help improve science and mathematics education in South-East Asian countries. This centre is also actively involved in conducting research on aspects of science education. Some research studies undertaken by these institutions include :

(i) The effects of inductive/deductive approaches in the teaching of two topics from Nuffield-based modern physics. (Lim meng Mui, M.Ed. Thesis, University of Malaya, 1976);

(ii) Relationships between cognitive development and the learning of science and mathematics. (Khoo Phon Sai, Ph.D. Thesis, University of Malaya, 1972);

(iii) Teacher perceptions of objectives for science teaching. (Cheong Siew Young & Wang Chee Seng, University of Malaya, 1977);

(iv) Summative evaluation of integrated science. (Ministry of Education, Malaysia, 1982);

(v) Environmental problems and orientations. A Malaysian case study. (Cheong Siew Young, University of Malaya, 1980);

(vi) In-science teacher education for curriculum innovation with particular reference to secondary school science in Malaysia. (Somasundaram, Indra, 1980, M. Ed. Dessertation, University of London);

(vii) Perceived use of inquiry teaching by a sample of Malaysian biology teachers. (Nor Asma Ismail & Peter A. Rubba, 1981 South Illinois University, U.S.);

(viii) An alternative approach to teaching the concept of field in secondary level physics. (Tamby Subahan, 1981, National University of Malaysia);

(ix) The development and field test of environmental education topics in biology in a grade X classroom. (Abdul Main Salimon, 1980. University Pertanian Malaysia); and

(x) Environmental control by legislation—A Malaysian case study. (Ariffin Suhaimi, 1980. University pertanian Malaysia).

Programmes for Out-of-School Youth and Adults and Popularization of Science and Technology

Various programmes are organized from time to time to cater for the out-of-school population and to popularize science and technology. The Young Scientist, which is televised, is one such programme. In this programme, selected science projects of upper secondary level students are televised. The students are given the opportunity to discuss their projects in terms of scientific methods used, observations made, results obtained and inferences made. Panel members then comment on the strengths and weaknesses of the projects and give suggestions for improvements. These projects cover areas of current interest in science such as environmental pollution, solar energy, hydroponics and food production. In this way, the programme not only serves the school population, but also the out-of-school population. It further stimulates interest in science and technology in the general public.

Information on science and technology us usually provided by the mass media. The television and radio are used to a considerable extent for the purpose of science education. In addition to the Young Scientist programme, there are other programmes of science on radio and television. This includes and education television series on school science curricula. Newsletters and articles on science and technology are published by various organizations and groups.

Current Innovations

Curricular Innovations. The Curriculum Development Centre of the Ministry of Education is currently engaged in conceptualizing a general education for the school level. In this context, due emphasis is to be given to the need for a balanced education, in particular the balance between the sciences and the humanities. The role of science education will, therefore, be re-examined in the context of a general education.

With the introduction of the new primary curriculum, which was implemented nationwide in grade I in January, 1983, the emphasis at the elementary level is on the basic skills in education. This is to continue throughout the first phase of elementary education (grades I to III). Science is to be incorporated as part of the subject of 'Man and his Environment', which would be introduced in the second phase of elementary education namely in grades IV, V and VI. Such a science curriculum would facilitate the acquisition of a broad prospective of science in relation to science-related social issues. In formulating a science curriculum within the framework of Man and his Environment due emphasis will be given to the child's experience and environment when considering criteria for content selection. Emphasis will also be given to learning skills of inquiry, fostering positive attitudes to science learning and developing basic concepts. The focus at this level would be on the observation and study of the environment.

At the secondary level, grater emphasis will be given to conceptual understanding and the acquisition of intellectual skills. Scientific concepts, principles, processes and critical thinking will be emphasized. Education through science is an important contribution to the totality of the individual's general education. Humanizing the scientific enterprise will be necessary for the provision of a values-oriented science education. This would be an essential ingredient of a balanced education. The science curriculum will thus have to highlight the relevance of science to the world outside the classroom. Social relevance, as an additional dimension in the science curriculum, will have to be given due consideration in the formulation of the secondary science curriculum. While experimental work and conceptual processes, which characterize science, will continue to remain central to science education, due emphasis needs to be given to the social dimension in science. A science curriculum in this context will have to provide for understanding the social implications of scientific activities and the contribution science and technology make to society. Such a science curriculum should provide for the incorporation of current social issues such as environmental degradation, energy conservation, consumerism and drug abuse, to name but a few. In a paper entitled, Towards a Science Education Policy, Prabhakar (1981) has deliberated on a number of these pertinent issues to be considered in the formulation of a science curriculum in the context of general education.

Fostering Scientific Talent amongst Students. Programmes are organized from time to time with the aim of nurturing scientific and technological talent amongst students and the out-of-school population, and for the development of scientific creativity amongst them. One such programme is the National School Science Exhibition jointly organized by the Ministry of education and Esso Production Malaysia Incorporated. This Science Exhibition is held biennially, and students from the upper secondary level in all schools in the country are given the opportunity to participate in the exhibition by sending in their projects. Some of the projects previously submitted, include: (a) electrical energy from solar energy; (b) river pollution; (c) biological nitrogen fixation: ways to improve production; (d) growth and reproduction of padistraw mushrooms; (e) study of the chemical components in the mango fruit; and (f) extraction of caffeine in tea and coffee; a quantitative study.

The Young Scientists programme is another such activity to promote the development of scientific creativity amongst school-children. Here pupils are encouraged to work on projects of social relevance such as projects on pollution, energy and food production.

Science societies in schools function as part of the co-curricular activities in science. Activities of these societies include, (a) visits to factories, research centres and other places of scientific interest; (b) talks on scientific topics; (d) project work on socially relevant topics such as water pollution. These activities help to cater for the development of scientific creativity amongst school-children.

The Ministry of Science, Technology and Environment, Malaysia, with the co-operation of the Science Centre in Singapore, organized a Science Exhibition in 1982 for the public. The exhibits included computing machines, electromagnets, transistors, batteries, plastics, synthetic dye and hormones. These exhibits were intended to show how scientific discoveries had conaged man's way of life over the years.

Role of Research Institutes and Industrial Concerns in Science Education. Research institutes such as the Institute for Medical Research, the Rubber Research Institute and the Science

Faculties of Universities contribute in various ways towards supporting and strengthening school and out-of-school science education programmes. From time to time, they organize exhibitions depicting their scientific research and the applications to everyday life. These exhibitions are open to the public. They provide speakers for school science society activities, to talk on various areas of scientific interest.

11

Maldives

Science as a separate subject is taught only in the English medium schools in Male. But some science concepts are incorporated in the environmental studies curriculum, which is used by all schools.

There is no specific official science policy statement but the concepts of science education are highlighted in the proposed educational plan and in the National Primary Curriculum which is presently undergoing a first major revision.

Science Education in Schools

At lower primary level (grade I and grade II) science concepts are integrated into environmental studies. From grades III to VII general science is taught, which includes physics, chemistry and biology. Up to grade VII all students take general science. At grade VIII level, science is divide into biology, chemistry and physics. At this level all the science subjects are compulsory. At grades IX and X students have the option of selecting science or arts subjects. Those who opt for arts subjects take history, geography and integrated science instead of biology, chemistry and physics.

In 1983 the percentage of students opting to take science was 60 per cent a grade IX level and 61 per cent at grade X.

There are altogether 40 periods of instruction per week at all levels. The table below shows the time devoted to science.

Grade	*Percentage of instruction time devoted to science*
	Per cent
III and IV	5.5
V	6.6
VI and VII	11.1
VIII	22.2
IX and X	33.3

Enrolment at the primary, secondary and pre-university stage (1982)

Level	*Number of Students*
primary	34, 090
Secondary	3, 745
Pre-university	55
Total	37, 890

Curriculum Aspects. The present science curriculum is organized as environmental science and integrated science for primary levels. In lower secondary and upper secondary the sciences are treated as separate subjects i.e. physics, chemistry and biology.

The Education Development Centre of the Ministry of Education is responsible for developing and evaluating the curricula for primary schools. Lower secondary and upper secondary schools follow the London GCE 'O' Level and 'A' Level syllabuses respectively.

There is no defined frequency with which the curricula are revised. It is carried out on an *ad hoc* basis. The present primary syllabus has been in use for about five years, but the Education Development Centre is in the process of renewing this syllabus.

In the primary curricula attention is being paid to real life problems and social issues. As the lower secondary and upper secondary curricula are governed by the London GCE there are very few social issues included. However a course in fisheries science was introduced at grade VIII in 1982 and it is being taught at grade IX in 1983 and grade X in 1984. It is hoped that this will make the students more aware of the problems of the fishing industry in the Maldives and the need to develop this industry further.

Evaluation. The school year is divided into four quarters and at the end of each quarter, the students' work is evaluated. The main examination is at the end of every year. At the end of grade VII the students take a public examination and at the end of grade X students sit the London GCE 'O' Level examination. Having passed this examination in at least two subjects, students may enter the Science Education Centre if they wish to proceed to university studies. At this Centre students follow the London GCE 'A' Level syllabus, which is a two year course. Evaluation is carried out throughout the two years. To enter the second year of the course students have to pass a mid-course test which is held at the end of the first school year.

Science Activities/laboratory Work and Equipment. In the primary and lower secondary there is no set time devoted to laboratory work. This is left to the individual teachers to decide but it is subject to availability of a laboratory. In the upper secondary school about 75 to 80 per cent of the curriculum time available for science is used for laboratory work. Laboratory work is not examined at primary and lower secondary levels but it is examinable at the upper secondary level. In the final examination, 33 to 40 per cent of the final marks obtained are for practical laboratory work.

The general provision of science equipment in the schools is very poor. Two government schools (primary and lower secondary levels) have science laboratories, but both are poorly equipped. Private schools have no science laboratories at all, so hardly any practical work is done in science subjects. The laboratory at the Science Education Centre (higher secondary level) is well equipped. Locally available materials are used as far as possible in the science laboratories but as the Maldives is a country relying on imports there are very few materials available locally; for example no chemicals or glassware are manufactured in the country so these have to be imported. This problem is most serious in chemistry and physics where almost all the equipment and chemicals have to be imported.

There is no institution or organization which is in charge of designing or producing science equipment.

Use of Educational Technology

At the primary and lower secondary levels, no sophisticated technology is used to reinforce or supplement teaching. At the Science Education Centre overhead projectors and cine film projectors are freely available to all teachers who wish to use them. In the science faculty, loop films are available to the students and these are used to reinforce teaching. Video films are also available to supplement teaching or widen the interest of students.

Teacher Training Qualifications

There is no specific science teacher training for the primary stage. Primary science is taught by primary class teachers along with other subjects.

At the lower secondary stage the teachers who take science are required to have a diploma/certificate in the teaching of science and three years teaching experience. At the upper secondary level the science teacher is required to hold a degree in the required science subject and to have had five years of teaching experience.

All teachers presently employed hold the minimum qualifications required but the majority of them are expatriates.

Attempts made to overcome the shortage of local teachers. Teacher training curses are conducted locally both in English and in the local language to teachers at primary level. Students are sent abroad on scholarships to graduate in science subjects and to follow up with a certificate or diploma in teaching.

Programmes and Innovations

Science teaching is a very recent development in the Maldives and no programmes have been conducted so far to popularize science and technology. The Science Education Centre conducts workshops/ seminars on the theme of making the curriculum more relevant to local needs and is studying ways of producing indigenous low-cost material for the teaching of science.

12

Mongolia

One in every four citizens of the mongolian People'sRepublic is attending a regular education establishment. All children of school age have compulsory education to the eighth year of school or the lower secondary stage of education. The main task facing the country is to create favourable conditions to introduce universal compulsory education throughout secondary level to the tenth year of school.

The People's Revolution of 1921 opened up a pathway for the development of cultural and scientific education. During the past six decades, illiteracy has been completely eliminated, and a real, democratic integrated education system has been established. Every citizen, irrespective of nationality, sex, race, social origin and position, has the right to education in the mother tongue. This right is guaranteed by the constitution.

Financial assistance for school age children is available from a Study Fund. This Fund is used to provide material assistance to pupils, when they are in need of it, by improving their health conditions, and also the cultural, educational and other aspects of their life. Pupils, who are unable to attend school regularly because of their parents' living and working conditions receive board and lodging with equipment and furniture free of charge for the academic years.

Secondary school pupils from villages are provided with free transport within the surrounding regions on their departure and return to school, at the beginning and at the end of the academic year, and also during the school vacations.

During the examination periods external students and evening school pupils are freed from their duties and fully paid by their organizations : (a) before the end-of-year examinations for five days; (b) during the eighth-year secondary school leaving examinations for two weeks; (c) during the examinations for the ten-year school leaving certificate for 20 days. Those who attend general secondary evening schools have the right to take one hour's leave, with full wages, for every lesson.

Orphans, or school age children without guardians, are provided by the State with free living accommodation. Weak children, in need of long term medical treatment, and disabled students (the blind, the deaf, the dumb and the mentally handicapped, are aprovided for in a similar manner).

The Ministry of People's Education is responsible for organizing, leading and developing all academic and educational work. The Executive Boards of local groups of People's Deputies are responsible for the organizational work pertaining to all school age children. The parents' duties are to send their children to school at the right age and to create good conditions for them to study.

School Education

General Structure. Primary schools take children up to the age of 8. After finishing the third year of primary school all pupils transfer and continue their studies in the fourth form of the general secondary school. Eight-year school-leavers are given a certificate of 'incomplete' secondary education, but on finishing grade VIII, pupils are able to continue their studies in upper secondary schools and in specialized secondary schools and then obtain a complete general or special secondary education certificate.

Some may study at vocational schools if they so wish and also may work or engage in industrial (productive) labour. Young people, who are working in branches of the national economy or culture, having finished the incomplete general secondary education, are provided with the necessary conditions for studying at general evening schools in shifts and at correspondence courses and seasonal schools. They are admitted to specialized secondary schools through entrance examinations. Such schools are organized in cities, towns, villages, big industry combines and farms. Evening schools are organized within the general education schools.

Evening secondary schools in shifts are organized within big industries, where shift work is practised. The academic year of the evening schools in shifts lasts 34 weeks with classes four days a week.

The aim of the seasonal school is to give those people with primary education who work at agricultural farms and associations, secondary education up to grade VIII level. The seasonal schools are attached organizationally to lower secondary or upper secondary schools of agricultural associations and state farms. A seasonal school is a school with a duration of three years and with 20 weeks of lessons from 1 October to 1 March each year. Adults, unable to attend seasonal and evening schools regularly because of industrial conditions, are covered by correspondence courses, and receive a general secondary education, at the extramural departments attached to general secondary education schools.

City and town dwellers receive the equivalent of an eight year education for five academic years (each academic year has 30 weeks) and full secondary education (upper secondary) for two years (each academic year has 34 weeks).

Science Education

All schools provide science education as part of the compulsory general education at all levels. The general primary schools offer arithmetic and the Monogolian language. In Form V (junior secondary school) biology, geography are introduced; in Form VI, physics is included; in Form VII students study chemistry and in Form VIII they study the principles of Public Law of the Republic, human anatomy, physiology and health education. In tenth year, students begin to study social sciences and astronomy in addition to the other disciplines.

All subjects are taught according to the programmes approved by the Ministry of the People's Education. Taking into account the age of the children, the normal school week for

Forms IV to VIII of general educational schools in fixed at 28 to 34 hours, and Forms IX and X, 35 hours at the maximum. Science education aims to develop fully the independent activities of children by providing them with laboratory work, seminar and practical tuition, as well as organized excursions.

Optional tuition among pupils is organized as follows : Form VII studies scientific principles of animal raising; Form VIII studies folklore, principles of agriculture, vegetable growing, chemical laboratory technology, mathematical logic, analytical geometry, logarithms and programming; Form IX studies literary criticism, physiological botany, quantitative and qualitative analysis, anatomy, chemical reactions, molecular physics and elementary astronomy. Form X studies complex numbers, conjuctive numbers, oscillations, waves, quanta, structure of organic substances, cosmology and so on. Additionally Forms VIII to X may attend optional subjects on Mongolian word-formation, Russian language and history of the Republic. Forms VIII and IX have optional tuition in geography. The optional courses take 134 hours in the lower secondary schools and 170 hours in the upper secondary schools.

This optional tuition aims to develop the ability of the individual and is organized on a voluntary basis. The curriculum of the optional courses is drawn up by the Research Institute of Pedagogy of the Ministry of People's Education. Taking into account the needs of the pupils and their parents, according to the decision of the Ministry of Education, advanced courses of physics, mathematics, chemistry and Russian language are organized for Forms VIII to X pupils of general secondary education schools which have the necessary materials and teachers.

The pupils who successfully complete Form VII and who pass the competitive examination, may take the advanced courses, and attend lectures by professors from the higher educational institutions and scientists invited from the scientific research organizations. Graduates of the courses have the right to continue their studies in the advanced courses of the complete secondary schools.

The Curriculum

The Law of People's Education states:

> A complete and incomplete secondary school is a single unit, whether general educational, labour, or poly-technical school, for instructing and educating children and youth, and for providing them with a general secondary education. This is ensured by organizing the process of education and upbringing, according to the generally established principles, so that the content and level of general education be uniform through the territory of the. Republic.

Unified study plans for general educational schools' adopted by the Ministry of People's Education, in 1979. Under this plan 43.8 per cent of all academic hours are devoted to humanitics, 38.9 per cent to natural and mathematical sciences, 5.7 per cent to labour training and 6 per cent to fine (imitative) arts and physical culture.

Primary level. The aim of arithmetic at this elementary level is to familiarize pupils with the four arithmetical processes and with solving simple problems.

General Secondary Level. The main themes of science education in Forms IV to VIII of general secondary schools are : (i) in arithmetic and the beginning of analysis, to give a knowledge of mathematics and its processes in connection with the notion of 'sets' and 'possessions'. In the first lessons the pupils study the topics of 'identity and 'transformation' at an elementary level; (ii) in geometry to study the rotation of flat figures round the axis of symmetry, projection of figures and formation of angles. Much attention is paid also to the transformation of figures and the problem of calculating angles. In Forms VI and VII they learn equality, expression of sets, and they also study the identical transformation of the expression process on the basis of the theoretical functional approach, the quality of equations, the linear quadratic equation, exponential functions and logarithms. The primary notion of the theory of approximate calculation is also included in the programme. Geometric transformation is a mutual similar reflection of the whole flat which is projected onto itself. Vectors and co-ordinates will be given here; (iii) in physics: to pay special attention to the molecular structure of substances; to study the fundamentals of molecular mass, density of a substance, weight, pressure, simple mechanism, heat-exchange, aggregative state of substances, electro-magnetic induction, kinematics and dynamics, heat capacity, thermal unit and calorific theory; (iv) in chemistry: to study the chemical elements of the periodic system, by explaining the character of substances and their compounds on the principles of the periodic table; (v) in biology: to study the structure of plants and animals, their state and comparative life, environment and historical adoption, the classification of plants and animals and their evolutionary development; and (vi) in anatomy and physiology: to teach the structure of the human body, paying special attention to the higher nervous activities.

Senior secondary level. In physics: to study the principles of conservation of energy, the retention law of charge, the laws of Coulomb, Ohm, the electro-magnetic induction laws of Faraday, the formula of Ampere and Lorenz, the rule of Lenz, the basis of determination of dimensions of the vibration and wave phenomenon process, the equation of the vibration charge, the model of atomic and nucleus structure, the law of connection between mass and energy, Einsteins equation, the analysis spectrum and various other spectra. In astrophysics, a basic component of astronomy, to study the features of matter beyond our planet earth.

The chemistry course provides a deeper knowledge of the periodic law and related system.

In biology, pupils study questions of physiogenesis and onto genesis, living nature, reproduction, heredity, variability and cytology.

Organization of Curricula. The programmes of study for each subject approved by the Ministry of Education, determine the content and time allocation. Each programme has a commentary describing the aims and objectives, methods and techniques, use of audio-visual aids and the general organization of instruction. In some programmes there is a list of books to be read by the pupils. Optional additional programmes are also included occasionally.

In order to discuss the main problems of instruction and education each school form a board of teachers to work according to rules approved by the Ministry of Education. Each school has its teaching unit of methodology which consists of a number of sections depending on classes and their pecularities.

The aims of the Teaching Unit of methodology are to study the achievements of science and pedagogy; to organize instructional processes; to improve teaching devices; to evaluate the implementation of study programmes and to make suggestions for improving the quality of educational and instructional work for the administrative boards of schools.

Revision of Curricula. In 1971, all educational establishments introduced new curricula and the Ministry of People's Education adopted a new curriculum for general educational secondary schools. In 1979, this plan was further improved by introducing some amendments. There is no fixed time for amending curricula.

Relevance to Society. In 1963 a law was enacted to strengthen the links between schools and life. In accordance with this law, education and industrial practices are closely correlated and students are expected to take an active part in social work. At the primary level pupils are acquainted with the work and activities of industrial workers. At the lower secondary level students learn about technical drawing, mechanics and hand-tools and they participate in some industrial processes. In Forms IX and X students work as probationers in training workshops, manual training centres and in agricultural co-operatives and state farms. This intensive manual training occupies up to 25 per cent of the curriculum time in Forms VIII to X.

Evaluation. In Forms III, VII and IX students have to pass an examination in order to progress to the next grade. At the end of each academic year every pupil is assessed in every subject. Assessment is based on a variety of techniques: oral interviews, written tests, completing or drawing tables and graphs and laboratory work.

Laboratory Facilities. In senior forms practical work occupies 13 per cent of the time available. In order to fulfil the updated curricular requirements, schools have established well-equipped laboratories and have introduced a study room system for instruction which is of great importance. Practical skills in science are given emphasis in final examinations, particularly in the oral examination.

Use of Educational Technology

At present all the general educational schools have been supplied with mechanical aids, equipment and audio-visual materials and 50 per cent of all school subjects have the opportunity of using study rooms and audio-visual aids.

There are 2, 300 items of approved equipment and audio-visual aids used for instructional work in the secondary schools. In the years 1976-1980 state investment in purchasing equipment and furnishings for schools increased by 2.4 times that of the previous 15 years. The Soviet Union rendered great assistance in the supply of school materials and school buildings. Some equipment, audio-aids and furnishings are now produced in Mongolia. Many audio-visual aids are constructed by teachers themselves.

At present 20 per cent of the required instructional equipment, audio-visual aids and other teaching materials are produced in the country, the rest are imported. There are some local workshops designing and producing educational devices. One of these is the educational device workshop in Ulan Baatar. It has different sections for radio, wood and metal. Here complex linguaphone booths and mechanical aids are produced. According to the state plan certain furnishings for classrooms and laboratories are also produced.

Audio-visual aids at the upper secondary school level include a wide range of photographic prints and slides. There are 900 filmstrips and 233 slides and also 911 cine films and cine extracts in the schools. Each local centre has film archives. Electronic computers are also used in advanced mathematics classes. Basic knowledge and practice in the use of electronic computers is given in Form X.

Teacher Training

Teachers in primary schools and the junior forms of general educational schools should have secondary education in pedagogy and are trained at the pedagogical colleges or specialized secondary schools for teachers. Teachers with higher pedagogical qualifications are required for general educational secondary schools.

Over 90 per cent of teachers in primary schools and junior forms of general educational schools, in the academic year of 1981-1982, possessed secondary pedagogical education. Seventy per cent of teachers in general educational secondary schools possessed a higher pedagogical qualification.

It is planned that by the year 2000, all primary and secondary schools will have fully qualified teachers. By the year 1990, 95.6 per cent of teachers in primary schools and 85.5 per cent of teachers in secondary schools will be qualified in the field of pedagogy.

Structure of Training. Teachers for primary schools are trained at pedagogical secondary schools. For enrolment those who are under 30 years of age with lower secondary education have to compete for places in the pedagogical schools by examination. The term of study at the pedagogical school is 3 years 10 months. During this period students will specialize in Pedagogy and at the same time will complete upper secondary education.

The science curriculum of the Pedagogical Secondary School is approved by the Ministry of Education. Twenty-three per cent of the total study programme is devoted to lectures, and 23.4 per cent to laboratory and practical work. Almost half the lectures and laboratory work are devoted to teaching methods and psychology, the Mongolian language, and mathematics. Additionally, students have teaching practice of ten weeks.

Teachers for secondary schools require a higher pedagogical education and are trained at universities and pedagogical institutes. Persons under the age of 35 with complete secondary, or upper secondary education, are admitted to the pedagogical institutes through a system of competitive examinations. Graduates of Form X of general educational schools and demobilized persons within the same year have the right to sit the competitive examinations, if they have an appointment as a teacher. Persons with pedagogical secondary education, if they have worked not less than two years as a teacher in primary schools, also have the right to enter the competitive examinations for the pedagogical institutes. Students who pass these examinations receive financial grants on a monthly basis.

The period of study at the pedagogical institutes is four years. The science curricula of the institutes are approved by the Ministry of People's Education. The actual study programme for each subject is worked out by the specialized departments concerned and are approved by the directorate of the institute.

At these higher teacher training institutions, methodology of teaching, psychology and specific science occupy 12-15 per cent of the time. Laboratory work and practical lessons take up 33.3 per cent.

In-service Training. Primary school teachers who have worked successfully for not less than three years after finishing at complete secondary schools are admitted to the extramural departments of the specialized secondary schools training teachers for primary schools. Those with complete secondary education, who have worked satisfactorily at rural primary schools for not less than five years, are permitted to take the graduate examinations at specialized pedagogical secondary schools training primary and nursery teachers. Teachers with pedagogical secondary schools for four years and in cities for not less than six years are admitted to the extramural courses of higher pedagogical institutes through competitive examinations.

Other ways in which teachers can upgrade their qualifications and increase knowledge and skills are by self-learning on a programme based on the curricula of the Research Institutes of pedagogy of the Ministry of Education. Such a programme contains aspects of teaching methods and psychology, reports on definite problems of pedagogy and published articles; and by attending short seminars on theory and methods of teaching.

After every five years of teaching, teachers must improve their qualifications by completing a one month advanced course. These courses are for those teachers who have completed their qualifications independently and who have taken part in two of the short term seminars.

The salaries of the successful graduates from the refresher courses are increased on average by 10-15 per cent.

In order to retrain teachers and to improve their qualifications, an Advanced Teacher Training Institute was established in 1983.

Research in Education

The Research Institute of Pedagogy was established in 1963 and has undertaken many investigations to improve the content and quality of science education, and also many studies to link practical work with independent thought and initiative in children. The Institute has been involved in the development of new science curricula and programmes for general secondary schools and with the use of educational technology in teaching. Teaching methodology has also been investigated by the institute and modifications introduced into teaching schemes, through practical handbooks of methodology, including: 'Pedagogical background of general education in a primary school', 'Leading and organizing tutorial work and inner-school control' and 'Instructional equipment and its significance in cognitive activities of pupils'. In recent years the Institute has published some helpful manuals on familiarizing pupils with the fundamentals of ethics and aesthetics, tutorial work in schools, and the structure and content of Young Pioneer organizations. The Institute co-ordinates the research work of all research workers in education.

Programmes for Extramural Youth and Adults and the Popularization of Science and Technology

The popularization of science and technology in the country is organized by the Mongolian Society for the Dissemination of Scientific Knowledge, the Society for Nature and Environment Protection, the Mongolian Revolutionary Youth League and by other public, educational, cultural, and scientific organizations.

The Mongolian society for the Dissemination of Scientific Knowledge is a voluntary public organization which aims to assist actively in the constant improvement of the political and scientific knowledge of the working people and in the upgrading of their educational level, by popularizing the great achievements of science and technology, and relating them to productive work.

The mongolian Society for the Dissemination of Scientific Knowledge, which has branches throughout the country, covers youth and adults at various people's universities. It disseminates information on science education using periodicals, radio, television, lectures, exhibitions, and by organizing meetings with advanced workers of industrial and cultural establishments. It has a periodical called 'Shingilekh ukhaan amidral' (Science and life) which is published bi-monthly.

The Society takes an active part in the preparation of regular broadcasts on a variety of science education themes for adult education.

Every year the Society carries out a month's campaign for the dissemination of scientific knowledge and two months' programme for the protection of nature and the environment throughout the country. It also issues a series of booklets for the herdsmen, who take their cattle to remote pastures for better grazing.

The Mongolian Society of Environment Protection is responsible for all activities related to nature and the environment. The Central Stations of young nature enthusiasts is fully responsible for environmental protection work among children and youth. Branches of the Station are organized at research institutes and schools. Attached to the Central Station and its branches are 15 kinds of cultural societies, the curricula and lesson programmes for which are worked out and approved by the Central Committee of the Mongolian Revolutionary Young League and the Ministry of People's Education.

The Central Station of young nature enthusiasts and its branches are engaged in many activities for providing theoretical knowledge by organizing excursions and trips, arranging exhibitions, and convening meetings.

They also form clubs of young naturalists, groups of young fire-fighters, and detachments of pioneers to combat agricultural pests. The Society also organizes radio and T.V. broadcasts on the theme of "nature and Man'.

With a view to improving the technical knowledge of children and youth, of creating research work in science and technology, and of developing technical sports; technician stations, clubs and cultural societies are organized, attached to industrial, economical, research and cultural organizations and schools.

Many stations, clubs and cultural societies are guided by the Young Technician House of the Central Committee of the Mongolian Revolutionary League.

The House, in addition to elaborating educational programmes for the stations, clubs and cultural societies, arranges competitions for the best invention among young technicians and propagates scientific and technological achievements. Young technician stations, clubs, and cultural societies have two hour classes twice weekly.

Educational Innovations

A session of the Mongolian People's Great Hural in December 1982 considered the further improvement of education in secondary schools and reaffirmed the commitment of the Government to scientific and technological progress. Specific innovations arising from this latest development are :

1. Diminishing the load on pupils by adjusting the hours devoted to different subjects, updating the curriculum and improving the interrelationship between subjects;
2. Improving the supply and qualifications of teachers for secondary schools, through extension of teacher training, and improvement of teachers' salaries and conditions of work. Also by introducing regular seminars for teachers—at local level to improve teachers' skills and knowledge, particularly in science and technology;
3. Using the Central Commission of the Children's Fund to finance the construction of well-equipped school buildings and to improve the children's way of life;
4. Developing industrial and co-operative training links and aproviding industrial training for senior students of general secondary schools; and
5. Organizing voluntary societies for pupils of mathematics, physics, chemistry and biology.

13

Nepal

The national goals of education are the guiding principles of science education at all levels of education. They aim to : (1) produce citizens who are loyal to the nation, the crown and national independence and who remain alert and ever active, concerning their rights and duties; (2) develop, preserve and extend such learning areas as science, technology and skills development, which are necessary for the development of the country and for producing a cadre of skilful workers and technicians to shoulder responsibilities in every area of national development; (3) inculcate qualities such as moral integrity, dignity of work, self-reliance, aesthetic awareness and cosmopolitanism; and (4) preserve and develop the national language, literature, arts and culture.

The Educational System

The systematic development of education spans a period of a little more than 30 years from independence from the Rana Regime in 1951. In 1951 there were two colleges, 11 secondary schools and 321 primary schools in the country. The number of students enrolled at the primary level was 8, 505, at the secondary level 1, 680 and at higher education level 1250.

Before the implementation of the National Education System Plan in 1971, there were 49 colleges, 1, 095 secondary schools with 120, 531 students and 7, 275 primary schools with 408, 471 students.

The educational structure consists of five years' primary, two years' lower secondary education and three years' secondary.

Although primary education is free it is not compulsory. Even so, enrolment is as high as 87 per cent.

In the recently revised structure of school education, grades VI and VII are designated as lower secondary education. Almost all the lower secondary schools are attached either to primary schools or to secondary schools.

The last three grades in the ten years school system constitute secondary education. At the end of schooling, students are required to take the School Leaving Certificate Examination.

Educational statistics 1982

	No. of schools	*No. of students*	*No. of teachers*
Primary	10, 912	1, 474, 698	32, 259
Lower secondary	2,964	199, 678	10, 820
Secondary	1, 031	170, 404	5, 634

Higher education is provided by the Tribhuvan University. There are also technical schools offering three years courses plus one year on-the-job training.

Science Education

Science is not taught as a separate subject in the first three years of primary education. In these grades science education is mainly hygiene, but some science concepts are also incorporated with social studies. From grade IV, health education is combined with science education. So in the first three years of schooling science learning is predominantly related to health. This strong emphasis on hygiene and health is given in response to the needs of society.

Science as a separate subject begins from grade IV, and is compulsory for all students from grades IV to X. It is an option for the last two years (grades IX and X). The main reason for making science optional is the shortage of trained science teachers. In the optional curriculum a large number of alternative groups have been provided for students to select from. These are : (a) science; (b) language; (c) social studies; (d) commerce; (e) Sanskrit; (f) home science; and (g) art and health.

To overcome this shortage the Ministry of Education is launching a five year programme, through the establishment of a science education development centre, to train and retrain more teachers of science.

Time Available. Four periods per week (10.25 per cent of instructional time) are allocated for teaching science in grads IV and V, the last two years of primary education, whereas in grades VI to X of lower secondary and secondary, five periods per week (12.8 per cent of instructional time) are devoted to the teaching of science.

Curriculum Aspects

Introduction. One of the significant features of the National Education System Plan 1971-1976, (NESP), was the establishment of the Curriculum Development Centre. It is currently called the Curriculum, Textbook and Supervision Development Centre (CTSDC). This Centre is solely responsible for developing implementing and evaluating science curricula for the primary, lower secondary and secondary stages of school education.

Currently an objective-based and centrally-directed model of curriculum development is practised. National goals are translated into curriculum objectives and programmes. The curriculum guides as prepared in various subject areas, including science.

The objectives of the new science curriculum are basically the acquisition of knowledge, skills and attitudes of direct use to the students in their daily life and undertakings.

Objectives of Primary Science Education. After the completion of primary level education the students will be able to : (a) develop fundamental scientific skills such as observing, classifying and recording data of things around them; (b) make scientific sketches; (c) use senses effectively in order to obtain information about the environment; (d) explain the fact that all living things are dependent on air, water, sunlight and soil; (e) describe the uses of soil, air and water and demonstrate their properties by simple experiments; (f) observe and describe the general characteristics and structure of living things and show the effect of the environment on plants and animals; (g) develop an awareness of and a curiosity about the properties of things around us; and (h) perform simple scientific experiments.

Objectives of Lower Secondary Science Education. After the completion of lower secondary level education the students will be able to: (a) sketch scientific drawings and do simple experiments; (b) observe natural phenomena and develop an awareness of those phenomena; (c) describe the properties and structure of matter and facts related to force and energy; (d) explain general facts regarding earth and space; and (e) describe the structure of plants and animals and show their interdependence within the environment.

Objectives of Secondary Science Education. After the completion of secondary level education the students will be able to : (a) describe fundamental scientific facts and concepts; (b) describe the structure and properties of matter; (c) describe general laws relating to work, force and energy and relate them to practical aspects of life, especially daily life; (d) explain the basic concepts related to earth science; (e) describe the structure and life processes of living things and the environment; (f) develop basic scientific skills and make use of them; (g) prove scientific principles and laws and make conclusions from experiments; and (h) develop scientific attitudes.

Organization of the Curriculum. The determination of the curriculum content is highly institutionalized and organized, with the major goals being set at the national level, by the Ministry of Education and with more specialized curriculum objectives being determined by specialists in the discipline area. The organization of the current science curriculum at primary level has given stress to the teaching of biology and environmental science. At the lower secondary level emphasis is laid on physical biological sciences, whereas at the secondary level the separate subject disciplines of physics, chemistry, biology, geology and astronomy are available.

In the CTSDC there are subject specialists who are fully responsible for developing and evaluating the curricula. The committee system is used to develop all three levels of school education curricula i.e. primary, lower secondary and secondary education. There are three types of committees. The first is the subject committee with members from different educational fields such as the Institute of Education, university campuses, Educational Directorate, and school teachers. The chairman is appointed by the Centre. The subject specialists of CTSDC first prepare a draft curriculum and this is discussed in the subject committee. Improvements will be made, if necessary, and the draft curriculum will be forwarded to the next committee known as Curriculum and Textbook Development and Innovation Committee organized under the chairmanship of the Chief of CTSDC. After the approval of this committee the draft curriculum will again be forwarded to the third committee called the Curriculum and Textbook Co-ordination Committee headed by the Honourable Minister of Education. Only after the approval of this third committee will the draft curriculum be finalized and ready for implementation.

Revision of Curricula. Curriculum developments is a continuous process and it has to be adjusted constantly to changing national needs, aspirations and values. For the improvement of the present curriculum, reactions were collected from personnel such as teachers, surpervisors and headmasters. On the basis of this information science specialists of CTSDC analysed the present science curriculum, and submitted revisions to a National Seminar on curriculum and textbooks, organized in 1977. The revised curriculum was restructured again in 1980-1981, and has been implemented since 1981 part by part. By 1983 the revised curriculum had been implemented throughout the country.

Relation to Society. There is a greater acceptance that the curriculum should be related to the life, needs and aspirations of the people. The current thinking is to organize the teaching of science in primary and lower secondary levels as environmental studies, with emphasis on hygiene and health, e.g. water; soil; air; plants around us; animals around us; plants, animals and the environment; effect and importance of the sun; relations of man with other living things and the environment; food and diseases.

Evaluation

Evaluation is a continuous and integral part of the whole teaching/learning process and helps teachers and curriculum developers to improve their teaching and curricula and thus enhance the learning of all students. Effective science teaching requires a strong evaluative base, which in turn demands well-stated behavioural objectives. Unless there is continuous feedback from the science teachers in the light of actual classroom experience, the improvements in science education to the desired level cannot be achieved. So it is a two way process.

An examination unit was established with the introduction of the NESP. Prior to this plan the examination administered at the end of each grade and the terminal examination such as School Leaving Certificate (SLC) were the only means of assessing progress of students. These examinations were usually of 2-3 hours duration and tried to evaluate the students' knowledge of the subject matter by means of about 12 to 16 essay type questions. The new scheme for student evaluation attempts to encompass all important objectives and considers evaluation as an integral part of the educational process. To perform this important task the examination unit has attempted to produce standardized achievement tests, but the process of constructing and standardizing comprehensive achievement tests has not yet gained the required momentum, mainly due to a lack of a pool of suitably-qualified professionals.

The new examination scheme for students' evaluation includes a provision for internal assessment. For this purpose, preliminary clarification of the objectives of each course at all levels of school education have been made and published in the form of curriculum guides. Internal assessment constitutes simple evaluation tools such as unit tests. The next step of the new evaluation scheme is to keep records of the progress achieved by individual students. For this work the examination unit distributes to the respective schools sample record forms for recording the progress made by individual students in different subjects and for compiling a cumulative record of their overall achievements.

Students are promoted from each education level on the basis of comprehensive examinations. At the end of primary education and again at the completion of lower secondary education, examinations are conducted on a district and zonal basis respectively.

In the final examination there is a provision for 25 per cent of the marks obtained in the internal assessment to be added to the marks obtained in the school leaving certificate examination organized by the examination unit. The questions cover only the cognitive domain, the psychomotor and affective domain objectives are neglected.

Science Activities, Laboratory Work and Equipment

Laboratory Work. Nepalese educators well understand the importance of activity-oriented science teaching. Since the introduction of science education at school level this understanding has been reinforced. Science students have been regularly taken to nearby science colleges for scientific activities and demonstrations. Later, when the schools acquired their own equipment and materials, demonstrations became possible in their classrooms. But classroom activities were not possible in all schools mainly because of a lack of qualified teachers and facilities and the textbook in use did not include simple activities.

With the emergence of the NESP in 1971 the new curriculum stressed, even more, activity-oriented science teaching and in accordance with this spirit textbooks were written with experiments and activities. For example the books now in use at different levels contain the following activities :

Grade IV (primary level) —22 experiments
Grade VII (lower secondary level) —79 experiments
Grade VIII (secondary level) —96 experiments

Although there are experiments and activities in the textbooks there is no separate time allocation for conducting experiments and practical work is not an examinable subject in the final examination.

Equipment and Materials. Before the introduction of the NESP, schools themselves acquired teaching equipment from their own resources. The schools compiled their own equipment lists and purchased the apparatus from neighbouring countries.

However, in the mid-1960s, under a joint project of Nepal and UNICEF, science equipment and kits were distributed to a few schools. It was found that this equipment was not consistent with the curriculum and textbooks and, furthermore, the apparatus was too sophisticated for Nepalese science teachers. The equipment was selected mostly from the 'Eve' list of UNICEF.

With the implementation of the NESP, schools were provided with equipment and other materials which the curriculum required. Every school obtained a set. There were 119 different items, including chemicals, for secondary level and 72 items for lower secondary level. This distribution was carried out only once, replacement being the responsibility of the school.

The equipment and material list was revised in 1981, to match the latest revision of the textbooks.

Facilities in the Schools. Very few schools have laboratory and storage facilities. Usually the equipment and other materials are kept in cupboards in the office. The facilities in lower secondary and primary levels are particularly discouraging.

Use of Locally Available Materials. Various efforts have been undertaken to encourage teachers to use locally available materials as an alternative source for science activities. Several agencies have conducted short-term training programmes, published guide-books, and arranged exhibitions and competitions to assist in this direction. Furthermore, the newly revised textbooks emphasize the use of locally available materials.

Procurement of Equipment. The CTSDC is mainly responsible for identifying, purchasing and distributing equipment and other materials. Almost all the equipment and materials are imported from India.

Some of the materials can be produced in the country by private organizations and at the Science Equipment Centre of Janak Educational Material Centre, which is a government-owned organization. In this regard, the CTSDC should play a major role in designing, testing and evaluating prototype equipment with the help of the Science Equipment Centre. Later such equipment may be mass produced by the Science Equipment Centre as well as by private enterprise.

There are no sophisticated technologies used in the majority of the schools. A few schools in the capital possess slide and movie projectors.

Teacher Training

Background Information. In 1966 at the request of His Majesty's Government, a Science Teaching Project was initiated by UNESCO with the aim of improving the quality of science teaching and science learning at all levels. Under this programme, facilities were provided for strengthening science teaching through in-service courses for science teachers, the supply of equipment, the provision of fellowships, and the establishment of a Science Equipment Centre.

As a first step towards upgrading the quality of science teachers, a special team of science teacher educators was trained at the College of Education. These key people were then involved in in-service as well as on the spot programmes for primary and secondary school science teachers.

Another programme was the Science Teaching Enrichment Programme, conducted by the joint effort of science specialists of the Ministry of Education and a Peace Corps Volunteer. There were no textbooks for the students as it was a totally activity-oriented programme.

After the implementation of NESP the Institute of Education undertook the responsibility of training teachers in all areas.

Teacher Training for Science Subjects. Teacher training is considered the most important part of education. Teachers play a vital role in the effective implementation of science curricula. Lack of qualified and trained science teachers in one of the greatest drawbacks in the field of science education.

The Institute of Education organizes different courses, at Certificate, Diploma and Degree level, to produce trained teachers. There are pre-service as well as in-service training programmes.

The production of science teachers from the Institute of Education is as follows : these students had taken science as a major subject in their B. Ed. or I. Ed. qualification.

In the year	*Secondary (B. Ed.)*	*Lower secondary (I. Ed.)*
1978-79	39	48
1979-80	81	135
1980-81	46	67

Qualification of Teachers. The qualification required for teaching science at the primary level is the School Leaving Certificate and additional training; at the lower secondary level; I. Sc. or I. Ed. with major in science; and the secondary level; B. Sc. or B. Ed. with a major in science.

The official data of qualified and trained science teachers are not available and not fixed. There are, however, very few trained and qualified science teachers; many of those who qualify with I. Sc. or B. Sc. prefer to take employment outside the teaching profession.

Programme for out-of-school Youth and Adult Science Activities and Popularization of Science and Technology

Publications, science fairs, and radio broadcasts are the major activities in out-of-school science. The publication of books and magazine is at an early stage; most of the publications are focused on the scientific community.

Science fairs are occasionally organized by various agencies for science students and teachers. A wider out-of-school science programme is still to be developed.

The radio broadcast programme is more popular. It has the advantage that transportation is not a hindrance which it is for activities such as science fairs. There are two radio broadcasts through radio Nepal. One is sponsored by CTSDC and the other by the Research Centre for Applied Science and Technology of Tribhuvan University.

Current Innovations

The Ministry of Education and Culture is launching a science project very shortly. The aim of the project is to upgrade science teaching and improve science education. The specific objectives as indicated in the Final Report of the Science

Education Project are to : (a) improve the teaching ability and science knowledge of practising teachers by in-service short courses, and by training 25 master teachers to provide on-the-job support to teachers; (b) improve science teaching facilities at a selected number of secondary schools; (c) improve the quality and use of science teaching equipment at all secondary schools in the country; (d) train and upgrade a number of key science educators; (e) improve the supply of equipment and to maintain it adequately; (f) provide a focus for science teaching activities throughout Nepal by the establishment of a National Science Education Centre; and (g) increase the supply of science teachers.

Meanwhile, the recently established Royal Nepal Academy of Science and Technology is also planning to launch science programmes at both the formal and non-formal levels. Similarly the Ministry of Education and culture is planning to undertake various science activities under the programme 'Science for All'.

14
New Zealand

The Education Act of 1877 set up a national system of public secular primary education, free and compulsory, with a three-tiered administrative structure. This consisted of a Department of Education (responsible for financing and inspecting the whole system), 12 (now ten) locally-elected education boards (responsible for training and appointing teachers and for oversight of education in their areas), and numerous local school committees.

Secondary schools charged fees, and remained outside this national system of public secular primary education. It was not until 1903 that these schools accepted 'free-place' pupils and public funding, and began the slow process of development into the typical multi-course co-educational secondary school of today. The secondary schools have guarded their administrative autonomy and principals of these schools retain a very large degree of independence in determining matters of classroom instruction and curriculum interpretation.

At various times there have been attempts to change the relationship between the Department of Education and the Education Boards but essentially the system now is very similar to that enacted in 1877.

Most New Zealanders (87 per cent) are of European origin, with descendants of the indigenous people (Maori) being the most numerous minority group (9 per cent). People of Pacific island Polynesian extraction form 3 per cent of the population, and are concentrated in major urban areas.

The Education System

In 1981 the government issued a general policy statement which emphasized the encouragement of growth through modern skills and technology. The statement acknowledged that the ability to compete successfully on world markets depends upon the continuing development of new technology to allow for more efficient production, processing and distribution of goods. Further, it noted the scope for growth in certain industries, namely micro-electronics, communications and information plant and animal breeding new materials microbiological development robotics oceanography and energy technology; and pointed out the New Zealand's skilled and educated workforce has the ability to provide specialist products, using technical ingenuity and innovation. The government's policy on education incorporates this theme of technological change, and specifically identifies certain areas of study (workshop technology, horticulture, computer science) as those in which modernization of the curriculum can be expected to meet the needs of technological advancement.

Organization of the Education System. The organization of the education system is a hierarchical one and at the peak of this hierarchy stands the Minister of Education. It is his responsibility, helped by the advice of his department, to formulate education policy for the approval of Cabinet and Parliament.

Next in the hierarchy comes the Department of Education, which has varying degrees of responsibility for the ten Education Boards, 2,000 plus primary school committees, 200 secondary school controlling authorities, 17 technical institutes, 6 teachers colleges and a large number of boards and committees appointed to oversee or advise on particular aspects of the system.

The Department of Education administers government policy at the national level, sees that standards are maintained throughout the country, and acts as an agency for the distribution of government funds. It is also responsible for the curricula in primary and secondary schools and sees that these are kept up-to-date with advances in technology and the needs of a changing society. The curricula are designed to cater for the requirements of New Zealand children growing up in their own country.

Private schools have their own funds from which the draw for their expenses, but they are assisted by government grants. Approximately 8 per cent of primary, and 12 per cent of secondary pupils, attend private schools. This proportion is lower than it was some years ago as 160 private schools have become integrated into the State system, under a scheme which allows them to retain control of their buildings, and to maintain their special character.

Although the department has general control over education on a national basis, district control of primary education is vested in ten education boards. These boards are statutory bodies and their members are elected by the school committees within the board districts. They administer government grants, employ the teachers, arrange school transport and are the initiating bodies in providing school sites and facilities generally.

Most secondary schools have their own governing bodies, which have the same degree of control and management of their schools as is exercised by the district education boards.

Structure of the Education System. The figure on the opposite page gives a summary of the structure of education.

Early Childhood Education. For children aged 2½ to 5 years there are free kindergarten schools and recognized play centres. Over two-thirds of the country's 4-year-old children attend. Both kindergartens and playcentres are initiated by groups of local parents whose continuing involvement is encouraged.

Primary Education. Education is compulsory from the ages of 6 to 15 but virtually all children begin school on their fifth birthday. The education provided in state schools is secular, there are no tuition fees and textbooks are provided.

The curriculum for primary and intermediate schools includes oral and written language, mathematics, social studies, art and crafts, science, physical education (including swimming), health education, music, home economics, workshop craft. The last two years of the primary school course may be taken at an intermediate school or an area school. The latter type of school exists in the smaller rural centres. It takes local pupils through their primary education and accepts pupils from a wider area for secondary education.

Secondary Education. Pupils enter secondary school at the average age of 13, and although legally obliged to remain only until their 15th birthday, a large proportion remain after the age of 15. Secondary education is free until the age of 19. During the first two years at secondary school pupils study English, social studies, science, mathematics, physical education, music and art and crafts. They also take a number of optional subjects.

Some specialization is introduced in the third year (Form V), when students can take a wide range of subjects. At the end of this year they sit the School Certificate Examination, which is widely regarded by employers as an indication of application and satisfactory progress. It can be gained by single subject passes, and permits entry to Form VI. At the end of the Form VI year students may obtain the University Entrance qualification either by accrediting or by examination. A Sixth Form Certificate may also be awarded, which is internally assessed.

Pupils who intend to go to university usually spend a further year in Form VII where they follow an advanced course leading to a Higher School Certificate which is awarded without examination. Suitably qualified students who attend university and other tertiary institutions receive government assistance in the form of a tertiary bursary.

Statistics. From New Zealand's total population of 3.1 million, one person in every three is enrolled in the education system either as a full-time or a part-time student. Enrolments in full years courses in 1982 were: 56,000 in kindergartens or playcentres; 486, 000 in primary or intermediate schools; 224,000 in secondary schools; 32, 000 full-time, 13,000 part-time and 9, 000 extramural students in universities: 4, 500 in teachers colleges; 7, 000 full-time, 36, 000 part-time and 30, 000 extramural students in technical institutes or community colleges; and 64,000 enrolments in evening classes at secondary schools. In addition

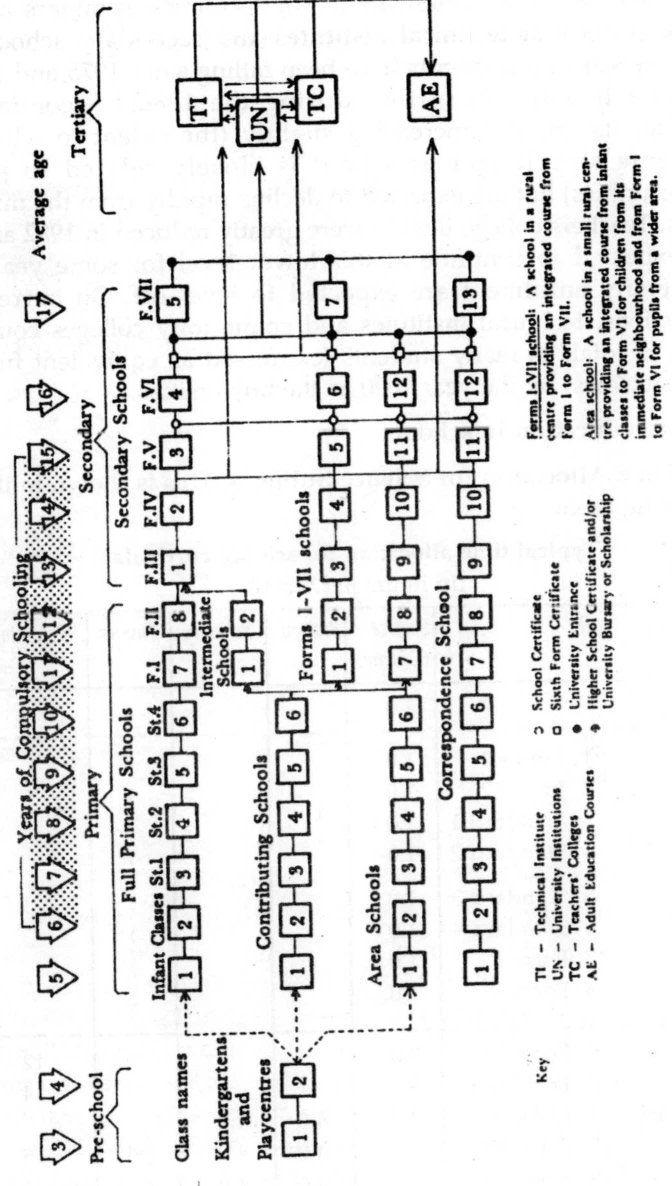
The New Zealand Education System
Average age
Years of Compulsory Schooling
Pre-school
Primary
Secondary
Tertiary
Class names
Infant Classes St.1 St.2 St.3 St.4 F.I F.II F.III F.IV F.V F.VI F.VII
Full Primary Schools
Secondary Schools
Kindergartens and Playcentres
Intermediate Schools
Contributing Schools
Forms I-VII schools
Area Schools
Correspondence School
TI
UN
TC
AE
Key
TI – Technical Institute
UN – University Institutions
TC – Teachers' Colleges
AE – Adult Education Courses
School Certificate
Sixth Form Certificate
University Entrance
Higher School Certificate and/or University Bursary or Scholarship
Forms I-VII school: A school in a rural centre providing an integrated course from Form I to Form VII.
Area school: A school in a small rural centre providing an integrated course from infant classes to Form VI for children from its immediate neighbourhood and from Form I to Form VI for pupils from a wider area.

there are 147, 000 enrolments in short courses, seminars and block courses at technical institutes and secondary schools. Primary school enrolments have been falling since 1975 and are forecast to fall still further during the 1980s. Secondary enrolments are still increasing slightly (the extent to which students stay longer at school is closely related to job opportunities) but are expected to decline rapidly from the mid-1980s. Teachers college intakes were greatly reduced in 1982 and are expected to continue at this lower level for some years. University enrolment are expected to level off. On current projections, technical institutes and community colleges could have, in total, as many students (expressed as equivalent full-time students) by the year 2000 as the universities.

Science education in schools

Time Allocation for Science Subjects. This is shown in the following table.

Typical time allocation for science curricula (in hours per week)

Year level		*Science (General)*	*Biology*	*Chemistry*	*Physics*	*Percentage*
Pre-school		1.0				
	1 Junior 1	1.0			)	
	2 Junior 2	1.0			)	
	3 Standard 1	1.0			)	
	4 Standard 2	1.0			)	
Primary	5 Standard 3	1.0			)	
	6 Standard 4	1.0			)	
	7 Form I	1.0			)	
	8 Form II	1.0			)	
	9 Form III	3.0				12
	10 Form IV	3.5				14
Secondary	11 Form V	4.0	4.0	4.0		
	12 Form VI		4.0	4.0	4.0)	16
	13 Form VII		4.0	4.0	4.0)	per subject

Organization of Science Education. Science (an integrated subject) is compulsory from junior primary years up to and including Form IV (grade X). At Form V science (integrated) is an elective subject, an is the third most popular subject (after English and mathematics), being chosen by half the girls and two-thirds of boys. These proportions have been rising steadily for several years. Smaller numbers of students study one or more of the separate sciences, which may be in addition to science (integrated). Biology is the most popular separate science at Form V, being taken by 20 per cent of girls and 10 per cent of boys, but it is being steadily replaced by science.

In Forms VI and VII (grades XII and XIII) students may choose one or more of the subjects biology, chemistry or physics, as part of a five-subject course. Approximately 60 per cent of Form VI students study biology, approximately 30 per cent study chemistry and 30 per cent study physics. In Form VII the percentage are 53 per cent, 46 per cent, 40 per cent respectively. More girls than boys study biology, and the reverse is true for chemistry and physics.

Aims of Science Education. The main aim of primary science ('Science Syllabus and Guide : Junior to Standard 4, 1980') is to help children develop inquiring minds and the skills for exploring and interpreting the accessible environment. This aim is further expressed in providing a science education that helps the child to acquire significant knowledge; develop basic concepts; develop process skill; develop in ability to communicate; and develop interests and attitudes.

The content areas of matter, energy, living things, time and space are used as the base through which concepts, skills, attitudes and interests are developed.

Most secondary schools now base their lower secondary science upon a draft 'Forms I-IV Science Syllabus and Guide (1978)', which is a revision of the official syllabus of 1969. For the purpose of this lower secondary syllabus, science is recognized as a set of attitudes to inquiry, a method of inquiry, and a body of knowledge. It is intended that students should acquire some knowledge of the empirical world about them; a little of the vocabulary and grammar of science; an ability to observe objectively; an ability to solve problem situations and think scientifically; and an awareness of the culture which is science.

During the Forms I to IV years (grades VII—X) the following content topics are studies: 'Nature of matter'; 'Earth science'; 'Community organization'; 'The animal way of life'; 'Energy'; 'Radiant energy'; 'Astronomy and time'; 'Chemical change'; 'The plant way of life'; 'Reproduction and growth'; 'Types of matter'; 'Electrical energy'; 'Force, motion and mass'; 'Resources and environment'; and 'Weather'.

In practice almost all students in the senior secondary school (Forms VI-VII) follow courses set by the Universities Entrance Board with three sciences in each of two years. These courses are set independently of one another. The aims of the physical science courses tend to emphasize understanding and application of the course content, whereas the biology courses aim to relate biology to some of the concerns of society (e.g. awareness of the role and responsibility of man in relation to the biosphere and of the relevance of biology to an understanding of man and human social relationships.)

Science Curriculum Development Procedures. The Department of education's Curriculum Development Division is responsible for keeping the school curriculum from the infant classes to Form VII under review. Its role includes co-ordinating the curriculum activities of all interested parties including the teacher unions, the inspectorate, the national examination boards, university interests and professional body interests. When agreement has been reached that revision is needed, revision committees, representative of all branches of the education service, are usually established under the authority of the Minister of Education. This initiative is taken within the Department of Education except for admonitions controlled by the Universities Entrance board, which establishes its own revision committees.

When a revision committee has completed its work, the Curriculum Development Division, alone or in association with the department's Publication Branch, Visual production Unit and National Film Library, is responsible for preparing guidelines and up-to-date teaching materials for the new courses. Private publishers frequently work in consultation with the Department of Education to prepare pupil texts, especially for high school courses. Where new or additional equipment is involved, the introduction of the new courses may be delayed until the necessary finance is approved by the Minister of Education.

Development procedures usually follow a common pattern involving the statement of precise objectives in terms of intended changes in pupils' cognitive and affective behaviour, the drafting of learning resources designed to achieve these objectives, the trial and appraisal of these materials in schools, and then revision in the light of the trials prior to formal publication and dissemination.

Fifty-two per cent of students spend some time in Form VI before leaving school. Here students may take any of the three specialist sciences (biology, chemistry, physics) offered for University Entrance (UE). The name 'University Entrance' is somewhat misleading as a description, because 80 per cent of those students who obtain this qualification never use it to enter university. However, the qualification is valued by the community and responsibility for it (and therefore for almost all of the Forms VI and VII science curriculum) rests with the universities. The universities do, however, consult widely with teachers, inspectors, and others, when contemplating curriculum change and will not proceed where there is significant opposition from teachers. Most UE examiners are school teachers.

Students in Form VII are those who have been successful in University Entrance and who choose to remain at school for a further year. Most students study five subjects during the year. Until recently this group consisted exclusively of those students intending to go to university (most leaving school from Form VII; not Form VI) after sitting the University Bursaries Examination. The curriculum at this level in the sciences is quite plainly preparation for university study. Syllabuses are devised in the same way as outlined for University Entrance, but at this level most examiners are university teachers.

Stability of Science Syllabuses. Science syllabuses are not changed easily or rapidly. New Zealand teachers are accustomed to being consulted frequently during the development of any new curriculum. The typical time between major revisions is 20 to 25 years. For example, work on the present primary science syllabus began before 1970, the final syllabus was introduced in 1980, and production of teacher resource units is expected to be completed by 1985. A summary of revision dates is given in the table on the following page.

Social Issues in Science Syllabuses. In general, science courses do not place an obvious emphasis on real-life problems or on social issues. There are exceptions, and individual teachers interpret syllabus statements in a variety of ways, but overall most importance is placed upon the development of conceptual understanding and investigative skills within the classroom, with little importance ascribed to the consideration of community problems or issues. There has been no strong expression of opinion from teachers seeking change to this position.

Within primary science, the syllabus discusses eight objectives concerned with the development of interests and attitudes. Two of these (care for the environment, care for living things) involve the consideration of values, and teachers are advised to limit this consideration to 'value judgements on matters in which they are directly concerned'. For example, the trees which shelter the playing fields also restrict vision on the road; should they be cut down?

Course		*Year of introduction*	*Minor revision*
Primary Science		1980	—
Form I-II	Science	1967	1978
Form III-IV	Science	1968	(draft)
Form V	Science	1983	—
	Biology	1944	1973
	Human Biology	1949	—
	Chemistry	1944	—
	Physics	1956	1979
Form VI	Biology	1966	1976
	Chemistry	1967	1976
	Physics	1970	—
Form VII	Biology	1971	—
	Chemistry	1068	1976
	Physics	1971	—

In Form VII biology, the consequences of man's evolution, in relation to population growth and to modification of the biosphere, and the future of man and the biosphere, constitute a minor part of the course.

Evaluation of Student Achievement. In primary schools, teachers are asked to assess a childs progress in the development of knowledge, skills and attitudes according to various criteria. They are required to make succinct statements on each child's 'Progress Record'.

To support the entries made on the 'Progress Record' teachers consider the results of tests, records of observations, assessment of practical work or written self-study assignments. All written tests used are teacher-made tests. Most schools issue regular reports to parents which indicate the child's progress, ability, and attitudes.

Similar considerations apply in the secondary school, but with greater reliance upon the use of formal school examinations. Secondary schools vary in the degree to which their evaluation procedures extend beyond the cognitive domain. Very few report formally upon the achievement of the affective domain objectives of their science courses.

Public examinations take place at:

Form V (grade XI)	(Department of Education—School Certificate)
Form VI (grade XII)	(Universities Entrance Board—University Entrance)
Form VII (grade XIII)	(Universities Entrance Board—University Bursaries and University junior scholarships).

Since 1976 three new school Certificate subjects (biological science, physical science) have been on trial in a number of approved schools. These subjects, collectively known as modular science, are based on a modular approach and after a very wide choice of courses. The subjects are internally assessed, but moderation between schools is the responsibility of the School Certificate Examination Board. This move has been welcomed by schools, but because of the variables—wide choice and internal assessment—it has taken a long time to achieve an acceptable system of moderation. Introduced for the first time in 1982, moderation is now based on performance in a science reference test, which is a general science ability test based on junior secondary science. Results of that test determine the internal grades which a school may award to its students. Wider implementation of this scheme is held up by the failure to resolve disagreement between the government and the teacher organizations over the question of time allowances for schools to carry out the desired internal assessment procedures.

Current Influences on the Curriculum. The strongest current influences on schools and on the curriculum are related to two factors : falling school rolls brought about by a decline in the birthrate, and the economic climate of the country as a whole. Falling school rolls, with consequent reduced requirements for teachers, means that teachers as a group are now more interested in preserving their own employment opportunities, and retaining previously allocated educational provisions. There is less interest by teachers in promoting curriculum change. The government continues to encourage and fund curriculum development by recognizes the need for restraint in expenditure. In recent years more attention has been given to some formerly neglected subjects, such as technical subjects, home economics, agriculture, and health; the present period is seen as one of consolidation.

Secondary schools have found their expected falling rolls to be cushioned by the fact that students are staying longer at high school. However, this is partly attributable to an attempt to obtain better qualifications while seeking employment and requires schools to devote more attention to counselling, and to programmes which will ease the transition from school to work.

In comparison with 1970, there is an older, better qualified teaching profession, whose members expect to remain longer in one school. Students and parents are keenly aware of vocational opportunities opened up or closed off by proficiency or weakness in certain school subjects. The New Zealand community in general is concerned to maintain or improve achievement in basic subjects, particularly reading and mathematics. Changing teacher attitudes make it less likely that curriculum change which requires any increase in out of school teacher time will be acceptable. In summary, curriculum change in science in the 1980s is likely to be gradual rather than dramatic.

Science Activities and Equipment. Although the emphasis of the primary science syllabus is on activity-based programmes, many teachers lack the confidence to exploit this potential to the full. On average about half of the total science curriculum time is devoted to practical activities, but there is wide variation. In the lower secondary school, about half the total class time is spent in practical activities, but this proportion falls in the upper secondary classes to about one-third or less. There is no practical or laboratory assessment component in any of the public science examinations. Examiners include written questions which require an understanding of practical techniques and experimental design.

Primary schools are not provided with laboratories and all science is undertaken in classrooms. Sets of simple equipment have been provided to all schools. These include 70 items in sets of six. A replacement scheme is in operation. Schools are able to use finance from their 'incidentals Grant' to purchase sundry items of equipment that are not included in the basic equipment sets. The purpose of the equipment sets is to provide basic materials (mostly imported) which will enable teachers to carry out an acceptable science programme. Teachers supplement this equipment with low-cost locally-available expendable items such as plastic-ware, matches, and glue.

Every secondary school is provided with laboratories, basic equipment, and annual maintenance grants, from government funds. Parent groups may provide additional money for special purposes, and science inspectors have limited discretion to supplement school grants in particular cases of need. A school of 1, 000 students will have six to eight laboratories in total.

Although the setting-up provisions for new laboratories are good, inflation since the year 1970s, and the declining value of the New Zeland Dollar* against the currencies of most suppliers

* Approximately New Zealand $1.53 = One US dollar.

of scientific materials, have made it difficult for schools to maintain their science equipment and materials at former levels.

About 80 per cent of secondary science equipment has to be imported, and rising costs have encouraged science teachers to exercise great care in purchasing, and in some cases to seek alternatives to traditional practical exercise. The potential cost of associated equipment and activities is likely to continue to be an important factor for consideration in any proposal to revise part of the science curriculum.

All science equipment, whether purchased by schools or by the department of education, is bought from private importers or manufacturers. There is no government institution set up for the design, production or evaluation of school science equipment.

Use of Educational Technology

In primary schools, teachers use little in the way of audio-visual aids other than the 16 mm movie projector and the slide/film-strip projector to support their science programmes. There are no educational TV programmes broadcast publicly for school use.

In secondary schools there is increasing use of the overhead projector in addition or as an alternative to the chalkboard. Although most secondary schools now own at least one micro-computer, they are not financed by the Department of Education. A small number of schools are using micro-computers for science simulation exercises in senior classes.

Teacher Training

Qualifications and Supply of Science Teachers. Primary teachers are generalists, rather than specialists, and all primary teachers are expected to be able to teach science.

Most primary teachers enter a teachers' college after having gained University Entrance or the Higher School Certificate and have studied at least one science subject (usually biology) while in Form VI. The three-year training period includes a minimum time of about 50 hours related to science education in primary schools and students elect certain major and minor courses. In this way a proportion of each intake receives some training in depth in primary science education, (up to 200 hours). These teachers eventually become resource staff in schools.

Although there are at present no regulations prescribing minimum qualifications for secondary science teachers, about three quarters are graduates in science, most of whom have undertaken a one-year post-graduate course of teacher training at a secondary teacher's college. The course of training contains elements of educational theory, teaching practice, and curriculum content studies. From 1985, entrants to the secondary teaching profession must be graduates with teacher training.

A recent survey of science teacher qualifications showed that the level of qualifications held had improved markedly in the past 20 years. Schools report that biology and chemistry teachers are generally well-qualified, and 75 per cent of the teachers teaching Forms VI and VII biology or chemistry hold relevant qualifications at final year B. Sc. level or higher.

On the other hand 35 per cent of Form VI physics teachers have only first-year tertiary level physics or less as their qualification in physics.

Pre-service Training. Primary teachers must include a science education component within their three-year training course, and this is shortly to be raised from 50 hours to 100 hours. Considerable proportion of most of these courses (the six teachers' colleges are independent of one another) is devoted to improving the teacher trainee's own understandings of science. Another major part consists of curriculum content studies related to the primary science syllabus. The focus of these programmes is course-based; teaching competencies are evaluated during teaching practice sessions, as a separate issue.

Most secondary teacher training consists of a one-year end-on course at the conclusion of university training at one or two secondary teachers' colleges. Typically the programme for a science teacher trainee consists of curriculum studies in lower secondary science, two senior sciences (or mathematics), general educational studies, and school practice sessions. By the end of the training year, course instructors are in a position to provide potential employing authorities with their judgement of a trainee's understanding and teaching competency.

In-service Training. In-service training is voluntary for teachers, and occurs in several ways. One national residential centre is available for week-long courses. District courses may be two or three -day residential ones, in school time, but the most common local courses are one day in duration only. Expenses for the above courses are met by the Department of education. Some teachers also attend courses during vacations, at their own expense, arranged by universities, teachers's colleges, or by groups of teachers themselves.

A continuing programme of in-service education in science for primary teachers is organized through the inspectors and science advisers attached to each education board district. There are 27 full time primary science advisers spread over the ten education districts. They conduct long term courses of 1-3 weeks duration; recall courses where teachers attend initially for up to a week and then return for 1-2 days every term; short courses of 1-3 days; and school-based courses.

The emphasis on in-service training varies, depending upon the stage of a curriculum project. At present in primary science, courses assume that the primary science syllabus will be in place for some time, and are directed mainly towards improving the competencies of teachers. With a number of different syllabuses and prescriptions, the secondary situation is more variable.

Research

Until recently the only research being carried out in science education comprised minor studies for post-graduate diplomas in education. However during 1979-1981 the Department of Education funded a research programme ('Learning in science Project', Freyberg and Osborne, University of Waikato) to investigate the teaching and learning of science at the Forms I to IV level. That project has revealed a hidden world of science unsuspected by most science teachers, particularly with respect to the ideas which children hold about scientific notions, and the persistence of these views into adulthood.

In 1982 the 'LISP Primary' research project was launched, which will similarly investigate various aspects of science in the primary school years. Already this project has produced some interesting material on children's questions about scientific topics.

Material from these projects is being incorporated into in-service, and into curriculum support materials, as funds allow. It is certain that the outcomes of the projects will have considerable influence upon science curricula in the future. The institution primarily responsible for this research is the Science Education Research Unit, University of Waikato, Hamilton, New Zealand.

Out-of-school Programmes

Extra-curricular Science Activities for School Children. Many senior primary and secondary classes go away from school for a three to five day field trip during the year. These field excursions relate to aspects of the curriculum which can be studied away from the school, such as forest duties, geology, outdoor skills, For safety an adult to child ratio of 1 : 6 is required. Accommodation is provided in lodges, some of which are owned by groups of schools. In a few cases a teacher is permanently stationed at the lodge.

There are over 100 museums, two general zoos, and a variety of aviaries, and aquaria, that have considerable educational value. The main museums and zoos have specially trained teachers attached to them, for school parties. The museums have a wide range of exhibits, with emphasis on local flora and fauna, both terrestrial and marine, and on science in general, and technology, past and present. One modern pleasing feature is that children in school parties are allowed to handle and use exhibits. The main museums also prepare special loan cases of items, illustrations, and replica material for loan to schools.

Many schools, both urban and rural, establish community committees to organize Agricultural Clubs to encourage children to adopt and care for calves, lambs, and suitable small animals at their homes. They are also encouraged to start small home gardens to learn horti-cultural science and also to provide food for the home table. Flower gardens, herb and alpine gardens, are also encouraged.

Science Fairs or Science Exhibitions for school children are now held in most regions of the country. These are organized by local science teachers, and supported financially by the local business community.

Formal Science Education for those who have Left School. Attendance at school is compulsory until the age of 15. After 15, young people in the age group 15-19 years fall into the following categories: unemployed; employed, with no study requirement; employed, with part-time study; or full-time study.

Some of the unemployed attend work skills training courses, which often include an element of simple applied technology, such as horticulture. Most of those doing part-time study are training for trades such as electricians or motor mechanics, and their classes are held at Technical Institutes or by correspondence. There is a strong applied science and technology orientation. Part-time study is also offered at the same institutes at technician level for the New Zealand Certificates in Science and Engineering. Full-time study in science and related fields in undertaken at a university or for some courses, such as during, at a technical Institute.

Each of the universities has a department of external studies, responsible for arranging short courses (often at weekends or during evenings) taken by university staff for particular interest groups. Science courses tend to be arranged for special interest groups, such as teachers, rather than for the general public.

Informal Science Education for Adults. There are regular ratio and television programmes on science and technology, including agricultural science. These TV programmes are screened in the early evening when they are more likely to be seen by young viewers. New Zealand television has a fine reputation in the field of documentaries, especially those related to natural science.

Scientific matters in newspapers and magazines are of minor interest, except where they relate to matters directly affecting New Zealand, e.g. production of synthetic petrol. In these instances writers and publishers have the difficult task of interpreting complex scientific ideas for the reading public.

Current Innovations

Curriculum, Materials, Equipment. The Department of Education has recently begun a major review and revitalization education in schools, from junior primary classes to Form VII. The first tasks have involved the revision of examination requirements in agriculture and horticulture at Form V and discussions are taking place about a possible course in agricultural science at Form VI. Alongside this, progress is being made on the integration of agricultural and horticultural ideas and concerns into the teaching of other subjects, particularly science and social studies. The primary science advisory service has been involved extensively in the design of preliminary draft teacher guide material. This project will take several years to complete.

An unusual feature of the primary science syllabus project has been the preparation of a series of some 130 Teacher Resource Units and Activity Cards. These small booklets were prepared by teachers, and developed in draft form in trials. Over half of them have now been produced in final form and issued to schools. They have also attracted considerable interest in Australia and elsewhere.

Rising costs have encouraged secondary schools to borrow equipment where possible, and this has been helped by the existence of two Science Resource Centres. In addition to lending science equipment, these centres act as repositories for school-based print materials, and also operate a system of loan kits for certain experiments in senior biology and physics.

National Science Fair. Most regions now run their own science fairs, for school children aged 10 years and upwards. A major commercial firm brings together the best from each regional fair to take part in a National Science Fair, which receives considerable attention from newspaper and television interests.

15
Pakistan

Immediately after the creation of Pakistan in 1947, the Pakistan Education Conference was held in Karachi to prepare the ground for bringing about major changes in the education system. The message from the father of the nation, the Quaid-e-Azam, to the conference was :

> There is no doubt that the future of our state will . . . depend upon the type of education we give to our children, and the way in which we bring them up as future citizens of Pakistan. Education does not merely mean academic education. There is immediate and urgent need for giving scientific and technical education to our people in order to build up our future economic life and to see that our people take to science, commerce, trade and particularly well planned industries. We should not forget that we have to compete with the world which is moving very fast in this direction.

During the same conference the Committee on Scientific Research and Technical Education recommended that every effort should be made to promote fundamental as well as scientific and industrial research.

A Commission on National Education, Set up in 1959, reported that secondary education is universally recognized to be the critical stage in determining the effectiveness of a national system of education. Regarding the existing curricula, the Commission observed that these were predominantly theoretical and bookish and recommended that the curricula should be changed to match the need of society more closely.

On the basis of these recommendations, the first efforts were made in the early 1960s to modernize the science and mathematics curricula at secondary and intermediate levels. An attempt was also made to introduce integrated, modernized science and mathematics courses. Books were revised accordingly in which inquiry-directed and open-ended approaches towards various problems of science were adopted.

National Education Policy

In 1977, a National Education Conference was held and recommendations of this Conference paved the way for 'The National Education Policy, 1979'. Realizing the importance of science in modern times, the Policy emphasized that the teaching of science should be improved at all levels of education. Recommendations were also made to popularize science among the masses through science fairs, exhibitions and competitions.

The Policy stated that among the factors influencing growth and development, science education is by far the most important as it provides a sound base for scientific research and technological development. In recognition of the vital role played by science education in national development, a National Centre for Science Education would be established. It would improve science teaching through research and innovation and promote and popularize science and technology among the masses through science fairs, museums and films. The National Education Equipment Centre was to be further strengthened in order to improve the quality and supply of equipment to school laboratories. Science equipment would be supplied to the existing laboratories in the schools and new science laboratories added to schools where they were required.

To achieve the above objectives the following programmes were planned :

(a) Under the supervision of the Curriculum Wing, develop modified Teaching Kits for use up to Class VIII.

(b) Develop inquiry-directed demonstrations and experiments for teachers and students for Classes IX-XII.

(c) Design and test innovative teacher education programmes and models for training science teachers and develop teachers' guides, handbooks, instructional packages, modules and other related materials.

(d) Develop a mobile-science laboratory to take science to the rural population, and organize on the spot in-service training programmes for science teachers.

(e) Organize science fairs at provincial and national levels and establish mini-science museums.

(f) Organize 'Future Scientists of Pakistan' awards for outstanding students who demonstrate creativity, imagination and critical thinking.

(g) Organize national seminars, symposia, workshops, working sessions and conferences for co-ordinating and promoting science education.

Education in School

The formal education system consists of the following distinct levels.

Level	*Age in years*		*Classes*	*Output*
	on Entry	*On leaving*		
Primary	5	10	I-V	Primary Certificate
Middle	10	13	VI-VIII	Middle Certificate
Secondary	13	15	IX-X	Matriculation Certificate
Higher secondary (Intermediate)	15	17	XI-XII	Higher Secondary Certificate
University 1	17	19		bachelor's Degree
University 2	19	21		Master's Degree
M. Phil.	21	22		Diploma in Philosophy
Ph.D.	22	23-24		Doctor of Philosophy

Entrolment at different levels along with the number of teachers for the year 1981-1982 are given in the following table.

Level	*No. of students*	*No. of teachers (in thousands)*	*No. of schools*
Primary	5,479,000	145,300	59,654
Middle	1,400,000	53,900	5,488
Secondary	543,000	69,900	3,570
Colleges	267,500	12,900	434

Science Education in Schools

Place of science. The place of science in the overall curriculum at various levels of education is given in Tables 1—4. From Classes I to VIII general science and elementary mathematics are compulsory (Tables—1 and 2). General science contains basic information about physical and biological science. Students opting for humanities from Class IX to Class XII have to study general science as well. (Tables—3 and 4).

Percentage of Science Students. After middle school, students proceed to secondary school where they have a choice of subjects according to their own aptitudes and inclinations. There is a general trend to study science subjects at this stage and only those who qualify in Class VIII with good grades are allowed to opt for science subjects. At this stage science is split into distinct fields such as: physics, chemistry, and biology. Mathematics is also divided into courses of elective mathematics and general mathematics. Students opting for the science group in Class IX have to study physics, chemistry, biology and elective mathematics.

Elective mathematics is of a higher standard than general mathematics. It is estimated that about 43 per cent of students opt for science subjects at the secondary level. The percentage of students gaining admission to the science group in the intermediate classes is slightly less, but in both cases more students would choose science if the number of science places could be increased.

After completing the intermediate stage in the science group, students may enrol at professional colleges in medicine or engineering. Again, the number of seats in these professional colleges is limited to the top students. The rest of the students complete their education in university to obtain a Bachelor's Degree in two years and a Masters' Degree in another two years.

Some students who qualify in secondary school in the science group and who are not admitted to intermediate colleges may join polytechnic colleges where they can learn trades such as automobile maintenance and repair, air-conditioning and refrigeration, electronics, electricity, metalwork, and woodwork. Such students are in great demand in industry.

Curriculum Aims and Objectives. Although the specific aims of teaching science at different levels of education vary, the main aims remain the same. They are to : achieve a broad and genuine appreciation and understanding of different aspects of science; promote scientific literacy and provide scientific and technological manpower in the country; develop a scientific approach in the young pupils so that they acquire ability to apply knowledge gained towards solution of problems; provide opportunity to an individual to determine his interests and aptitudes in science as a vocation; and improve the general economy of the country and raise the living standard through the application of science and technology.

Table—1. Scheme of studies for elementary classes

Subject	*Classes I and II Age 5 and 6 +*		*Class III Age 7 +*		*Classes IV and V Age 8 + 9 +*	
	No. of periods per week (39)	*percent-age of total time*	*No. of periods per week (39)*	*Percent-age of total time*	*No. of periods per week (39)*	*percent-age of total time*
Languages:						
(a) Ist language	12	30.7	6	15.3	6	15.3
(b) 2nd language	—	—	6	15.3	6	15.3
Mathematics	6	15.3	6	15.3	6	15.3
Science	5	12.3	6	15.3	5	12.3
Pakistan/ Social Studies			3	7.69	4	9.23
Health and Physical Education	5	12.30	3	7.69	4	9.23
Islamiyat	6	15.30	6	15.3	6	15.3
Arts	5	12.30	3	7.69	3	7.69

Table—2. Scheme of studies for middle classes

Subjects	*Classes VI to VIII age 9 to 10 + 11 +*		
	No. of periods per week (45)	*No. of hours per week (30) each period of 40 minuts*	*percnetage of total time*
Languages:			
Ist language	6	4.00	13.33
2nd language	4	2.40	8.88
English compulsory	6	4.00	13.33
Mathematics	4	2.40	8.88
Science	3	2.00	6.66
Pakistan/Social studies	3	2.00	6.66
Health and Physical Education	3	2.00	6.66
Islamiyat	4	2.40	8.88
Arts/Arabic/Persian	2	1.20	4.44
Vocational	10	6.40	22.22

Table—3. Secondary level science option

Components	*subject*	*papers*	*Marks*	*Weekly periods*
I	Urdu	One/two	100 to 150	4-6
	English	-do-	-do-	-do-
	Pakistan studies	One	75	3
	Islamiyat	One	75	3
II	Mathematics	One	100	4
	Physics	One	100	4
	Chemistry	One	100	4
	Biology	One	100	4

Table 4. Intermediate classes (for science students only)

Subjects	*Paper*	*Marks*	*Periods Per week*
Urdu	One	100	4
English	One	100	4
(a) Islamiyat/Civics*	One	50	2
(b) Pakistan Studies			
Part I			
**Pakistani Culture	One	100	4
*** Sindhi	One	100	4
Mathematics or Biology 1	Two	200	8
Physics	Two	200	8
Chemistry	Two	200	8

* For non-Muslim students only

** Option for foreign students in lieu of Urdu

*** Option for Sindhi students in lieu of Urdu.

1. At present science students elect only one subject out of mathematics and biology. From 1984 onwards there is a proposal to make the study of mathematics and biology compulsory for science students.

The general objectives for teaching science up to the middle stage are to : develop the spirit of inquiry and inquisitiveness; help children understand the physical environment and the interrelationship that exists in nature; develop an ability to observe carefully and to report facts accurately and with understanding; acquaint the children with the various subject areas of science and integrate the broad subject matter areas of science so that the children can begin to see science in its total perspective; help children acquire and apply knowledge and manipulative skills; develop scientific attitudes and aesthetic awareness; develop the habit of critical thinking and the ability to draw inference from observations; and help children develop basic concepts of various disciplines of science.

At secondary and higher secondary (intermediate) level, separate science subjects are taught and each has different objectives. However, some common objectives of teaching physics, chemistry and biology at secondary and higher secondary levels are to: present physics, chemistry and biology to the students as stimulating subjects, intellectually satisfying and significantly related to their experience of life; help students to participate more effectively in solving the problems of society; help the individual become a more productive member of society; and prepare scientifically educated individuals as useful members of society.

Organization. Up to Class VIII science is taught as a single subject and in most cases a single teacher teachers all aspects of science at these levels. At secondary and higher secondary levels the separate science disciplines are taught by different teachers. Practical work is performed in separate laboratories.

Environmental studies has also been developed as a curriculum subject but as there no trained teachers in this field, the subject has not yet been introduced.

Methodology. Each of the four provinces in Pakistan has its own Bureau of Curriculum Research and Development. At the Federal level there is a National Bureau of Curriculum. This Bureau is a part of the Federal Ministry of Education. With the help of expert subject committees each provincial bureau prepares the initial drafts of curricula for various subjects at different levels. After the preparation of initial drafts National subject committees are set up to consolidate provincial drafts and prepare a final version of the curriculum for each subject. This curriculum is then followed by the entire country.

Frequency of Revision. Revision of curricula is a continuous process and steps have to be taken to keep the process going. How ever the last revisions of curricula from primary to secondary levels were made during the period 1973-1976. The curricula for higher secondary were revised during 1982.

Relating the Curricula to Real-life Problems. Pakistan is basically an agricultural country. About 80 per cent of the population live in villages and small towns. From Class I up to Class XII many concepts are taught concerning the growing and protection of various crops and plants. More emphasis on practical aspects of these concepts could help many students acquire skills as farmers. Similarly if studies in salt analysis for higher secondary students were extended to include soil analysis, it could help many students to test the soil in their own fields and thus to suggest remedies for various shortcomings.

Evaluation. Up to Class VIII most of the schools follow an internal evaluation system. In a few cases examinations are also conducted by the Regional Directorates of Education. The first recognized public examination, for Class X, is conducted by the Boards of Intermediate and secondary Education. The same Boards also conduct examinations for higher secondary level. The examinations in science subjects consist of theory and practical. Practical examinations contribute about 25 per cent. All Boards of Education have their own research cells. These cells undertake research work to improve the evaluation system.

Current concerns include the following questions :

(a) Is the present system of examinations satisfactory? If not, what measures should be adopted to improve it?

(b) Should the essay type questions be replaced by objective tests? Or should the two be blended harmoniously to form one question paper?

(c) Since the introduction of objective tests would be a novel experiment, what measure should be adopted to familiarize students and teachers with them?

(d) Since preparing objective tests is a very laborious and technical task what methods should be adopted to prepare them on a large scale

(e) What system of grading the papers should be adopted?

Objective type tests have been developed, and a bank of test items has been established. At present, theory papers have essay the tests only. However, during practical examinations teachers usually judge the knowledge of the students through objective type questions.

Science Activities, Laboratory Work and Equipment. Up to middle level no separate periods for science practicals are allocated. Usually all activities in and out of class are arranged by the teacher. As such it is rather difficult to assess the percentage of time devoted for practical work. At secondary and higher secondary levels 25 per cent of the total time is usually available for science practical work.

Examination in practicals or laboratory work in any science subject is a compulsory part of the public examination. Usually these examinations of practical work carry 25 per cent weightage, including 5 per cent for work done in the laboratory.

Science Equipment and Low-cost Teaching Aids. Schools and intermediate colleges situated in large cities are very well equipped to meet the needs of the latest curricula, but very few village schools have laboratory facilities. In most of the secondary schools, laboratory buildings and science apparatus are practically non existent.

With this factor in view a 'National Teaching Kit' was developed for primary classes in 1976. The kit consists of about 100 items which are packed in a metal box. It contains enough material to facilitate teaching of all the concepts in all subjects at primary level.

In collaboration with UNDP, the National Educational Equipment Centre, Lahore has produced about 60, 000 kits and distributed them to primary schools all over the country. Some teachers have also been trained in the use of this kit, but since the number of teachers at the primary level is very high a substantial number of teachers are still untrained.

In view of the lack of funds it is not possible to provide science equipment to all the middle and secondary level schools. The Ministry of education therefore began, in 1982, a small research project to develop low-cost aids to teach various concepts in science subjects. About 40 experiments have been developed, using locally available inexpensive materials. The basic idea in developing these aids is to train teachers and give them skills to produce their own teaching aids from inexpensive materials available in and around their schools. Experiments developed by the Ministry of Education are suggestive only and will be used as models during in-service teacher training programmes to stimulate the teachers to think creatively and develop their own aids wherever possible.

Most of the equipment needed up to Class XII is available locally. Sophisticated electronic equipment is not manufactured locally.

A National Educational Equipment Centre has been set up in Lahore. The Centre produces many items of apparatus needed for the schools. The mass production of this equipment is done only after thorough checking and testing in schools. On the basis of feedback, the design of such equipment is improved.

Educational Technology

Very few schools used sophisticated educational technology equipment. Closed circuit television (CCTV) is not available, even in urban schools. Most schools use charts or models to facilitate the teaching of science subjects. However, in teacher training programmes organized by the Federal Ministry of Education, equipment such as CCTV, 16 mm films, overhead projectors and many other aids are used. The Ministry of Education plans to set up some mobile science laboratories, which in addition to science equipment will have audio-visual aids. Two or three science education experts per mobile science laboratory will be recruited to give training to science teachers in their own schools. This project is in its initial stage.

The teaching of science subjects with the help of computers has not yet begun in schools or colleges.

Teacher Training

Minimum Qualifications for Science Teachers. The minimum qualifications prescribed for science teachers at different levels of education are as follows.

Level	*Classes*	*Qualifications*
Primary	I-V	(i) Secondary School Certificate
		(ii) Primary Teacher Certificate
Middle	VI-VIII	(i) Intermediate with science subjects, and
		(ii) Certificate in teaching
Secondary subjects, and	IX-X	(i) Bachelor's Degree with science
		(ii) Bachelor in Education
Higher Secondary		
Intermediate	XI-XII	Master's Degree in the subject to be taught

Percentage of Qualified and Trained Teachers. Exact figures for the ratio of trained and untrained teachers are not available. An analysis of staff members working in different schools, and also of teachers called for various training programmes shows that at school level a high percentage of teachers do not possess adequate qualifications, especially at the secondary level. A good proportion of science teachers at this level do not possess degrees in science. In some cases teachers are teaching science subjects which they themselves never studies as students. At higher secondary or intermediate college level there is no shortage of qualified teachers.

To over come the shortage of teachers the following stratgies have been developed :

(a) The subject of education has been introduced from Secondary to University level.

(b) About 110 Teacher Training Schools and Colleges of Education Extension Centres provide both pre-service and in-service teachers training.

(c) Allama Iqbal Open University, Islamabad has launched distance learning programmes for the training of primary and middle level teachers.

(d) The Teacher training Sector of the Federal Ministry of Education launched a scheme in 1979, for the training of senior teachers at the national level. These teachers, are used in the provinces for the training of teachers working at the grassroots level.

There are about 80 Elementary Teacher Training Schools in the country. Potential primary level teachers enrol in these schools after the secondary level examination. The duration of the training is about one year. Similarly, potential teachers at secondary enrol in teacher training colleges after completing their degree. A period of one year is needed to complete the Bachelor's Degree in education.

In service teacher training programmes are organized essentially by Provincial Education Extension Centres. The courses are usually of two to three weeks duration. Attention is paid to : methodology of teaching; course content in which the students or teachers are experiencing difficulty; and production of low-cost teaching aids.

Research Projects

Pakistan is faced with many problems pertaining to the quantitative expansion and qualitative improvement of its educational programmes. Perhaps the first and the most important question in the field of science education is the relevance of the existing science curricula to real-life problems. Questions, such as the following, are often put forward at various educational conferences and seminars.

(a) Are the science curricula for various levels of education relevant to the specific needs of the students and society?

(b) Are the textbooks, teacher's guides and science equipment of a satisfactory standard?

(c) Are the teachers adequately qualified and trained to implement the curricula in letter and spirit?

(d) Are the teachers dedicated to the profession?

(e) If the answers to the above questions are not in the affirmative, what can be done, within the limited resources, to implement the curricula more effectively?

Institutions engaged in research work. Besides the Curriculum Research Wing, all Institutes of Education and Research (IERs) in various universities and the Education Extension Centres are doing basic research work in the field of science education. For example:

(a) The IER, Punjab University, Lahore has undertaken a Science Education Project (SEP) on improvement of methodology of training science teachers.

(b) The Education Extension Centre, Lahore, has undertaken a research project on the assessment of needs of science teachers. It intends to improve its in-service training programmes for science and mathematics teachers, as a result of this survey.

(c) The education Extension Centre, Lahore is also trying

to establish a number of Teacher Training Centres and thereby to launch a massive teacher training programme.

(d) The IER University of Sind, Jamshoro, and Education Extension and Research Wing, Jamshoro, are also engaged in developing better models of teacher training programmes.

(e) The Curriculum Wing, Islamabad has undertaken a research project to improvise science apparatus from inexpensive low cost materials.

(f) The Education Extension centre, Abbottabad is also doing research work in curricula for teacher training programmes.

Programmes for out-of-school Youth and Adults and Popularization of Science and Technology

Due to lack of resources and stringent economic constraints it has not been possible for the educational planners to keep pace with the ever growing rate of population. Moreover, the number of out-of-school children is very high, since the rate of drop-outs at the primary stage is almost 50 per cent.

The Mass Literacy Commission, Islamabad, and the Allama Iqbal Open University (AIOU) are engaged in adult literacy programmes. The Mass literacy Commission has launched many programmes for adult literacy using literacy teams. The AIOU has launched its distance learning programmes through correspondence, mass media and literacy centres which are available throughout the country. AIOU Islamabad has also begun specific programmes on radio and TV for school and college students and teachers. These programmes are equally popular among students and teachers.

In order to make science popular among the masses, science exhibitions are organized by some teachers' association, and the Boards of Intermediate and Secondary Education. A science museum with latest innovations in science has also been opened in Lahore. In addition to these efforts a good number of urban schools have science clubs where students are given the opportunity to undertake project work.

Locating Talented Students. There are various organizations and schools which organize competitions among science students. Besides these, students with good results in public examinations are awarded scholarships to encourage them to continue their pursuits in the field of science.

On the special instructions of the Federal minister for Education a scheme for talent farming has been initiated. Under this scheme students will be picked on the basis of their performance at the middle level. These students will be given the best possible education and their entire educational expenses will be borne by the Government. Efforts will be made to provide them with opportunities to interact with senior scientists.

Science Clubs. The Educators' Club, Rawalpindi is an organization of teachers engaged in various activities both for students and teachers. The Club organizes an annual science exhibition where students display their projects. A team of scientists judges the exhibits and awards prizes to students on the basis of their original thinking and creativity.

Innovations

The Curriculum Research Wing of the Federal Ministry of Education, which is responsible for formulating and revising curricula, has revised the curricula for Classes XI and XII.

The National Educational Equipment Centre, Lahore has produced a number of items of equipment and is improving the designs through regular research and testing.

On the special instructions of the Federal Minister for Education, a project entitled Vertical artculation of curricula from Classes VI to XVI' has recently been launched . The project envisages the analysis of curricula for these classes and making recommendations for improvement. This task has been entrusted to a team of senior scientists and university and college teachers who will make recommendations for vertical as well as horizontal improvement of the curricula.

16

Papua New Guinea

Papua New Guinea (PNG) is a very diverse country both geographically and culturally. This is most strikingly illustrated by the fact that in a population of just three million there are more than 700 languages, which is more than a quarter of the languages of the world. Despite this—indeed because of it—the official language of instruction at all levels of the formal education system is English.

The PNG education system itself is a relatively Young one. This in turn is illustrated by the fact that until after the Pacific war virtually all schooling was provided by mission agencies and that secondary school education began only in the 1960s.

The legislative basis for the education system in Papua New Guinea is the Education Act, 1970. This Act provides a National Education System to include Government and church agency schools which meet prescribed conditions in terms of student enrolment and teacher qualifications. Under the Education Act, the Government Financially underwrites all schools within the system by paying teachers' salaries. Schools accept national control over planning and professional staffing matters. Non-government agencies retain supervisory responsibility over their schools and colleges with appropriate staffing safeguards.

The 1982 National Budget for education was K. 115.4 per cent of the total government expenditure. Papua New Guinea does to have a well-enunciated science policy statement

However, Papua New Guinea's Eight Aims, announced in December, 1972, constituted the first real attempt to formulate a strategy for development, and therefore are a precursor to any science policy. They are :

(a) A rapid increase in the proportion of the economy under the control of Papua New Ginean individuals and groups and in the proportion of personal and property income that goes to Papua New Guineans;

(b) More equal distribution of economic benefits, including movement toward equalization of incomes among people and toward equalization of services among different areas of the country;

(c) Decentralization of economic activity, planning and government spending, with emphasis on agricultural development, village industry, better internal trade and more spending channelled to local and area bodies;

(d) An emphasis on small-scale artisan, service and business activity, relying where possible on typically Papua New Guinean forms of business activity;

(e) A more self-reliant economy, less dependent for its needs on imported goods and services and better able to meet the needs of its people through local production;

(f) An increasing capacity for meeting government spending needs from locally raised revenue;

(g) A rapid increase in the equal and active participation of women in all forms of economic and social activity; and

(h) Government control and involvement in those sectors of the economy where control is necessary to achieve the desired kind of development.

The basic thinking behind the Eight Aims was that rural development should be emphasized as a vehicle for promoting a more equal distribution of social and economic opportunity. The Government provided further broad guidelines for future policy when they promulgated the National Development Strategy (NDS) in October, 1976.

There is at present no body equivalent to a National Science Council in the country. New public sector scientific activities are all subject to the broad developmental objectives as per the NDS. On going scientific activities in the public sector are dealt with by government departments and statutory bodies according to their own perception in their respective areas of competence.

Proposals for the establishment of a National science structure have been made after considerable national deliberation and the seeking of expert advice from UNESCO. Ministerial responsibility for science has in the last five years passed from the Ministry of Education, Science and Culture through the ministry of Science, Culture and Tourism to the present time where no single Ministry has responsibility for it. Science policy *per se* now largely remains in abeyance.

Science Education

Science is a compulsory subject in all of grades I-XI of the National education system. There are nationally prescribed curricula in science throughout and the language of instruction in English.

Primary Education. The task of community primary education is to equip the child with basic knowledge and skills which will be of use to him in his home community, regardless of whether he proceeds to high school. Hence primary schools have been renamed Community Schools.

Children enrol in the six year (grades I to VI) Community School programme at age 7. The curriculum includes a core of English, mathematics and science controlled by the National Government alongside 'community based' subjects including community life, expressive arts, health, Christian religious education and physical education which are under the control of Provincial Governments.

In 1982, 317,814 PNG children (61.0 per cent of the 7-12 year old population) were enrolled in 2, 186 community schools taught by 9,955 teachers all PNG nationals. Basically coastal provinces which have been longer in contact with the outside world show much higher enrolment levels than highland (inland) provinces. Three boys are enrolled in community schools for every two girls.

The long term objective is Universal Primary Education by the end of the century. Only slow progress is being made towards this goal. Annual recurrent per capita cost of community schooling is about K. 170.

At the Community School level science receives only a small allocation of time, 30 minutes per week in grades I-IV, and 40 minutes in grades V and VI out of a total weekly time allocation of about 1, 800 minutes. In addition, there is a 30 minutes science radio broadcast for grades V and VI. The science lessons are activity based, designed to expose pupils to a range of science-related experiences with stress on the immediate environment. The broadcasts relate the science concepts introduced in the activities to broader issues and applications. There is also a health programme for community schools and practical work in agriculture is undertaken.

Secondary Education. The aim of the four year secondary education programme (grades VII to X) provided by Provincial High Schools (PHS) is to provide adequate preparation for post-secondary training courses, direct employment needs an responsible participation in community life. The PHS course is organized in two stages of two years each, with 40 per cent of students leaving at the end of grade VIII.

Selection into PHS is through a nationwide high school, selection examination. Grade VI community school pupils take this examination in September each year and about 30 per cent are selected for entry to high school. Provincial Education Boards use the examination results in order to select pupils for high schools. In 1982, 67 per cent of selected students were allocated places solely on their performance in the examination. The remaining places were granted on a quota basis to ensure that all community schools obtain some representation in high schools.

Total enrolment of students in PHS in 1982 was 39, 722 (15.1 per cent of the age cohort; who were accommodated in 105 high schools, 75 of which were Government agency operated). There were 1, 556 teachers (1,146 nationals) and the ratio of boys to girls was 2:1.

The core curriculum includes English, mathematics, science and social science, while options include expressive arts, commerce, health, manual arts and agriculture. Modification of curricula for use in high schools is a continuous process. Annual per capita cost at PHS is about K.460.

In Provincial High Schools (PHS), science is taught as an integrated subject, which is part of the compulsory core, for five 40 minute periods of a total of 40 periods per week throughout the four years. All PHS have at least one laboratory provided with gas and running water. Teaching is based on a syllabus and detailed teacher's guides produced by the Curriculum Unit of the national Department of education teachers may make radical departures from this syllabus only with the consent of, and in consultation with, their inspectors. Few, if any, do so.

National High Schools. About 15 per cent of grade X students are selected on the basis of School Certificate results to enter the four national High schools each of which enrols 200 students in grade XI each year. These schools provide grades XI and XII mainly as an academic preparation for tertiary study. All students take English, mathematics, social science, science and expressive arts in grade XI whilst in grade XII a system of options operates whereby students choose from 'major' offerings in most of the five subjects. All students are required to take English and at least minor mathematics in grade XII. At the end of grade XII more than 60 per cent achieve matriculation to the two Universities and 80 per cent continue with some form of post-secondary education. A National Curriculum and examination system has recently been developed for these schools through a system of Subject Advisory Committees made up of NHS, University and National Department of Education headquarters staff. Total enrolment in National High Schools was 1, 680 in 1982 staffed by 97 teachers. Annual per capita cost at NHS is about K. 2,200.

The compulsory grade XI and major grade XII science courses contain separate strands of physics, chemistry and biology, each usually taught by a different teachers. At grade XI each strand has two 50-minute lessons per week while in grade XII each strand has three 50-minute lessons per week. The minor science course offered in grade XI consists of a range of suggested modules grouped under the three main themes of (a) human biology; (b) evolution; and (c) technology; and is allocated a total of four lessons per week.

Minor science is taken by only very small number of students (about 20 per cent) whereas because of University entry requirements a majority (about 60 per cent) undertake major science in grade XII. National High Schools are staffed almost exclusively by expatriates. It is planned to recruit national graduates with experience in PHS into the NHS teaching force.

Technical Education. Technical colleges provide training to meet identified manpower needs for semi-skilled and sub-professional technical employment. In 1982 the nine technical colleges, including two secretarial colleges, had a total full-time enrolment of 3, 778 students taught by 252 instructors (62 national).

The Education Department plans to greatly expand the number of pre-employment technical training PETT courses of variable duration, usually 20 or 40 weeks, and catering for grade VIII and grade X school-leavers. PETT students can obtain formal trade qualifications by obtaining employment in an area related to their course and returning to a technical college for prescribed formal extension courses.

Courses in technical colleges are developed by trade panels which include industry, commerce representatives and National Boards of Studies with the assistance of curriculum unit officers. Most certificate and PETT courses have a basic science component.

Adult and Vocational Education. Various adult education courses have been established to meet the needs of the community. Vocational centres provide courses of one or two years duration in basic technical and/or agricultural skills with the object of developing more productive citizens either in the monetary or 'informal' sectors of the economy. They are mainly based in rural areas and in 1982, the 89 centres had a total enrolment of 5,362 students.

Formal correspondence studies in grade VII to X core subjects (except science) and a Commerce Certificate are offered by the College of External Studies which has about 7,500 part-time students. Sixty students followed a grade VII trail science course in 1982 and it is hoped that many more will enrol when the course is offered to the general public. A community secondary education programme has been set up through 33 study centres to assist people undertaking correspondence secondary education.

Tertiary Education. The Office of Higher Education advises the Government on post-secondary education with a view to meeting the nation's needs for trained manpower and to ensure the balanced development and use of post-secondary educational resources. The office is responsible for advising on levels of funding to be recommended on behalf of the universities.

There are two universities and a total of about 60 government and non-government institutions offering post-secondary (grade X) level courses. The two universities offer a range of four year first degree programmes following successful completion of grade XII.

Curriculum Aspects of Science Education

Primary. The Educational aims adopted in the development of the primary science curriculum arose from the belief that experience was of value for its own sake and that in the situation in which the project would operate any new experience of the physical world would be of value. The course would 'educate the children through science rather than teach science to the children'.

The basic aim of the course as set out in the Teacher's Handbook is as follows :

> To allow children to gain knowledge and understanding of the world about them in as interesting a way as possible through activity and enquiry. To develop this attitude of enquiry.

Another document sets out rather more specific objectives as follows : enrichment of experience; establishment of awareness of cause and effect relationships; development of skills of manipulating, observing, measuring, recording and communicating; and problem solving and learning how to learn.

The six year course is divided into three two-year stages or phases (hence the name Three Phase Primary Science—TPPS). The nature of this programme is further defined as follows :

(a) Phase I is a series of activities during and after which discussions and questions should be encouraged;

(b) Phase II is a series of simple experiments. Pupils will be expected to observe and report what they have observed. If any child wants to make notes or drawings he should be encouraged to do so and be given a book to keep his work in; and

(c) Phase III is a series of more formal experiments involving comparison, measurements, recording data, simple graphing, voluntary sketching and recording. The sketching and reporting will be in notebooks given to all pupils for this purpose.

The content of the course was determined by its relevance to the local environment; capability of stimulating interest and enjoyment; and being within the competence of the teachers.

The first major development of the primary science curriculum in PNG was a UNICEF/UNESCO assisted education project initiated in 1968. This project provided a full-time UNESCO science curriculum adviser who was funded for three years and who set up a Science Curriculum Development Panel consisting of himself, a number of primary teacher's college science lectures, one primary school headmaster and one primary science teacher from a pilot school.

A major evaluation of the material produced was carried out in 1977. This evaluation generally supported the material but made several recommendations.

As a result of the evaluation, the Community School Science Advisory Committee (CSAC) which consists of teachers' college science lecturers, science curriculum officers from the curriculum unit of the National Department of Education and experienced science teachers, recommended that the original aims, methods and content be maintained while the programme be revised beginning with Phase III. This revision is now complete.

The revision provides 'paper in-service training' for teachers in the form of background notes (explaining the aims and concepts underlying the activities) questions to ask the children (with answers), diagrams and worksheets. An attempt has also been made to reduce the amount of imported materials needed through the use of locally available substitutes. Wherever possible links with traditional practices, methods and experiences have also been strengthened.

Thus there is a continuing move in Community School Science to Provide teachers with more assistance both with science and with teaching; and relate the science programme still more closely to the pupils' environment.

At the end of the community school programme there is a selection examination for entry into secondary schools and one of the three papers taken by the students contains questions based on the prescribed science curriculum.

Lower Secondary. As there is an exit point for 40 per cent of students at grade VIII the programme is planned in two stages—grades VII and VIII and grades IX and X. At the first stage particular efforts are made to relate the programme to the needs of those who will not continue with formal schooling. This means stress on qualitative science related to applications and the environment rather than quantitative, academic science.

The aims of this science syllabus include a development in the student of :

(a) An awareness of interest in and curiosity about the natural phenomena of his environment and a commitment to seek a scientific explanation of these phenomena;

(b) An understanding and appreciation of his relationship to his environment and confidence in his ability to effect changes and improvement in the environment;

(c) His critical thinking ability, and reducation in any tendency to adopt opinions based on unsupported or unreliable evidence; and

(d) An understanding and appreciation of the methods of science, and the past, present and possible future contribution of science to mankind.

The materials produced and presently used in schools consist basically of a series of Teachers' Guides one for each of the six units in each of the four grades VII—XII. The Guides set out the programme as a number of student 'Investigations' each intended to occupy a double period of 2 x 40 minutes. The Investigations usually have a teacher introduction, student group activities and concluding discussion; all set out in some detail, including specifications of what students are intended to learn from the Investigation.

Increasingly, student activities are organized on the basis of student worksheets. The original VII and VIII units were accompanied by short illustrated student readers which were issued in class sets to all schools. This has not been done with the more recent grades IX and X units mainly due to lack of resources. There has been a policy that textbooks should not be used in PHS science in PNG partly because it was feared this would encourage teaching and learning for rote memory rather than understanding and partly because no suitable text could be identified. The benefits of a student text as a support for activity based science teaching is now recognized but a decision on adoption or production of a suitable text has not been made. Recently a start has been made in the production of an 'Item bank' of mainly multiple choice test questions for each unit.

The secretary for Education authorizes all science courses taught in Provincial High Schools. A body of science educators now called the Provincial High Schools Science Advisory Committee (PSAC) develops Provincial High School Science Syllabuses and material and submits these along with recommendations concerning future science education policy to the Secretary for his approval. While the membership of the PSAC has constantly changed over the years, it generally includes curriculum officers, teachers, inspectors, staff of the universities and other interested individuals from the science education community. The PSAC meets at least once each year-usually for a week.

Science was first taught in high schools in Papua New Guinea in 1960 when an interim measure was adopted whereby teachers had the option to follow either the Australian New South Wales Wyndham Science course or the Sarawak Secondary Science Syllabus. The Wyndham scheme was the first attempt in New South Wales at an integrated four year course containing elements of physics, chemistry, biology, geology and astronomy.

In 1966 a new syllabus designed in Papua New Guinea for grades VII and VIII was introduced into all schools. This syllabus was also an integrated course which had been somewhat reorientated to the Papua New Guinea environment. In 1968 a new syllabus for grades IX and X was introduced. This syllabus was a radical departure from the conservative content-orientated grades VII and VIII syllabus that had been introduced two years earlier. This new grade IX and X syllabus was developed around a framework consisting of a basic core; a development area; and a research area.

Teacher reaction to both syllabuses was both swift and mixed. The grades VII and VIII syllabus was excessively content loaded and resulted in teachers either trying to cover large quantities of content poorly or having to try to work out for themselves which were the most important areas. The grades IX and X syllabus gave teachers a great deal of freedom and consequently a great deal of responsibility in organizing the most suitable methods and areas of study. Neither syllabus contained much background material for teachers nor did they take into account the general level of inexperience of most teachers in the country, both Papua New Guinean or expatriate. The lack of materials and guidance provided by these syllabuses were compounded by the Comparatively limited educational background of many science teachers coming from Goroka Teachers College.

Thus in 1970 the Secondary Science Curriculum Committee (a forerunner of PSAC) decided to scrap all existing science curricula in high schools and undertake radical rewriting and restructuring of the secondary science syllabus.

A hastily prepared interim syllabus was produced and introduced into all high schools at the beginning of 1971 as a holding measure. This stop-gap device was the science syllabus followed in most Papua New Guinea High Schools until it was progressively phased out by the present material.

Preparation of material for grades VII and VIII began in 1971. It consisted of a 12-Unit course of work which was intended, when taken together to provide a self-contained general science course. It provided all students (whether they were leaving school or continuing on with the next two years of the course) with a basic background in scientific understanding that would enable the student to live a better life in his local environment. Emphasis was placed on human biology and nutrition, ecology and the physical environment, concepts of energy, force, work and simple machines and the working of simple electrical circuits. Each unit of the new course was prepared, tried out on a pilot scale for at least two years, modified, then printed and distributed to all provincial High Schools, and is basically the material which is presently used in schools.

By the end of 1981 all units from grades VII to X had been given trials, evaluated, modified and put back into the schools. However, science courses in Papua New Guinea (and those in other subject areas) have remained open to further change and development as conditions and ideas change. A revision of the grades VII and VIII material is already underway. This revision is attempting to :

(a) Identify those scientific concepts which are most important to students both in terms of their immediate environment and beyond;

(b) Identify the form and level at which it is appropriate that these concepts be understood;

(c) provide a series of activities which relate to these concepts and illustrate various aspects of the concepts leading to a well rounded understanding of them;

(d) Involve students in using the 'scientific method' for themselves, formulating hypotheses, collecting data and testing hypotheses;

(e) Identify aspects of the students environment and beyond which can be understood in terms of the concepts; and

(f) Draw up a revised teaching programme.

This process has not involved a departure from the present programme but rather a reconstruction and modification within the basic framework of the present units. It is expected that the revised grade VII units will be in schools in 1984.

Development of high schools is now taking them in the direction of a closer relationship with the communities they serve, whether they be urban or rural. Most PHS are rural boarding schools of 250-600 students. A recent attempt to establish rural day high schools was neither popular not successful academically mainly due to the generally scattered population pattern. It has been largely abandoned. Some boarding schools have become self-sufficient in food supplies and other are encouraged to be self-reliant through agricultural and commercial projects.

Examinations. A School Certificate is awarded after grade X. Up to 1981 this was largely internally assessed and moderated by a mid-Year Rating Examination (MYRE). This examination, in multiple choice format, covered English, Mathematical Thinking and Scientific Thinking and was intended to be 'content free'. On the basis of this examination schools were awarded an appropriate number of distinctions, and credits. These were awarded to individual students mainly on the basis of internal assessment.

In 1982 students sat for four end-of-year multiple choice papers covering English, mathematics, science and social science based on the stated syllabus objectives. The results of these examinations were used to moderate the internal assessments which were then combined with the external marks. These combined results were then used to rank and apply a national distribution of distinctions and credits to individual students.

Item Banks are available for all Science units in grades IX and X. These are used extensively by teachers in the compilation of instruments for internal assessment.

Upper Secondary. The National High Schools offer compulsory grade XI and non-compulsory grade XII science courses containing separate strands of physics, chemistry and biology.

The general aims of all National High School science courses are as follows:

(a) To help students:

(i) Acquire a body of scientific knowledge;

(ii) Acquire an understanding of certain scientific concepts;

(iii) Acquire attitudes based on scientific principles;

(iv) Understand the general use of the terms 'law', 'fact', 'hypothesis' and 'model' and especially that 'theory' means an attempt to synthesize a collection of facts into an overall structure;

(v) Acquire basic scientific skills; and

(vi) Become familiar with official scientific definitions of words and their relationship to lay interpretations and usage.

(b) To develop in students the ability to adapt a new situations, to absorb and understand relevant scientific information, and to cope with an increasingly technological society.

(c) To encourage students to :

(i) Use an experimental approach and to take responsibility for the design of their own experiments, including the use of controls;

(ii) Acquire the habits of observing, recording accurately and reporting accounts of experimental work in a clear and objective manner; and

(iii) Use graphical and diagrammatic means to represent data.

(d) To develop the following scientific skills: (i) manipulation of apparatus; (ii) observation; (iii) measurement; (iv) recording of data; (v) computation of results; (vi) drawing of conclusions from data; (vii) reporting of results; and (viii) problem solving.

The minor science course, non-compulsory, offered in grade XII consists of a range of suggested modules, grouped under the three main themes of human biology, evolution, and technology. The general aims of this course are to reinforce those of other science courses in National High Schools and are particularly directed to: reinforce and extend relevant scientific concepts;

continue development in scientific literacy; encourage appreciation of the impact of science and technology on society, and their application in PNG; forster an active concern for man and his environment; encourage an interest in, and an inquiring attitude towards, scientific matters; and increase the knowledge of oneself.

The first grades XI and XII science courses in Papua New Guinea were developed in 1969 at Sogeri National High School. The Opening of other National High Schools led to a period of syllabus anarchy during which different science courses were taught even within each school. This situation was incompatible with the education strategy. The formation of the Curriculum Unit and the appointing strategy. The formation of the Curriculum Unit and the appointment of a Senior Curriculum Officer (SCO) for science enabled the Board of Studies (BOS) to recommend the development of common science courses in 1976.

The National High Schools Science Advisory Committee (NSAC) under the chairmanship and direction of the SCO Science was responsible for the development of curricula, support material and the examinations. The NSAC makes recommendations through the National High Schools to the Secretary for Education for his approval. Representatives of all National High Schools, both universities and other organizations make up the NSAC team which meets two or three times a year.

On reaching a consensus, the enormous workload of curriculum and examinations is delegated to practising field officers. The NSAC prepared draft outlines for all courses, and trials began in 1977. These draft outlines were further modified by the NSAC and resulted in the National High School Science Syllabus Grade XI and the National High School Science Syllabus Grade XII Major and Minor courses which were approved by the Secretary in 1979.

A Higher School Certificate is awarded after grade XII. Three separate external examinations are set in science covering biology; chemistry and physics. External examiners from the two universities set these papers, while teachers can provide model questions. The examinations are based on the detailed syllabus objectives. The results of the external examinations are used to moderate the schools' internal assessments which are then combined with the external marks. The moderated internal assessment at present provides for 75 per cent of the final mark. The internal assessments are derived from school assessments comprising 70 per cent written tests, 20 per cent assignments and 10 per cent practical assessments. The Minor course is examined internally.

Science Activities, Laboratory Work and Equipment

Primary. The major emphasis of all primary science lessons is on child activity and experience, and is based on the assumption that children learn best by doing things rather than by hearing about them. To ensure that child activity is the main ingredient of each lesson, all lessons are organized around a simple common lesson procedure which is to :

(a) Make sure the groups are settled;

(b) Tell the class in a few words what they are going to do—not what will happen;

(c) Get group leaders to collect the materials;

(d) Move amongst the groups;

(e) Listen for comments and questions; and

(f) Collect materials and complete the lesson with discussion and questions.

There is no practical component in the examination taken by grade VI students. Some of the multiple choice items relating to science assess the understanding by students of practical activities prescribed in the science syllabus.

Materials for the activities come from a number of sources. First, there is a kit of teacher and pupil materials which is supplied to all schools (*e.g.* lenses, syringes, magnets, candles). Second, much material has to be collected by the teachers and pupils (*e.g.* bottles, tins, rocks, seeds) and lastly there is a list of locally available substitute materials (Bamboo strips instead of forceps and bush thorns or fish bones instead of pins) and items which could be made by the teachers (*e.g.* substitute school or coconut oil burners, funnels and simple pulleys).

The National Government has supplied all schools with one basic science kit. These are purchased from the UNICEF Packing and Assembly Centre, Copenhagen. The purchase of either replacement kits, individual items or consumables is now the responsibility of the various Provincial Governments' Education Divisions. Similar kits are also available through local suppliers. All items in the kits are imported as there are no local manufacturers of science equipment in the country. The Curriculum Unit, the Port Moresby In-service College and numerous individual teachers design substitute items of equipment and these designs are circulated to teachers for their information and use.

Although the government has supplied all primary schools with a basic science kit, many of these were supplied in the early 1970s. Since then numerous replacement part have also been issued, but these have not been able to keep up with the rate of loss. Surveys have shown that as many as half the schools in the country do not have complete kits. The lack of science background of the teachers and hence confidence to teach science has led to many using the excuse of not having the proper equipment to teach science. Recent revisions in the curriculum, teachers' guides and in-service programmes have therefore made serious attempts to reduce the amount of imported or 'formal' science materials needed by placing emphasis on the use of locally available substitutes.

Lower Secondary. More than half of the lower secondary curriculum requires the students to be involved in practical work. Most schools hold all the science lessons in a science laboratory. All schools have at least one laboratory provided with gas and running water. Most schools have a science block consisting of two laboratories and a preparation room. Many of the older schools have four science laboratories.

There is no practical component in the end of year external examination which is of a multiple choice format. Like the grade VI examination, questions pertaining to practical activities prescribed in the syllabus are often included. The internal assessment counts towards 50 per cent of a student's final mark and teachers are encouraged to include tests of practical skills such as observation, recording results, manipulation of equipment, and devising experiments as well as subjective assessment of the students' attitude to practical work.

All schools are supplied with a basic science kit which in 1982 cost the government about US $ 10,000. Consumables, replacements and additional equipment have to be purchased by individual schools with funds obtained from the Provincial School Equipment Trust Fund, Boards of Governors and the Government Stores Account. Most high schools are well equipped. New schools which have not yet received their basic science kit are usually assisted by a nearby school until their equipment arrives.

The components of the basic science kits are completely supplied from overseas. Most teachers' guides contain instructions and plans for teachers to construct simple pieces of equipment, some items of which are essential for their teaching. No locally-manufactured equipment is currently available in the country although recently the government placed an order with a sheltered workshop' for a trial batch of student electricity kits which were designed by the University of Papua New Guinea.

Upper Secondary. All science lessons in the National High Schools are taught in well-equipped science laboratories. The four National High Schools have, on the average, five laboratories each. An estimate in 1982, for the equipping of a new school was approximately US $ 50,000. These schools have a recurrent budget for science equipment of about US $ 4,000 per annum.

There is no practical component in the end of year examination but the internal assessment counts 75 per cent towards a student's final mark; 10 per cent being for compulsory practical tests.

All equipment in NHS, apart from the teacher and student constructed complement, is purchased from overseas.

Use of Educational Technology

The only audio-visual aids used widely in primary science teaching are charts. A series of these have been prepared by the Curriculum Unit and are supplemented in some schools by others made by teachers. Some urban schools use 35 mm slides and 16 mm films which are either bought, borrowed or hired.

Most schools in the lower secondary section have overhead, 35 mm slide, and 16 mm projectors. The curriculum Unit produces sets of 35 mm slides and accompanying notes for many of the science units. Films are available through the University of Papua New Guinea, the National Library and commercial outlets. An increasing number of schools now have video facilities and films are available through the National Library and numerous commercial outlets. Some schools have their own Apple II computers but very few use these for teaching purposes.

All National High Schools have overhead, 35 mm slide and 16 mm projectors as well as video and computer facilities. Numerous slide sets, 16 mm and video films are held in the schools and are used in the teaching of science. Again, commercial hiring is used extensively. The introduction of computes in science teaching is in its infancy.

Teacher Training

Primary. The training of community school teachers in carried out through a two year post-grade X programme. The grade X requirement is very recent and is still not always meet. Of the eight community teachers' colleges in the national Education System, seven are administered by church agencies. In 1981, enrolment in the two year primary pre-service course totalled 1,649 students taught by 165 lecturing staff of whom 61 are Papua New Guinea nationals.

The teacher's college programme science 1970 includes a component for all students, on the methods and content of the prescribed science course. Entrants to the programme often have a weak background in science and in other subjects.

In 1979 one of the then two government agency community school teachers' colleges was converted to become the sole in-service training institution. In-service training of community school teachers is conducted at this college mainly through six month courses which include a science component. The college also runs courses with a science component to upgrade teachers to the equivalent of grade IX. Short in-service workshops, especially during the National In-service Week are also held in the provinces by Teacher's College or Curriculum Unit Science staff. Background notes and in-service guidelines are produced by the Curriculum Unit as 'paper in-service' for these short courses and assist individuals and school staff groups to upgrade their weak science background.

Lower Secondary. Teacher education for secondary education is conducted by the University of Papua New Guinea (UPNG). The Goroka campus of UPNG offers a two year Diploma in Secondary Teaching following the completion of grade XII in school or the preliminary year at the Goroka college. Students in the diploma programme choose two teaching subjects *e.g.* science and mathematics or social science and language. The preparation in science is based very closely on the teachers' guides for the secondary science syllabus. It is generally recognized that Goroka Diplomates are weak in their subject areas—particularly in science and mathematics but stronger in practical teaching skills. More than 90 per cent of Papua New Guinea teachers in lower secondary schools are diplomates. UPNG also offers a four year pre-service B. Ed. degree programme for prospective secondary school teachers. This is a post-grade XII or a post-preliminary year course. This programme involves three years of study of selected courses offered by the Faculties of Arts or Scence and a year of professional study and preparation in the Faculty of Education. B. Ed. graduates have a comparatively strong subject background. Fewer than 2 per cent of Papua New Guinea nationals teaching in secondary schools are graduates.

In-service training for PHS science teachers is also provided by UPNG. Diplomates may return to the University for a further two years, (after a minimum of two years teaching) to complete an In-Service B. Ed. degree. This programme concentrates on upgrading the science background through courses in the Science Faculty, although advanced professional courses are also included. A six month in service programme for science teachers is also offered at Goroka. This too concentrates on subject background.

Ongoing science in-service training at the provincial or school level is sporadic and varied and depends on the location of interested and able individuals who form the core of various groups. The most successful of these have negotiated with local education authorities and hold in-service meetings at the beginning of each term during which teachers go through and often learn the topics scheduled for the following term's teaching. Others still hold annual in-service courses during the National In-service Week.

Teachers' Guides, which form the basis of the lower secondary science curriculum, are developed as 'paper in-service' documents whose content and structure are such that they enable the weaker teachers to develop their own content background and their skills of lesson planning and presentation.

Upper Secondary. National High Schools are staffed almost exclusively by expatriates and all but one of the science teachers are from overseas. Plans are underway to recruit more national graduates with experience in lower secondary and to provide scholarships to experienced teachers to gain degrees before taking up teaching in the upper secondary area.

Research

Research into science education is carried out in PNG by and in affiliation with the Research Branch of the Department of Education, the Mathematics Education Centre, the Research Committees of the University of Papua New Guinea and the Papua New Guinea University of Technology, and the Education Research Unit of the University of Papua New Guinea.

Researchers have carried out investigations into Piagetian conservation, the differences in cognitive development in bilingual children, differences in science achievement over time and with changes in curriculum, and the structure of the school population, the development of scientific attitudes, curriculum evaluation, ethno-science and its relevance to science education.

The most significant research into science education currently being undertaken in PNG is a result of participation in the Second International Association of the Evaluation of Educational Achievement Science Study (SISS). PNG has organized trial testing of the international science tests at all three levels and has been able to make a considerable contribution to the finalization of the international tests. Largely due to representations from PNG, based on the results of the trial testing, the population definitions for the survey have been made more flexible.

Out-of-school Science Activities

There is no programme of non-formal science education other than the indirect effort of agricultural and appropriate technology extension work carried out by various government departments and church agencies.

The massive illiterate rural majority do not benefit from the various publications aimed, in the main, at school-leavers and the literate minority, although the publications usually contain a science and technology component. Increasingly, educators are realizing that knowledge from the traditional societies has an important role to play in the learning of science. The most recent Teachers' Guides draw, where applicable, upon much of this traditional knowledge and use it to establish links with the applications and teaching of science.

This will hopefully, not only give status to this storehouse of knowledge, but also establish channels of communication between the formally educated and the rest of the community resulting in a mutually beneficial transfer of knowledge.

Current Innovations

The revision of the grades VII and VIII science curriculum to include, where applicable, traditional knowledge as a launching point in science teaching is the most exciting current innovation at the lower secondary level. The identification of traditional astronomical data, and classification and counting systems, give powerful foundations to the development of important science concepts.

The development of a broad range of 35 mm slide sets and accompanying notes continues, and experimental work on the production of video science programmes will continue with the final introduction of a much discussed television network and facilities.

The development of textbooks and student material in the lower secondary sector is in its infancy and will be the thrust of future curriculum development. A project for the development of laboratory manuals in the upper secondary sector is underway and should be completed by the end of 1984. This will go to long way towards ensuring the standardization of laboratory experience and will assist in the future inclusion of a practical component in the external examination process.

One province has taken the lead in in-service training and appointed a full-time Provincial In-Service Training Officer for science. The programmes developed in this province could form the vanguard for a future national in-service training project.

Generally, while science is seen as an essential core subject throughout the education system, it does not at present receive the emphasis in terms of time allocation which it often does elsewhere. There are a number of reasons for this. The limited science background of community School teachers influences the amount of science that can be attempted at that level. Due to the wide aims of the curriculum at lower secondary level, specialized subjects stressing preparation for the next level, receive low priority. Even at the National High School level where academic preparation for further studies is a high priority, there is less time devoted to science than would be the case in pre-tertiary programmes elsewhere.

17

Philippines

In 1981, leaders from various sectors of society came together in a series of workshops to deliberate on the directions of science and technology in the country during the period 1983-1987. A final draft for a five-year plan resulted from all these deliberations. Under the section on developmental patterns and directions, a sub-topic of the plan is devoted to the development of science and technology and includes several proposals relating to the first two levels of education. These proposals are that (a) the recruitment of potential scientists will begin at high school level; (b) support and expansion of science teachers' programmes will be carried out in consultation with the country's scientists; (c) given that education is the primary responsibility of the state, support will be given to elementary and secondary science education by involving scientists in curriculum and training, identifying pilot elementary schools with adequate science components, and strengthening the Philippine Science High School and other science-oriented high schools; and (d) science education for policy-makers will be considered.

In considering programmes and projects for the near future, two specific projects were included under the programme to develop science and technology. These were (a) science promotion and apprenticeship (*e.g.* science camps, fairs, clubs, quizzes); and (b) science promotion for decision makers and the public.

The above projects are not new; several efforts along these lines have been undertaken for some time but they have received new vigour through the reorganization of the former National Science Development Board into the National Science and technology Authority (NSTA). A Science Promotion Institute has been constituted as one of the offices in NSTA. This office has responsibility for all projects and activities sponsored by NSTA which are concerned with the popularization of science.

Late in 1982, the Ministry of Education, Culture and Sports and the NSTA undertook an 18-month project entitled, 'Science Education Development Plan' which aims to develop guidelines for the improvement of science education at three levels of education for both public and private sectors. Policies, programmes and projects will be identified with respect to the following areas in science education: organization, finance, curriculum, staff development, textbooks and instructional materials, equipment and facilities, research and linkages with government and non-government agencies. This project is ongoing and is expected to come up with a development plan by 1984.

Science Education in Schools

The figure on the following page shows the structure of the ten-year school education system, six years for elementary and four years for secondary. There are 31,455 elementary schools and 5,156 high schools according to the statistical bulletin of 1981. The enrolment figures are : 8,290,440 for the elementary level (grades I to VI) and 3,018,568 for the secondary levels (Years 1 to 4).

Primary level. Science is taught from grade III but arithmetic is part of the curriculum in each year from grade I. Furthermore, although there is no science in grades I and II within the new curriculum, pupils at grades I and II read about science in their English language subjects.

Science is taught with health education as a separate subject from grades III to VI. Forty minutes daily is allotted to this subject. The school year is generally about 180 days. The science courses at this level may be considered integrated in the sense that the subject, in addition to health concepts, includes concepts from the biological and physical science as well as from the earth and space science, environmental sciences and some population education concepts. The proportion of time available for science and health is grade III, 13.33 per cent; grade IV, 11.76 per cent; and grades V and VI, 11.11 per cent. (*Table 1*, page 24).

Secondary level. At the secondary level, the teaching of science and mathematics has been strengthened since 1973 when both were made required subjects at each year level. The science courses taught at this level are :

Year 1 — Integrated general science — 180 minutes per week
Year 2 — Biology — 180 minutes per week
Year 3 — Chemistry — 300 minutes per week
Year 4 — Physics — 300 minutes per week

Table 2 gives the overall curriculum of the secondary schools. The curriculum of the public secondary vocational (trade and industrial, agricultural and fishery) schools differs for the prescribed revised secondary education programme of 1973 in the practical arts and vocational components. More time is allocated to these subjects.

Environmental science is not taught as a separate subject but some topics are included in biology and chemistry. Also, an earth science course (with focus on the Philippine environment) is offered as an elective in some public schools at the Year 2 level. Other optional science courses are astronomy and botany for Year 3 and applied chemistry, environmental science or applied science for Year 4. No optional courses are offered for Year 1 of high school.

The percentage of time for science at secondary level is : Year 1, 11 per cent; Year 2, 10.7 —10 per cent; Year 3, 15.15—13.5 per cent; and Year 4, 15.15—13.5 per cent.

The special science schools which offer more science courses for their students (who are selected) show a much higher percentage of instructional time devoted to science compared with the general high school as shown by the sample of three science high schools below.

The structure of school education in the Philippines from primary to pre-university stage

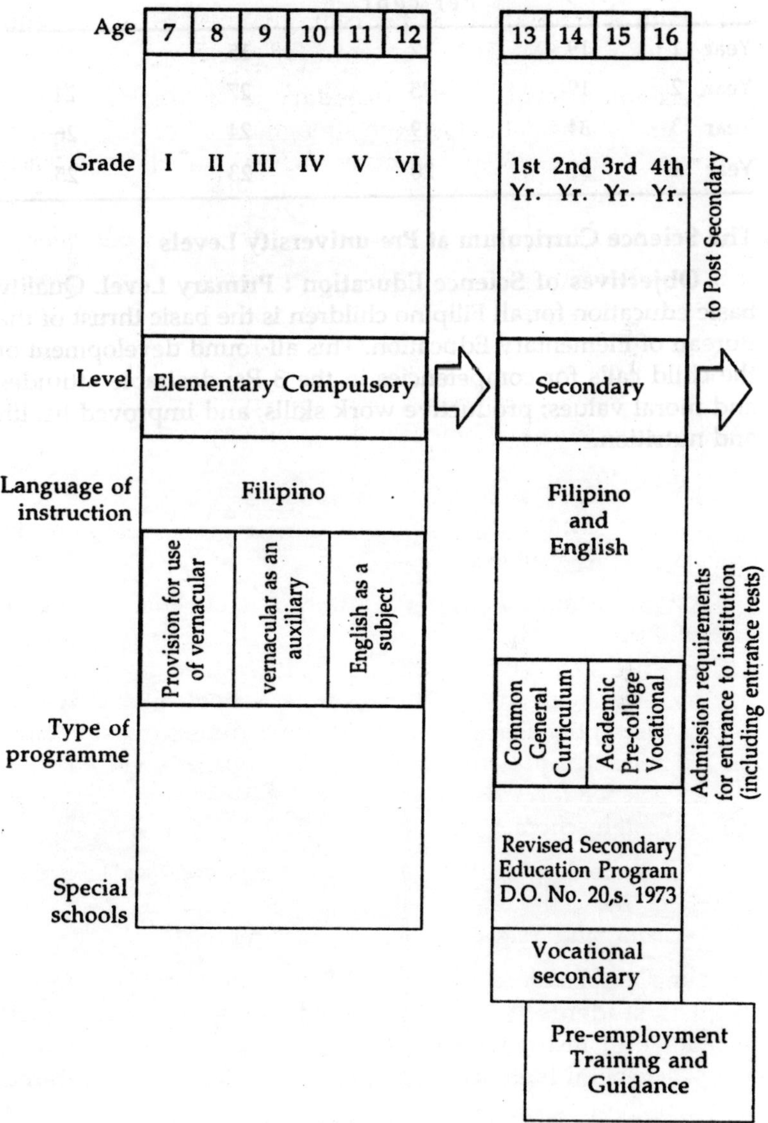

Source : Adapted from: Secondary Education Program in the Philippines from primary to pre-university stage.

	PSHS (Philippine)	*MSHS (Manila)*	*QCHS (Quezon City)*	*Average*
		Per cent		
Year 1	19	17	15	17
Year 2	19	25	27	24
Year 3	34	19	24	26
Year 4	31	20	23	25

The Science Curriculum at Pre-university Levels

Objectives of Science Education : Primary Level. Quality basic education for all Filipino children is the basic thrust of the Bureau of Elementary Education. This all-round development of the child calls for competencies in the 3 Rs; desirable attitudes and moral values; productive work skills; and improved health and nutrition.

Table—1. The new Elementary School Curriculum

Learning areas	Daily and weekly time allotment in minutes per grade level*											
Grade	I		II		III		IV		V		VI	
	D	Wk	D	Wk	D	Wk	D	Wk	D	Wk	D	Wk
Character building Activities	20-30	100-150	20-30	100-150	20	100	20	100	20	100	20	100
Filipino	60	300	60	300	60	300	60	300	60	300	60	300
English	60	300	60	300	60	300	60	300	60	300	60	300
Mathematics	40	200	40	200	40	200	40	200	40	200	40	200
Civics and Culture (History/Geography/ Work Ethics)	40	200	40	200	40	200						
History/Geography/ Civics							40	200	40	200	40	200
Science and Health					40	200	40	200	40	200	40	200
Arts and Physical Education					40	200	40	200	40	200	40	200
Home Economics and Livelihood Education							40	200	60	300	60	300
Total	220-230	1100-1150	220-230	1100-1150	300	1500	340	1700	360	1800	360	1800

* Implementation begins in 1983 for grade I, 1984 II and so on to 1988 for grade VI.
D—daily; Wk—weekly..

Table 2. The revised secondary curriculum

Subjects	Year 1		Year 2		Year 3		Year 4	
	Units	Minutes/ Week	Units	Minutes/ Week	Units	Minutes/ Week	Units	Munites/ Week
Communication arts (English)	2	300	1	180	1	180	1	180
Communication arts (Pilipino)	1	180	1	180	1	180	1	180
Social studies	1	180	1	180	1	180	1	180
Science	1	180	1	180	2	300	2	300
Mathematics	1	180	1	180	1	180	1	180
Practical arts/ Vocational course	1	300	1	300	1	300	1	300
Electives (Academic/ Vocational)	—	—	1	180/ 300	2	360/ 600	2	360/ 600
Youth development training (I-III)	1	300	1	300	1	300		
Citizens army training (IV)							1	300
Total	8	1620	8	1680/ 1800	10	1980/ 2220	10	1980/ 2220

Source : Bureau of Secondary Education, Ministry of Education, Culture and Sports.

The following objectives for science education are in support of the major thrust of the Bureau in the context of science and mathematics education.

To enhance his functional literacy and his capability as a responsible and productive member of his community an elementary school child should be able to :

(a) Demonstrate acquisition of intellectual processes such as the following, by applying these processes to broaden knowledge : (i) observing and describing, (ii) inferring, (iii) measuring, (iv) classifying, (v) experimenting, (vi) controlling variables, (vii) defining operationally, (viii) seeking patterns and relations, formulating conjectures or hypotheses from observed patterns and verifying them, (ix) arriving at conclusion by inference, (x) describing quantitative relations in words or in mathematical symbolism—*e.g.* charts, graphs, expressions, equations, (xi) visualizing or constructing and interpreting conceptual models, (xii) estimating, and (xiii) calculating or performing mathematical manipulations;

(b) Demonstrate understanding of basic mathematical knowledge : (i) numbers and number systems, and (ii) some properties of geometric figures;

(c) Demonstrate comprehension of fundamental concepts and principles in the physical and biological science and their intelligent application to appropriate life situations and the local environment;

(d) Apply mathematical and scientific knowledge in seeking answers to problem situations encountered in relation to the home, family and the country; and

(e) Display scientific attitudes such as : (i) open-mindedness, (ii) curiosity, (iii) persistence, (iv) intellectual honesty, (v) recognizing the approximate nature of measurement, and (vi) recognizing the tentativeness of inductive conclusions/scientific information.

Objectives of Science Education : Secondary Level. In the ten-year system of education, no distinction is made between upper and lower secondary. The four-year high school period is considered as a four-year continuum; objectives are stated in terms of the entire four-year secondary period.

To attain potential as a rational human being and to acquire the essential foundation for development into a productive and versatile citizen, the student in the secondary school science should be able to :

(a) Demonstrate understanding of basic science concepts in such ways as : (i) describing and explaining natural phenomena, (ii) identifying scientific principles involved in a particular situation, and (iii) applying concepts to new situations;

(b) Apply the processes of sciences in such ways as : (i) identifying a problem and defining and delimiting it, (ii) constructing hypotheses, (iii) making accurate observations, (iv) collecting, recording and organizing data, (v) analyzing and interpreting data, (vi) designing and performing simple experiments/investigations, (vii) making independent conclusions based on relevant data, (viii) making inferences, (ix) making predictions based on a given set of data, and (x) making and using conceptual models in science;

(c) Display scientific attitudes such as : (i) recognizing the limitations of science, (iii) weighing evidence, (iii) suspending judgement when evidence is insufficient, (iv) willingness to be convinced by evidence, (v) open-mindedness, (vi) persistence, (vii) tolerance, (viii) curiosity, (ix) recognizing the tentativeness of conclusions/scientific information, (x) respect for life, (xi) intellectual honesty, (xii) co-operating in working with others, and (xiii) objective, unemotional discussion of controversial issues;

(d) Enhance the range and quality of the individual and group participation in the basic functions of society by recognizing the social implications of science in relation to man and his environment such as those related to conservation, population, health and sanitation, agriculture, medicine, and advances in technology; and

(e) Demonstrate work skills by utilizing science and health concepts as applied to: (i) community health, (ii) conservation of natural resources, (iii) drug action, (iv) food production, (v) malnutrition, and (vi) population growth.

Development and Revision of Curricula

The development of curricula is based on syllabuses, outlines, or writing briefs prepared by the curriculum units of the Bureau of Elementary and Secondary Education. The actual preparation of textbooks may be undertaken by the private sector (individual authors and publishing companies). The curriculum development centres may or may not choose to participate in textbook writing but their staff are used as consultants in determining objectives content and organization of the curriculum as expressed in the writing briefs. The bureaux may themselves undertake preparation of textbooks particularly for new or experimental courses.

The curricula are revised approximately once in a decade; for example, new science textbooks were completed from the mind—1970s to the end of the 1970s. A new elementary curriculum goes into effect in 1983 for grade I, and one grade yearly will be introduced until 1988 when the full grades I to VI curricula will be implemented. The new curriculum for the Bureau of Secondary Education was implemented in 1973. New textbooks in science and mathematics (and in other subject areas, too) become available from the curriculum centres during the period 1976-1980. The Bureau has now commissioned a nation-wide study to determine, among other matters, whether or not the curriculum needs improvement or revision.

Curriculum Content

The concern for real-life problems and attention to social issues (science-related) are evident at the primary level in the Elementary *Learning Continuum.* Key behaviour indicators in terms of desirable habits, attitudes and values are identified in each learning unit. One example from each grade level will illustrate this point : grade I, practice habits of cleanliness; grade II, practice health habits that make one grow; grade III, practice ways of keeping one's surroundings clean; grade IV, help in the conservation of soil, grade V, help conserve electricity at home; and grade VI, co-operate with some government agencies in their efforts to control floods.

At the secondary level the first two science courses are environmentally oriented. The first year high school courses deals with physical science content in the context of the student's own experience and his environment. For example, the concept of measuring forces is introduced in 'How many newtons do you weigh?' and matter is studied in 'What are things made of?' This first year textbook includes current concerns like : going metric, source of energy in the Philippines, slow down soil loss, make poor soil rich, salt making, and typhoons. The second year textbook has one whole chapter on human reproduction which includes family planning and methods of birth control. The last unit, Man and his Role in the Environment, provides basic concepts regarding man and his ecosystem, then goes into applications and implications of these interactions such as : improper disposal of waste, chemicals to kill insects, dirty air, improper logging, increase of eloping population, and how can a Filipino conserve his environment?

Although the third year chemistry textbook, Chemistry in your environment, deals with the basic chemistry concepts, these are well illustrated in terms of the student's real life experiences and social issues. For example, the concept of colloids is related to everyday colloids the students are likely to encounter like paints, fruits jellies, India ink, mayonnaise, milk, soapsuds, butter, cheese or smoke. Also, applied and socially-oriented modules are introduced. For example the flow chart for Chapter One, Chemistry and You, shows at what points the following modules may be introduced: about burning, potable water from sea water, refined salt from coarse salt, salt from sea water, chemical language, nata de arroz, waste not, want not chemical arithmetic, money in rabbits, and fish conservation and preservation.

The physics course uses the book Physics in your environment, which is written so that even schools with minimal facilities should be able to use it. Also some activities can be carried out at home using ordinary household items. Some topics which are socially oriented are introduction in comic book style using real-life situations, for example, energy conservation is introduced in terms of a dialogue between a teacher and a student on the local situation concerning the energy crisis. A visit to a nuclear power station is also in comic-book style, illustrating in the context of a local power plant what questions students are likely to ask and the answer they are likely to get from such a visit.

All of the foregoing examples are based on the government text books widely used in the public schools and in several private schools. The teachers' guide for these books serves as the detailed syllabus. Every teacher who uses these books is provided with the teachers' guide.

Evaluation

Student achievement is evaluated at school level. Large schools, with several classes at each grade level may have departmental tests. These are tests to which each teacher contributes, *e.g.*, science teachers will all contribute to the science departmental tests. These are 'long' tests and are given at each grading period (there are usually four grading periods a year). At this level, the tests are all teacher-made tests.

There are no public examinations either at the end of the primary or the secondary levels of education. However, those who wish to proceed to tertiary level institutions must pass a national college entrance examination conducted by the National Educational Testing Centre of the Ministry of Education, Culture and sports. Those who pass this examination qualify to seek admission in the different institutions of higher learning. However, some institutions have their own entrance examination which students must pass to gain admission. A third examination is given in some universities by some of the professional colleges which administer their own entrance examinations and interview applicants for admission. Thus, at the ranking institutions of higher learning, a student must pass there entrance examinations. At the tertiary level, including entrance examinations, the examinations world tend to be mostly cognitive, but during interviews (at some colleges) attempts to probe into the affective domain are made.

At the elementary and secondary levels, apart from the long or periodic tests, teachers tend to give several short, quizzes, which may be given weekly, every few days or even daily. Long or short quizzes are mostly cognitive tests. Affective evaluation tends to be observational; anecdotal records may be kept by some teachers or some other means of recording may be used.

At these levels, the report cards of the students usually include some record of behaviour which belongs to the effective domain (courtesy, effort, co-operation, sociability, punctuality, conduct and others which demonstrate growth in desirable attitudes). Grades (or marks) are given for these affective behaviours at each grading period. The marks may be in percentages or in the form of qualitative statements like poor, fair, good, outstanding.

Science Activities, Laboratory work and equipment

Elementary Level. At the elementary level, the curriculum is heavily activity oriented. Assuming the teachers follow the guide and the textbooks, the time available for experiments and activities is grade III, 64 per cent; grade IV, 65 per cent; grade V, 50 per cent; and grade VI, 50 per cent. This is based on the existing books and teaching guides used in the schools. It may change during the years 1985-1988 when the new curriculum will be implemented gradually through to grade VI.

Secondary Level. At the secondary level the time devoted to laboratory or practical work and activities varies approximately as follows (depending on the required number of experiments and activities): Year 1, 13-21 per cent; Year 2,22 per cent; Year 3, 10 per cent; and Year 4, 9 per cent.

The one national and four city special science high schools, devote more time to laboratory work for two reasons : (i) they offer more science courses enabling students to take two or more science courses per year; and (ii) most of them require students to take two science course at each year level of the last two years of secondary school.

Teachers evaluate practical work almost wholly on the basis of the laboratory reports which students submit. Practical examinations are rare, although the grades given to laboratory reports are considered in determining the student's grade in a science course. In national examinations, practical items (laboratory oriented) are generally not included. However, once a year, provincial regional and national tests are given to select the outstanding science students (cash prizes and other incentives are given). This selection involves quizzes and practical laboratory exercises or problems which involve practical work.

Regarding laboratory facilities in the secondary schools the following is a rough estimate of the situation.

	General science	Biology	Chemistry	Physics	Average
	Per cent				
Practically no equipment	50	40	22	20	33
Poorly equipped	40	35	55	60	48
Moderately equipped	9	23	20	17	17
Well equipped	1	2	3	3	2

The School Science Equipment Development Project (SSEDP), a UNDP/UNESCO—supported project was officially approved in June, 1975 and implementation began towards the end of the same year. The National Science Development Board, (now the National Science and Technology Authority) was the main proponent with the University of the Phillippines System (University of the Philippines Science Education Centre and College of Engineering) and the Ministry of Education, Culture and Sports as co-operating agencies.

The project provided for the establishment of a centre for the design and production of science equipment for the elementary and secondary levels at the national Institute of Science and Technology. The SSEDP collaborated with the University of the Philippines Science Education Center (UPSEC) in the development of curriculum materials.

The project developed a kit each for elementary science, high school science, chemistry, biology, and physics.

Sub-projects for the distribution of the elementary science and high school science kit were undertaken in 1979-1980 and 1981-1982 respectively. The goal was to give the 30,000 public elementary schools and about 5,000 high schools one kit each. To-date, about 12,000 elementary schools have received the elementary kits and about 1,000 high school science kits are about ready for distribution.

The SSEDP officially terminated in December, 1982 and the production technology has ben transferred to the private sector.

The percentages of locally produced and imported items in each kit are as follows :

	Elementary science %	*Biology* %	*Chemistry* %	*Physics* %	*General science* %
Items available from local manufactures	90	70	40	90	90
Imported items	10	30	60	10	10

Educational Technology

The Science Education Centre conducts in-service education (short-term, non-credit mini-courses) in the use of the VTR system, overhead projectors, slides, and tape-recorders as well as in the production of materials using these audio-visual technologies. Clientele for such courses are generally from teacher education institutions, the Regional Science Teaching Centers (RSTCs), tertiary level teachers of science and selected high school teachers. The latter group, in addition, generally request simpler visual aids which do not rely on the availability of hardware. This is particularly true of groups teaching in disadvantaged areas. So, making charts and similar low-cost teaching aids, and using some science education games are also included in such courses, depending on the participating groups.

At present, UPSEC and seven RSTCs have VTR systems. The one at UPSEC is sophisticated and is production oriented. Teacher education and student lessons which will be shared with the seven RSTCs are being prepared. The RSTCs are well located in the sense that they serve different geographical areas. Their VTR systems are used in micro-teaching and (with the Betamax unit which they all have) are able to show concept films and films illustrating teaching methodologies in science which they can produce themselves or purchase from UPSEC. UPSEC assists some of the centres, which request help, to edit their own VTR lessons.

A continuing project of UPSEC is the production of single concept VTR lessons in science and mathematics which can be used independently of the classroom or as a supplement. It is hoped that some of these VTR lessons may be broadcast during 1983-1984.

Computer education is in its infancy in teacher education. It is practically non-existent in the schools. But in the summer of 1983 some private schools offered summer courses for children in computer education. This occurred only in Metro manila but it is likely to continue and spread henceforth. These programmes were conducted with groups external to the school system.

UPSEC has a plan to train teachers, but teacher education mini-courses must be prepared first. There will probably be a time lag of at least a year before UPSEC can begin microcomputer lessons for teachers. The overall plan is to integrate educational technology with microcomputers in order to reach a wider audience who have no access to microcomputers. But this will come much later, after expertise had been developed not only in its use but also in the production of software applicable to the local situation.

Teacher Education

The minimum qualification prescribed for teachers at both the elementary and secondary level is a bachelor's degree in elementary education and in secondary education respectively. All teachers have these degrees; there are some exceptions—teachers without their degrees in education but with a basic degree in some other field like pharmacy, engineering or commerce. In such cases, the teachers are required to take 18 units of education if they expect to remain in the teaching profession. It is safe to say then that in the country as a whole all teachers have a basic four-year undergraduate (bachelor's) degree. A number of teachers have master's degrees or several units towards a master's degree. Since all teachers have bachelor's degree, 'unqualified' teachers in the country refer to those teachers who do not have majors and minors or at least 12 academic credits in the subject area they are teaching. This is often true of science teachers in the last two years of high school, i.e., chemistry and physics teachers. Extremely few graduates finish with majors in these areas. So, these subjects are likely to be taught by a non-majors; some may not even have a major in science or mathematics and would have specializations in language or special sciences or home economics. This situation is not uncommon in small rural schools.

The overcome this situation the National Science and Technology Authority (NSTA) has been funding summer institutes since the late 1960s in about seven to ten regional science teaching centres located all over the country. In 1975-1979 the World Bank project on science education strengthened the physical facilities of the most disadvantaged centres. These NSTA-supported in-service programmes for science and mathematics teachers have emphasized the learning of science subject matter, teaching techniques, use of educational technology, improvization of apparatus and laboratory techniques. The NSTA has, from the same period, been supporting master's degree programmes for teachers from the RSTCs and from the regional offices of the Ministry of Education, Culture and Sports. About 472 teachers have been trained in this programme. In addition to these programmes the Ministry meets the problem of unqualified teachers through : (a) mass training (whenever new curricula are introduced) which reaches almost all teachers of a given subject; (b) specially designed training programmes (short-term competency-oriented intensive courses) at the Philippine Normal College and in the University of the Philippines (the Science Education Center has charge of the science and mathematics programmes) to learn specified skills and concepts; (c) distance learning which uses radio and print materials (only two or three regions have opted to use this strategy); (d) echo seminars conducted by Ministry supervisors and other staff; and (e) the Bagoi Vacation Normal School which had an enrolment of over 900 in 1980-1981, 62 M.A. graduates in 1980, and 52 M.A. graduates in 1981.

Special summer institutes have been supported by the NSTA in seven to ten RSTCs each year for over a decade. These institutes are intensive six week training programmes for which attending teachers may earn about 56 graduate units. Statistics collected over the period 1971-1981 show that the 1,562 chemistry teachers who have attended comprise the largest number of participants followed in order by physics teachers, integrated science, biology and mathematics teachers. The following figures show that when comparing the number of teachers in each subject area there has been a much larger proportion of integrated science teachers attending the institute than any others.

Subject area	*Year level*	*No. of teachers*	*Percentage trained at Science Institute*
			Per cent
Mathematics	First to fourth year	9,645	5
Integrated Science I	First year high school	2,411	60
Biology	Second year high school	2,411	37
Chemistry	Third year high school	4,822	32
Physics	Fourth year high school	4,822	31

The total attendance of 5,898 science teachers show that the NSTA/RSTC-supported special summer institutes have reached a substantial number of teachers. The programme needs to be periodically revised and updated in order to enable the teachers to keep on returning to the institutes after so many years. A renewal period of five years would be desirable.

The minimum requirements set by the Bureau of Higher education for the undergraduate degrees in elementary education (BSEE) and in secondary education (BSE) are shown on the following page.

	Elementary units	*Secondary units*
General education	102	93
Professional education	36	30
Electives	0	0
Area of specialization/ concentration		

	Elementary units	*Secondary units*
(a) major	18	24
(b) minor	-	9
Total	156	156

The programmes of the state university for the same degrees follow :

	Elementary units	*Secondary units*
General education	54	58
Professional education	55	37
Major/Area of concentration	18	31-37
Minor	-	12
Others	10	
Total	137	150

The minimum requirement for laboratory work is 2 per cent of the total curriculum (four units) but most of the larger colleges and universities require much more. In the University of the Philippines, from 8 per cent to 29 per cent of the total programme time is spent on laboratory work depending on the major area of study.

Practice teaching or teaching internship is usually carried out during the last semester of the senior year (fourth year). Some institutions require students to undertake in-campus teaching first before doing practice teaching in actual schools. For these courses, the evaluation of students is performance-based.

For science majors, the required laboratory work varies from a minimum of 2 per cent to about 29 per cent of the total programme.

Performance in the laboratory is generally considered as part of the total rating for a course.

Teachers who wish to have permanent appointments in the public schools, or who wish to receive priority in applying for a given position, must pass the civil service examination for teachers. Teachers in the private schools do not need this qualification.

Research

Research in science education related to the elementary and secondary levels of education and the teachers concerned with these levels are conducted by students at the master level and by a few at the doctoral level. Some staff members of the College of Education also conduct some studies but these would be minimal; most studies are conducted by their students. Being a research and development centre, the staff of the Science Education Centre of the University of the Philippines conduct research studies as part of their regular duties.

Research in science education is of the following type:

(a) Learning studies (e.g. learning styles of students, environment factors that effect learning, cognitive development in children, concept learning, students' misconceptions in science, difficulties of students in learning science subjects);

(b) Competencies of teachers and students in science and mathematics (e.g. teaching competence in terms of concepts and professional skills);

(c) Impact of training programmes;

(d) Language studies (mostly on problems in learning science);

(e) Curriculum evaluation;

(f) Student performance (achievement tests on selected concepts and skills);

(g) Vocabulary studies, including reading levels in science;

(h) Needs and assessment studies of rural communities (as a basis for curriculum development);

(i) Classroom interaction;

(j) Survey of facilities in science;

(k) Status survey (of science education); and

(l) Policy level study—a research-based study to develop a science education development plan for the Philippines. It is a joint project of the Ministry and NSTA. The aim is to produce a plan that will provide guidelines for policies, programmes, projects.

The results of these studies are available mainly in the libraries of the College of Education. In the case of the Science Education Centre, the studies are available in monograph form; usually summaries of research studies conducted by the staff. The clientele for these monographs are graduate students, teachers and educational institutions, both local and foreign. Technical reports of studies are available from the Centre's staff but are not for general dissemination.

The Science Education Centre itself uses many of these studies for its own work. Several of these are used as baseline data for developing materials, for planning, and for designing short-term courses.

Other institutions involved in research, mostly large scale surveys, are the Centre for Educational Measurement (a private organization) and the Ministry of Education, Culture and Sports, which conducts national surveys on such topics as the textbooks used by schoolchildren, on student performance, evaluative studies of various aspects of education.

Popularization of Science and Technology

There are several ways employed to popularize science and reach out-of-school youth. Science clubs and science camps are well organized and receive encouragement and support from the Science Promotion Institute of NSTA. Science club advisers meet to plan activities for their clubs. During the long vacations, science camps are organized for students and teachers where many opportunities for learning outdoor science are provided.

Perhaps one of the best organized activities is what is known as TOYS (The Outstanding Youth Scientists) each year. Through the conduct of a series of science fairs and science quizzes, starting at municipal level through provincial, city, regional and up to national levels, participants from all over the country undergo a series of selection activities. The board of judges usually comprises science academics and the scientific corporate communities. At the final selection stage, seven outstanding participants from the science fairs (two from the colleges, three from secondary and two from elementary) and three from the science quiz are selected, making a total of ten. These ten are then adjudged The Outstanding Youth Scientists (TOYS) of the year. This programme reaches practically all schools. Furthermore, the venue for national selections is rotated; the 1982 selection, for example, took place in Leyte.

The funding of TOYS has been a co-operative venture between the NSTA and the Phillipine Jaycees. Ogranization and operation of the activities in the field are accomplished by staff of the NSTA and the Ministry.

The objectives of TOYS are to : (a) develop and sustain youth interest in the pursuance of scientific endeavour; (b) provided an attainable goal in the scientific world of the youth; and (c) provide appropriate recognition for potential leaders in science.

Other ways of reaching the general public include the use of TV programmes. The NSTA has sponsored programmes for adults such as Carl Sagan's series on the universe. Currently, the National Media Production Centre,.with UPSEC, plans to try out a science programme for children.

The private sector has also continuously supported and organized a science Quiz Bee every year. Recently this has become regional; Asian countries have been invited to participate.

Another way of disseminating science to the countryside is through science and technology modules which deal with the concerns of individuals and society, either urban or rural Examples are health, nutrition and sanitation modules as well as those dealing with livelihood projects. UPSEC has produced some of these and they are sometimes used by organizations that work with population groups that need such inputs. There are several agencies of government with similar modules in their extension programmes like University of the Philippines, Los Baños; the Ministries of Agriculture and Natural Resources; Bureau of Fisheries. The difference between these and UPSEC modules is that the latter are more pedagogically oriented, attempt more to present materials to suit the target group and illustrate whenever possible the relation to science principles.

Current Innovations

There is a nationwide attempt to teach values and change the attitudes of teachers. This is different from earlier attempts, in that the effort is concerted, organized, monitored thoroughly and well funded by the Ministry. A select group of some 350 teachers were trained intensively for several months in the Development Academy of the Philippines. This group will now be travelling all over the country conducting training sessions for groups of teachers. This will take approximately four years at the end of which all or most teachers will have undergone training.

Outstanding science and mathematics teachers are selected from regional and national levels all over the country. From the regional group (one outstanding teacher per region) the most outstanding two or three are selected for these awards which include cash as well as trophies.

The private sector (Jaycees) and the NSTA select and award prizes to outstanding youth scientists. Another example of private (industry) effort is the National Quize Bee which began as the project of a group of business companies and which has now expended its activities to the ASIAN region.

In research, the UPSEC is undertaking a study of all the science books which are now widely distributed by the Textbook Board Secretariat. The study proposes to analyse the match between the curriculum demands and the cognitive level of the students.

The University of the Philippines and a few other leading universities are offering degrees in computer science, UPSEC, and a few other leading teacher education institutions, conduct staff seminars on the use of micro-computers.

Seven of the RSTCs are using VTR systems as part of their regular teaching methodology. Further VTR system will be made once UPSEC finishes the series of teacher education VTR lessons it is preparing. An exchange of VTR lessons with RECSAM* in Malysia is planned as a way of speeding up the collection of relevant VTR science lessons, and of improving them.

* Regional Centre for Science and Mathematics, Penang.

18

Singapore

Singapore has embarked on an industrial development programme emphasizing high technology and skills. As the country depends only on its manpower resources, no effort has been spared to ensure that science education, both formal and non-formal, is provided for the young and for adults in order to met the needs of an industrializing society. In the schools and colleges, science education is aimed at cultivating the enquiring mind and developing scientific literacy and creativity. Out-of-schools, science programmes and activities are conducted by various institutions and organizations to promote awareness and appreciation of science and technology and their implications in society.

Structure of School Education

The New Education System in Singapore was phased in for Primary 1 and Secondary I in 1980 and 1981 respectively. This new system takes into account variations in intellectual ability among pupils and makes allowance for them to proceed at their own rates of progress. It also gives emphasis to the bilingual policy of the government. Pupils are given six to eight years to complete primary education, four or five years to complete secondary education and two or three years for pre-university education.

Primary Education. Formal primary education begins at age 6. All pupils follow a common curriculum for the first three years of primary education which emphasizes language learning in English and a second language which may be Malay or Chinese or Tamil. At the end of Primary 3, pupils are streamed into one of three courses according to their academic attainment :

a) *Normal Bilingual Course (N—course)*. This course is for average and above average pupils and leads to the Primary School Leaving Examination (PSLE) after three more years, at the end of Primary 6.

b) *Extended Bilingual Course (E-course)*. This is for slow learners and leads also to the PSLE but after five more years, at the end of Primary 8.

***Figure 1.* Structure of the new education system Primary level**

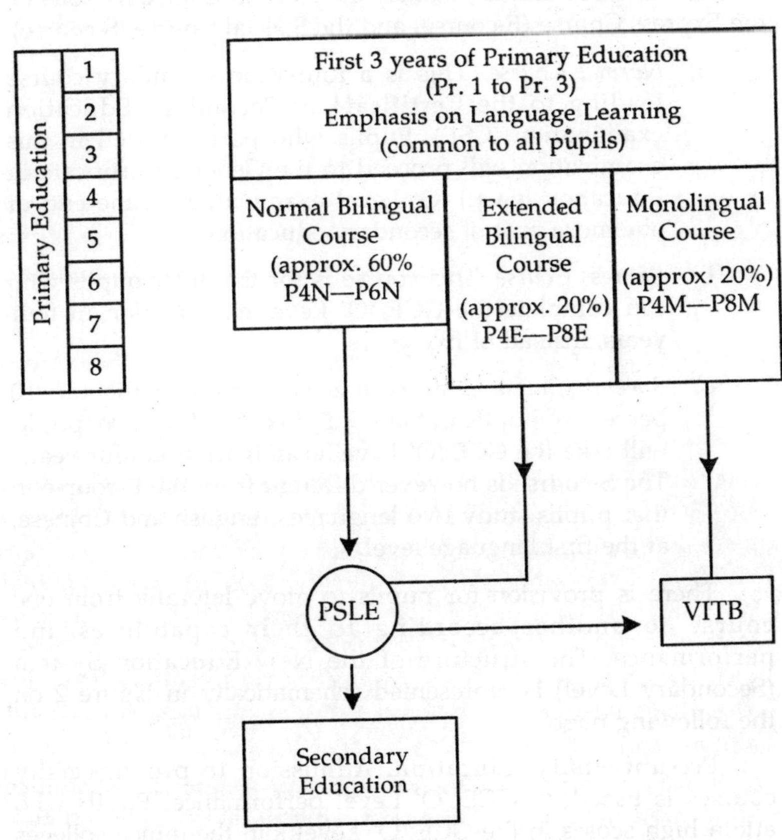

c) *Monolingual Corse (M-course).* This course is for very slow learners and emphasizes the study of only one language. At the end of five years in the course (Primary 8) pupils will be given an assessment and then channelled to the Vocational and Industrial Training Board (VITB) for vocational training.

The structure of the New Education System (Primary Level) is given schematically in Figure 1. Lateral movements between courses may be decided by school principals based on the progress of the pupils.

Secondary Education. Based on the results of the PSLE, pupils are promoted to the secondary level and join Secondary I for one of three courses, namely the Normal Course (N-cousre), the Express Course (E-course) and the Special Course (S-course).

a) *Normal Course.* This is a four-year secondary course leading to the Certificate in Secondary Education examination (CSE). Pupils who perform well in this examination will proceed to the General Certificate in Education (GCE) 'O' Level examination at the end of one more year of secondary education.

b) *Express Course.* This course is for the abler pupils who can complete the GCE 'O' Level examination in four years, instead of five years.

c) *Special Course.* This course is offered to the top 10 percent of pupils in the PSLE. Like the E-course, pupils will take the GCE 'O' Level examination in four years. The S-course is however different from the E-course in that pupils study two languages, English and Chinese, at the first language level.

There is provision for pupils to move laterally from one course to another according to their capabilities and performance. The structure of the New Education System (Secondary Level) is represented schematically in Figure 2 on the following page.

Pre-university Education. Admission to pre-university courses is based on GCE 'O' Level performance. Pupils who attain high scores in the GCE 'O' Level join the junior colleges which conduct two-year courses leading to the GCE 'A' Level examination. Pupils of average ability who satisfy the admission criteria for pre-university education are admitted to secondary schools offering three-year courses leading to the GCE 'A' Level.

Pupil Enrolment. In 1983, three were 289, 346 pupils at the various primary levels, 158,796 pupils from Secondary I to IV and 19,394 pupils at the pre-niversity level.

Science Education in Schools

Science as a Subject in the Curriculum

a) *Primary level.* Formal Science is not included in the Primary 1 and 2 curriculum but is taught and learned indirectly through language and other activities. Science is taught formally from Primary 3 onwards and it is one of the four subjects offered at the PSLE.

b) *Secondary level.* At the lower secondary (i.e. Secondary I and II) General Science is one of eight core subjects in the curriculum.

A science subject is compulsory at the upper secondary levels (*i.e.* Secondary III and IV) for the Special and Express Courses. Pupils may choose one, two or three science subjects from biology; chemistry; physics; science (physics, chemistry); science (physics, biology); science (chemistry, biology); combined science; science/integrated science offered as a double subject); and human and social biology.

As a balanced curriculum is stressed at the upper secondary levels, pupils usually offer one or two science subjects at the GCE 'O' Level with a number of pupils taking three science subjects out of a seven-or-more subject curriculum.

For the N-course, a science subject is not compulsory from Secondary III level. Science (physics, chemistry), science (physics, biology), science (chemistry, biology) and human and social biology are offered as electives. A recent survey on the first batch of Secondary III N-course pupils shows that only 47.5 per cent of classes at this level offered science as a subject.

At the pre-university level, the science subject options are : biology, chemistry, physics, physical science, computer science, additional chemistry, and additional physics. Pupils are normally

Figure 2. Schematic representation of new education system Secondary level

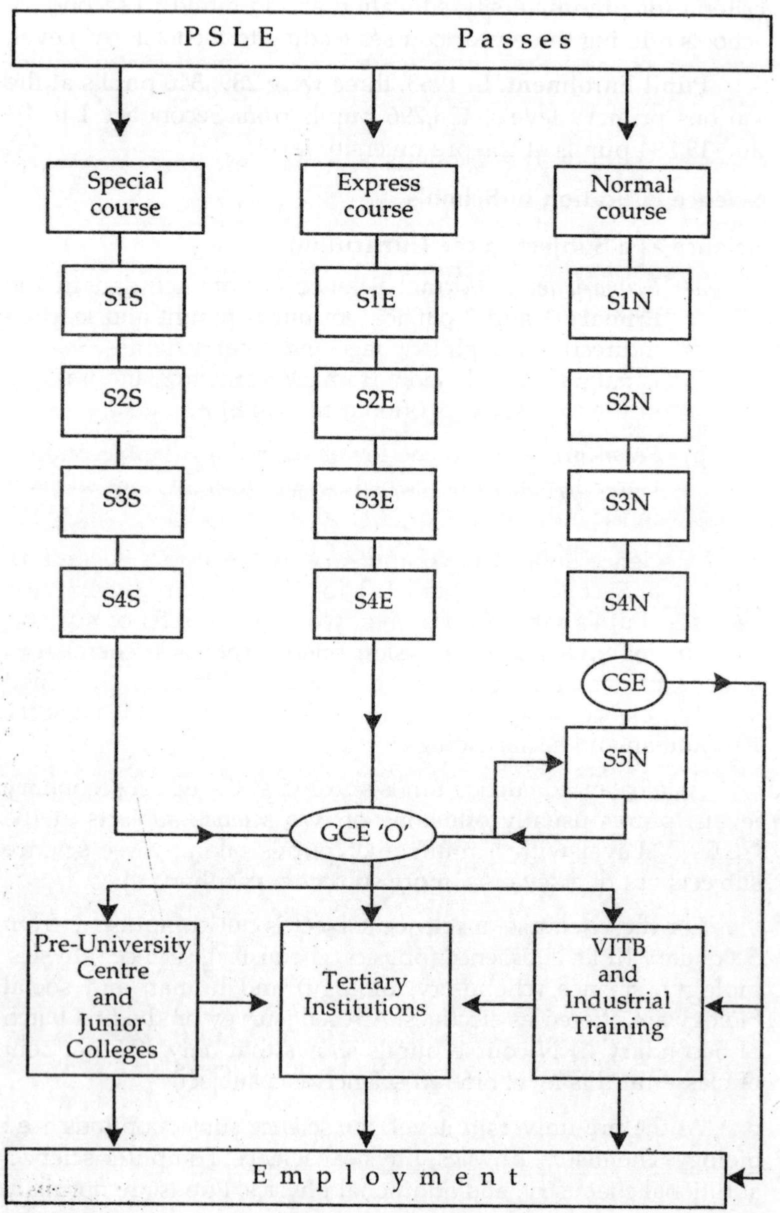

permitted to enrol for a maximum of three science subjects provided that physical science is not taken together with physics or chemistry.

Curriculum Time for Science. The school curriculum time for the teaching/learning of science ranges from 1¾ hours a week at Primary 3 level to a maximum of 21 hours a week at pre-university level. The number of hours per week of formal instruction in science at the various levels is shown on the following page.

Medium of Instruction. Since most of the advances in scientific knowledge are reported in English, Singapore has adopted the policy of teaching mathematics and science only in English to both English-medium and non-English-medium schools. The implementation of this language policy was phased into all schools in 1978 for Primary 1-3 and in 1981 for Secondary I. In 1984 and henceforth, mathematics and science subjects will be taught and examined in English in all schools up to the GCE 'O' Level.

Table 1. Instruction time for science in schools

Level	*Total curriculum time per week (hours)*	*No. of teaching hours for science per week*
Pr. 3	23¾	1¾
Pr. 4N/E-6N/8E	23¾—24 $\frac{7}{12}$	2¾
Sec. I—II	25	3¾-4
Sec. III—IV	25	3—4*
Junior College	37½	5—7*
Pre-U Centres	25	4—5*

* Hours per week per each science subjet taken

The Science Curriculum. Science syllabuses for the primary and lower secondary levels of all courses and upper secondary levels of the N-course are prepared by the Ministry of Education for use in the schools. At the pre-university levels and the upper secondary levels (*i.e.* Secondary III and IV) of the E-course and S-course, no formal teaching syllabuses are prescribed and schools are guided by the examination syllabuses set for the GCE 'A' and 'O' Level examinations respectively.

Primary Science Syllabuses. Since the introduction of science as a formal subject in the primary school curriculum in 1958, the primary science syllabus has undergone four revisions. In the 1961 revision, contents for Primary 1 and 2 were trimmed down. In 1971, a new syllabus aimed at teaching basic science concepts, fundamental scientific skills and correct scientific attitudes was introduced. With the emphasis on language learning at the primary levels, the science syllabus was further modified in 1978 to enable non-English medium pupils to cope with the science programme that was being taught in English. With the implementation of the New Education System a new syllabus was introduced in 1982 tailored for the N-course and E-course pupils. This syllabus was first phased into Primary 3 (N-course) and Primary 4 (E-course) in 1982 and will be extended to all other levels by 1985. Table—2 shows the time frame for the phasing-in of the new syllabus.

Table—2. Time frame for phasing-in the new primary syllabus

Year	3N	4N	5N	6N	4E	5E	6E	7E	8E
1981	X	X	X	X	X	X			
1982	/	X	X	X	/	X	X		
1983	/	/	X	X	/	/	X	X	
1984	/	/	/	X	/	/	/	/	X
1985	/	/	/	/	/	/	/	/	/

Key: X—Existing syllabus/ — New syllabus

The primary science course is intended to help pupils:

a) Acquire simple scienctific skills, namely, observation, classification, ways of finding out, collation and interpretation of observations, making inferences and communicating their experiences in writing as well as orally;

b) Develop an interest to learn about objects and events in the environment by asking questions, formulating ideas and performing purposeful activities;

c) Develop a progressive understanding of the ideas of change, cause and effect relationships, energy, matter, the characteristics of life and the interactions between the living and non-living systems of the environment; and

d) Become aware of science as part of human activity and the contribution of science to daily life.

The theme throughout the new syllabus is 'Man in his environment'. The content structure of the syllabus focuses on man's constant interactions with living and non-living objects which exist in his environment. The concept of matter and energy as components of the environment which are constantly undergoing interaction and change flows through the whole science programme.

Learning situations that are correlated to life situations are provided in many instances. Pupils are made aware of the importance of fuel as a source of energy in their life, and of the need to conserve energy at all times and in various ways. The topics on force, energy, work and simple machines link the concept of energy to the scientific applications of science and technology. It is intended to teach pupils to appreciate how man, as opposed to other animals, is able to make use of technology to manipulate the living and non-living systems.

The syllabus also includes a section on the dependence of all life forms on a healthy and balanced environment. The pupils' attention is drawn to the causes and ill effects of pollution as an undesirable change in the environment. On the whole, the syllabus provides ample opportunities for the learning of process skills and for the development of creativity and intellectual growth.

Lower Secondary Science Syllabus. The General Science syllabus for Secondary I and II was first implemented in 1962. Except for the introduction of SI units in 1972, the contents of the syllabus remained unchanged until the end of 1982. The revised lower secondary science syllabus is designed for pupils in the Special, Express and Normal course. First introduced to Secondary I Pupils in 1983, it will be phased-in at both Secondary I and II levels by 1984. The aims of science education at the lower secondary stage are to :

a) Provide pupils with the essential scientific knowledge and skills that will meet their educational and vocational needs;

b) Develop science concepts and an understanding of our physical and biological environment;

c) Develop the pupils' ability to use the methods of science;

d) Provide a science course which is both relevant and meaningful in the technological environment of today; and

e) Enable pupils to appreciate the humanistic aspects science.

e) Enable pupils to appreciate the humanistic aspects of science.

The revised syllabus embodies not only the fundamental principles of physics, chemistry and biology but also includes some environmental and ecological concepts. Unlike the traditional and contemporary science curricula, the lower secondary science syllabus is updated to include conceptual schemes and scientific processes. The concepts found in the various disciplines are integrated into unified themes to provide a multi-disciplinary approach. The emphasis is on the development of an inquiring mind by which pupils are guided to discover things for themselves, analyse data collected and draw inferences which they may apply to new situations logically and creatively. Included in the syllabus are a number of topics which focus on social issues relevant to the learners and draw the learners' attention to the moral obligation they have to their community.

Among such topics is one on water consumption in which pupils are made aware of the heavy demands made on their water supply by rapid population growth, urbanization and industrialization, and hence the necessity for water conservation. Another illustration of topics related to life's problems is one on ecology. The pupils' attention is drawn to the interference of over-population, urbanization, industrialization, pollution and depletion of natural resources on the balance in an ecosystem and how the environment, such as the school or the community, can be improved by organized action, conservation and wise management.

Upper Secondary and Pre-university Levels. The N-course pupils in the upper secondary levels follow the Certificate in Secondary Education (CSE) syllabuses in the subjects science and human and social biology. The syllabuses of both these subjects include about 60 per cent of the GCE 'O' Level syllabus content and were introduced for the first time in 1983. As many pupils in the N-course will terminate their education at the CSE level and hence will not pursue a formal science education after that, the syllabuses are aimed at providing a basic scientific literacy with sufficient science content to enable most of these pupils to follow further vocational training courses. The functional aspects of science are stressed and there are opportunities provided for pupils to develop a scientific approach to the solution of everyday problems. Issues such as breast-feeding, family planning, infection, diseases immunity, individual and community responsibilities are included in the human and social biology syllabus. The science course at the upper secondary (E - and S—course) and the pre-university levels are guided by the long established GCE 'O' and 'A' Level syllabuses.

Evaluation. Evaluation of pupil achievements at all levels is through continual assessments and semestrial examinations. Pupils are continually assessed throughout the year by way of daily exercises, class tests, practical assignments and projects. Two semestrial examinations are conducted, one at mid-year and the other, the final examination, at the end of the year. Besides being a formative evaluation, continual assessments are used, together with the semestrial examinations for promotion of pupils to the next grade level.

At the Primary 6 level, science is offered as one of the four subjects in the PSLE. The mode of the examination is a written paper of 1½ hours duration consisting of both objective and structured-type questions. The CSE examination, a joint examination of the Singapore Ministry of Education and the University of Cambridge (United Kingdom) Local Examinations Syndicate, will be held for the first time for N-course pupils in

1984. The examination for each science subject will consist of one written paper which is graded. There is no practical examination for science in the CSE.

The GCE 'O' and 'A' 'Level examinations are long standing examinations jointly conducted by the Singapore Ministry of Education and the Cambridge Local Examination Syndicate. The syllabuses and specimen papers for the various science options at these two levels are widely known. Generally, the public examinations take into consideration the instructional objectives of the science programmes at the different levels and stages. As the syllabuses change from content bias to the understanding of broad concepts and the learning of process skills, the style and emphasis of the examination are modified accordingly.

Activities and Laboratory Work. Science is basically an experimental discipline and practical activities form an integral part of science teaching/learning. At all levels, pupil or activity-centered science teaching is advocated and at least one-third to one half of the instruction time is generally set aside for practical work.

At the primary and lower secondary levels the revised syllabuses emphasize the importance of involving pupils in problem-solving through observation, inquiry and discovery. This is coupled with the use of materials such as workbooks published by the Curriculum Development Institute of Singapore (CDIS); a Division of the Singapore Ministry of Education. Teachers are moving from a teacher-centred and content-oriented teaching style to the inquiry/activity-centred teaching approach. Activities which include simple projects designed to promote investigation and discovery rate introduced in lessons aimed at stimulating critical and creative thinking through the use of process skills.

At the upper secondary and pre-university leaves, practical work is conducted more intensively in subjects requiring practical examinations. Of the science subjects offered at GCE 'O' and 'A' Levels, general science, combined science and human and social biology have no practical examination. Instead they have written questions that test the practical applications or laboratory work done during the course. For subjects where practical work is examinable, the practical examination carries a weighting of 20-25 per cent. In all cases, the practical examinations require pupils to carry our experiments with given instructions.

Equipment and Facilities. With the stress given to the teaching of process skills, schools are aware that appropriate equipment and facilities must be provided for effective science teaching. Where funds and space are available, primary schools have set up science rooms. These science rooms, which are suitably equipped, provide a conducive environment for group activities. In July 1983, a primary school science room was set up at the Singapore Science Centre to serve as a model for schools wishing to set up one of their own. In schools where it is not possible to have a science room due to the shortage of space, the requisite equipment is either stored in multi-purpose resource rooms or mobile cupboards which can be moved to classrooms for science lessons.

Science gardens have also been set up in about 60 per cent of primary schools to enable pupils to observe and study plant life and habitats. Science lessons are therefore sometimes conducted out-of-doors. Additionally, the science gardens provide specimens for indoor lessons. It is apparent that the functional value of the science garden in teaching process skills has been recognized by teachers and more schools are now developing such gardens.

All secondary schools are junior colleges are provided with standard physics, chemistry, biology and general science laboratories which are amply stocked with apparatus and equipment is imported through local agents and their cost met by school funds. There are, however, modest attempts by teachers to improvise equipment for use as teaching aids to meet the needs of the science syllabuses.

Instructional Materials. All science books used by primary and secondary schools must have the approval of the Ministry of Education. This is to ensure that books used by the pupils are of suitable standard and quality and that they cover the respective science syllabuses. Up to lower secondary level, the science textbooks are locally produced. The materials published by the CDIS for the primary and lower secondary levels are very popular in the schools. These materials comprise pupil's textbooks and workbooks, teachers' guides and some audio-visual aids. The contents of these materials closely follow the newly-revised syllabuses.

Science books in use in the upper secondary and pre-university levels are mainly written by overseas authors and selected for their suitability *vis-a-vis* the science syllabuses examined at the GCE 'O' and 'A' Levels.

Use of Educational Technology

Audio-visual Libraries. Schools have been provided with ample funds to develop their audio-visual resources. The CDIS has an instructional media library which loans audio-visual science materials to all schools. Films, film-strips, slides, multi-media kits, film-loops, video cassettes and transparencies can be easily loaned from the library for schools use. The CDIS also telecasts daily educational science programmes to enrich and supplement science teaching in the classroom for the primary and lower secondary pupils in the schools. In addition, science films are also readily available from various external sources such as foreign missions, cultural organizations and commercial companies. With all the support given by the Ministry of Education and external organizations, schools are upgrading their audio-visual resources and encouraging teachers to use more aids to reinforce, enhance, enrich or supplement the science teaching programme.

School Resource Libraries. Teachers are developing materials by themselves for their school resource libraries. Many schools now have a good stock of transparencies, slides, and video tapes, and these materials are often incorporated into the lessons for more effective teaching. To assist teachers, the lower secondary school science project team of CDIS has developed a media kit which contains all the audio-visual materials for use with the lower secondary science text-books. The Science Teachers Association of Singapore has also developed a set of slides on public health together with a handbook for the teaching of biology and human and social biology at the upper secondary levels.

Computer Literacy. Although no computer science is taught at the secondary level, every school is provided with at least three micro-computers by the Ministry of Education to teach pupils computer appreciation. Individual schools may have developed their own programmes or purchased various computer software for science teaching. At the pre-university level, computer science is offered as a curriculum subject and a minicomputer is provided for the use of candidates in examinations.

Teachers and Teacher Training

Staffing. There are 6,932 science teachers of whom 75.6 per cent teach science at the primary level, 21.6 per cent at the secondary level and 2.8 per cent at the pre-university level. Only 15 per cent of the science teachers have a degree in science and most of these (98 per cent) are deployed in secondary schools and junior colleges. Among these science graduates, 26 per cent teach the biological sciences, 50 per cent teach the physical sciences and 24 per cent teach general or combined science. At the pre-university level, all the science teachers are graduates and many have post-graduate qualifications. At the secondary level, 44 per cent of the science teachers are non-graduates, with the majority (81 per cent) of them teaching general science (lower secondary science) as their main teaching subject. Nearly all the primary science teachers are non-graduates and about one-third (30.3 per cent) do not have a pas in a science subject at 'O' Level. Nevertheless, all science teachers are given both pre-service and in-service training.

Pre-service Training of Primary Science Teachers

Science Courses Offered. The pre-service training of primary science teachers is incorporated in the two-year full-time Certificate in Education programme for GCE 'A' Level holders. This programme provides for both professional and academic training and prepares trainees to teach in the primary schools. In the first year of the programme, all trainees are required to take a compulsory course on the teaching of science in primary schools. In the second year, trainees may opt to do a course either on the teaching of science in lower secondary classes or on academic studies in science.

Nature of the Science Courses. Trainees are provided with the necessary skills to teach science at the primary level. While methods of teaching form a major part of the course, there is also a content component built into it. This component gives trainees the science concepts taught in primary schools. Where possible, these concepts are related to teaching materials used in schools especially those produced by the CDIS. Course work includes lectures, practicals and microteaching sessions. The microteaching and workshop sessions on worksheet preparation, improvization of teaching aids and materials are performance-based and aimed at developing the needed competencies.

School Experience and Teaching Practice. Trainees are exposed to three weeks of initial school experience to enable them to appreciate the actual situation and problems faced by teachers in the classroom. The experience gained in the three weeks helps them to see classroom implications of the course work which follows in the subsequent term. It also enables trainees to fit more easily into the life of the school when they begin their teaching practice. The amount of direct teaching carries out by them during the initial school experience is determined by their readiness to assume responsibility for conducting lessons, as well as by the needs to the schools to which they are assigned. Throughout the three weeks, they work with experienced teachers in the school. Trainees are posted to schools for a total of 20 weeks of teaching practice in their two-year course. This programme, which enables trainees to have direct teaching experience in schools, aims to help them develop their teaching skills, broaden their experience and gain insights into the theory and practice of teaching.

Evaluation Procedures. Trainees are assessed on their practical assignments and project work. In the course on academic studies in science, trainees take a three-hour written examination (80 per cent) and submit an assignment on a selected area in science (20 per cent).

Pre-service Training of Secondary Science Teachers

Science Course Offered. The IE offers a one-year full-time Diploma in Education programme to university graduates intending to become secondary school teachers. In addition to the normal professional education courses, the institution offers the following methods courses (called curriculum studies options) in science to intending science teachers : curriculum studies option in biology (90 hours); curriculum studies option in chemistry (90 hours); and curriculum studies option in physics (90 hours).

Nature of courses. The overall guiding principle is, initially, to steer the beginning teacher towards appropriate personality traits of dedication, self-control and sensitivity, and to impart skills in inter-personal relationships. While sociology, philosophy and psychology courses in their professional education studies emphasize the teacher's role in the educational system in general and his role in the school in particular, the methods courses are to be seen in the light of preparing the teacher for his role in the classroom.

Methods courses teach the trainees to apply their knowledge of 'subject' and 'education' to actual classroom situations. In this light the role of the methods courses can be conceptualized as shown in the following diagram.

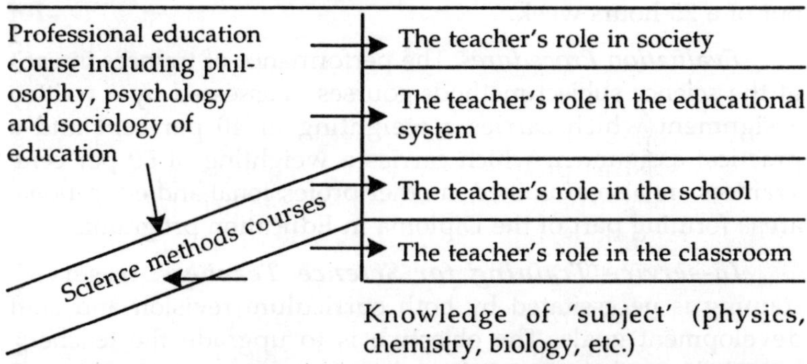

The science methods courses are designed to prepare the trainee to be a competent biology, chemistry and/or physics teacher. In this context the trainee should be able to: (a) set realistic goals and objectives for himself, as well as for his charges; (b) identify various techniques and resources available in the teaching of the science subjects; (c) formulate organizational and safety aspects in school laboratories; (d) develop skills for effective preparation of teaching aids or improvization of simple apparatus; (e) Plan and construct a test paper; (f) analyse and interpret a set of data using various evaluative techniques; and (g) present a logical review of curriculums projects or packages.

Course Content. The course concentrate on teaching methodology and focus on the development of the necessary competencies to bring about effective learning in the classroom. More specifically, they prepare trainees for teaching the various science syllabuses at the secondary and pre-university levels. Trainees are exposed to appropriate teaching methods and guided in the construction of aids for effective teaching. Skills on management of laboratories and maintenance of laboratory equipment are also taught. Microteaching sessions are included to enable trainees to try out various teaching ideas and skills and microcomputers are also available.

School Experience and Teaching Practice. All Diploma in Education trainees are posted to schools for three weeks of initial school experience and ten weeks for teaching practice. During the teaching practice, trainees normally teach about ten hours out of a 25-hours week.

Evaluation Procedures. The performance of trainees in each of the science subject methods courses is assessed by a written assignment which carries a weighting of 40 per cent and a practical assignment which carries a weighting of 60 per cent. Trainees are also examined in other professional and educational areas forming part of the Diploma in Education programme.

In-service Training for Science Teachers. In-service training is necessitated by both curriculum revision and staff development goals. The objective is to upgrade the teachers' knowledge and competencies.

The Institute of Education conducts a one-year full-time Further Professional Certificate in Education (FPCE) programme which pursues a more intensive study of both theory and practice in selected area of primary school work. Teachers in this programme are required to do a 60-hour course in science or mathematics. The science course provides an in-depth study in the methodology of teaching science in primary schools. Teachers are exposed to various techniques and resources for teaching primary science, and they are made familiar with the preparation of teaching materials, evaluation techniques, and current developments. Appropriate emphasis is given to the teacher's role in the classroom and science room.

The Institute also offers a 30-hour in-service course entitled 'Developing skills and concepts in primary science teaching' for primary science teachers. Through lectures, workshops and practical laboratory sessions, participants are helped to upgrade their knowledge and skills in the following area: preparation of simple aids; new primary science curriculum; and development and assessment of process skills.

Optional topics such as those listed below are also available : preparation of teaching units; concept formation; organization of field studies; role of local resource centres; evaluation techniques; studies of animals and plants; studies in energy; and studies in matter. The Institute staff also assists the Ministry of Education and the Science Teachers Association of Singapore in conducting workshops for teachers teaching the new lower secondary science syllabus.

School Based Workshops. In addition to formal in-service courses, school-based workshops are regularly organized by individual schools or groups of schools to meet the needs of teachers in specific areas of science teaching. For these workshops, inspectors and text-book writers from the Ministry of Education, and science staff from the Institute of Education are often invited by the schools to act as resource personnel. These school-based staff development activities are becoming increasingly important and serve to upgrade the teaching competencies of teachers in the various subject disciplines.

Research in Science Education

Research in science education is mostly carried out at the Institute of Education. Research activities in the Department of Science Education focus principally, but not exclusively, on problems concerned with meaningful and efficacious methods of teaching and learning science in the context of the Singapore curriculum. These can broadly be identified as innovative methods of teaching science, with particular reference to computer-assisted instruction; and nature of science and the learning process, with particular reference to Piaget's theory of cognitive development.

Staff that were involved in the computer-assisted instruction project found from their experimental studies that a drill and-practice programme produced a significant gain in pupil performance. Feedback from the experimental group showed pupils enjoyed the programme and found it helpful. The following publications resulted from this study : Handbook on computer-assisted instruction; Computer-assisted instruction in chemical education—final report; and Computer-assisted instruction in chemical education—user's manual.

Other research reports from this department include an analysis of the pre-university integrated physical science curriculum in terms of its relevance to first year science at the University of Singapore; and a Piagetian-based programme for learning 'elements and symbols'

Programmes for Out-of-school Youth and Adults and Popularization of Science and Technology

Science Clubs and Societies in School. All schools carry out their non-formal science programme through science clubs and societies. Activities are conducted outside formal school hours and are usually not tied down to a syllabus. The clubs and societies provide opportunities for teachers and pupils to explore areas of science for enrichment. Some of the activities organized by the clubs and societies are visits to places of interest, science talks, quizzes, film shows, exhibitions, project work and gardening.

The Science Teachers Association of Singapore and the Singapore science Centre have both contributed much in promoting enrichment activities in the school science clubs and societies. Through *Science centre bulletin* (a quarterly publication of the Singapore Science Centre) interesting articles on scientific discoveries, puzzles and simple projects provide ideas and resources for activities. The Science Teachers Association of Singapore and the Singapore Science Centre under the sponsorship of the Singapore Association for the Advancement of Science and the Singapore National Academy of Science have initiated a scheme for primary school pupils to conduct meaningful and interesting science projects. Under the scheme, pupils are required to work on simple projects on subjects such as botany, zoology, meteorology, geology, astronomy and ecology. Stars are awarded for each completed project and the accumulation of the requisite number of stars entitles a pupil to be awarded a 'Young Scientist' badge. Since the introduction of this scheme in 1982, many primary schools have undertaken related projects as part of the activities in the science clubs.

Singapore Youth Science Fortnight. This is an annual event organized unity by the Singapore Science Centre and the Science Teachers Association of Singapore. The programme which caters to all levels of pupils in the schools and junior colleges aims to (a) give youth a deeper insight into science and technology; (b) allow young scientists to discuss scientific problems and the implications of science on society among themselves and senior members of the scientific community; and (c) allow educators of youth to exchange views and experiences in science education. Held during the June holidays, the activities vary slightly from year to year. Included in the programme are the science fair, science forum, science fiction writing competition, science circus, science fiction film festival, science olympiad, science camp, nature ramble competition and science seminar. About 100,000 students participate directly or indirectly in the various activities of the Science Fortnight annually. The activities have successfully provided the imaginative and creative youth in society with an opportunity to appreciate that science is a living and dynamic body of knowledge

The science fair is aimed at a different group of pupils each year. In 1981 the participants were pre-university pupils; in 1982, it was for primary pupils and in 1983 the participants came from secondary schools. Pupils are given about six months to work on their science projects. Judging is based on a written report and a display of the project work at the fair. The project work submitted at every science fair has been of a reasonably good standard and varied in subject matter and complexity.

Science forums and seminars are conducted for secondary and pre-university pupils. Topics chosen are usually related to social and economic implications of science on society. Issues on pollution, population control and man and his environment have been discussed.

A science camp is organized at the Science Centre ground each year to expose pupils to the study of ecology. The programme includes lectures, film shows, discussions and various other activities. Practical work is centred around the Singapore Science Centre surroundings. A three-day camp was conducted in 1983 for upper primary pupils to expire how nature works at the Science Centre's new ecogarden.

Science olympiads are held to challenge pre-university participants to tackle problems on various aspects of science. There are short questions to test the participants' speed, knowledge and accuracy, long questions to test their analytical abilities in solving problems and project work which requires creative skills and team effort.

The nature ramble competition was introduced for the first time in 1982. Open to all pre-university students, it hopes to generate an appreciation and awareness of the wonders of nature and develop an understanding of how nature works. Participants are required to make a study of a chosen habitat and prepare a handbook based on the observations or studies made in the nature ramble.

Singapore Science Centre. The Singapore Science Centre has played an important role in providing science and technology education to both youth and adults. As an exhibition centre, it displays a wise range of exhibits centred around two main ideas, energy and life. Exhibits are broadly categorized under physical sciences, life sciences, special exhibits and solar radiation. About 40 per cent of the exhibits on display are participatory and visitors are treated to a hands-on approach in discovering sciences. Exhibits in the physical sciences gallery include nuclear power, automotive engineering, communication and information systems, time, and man into space. Exhibits in the life sciences gallery explain biological principles and their applications in daily life. They consist of graphic panels and audio-visual shows, models and life specimens on such topics and themes as cell, human birth, genetics, evolution and population. The special exhibits gallery houses exhibits demonstrating the wave phenomena of light and sound. There is also a newly-developed ecological garden which enables the public to learn about nature and the dependence and influence on life of one species on another.

Besides being a tourist attraction, the Science Centre is very well frequented by the local public. Indeed its exhibits and activities form an integral part of the science education for pupils in the schools. This is recognized by all schools, nearly all of which are institutional members of the Science Centre. Schools organize frequent visits to the Centre for their pupils throughout the year.

The science Centre also provides special programmes for pupils including science talks; laboratory courses; science lectures-cum-demonstrations; forums; film shows; science club activities; and exhibit guided tours. These activities are meant to enrich, extend and supplement the programmes in schools. Workshops, forums, seminars, and short courses are organized by the Centre staff for science teachers to help upgrade their knowledge and teaching skills.

The publications of the Science Centre aim to arouse an interest in science through reading and they are well supported by the schools. There activities are meant to enrich, extend and supplement the programmes in schools. Workshops, forms, seminars, and short courses are organized by the Centre staff for science teachers to help upgrade their knowledge and teaching skills.

The publications of the Science Centre aim to various an interest in science through reading and they are well supported by the schools. There is a scheme in which the public can enrol as 'Friends of the Science Centre' by paying an annual subscription. 'Friends' are exempted from entrance fees when visiting the Science Centre, kept informed of the Centre's activities through its publication, Science Centre news and are entitled to join the special activities conducted by the Centre.

Singapore Zoological Garden. At the Singapore Zoological Garden, informal science education about animal life is made available to the public through various means. All enclosures are provided with aluminium signboards which provide information about the animals such as their distribution, common names, diet, social system and breeding cycles. For those unable to read, talking booths give, at the press of a button, a brief commentary in English and Mandarin about the animals.

Educational legends such as one about relationships between dogs and wolves are posted on signboards at various locations in the zoo. There is an 'Animal show-time' held daily with a running commentary given over the public announcement system. Slide shows are provided for the public in the air-conditioned theatrette during week ends. The Zoological Garden also conducts special educational programmes for pupils. Slide shows and discussions are arranged for organized groups of pupils at all grade levels. Worksheets are also prepared for pupils who wish to learn more about the animals. A termly newsletter is sent out to all schools providing information about happenings in the Zoological Garden and the schedules of the educational programme for the coming term. The activities conducted are particularly popular with the primary and lower secondary pupils. Primary and secondary schools can enrol as institutional members of the Zoological Garden and enjoy certain privileges.

The Zoo-Ed, a quarterly publication of the Zoological Garden is very well received by pupils. For each issue, about 30,000 copies are sold. Other publications produced include a book on snake encounters, maps of the zoo and posters on Singapore snakes, hoofed animals and apes. All publications are available to the public.

Science on Television. Besides transmitting science programmes to schools under the Educational Television (ETV) programmes, the Singapore Broadcasting Corporation also telecasts non-fictional and fictional science films to educate and entertain the public.

Current Innovations

Instructional Materials Development. With the introduction of the revised science syllabuses for the primary and lower secondary levels, there is a need to produce teaching and learning materials. Two project teams have been formed in the Curriculum Development Institute of Singapore to write materials based on the revised syllabuses.

The Primary Science Project. Materials comprising textbooks, workbooks, teachers' guides and audio-visual aids have been produced for the first few levels. The materials stress the importance of acquiring the process skills associated with problem-solving and provide pupils with a variety of activities to aid them in the learning and mastering of science concepts. Consultancy advice has been sought regarding the development of the curriculum materials.

Lower Secondary Science Project. The lower secondary science project was initiated as early as 1970 by a standing committee comprising specialists from both the Ministry of Education and the Science Teachers Association of Singapore. The committee was set up to develop science materials for the lower secondary pupils taking general science. Progress was slow, as work was undertaken by serving science teachers working on a part-time voluntary basis. Nevertheless some materials were developed and tried out in some schools in 1977.

With the setting up of a project team in the CDIS, the first generation materials were modified to be in line with the revised lower secondary science syllabus. The project team has since designed and developed an integrated package of curriculum instructional materials consisting of pupil's textbooks and wordbooks, a teachers' guide and supplementary instructional materials. There is also a media kit consisting of specially designed wall-charts, slides, transparencies and card games. The revised materials were first tried out at Secondary I level in three schools in 1981 and at Secondary I and II levels in 15 schools in 1982. Nearly all schools are now using these materials for their Secondary I classes. From 1984, the complete lower secondary science package including AV materials will be ready for use at Secondary I and II levels.

The project materials are characterized by the interdisciplinary treatment of science topics; the emphasis on enquiry-based science learning; the selective emphasis on technological aspects of science content e.g. water purification and conservation, alternative energy sources; and the inclusion of ecological and environmental aspects of science, such as problems related to urbanization, industrialization and safety at home and at work.

Special Programmes for Locating and Nurturing Scientific and Technological Talents. There are many national science competitions and quizzes organized throughout the year which pose challenges for the talented and scientifically-inclined pupils. The Singapore Science Fortnight activities provide ample opportunities for pupils to develop their scientific potential. The Singapore National Institute of Chemistry organizes chemistry speech contests biennially for the eloquest and scientifically knowledgeable secondary pupils. Each year too, the Ministry of Education sends four outstanding pre-university students to participate in the London International Youth Science Fortnight, a residential conference held in London aimed at developing among young people of all nations, a deeper insight into science and its application for the benefit of mankind.

Role of Industrial and Professional Organizations. Support from both the public and private sectors in science education programmes has been forthcoming. Many of the projects and activities might not have been conducted without the ready sponsorship of industrial and professional organizations. Singapore is fortunate to have big oil companies coming forward to share the responsibilities of promoting science education. Among the projects sponsored by these companies are the Singapore youth Science Fortnight, publications and activities organized by the Singapore Science Centre and the Science Teachers' Association of Singapore. Professional organizations, too, play their part by providing expertise aimed at the advancement of science and at achieving excellence in science education.

Resource materials for supplementing science teaching in schools are developed quite extensively by the educational services divisions of the large industrial and commercial companies, quasi-government organizations and information services of various foreign missions. Magazines, films, science kits, wall-charts and audio-visual packs are made easily accessible to teachers for loan.

19

Socialist Republic of Viet Nam

In August, 1956, the Government of the Democratic Republic of Viet Nam (now the Socialist Republic of Viet Nam) promulgated a policy for general education. It provided the objectives, tasks and guiding principles for general education, the statutes of general education, content of education, and the training of teachers. It outlined the objectives of general education; the duties of general education schools; the guiding principles of general education in particular and of education in general; the change in the school system from nine years to ten years; and the curricula of general education subjects, which included providing pupils with basic, modern and systematic scientific knowledge.

Science and Technology Policy

The science and technology policy aims to bring the role of science in economic, cultural and social activities into full play; to step up the scientific and technical revolution in close co-ordination with the revolutions in relation to production, ideology and culture; to make science a direct productive force actively serving the implementation of the policies of the socialist revolution; to satisfy at an ever higher level the people's material and cultural demands; and to meet the requirements of initial defence and security. At the same time, efforts should be made to build advanced science and technology.

Throughout the period of transition, every scientific and technical activity must be devoted to serving industrialization, and making contributions to building the material and technical basis for socialism in forthcoming five-year plans. In the years to come, science and technology must, at all costs, fulfil the top-priority task of developing, at tremendous speed, the all-round agricultural production for Viet Nam, and bring into full play the development of the country in terms of manpower, land, and tropical natural resources.

A group of scientists, technicians and skilled workers must be built up and highly-qualified specialists trained in research teaching and production, competent for the organization and management in the various fields of natural sciences, and technology and social sciences.

Science and technology must make a significant contribution to re-organizing production, improving economic and social management, and scientific and technical management. International co-operation in science and technology must be expanded.

Creativeness in science and technology must be promoted in order to bring into full play present and future productive potentialities, to increase the quality of products, to make full use of domestic sources of materials and to use manpower resources and materials economically.

Structure of Education in Schools

The education structure in general education schools in the North is different from the South. In 1975, after total liberation the 12 year system was maintained in the newly-liberated areas and new curricula and textbooks introduced. In North Viet Nam the ten-year system, consisting of four years of first-level, three years of second level and three years of third level was followed. Since the school year 1981-1982, educational reforms have been introduced shifting the whole country educationally to the 12-year system consisting of five years of first level or primary education, four year of second level, together giving a nine-year basic general education; and three years of third level, called secondary general education.

As the reform has only just been effected, there has not yet been a new Form IX in the North. By 1983, the reform had been carried to form II so it will be some time before education is completely unified in the system.

The basic general education school aims to provide pupils with an all-round education, making it possible for them to do general, simple work of all kinds, to choose a career, to join social activities or to go on with their study in secondary general education by different methods.

Primary education, which used to prepare pupils for life, is now only to prepare pupils, in knowledge, methods and psychology, for their study in a second-level general education school.

The secondary general education school, from X to Form XII, is to improve and complete the general culture of pupils finishing the basic general education school. Following the secondary general education school, pupils can enter universities, colleges, a number of intermediate vocational schools and trade schools or join productive work immediately.

In the network of secondary general education schools, apart from the ordinary schools, there are the work-and-study schools for young people. In terms of the content of education, they are the same as the ordinary schools. But the periods of technical education are greater and especially those devoted to production (agricultural or industrial) take up much more time. Pupils work two to three hours a day, or work for a definite period in the year, and are, in the main, self-sufficient in their everyday necessities.

Finishing this school, pupils with a trade can join productive work immediately or continue their study in colleges or university through general selective examinations.

Six-years old children, regardless of whether or not they have been through kindergartens, are admitted to Form I of primary school where they are taught the three Rs.

Pupils finishing Form V with the necessary marks are automatically promoted to second-level schools. In secondary schools the selection of pupils is carried out every year by selective examination in two subjects : mathematics and literature. Candidates are pupils finishing basic general education schools. Every year, about 30 per cent of pupils finishing basic general education schools are admitted to secondary general education schools.

Science Education in Schools

General Structure. In the first-level, as early as Form II, pupils are provided with very elementary, unsystematic and synthetic knowledge, on familiar fauna and flora, the earth, stones, air, water and the natural environment around them, and on the activities of people exploiting, utilizing and transforming local nature.

In Forms II to IV, pupils learn the same knowledge through texts in national literature, outdoor excursions, simple experiments and work in school gardens.

In Form V, scientific knowledge is classified rather systematically and detached from national literature to become a separate subject with a synthetic character. With this basic science, there is geography that gives pupils an elementary knowledge of the local physical geography (villages, districts and the physical geography of Viet Nam).

In Form VI, the introductory class of the second level, there are another two subjects : biology and general physical geography, including some knowledge of geology.

On the basis of the knowledge accumulated in mathematics and other subjects, pupils begin to study physics from Form VII and chemistry from Form VIII. Up to Form VIII the scientific subjects to be learned at general education schools are taught as compulsory subjects.

So far only a limited number of curricula have been developed; others will follow as the educational reforms take effect.

Time Available for Science. At the first level, science education takes up 5.2 per cent of the teaching periods at schools in the North and 5.4 per cent at schools in the South. At the Second level, science education takes up 21 per cent of the teaching periods in the North and 27 per cent in the South. At the third level the percentages are 24 in the North and 28 in the South.

The weekly teaching periods for all three levels are shown in Tables 1, 2 and 3.

Table—1. Science teaching periods at first level

	North					South				
Subjects/Forms	I	II	III	IV	V	I	II	III	IV	V
Basic science		1	1	2	2		1	1	2	2
Geography					1				1	1

Table—2. Science teaching periods at second level

	North				South			
Subjects/Forms	VI	VII	VIII	IX	VI	VII	VIII	IX
Biology	2	2	2		2	2	2	2
Geography	2	1,5	1,5		1,5	1	1	1
Physics		2	3			2	1.5	2
Chemistry			1,5				2	2

There has not yet been a new Form IX North Viet Nam.

Table 3. Science teaching periods at third level

	North			South		
Subjects/Forms	X	XI	XII	X	XI	XII
Physics	2,5	3	4	4	4	4
Chemistry	1,5	2	3	2	2	2
Biology	2	1,5	1,5	1,5	1,5	2

Science Curricula at the Primary Level. The objectives of science are to : supply pupils with preliminary knowledge of living creatures and inanimate things and guide them to observe natural phenomena; kindle and develop in pupils a love for nature, the country, and the working people; and encourage them to fight superstition.

Scientific subjects at primary schools are not taught separately but are integrated into the rest of the curriculum. In Forms I to III, the subject is not taught systematically, the first scientific knowledge is learned through national literature in stories told by teachers, and through excursions. In Form IV, science is taught separately, independent of national literature, under the name, 'The ABC of science'.

The four-year curriculum provides pupils with concrete ideas of the four seasons, living things (the most common cultivated and wild plants, domestic animals, wild beasts, birds, insects, cultivation, livestock breeding), structure and activities of the human body, preventive hygiene, inanimate things (water, air, soil) and a basic knowledge of electricity.

This content is selected and classified and the method of teaching helps the pupils take in scientific knowledge and skills intuitively. Thus, first of all, pupils learn the typical facts in the locality, the particular characteristics of each season, what they see with their own eyes and hear with their own ears.

In Forms I and II, in autumn, children learn about autumn weather, autumn fruits, farming and gardening. They observe the weather, life and growth of plants and animals and study human efforts to transform nature. Through the subject 'air' in Form IV, children learn the properties of air, and such relevant natural phenomena as wind, storms, and human impact (man making full use of the force of wind), the composition of air and environmental hygiene and the effects of green trees.

The children's knowledge is expanded and gradually systematized. In Forms I and II, pupils learn something about particular animals. In Form III more general knowledge about a number of important animals—birds, fish, insects—and some particular features of these species is taught. In hygiene, for example, they learn external bodily hygiene in Form I, hygiene and the senses in Form II, and preventive hygiene of some common disease, including environmental hygiene, in Forms III and IV.

The above-mentioned content structure calls for a suitable organization of teaching and learning and teaching methods.

In Forms I and II, scientific knowledge is introduced through reading texts, not quantitatively and not yet systematically.

In Form III lessons on science are included in national literature in separate chapters with rich scientific content. The method used is one peculiar to science, with direct observations and necessary practical experiments.

In form IV, there are separate textbooks for the subject with the lessons following the subject-matter in the curriculum.

In all classes, science education is closely linked with practical work, for example, production periods in the school-garden, toy-making periods, simple experiments, collections of soil, rocks and plant samples, visits to fields and factories, and social activities such as looking after parks, taking care of trees planted by grandfathers, worm-catching festivals and cattle shows.

Secondry Level Science. At the secondary level, natural sciences are taught as three separate subjects; physics, chemistry and biology.

The objective of teaching physics and chemistry are to : impart systematic, basic general knowledge of physics and chemistry; educate pupils in dialectical materialism and proletarian internationalism; make it possible for them to understand, theoretically and practically, the basic applications of the laws of physics and chemistry to life and production; train them in the skills of using measuring instruments in physics and chemistry and making common physical and chemical tests; foster in them the passion for science, creative curiosity, ability to work independently and the sense of getting near to nature and production.

The objectives of teaching biology are to : impart systematic, basic and general knowledge of living creatures and the part they play in agricultural economy, other branches of the economy and health protection; enable the pupils to understand the laws governing the evolution of living creatures, on which basis to build a scientific world outlook, to fight down idealist viewpoints and superstition; enable them to grasp the basic points of Mitchurin's and Pavlov's theories in order to apply them to cultivation, livestock breeding and preventive hygiene and train them in the basic skills of laboratory work, cultivation and livestock breeding; and make it possible for pupils to know the richness of fauna, its importance and prospects in agriculture, achievemens in health protection and transforming fauna.

In the first level secondary schools, natural sciences are taught as three separate subjects. Pupils begin to learn biology from Form VI, physics from Form VII and chemistry from Form VIII. In the second level secondary schools, physics, chemistry and biology are taught simultaneously from Forms X to XII. All secondary school pupils follow the same curricula and use the same textbooks for physics, chemistry and biology. These curricula and textbooks are compiled and controlled by State organizations.

The teaching/learning of all scientific subjects at secondry level is carried out in the following way :

a) *Class activities.* Listening to explanations; training in theoretical skills; following demonstration experiments; carrying out simultaneous experiments; and practice.

b) *Outdor activities.* Practice; visits to scientific, technical and production institutions, economic and scientific exhibitions and museums.

c) *Activities in extra-curricular groups.* Participation in scientific evenings and exhibitions of collections of wall-news papers.

Physics. The curricula of physics at first level secondary schools covers the most elementary knowledge of mechanics, heat, electricity, magnetism and geo-optics. At this level, knowledge is imparted mostly through the description of phenomena, qualitative rather than quantitative explanation.

At second level secondry schools more knowledge on mechanics, heat, electricity, magnetism, geo-optics, physico-optics, atomic and nuclear physics is imparted. At this level, apart from methods of observations and experiments, the role of theories, mathematical deducation, and the quantitative approach are strengthened.

Chemistry. The curriculum of chemistry at first level secondary schools consists only of simple knowledge of inorganic chemistry in order to provide pupils with elementary concepts of the properties of a number of important chemical elements and the classification of inorganic substances.

The curriculum of chemistry in second level secondary schools has a comparatively integral structure, including both inorganic and organic chemistry. Particular attention is paid to modern theories of chemistry, important processes of production and application of chemistry to the national economy.

Biology. The curricula of biology in first level secondaary schools consists of knowledge on vegetation, simple micro-structures and plant physiology; and knowledge on the structure, life and development of the most important groups of animals.

In second-level secondry schools, the curriculum includes human physiology, anatomy and modern theories of biological evolution, the origin of species, and methods of transforming old species and creating new ones.

Apart from the ordinary curricula, there are higher curricula for gifted pupils in each separate subject.

Modification and Renewal of Curricula. The current curricula of physics, chemistry and biology have been in use since 1956. They are basically unchanged. However, every three to five years, there are minor alterations guided by the principles of simplifying the curricula in harmony with the teaching and learning by removing a number of lessons too detailed in theory and less significant in practice and reducing the demands on fundamental knowledge and a number of skills; and bringing them up to date with the modern theories of the respective subject by eliminating some old-fashioned ideas and explaining some topics in the light of modern viewpoints.

Relation to Society. The relation of scientific subjects with everyday life is carried out, first of all, in the teaching process through curricula content and teaching methods. Apart from providing an understanding of the phenomena, concepts, theories and fundamental laws of science, the teaching process must also provide pupils with simple knowledge of the techniques, technology and organization of products and goods; form and consolidate practical skills; and develop the ability to apply the theories learned, to production.

The combining of scientific subjects with practice is also carried out through extramural activities (production and social activities). It is necessary to systematically introduce pupils to the scientific basis of all practical activities and at the same time help them apply the knowledge learned to the activities of everyday life, such as methods of cultivation and livestock breeding.

Evaluation and Examinations. The evaluation of pupil's records is carried out by an oral control in each teaching period, written control after one or two chapters, written control at the end of each term, and a written examination (final examination) at each education level.

Generally speaking, evaluation and examinations only centre on the theoretical knowledge of pupils.

The National Institute of Educational Science has developed a project for improving the examination system in order to achieve all the objectives of general education schools.

Science Activities, Laboratory Work and Equipment. Demonstrations are given by classroom teachers to orientate, illustrate, study and experiment with the main contents of each lessons according to the requirements laid down in the curricula and textbooks. Demonstrations are most common, relatively easy to cary out, and make up the highest percentage in science practical activities at all educational levels. Demonstrations are provided for in about 25 per cent of the teaching periods in the curricula of elementary science subjects at the remarry stage and in biology, physics and chemistry at the secondary stage.

Practical experiments by school pupils in laboratories, school-gardens and on the fields do not yet constitute a high percentage of the science curricula. Owing to a shortage of laboratory equipment and tools, the curricula only provide for a small number of selected practical experiments for groups of two or three pupils. The percentage of the periods spent on compulsory experiments is shown in Table—4.

Table—4. Percentage of periods of compulsory experiments

Subjects	*Lower Secondary (in %)*	*Upper Secondary (in %)*	*Average (in %)*
Biology	18	12	15
Physics	8	8	8
Chemistry	8	5	6

Practical experiments by pupils at home are provided for in curricula or textbooks in the form of experimental exercises and observations. Such activities only requre simple facilities. For example, the curricular of 'The ABC of Science' in the final class, first level, has 63 lessons which requre pupils to complete eight experimental-observation exercises by themselves at home and nine practical experiments at home.

The curricula for science also provide for sight-seeing activities to study the natural environment and local agricultural and industrial establishments to relate science to everyday life, e.g. the curricula of physics in Forms X, XI and XII, upper secondary level, devote 16 period to pupils sight-seeing tours, observations and practice in production, making up about 5 per cent of the teaching periods for physics.

Recent Developments. Since 1981, general education schools have carried out educational reforms. The periods devoted to science practical activities—especially pupils' practical experiments-in all classes and subjects, have increased to become 10 to 12 per cent of the total periods available for science.

For special classes majoring in physics, chemistry and biology, the curricula provide for 25 to 30 per cent of the periods for pupils' experiments.

Assessment. In public final examinations, there is no practical test. In selective examinations for pupils good at biology and physics, practical work provides 30-40 per cent of the marks in the examinations. Pupils selected for special classes must sit for examinations in practicals after the examinations in theory.

Equipment. To meet the requirements of content and methods of the curricula the Ministry of Education has published lists of teaching aids for each subject at all levels.

The lists specify the equipment in common use : pictures, lantern slides, educational films, demonstration instruments, apparatus, and the materials and tools necessary to assemble and repair teaching aids.

Each item includes details of the quantity required and how to acquire it. Expenses for teaching aids are ear-marked in every budget of the local education authority.

To supply schools with equipment, the Ministry of Education has, for more than 20 years, taken active measures to establish institutions for study, design, production, import, and distribution, of teaching aids. Equipment guides are published. International assistance has been secured.

In the years 1976-1980 alone, the Ministry of Education provided various schools with mechanics sets for lower secondary schools (4,000); electro-magnetism sets for secondary schools (6,000); physics practice sets (10,000); electric motors for secondary schools (2,000); dissecting sets for biology (15,000); models; samples of animals; samples of bones; and various kinds of charts for biology, physics and chemistry.

In spite of the many efforts and the active assistance of may agencies and countries (especially UNICEF and the Ministry of Education of the German Democratic Republic) the general education schools have not been able to meet the demands of science teaching.

Statistics of the equipment available in general education schools are being compiled and the items evaluated, but the following general remarks can be made on the state of equipment at all education levels :

a) At first-level general education schools, there are only charts, simple teaching aids and samples made or collected by teachers and pupils.

b) In lower secondary schools, every town has one centre well-equipped with physics, chemistry and biology experiments to serve pupils of four to five neighbouring schools for practical work. Every province has two or three large second-level general education schools that are well-equipped. About 40 per cent of the schools in cities and towns and villages in the plains have enough equipment for demonstration experiments. The schools in the mountainous areas, the border areas, the water-logged parts of the Mekong River plains and the newly-established schools do not have enough teaching aids.

c) As far as upper secondary schools are concerned, every province and town has one or two comparatively well-equipped schools. There are hardly any schools without teaching aids. Generally speaking, most schools are equipped well enough to carry out the most important demonstration experiments and about 50 per cent of the compulsory practice exercises.

Manufacture. Special technical equipment, precision balances, measuring instruments, and microscopes are imported. Otherwise, simple, inexpensive equipment is mass-produced in the factories, print-shops and film laboratories of the Ministry of Education and other Ministries. There organizations comprise the : (a) Company for School Equipment, Ministry of Education and its branches in the different provinces; (b) National Institute of Educational Science; (c) Department of Professional Supervision and Inspection of General Educational Schools, Ministry of Education; (d) Television and Broadcasting Department, Ministry of Education; (e) Teaching Aids Workshop of the Ministry of Education and the Teaching Aids Workshops of the Provincial Education Departments; (f) School Films and Tape-recording Studio, Ministry of Education; and (g) production establishments of the various ministries, branches and localities.

The Company for School Equipment, Ministry of Education supervises the production of equipment and teaching aids; co-ordinates with professional departments to guide the self-production, maintenance and use of teaching aids; co-ordinates with the National Institute of Educational Science to work out lists of teaching aids for all subjects and designs models of teaching aids for each subject; and directly supplies and distributes teaching aids to northern provinces.

The equipment made by teachers and pupils do not constitute a grant percentage in the stipulated lists but are an important part of the total. They include samples of animals, vegetation, raw materials, machines, common tools. There are also school-gardens, cultivation and breeding corners, and weather sections built up by each school.

The making of teaching aids by teachers and pupils is a long term important strategic policy aimed not only at solving the shortage of equipment but also at achieving educational purposes, strengthening practical work and improving the teaching of science. The various education departments give instructions, hold training courses, exhibitions and competitions on self-made teaching aids from schools to national levels. There were four such exhibitions and competitions in 1971, 1976, 1978 and 1981. In 1981 alone, more than 500 kinds of teaching aids received certificates of commendation from the Ministry of Education.

Use of Educational Technology

In present day general education schools, there are hardly any audio-visual aids and other sophisticated technologies because of their high cost and maintenance.

In a number of provinces, there is only one centre equipped with such common audio-visual aids hardware as slide projectors, overhead-projectors, sound film projectors and tape-recorders and a few software comprising slides, slide-tapes, films and tape-recordings produced by the School Films and Tape-recording Workshop, Ministry of Education.

There have not yet been any TV or radio programmes on science for general education pupils, nor has there been any school using computers in teaching science.

Teacher Training

Qualifications. The minimum professional capacities executed in knowledge; able to drill pupils in skills, and in applying knowledge linked to life and local conditions; and professionally qualified, with the ability to use good teaching methods and to be able to develop pupils' thinking during the process of teaching.

Extent of Qualified Teachers. All teachers are not fully qualified, owing to war-time difficulties, shortening of training courses or lack of equipment and facilities.

It is difficult to assess the teachers' capacities and no reliable official figures have been obtained. However, it is estimated that about 30-40 per cent of primary teachers, 50 per cent of lower secondary school teachers and 70 per cent of upper secondary school teachers can meet the qualifications listed. Thus there are many thousands who are still unqualified.

Pre-service Training. To overcome the shortage of qualified teachers, the Ministry of Education has standardized the courses of training-upper secondary school teachers (third level) must have four-years of university training; lower secondary school teachers (second level) must have three-years college training; and primary school teachers must have two-years pedagogical training after the post-secondary schools.

In-service Training. Various options are available for in-service refresher courses :

a) ***Correspondence Courses.*** These follow the in-service training course of a regular teacher training college and allow teachers to remain in their schools. Every year, conditions, permitting, some time is available for concentrated studies at the teacher training college.

b) ***Local in-service Training Refresher Courses.*** These are held during summer holidays.

c) ***Collective Study Activities.*** These are regularly organized by local educational authorities for teachers of the same subject from a group of schools.

Teacher Training Colleges. There is a network of teacher training colleges for the regular training of teachers at primary, lower secondary and upper secondary level.

a) ***Teacher Training Colleges Run by the Ministry of Education.*** These collegs run a programme of four years duration. Students are chosen from among those finishing secondary school. They may choose a subject to study and, later, to teach at secondary schools. Three are departments of mathematics, physics, chemistry, geography and technology. The curricula of each Department consist of many subjects belonging to the following groups of science: politics-economics—philosophy, economics, the history of the Communist Party; basic sciences in the speciality chosen by the student—theory and practice; professional science-pedagogy, psychology, teaching methods; and other subjects such as foreign languages, physical training, and military drill.

b) ***Teacher Training Colleges in the Provinces.*** There are one or two in each province run by the local authorities. Students are selected from among those finishing secondary schools. Students may choose a department where they will spend three years. After graduation, they will be teachers of two subjects at lower secondary schools (second level), *e.g.* mathematics and physics, and chemistry, chemistry and biology or biology and geography.

The curricula of these departments also consist of four groups similar to those in the centrally organized teacher college.

c) ***Secondary Teacher Training Colleges in the Provinces.*** These are also run by the local authorities. Students are selected from among those finishing secondary school to be trained for two years as primary school teachers. Student teachers at these schools must study natural and social sciences at the same time.

To train students in practical educational skills at teacher training colleges, from the second year, students must attend periods with experiences teachers. In the final year, they must undertake practice teaching for four to eight weeks at secondary schools. They must teach the subject they have been taught at the training college under the guidance, help, supervision and evaluation of guiding teachers.

Research

Research into educational science is given particular attention because through research, conclusions can be drawn and improvements made.

One of the research studies being carried out is, 'The optimization of the contents of teaching'. This research is being conducted by means of three investigations: (a) study of teachers with different backgrounds, qualifications and experience; (b) study of pupils capabilities in different localities and social backgrounds; and (c) study of control groups. The conclusions, so for, from the research point to the need for optimizing the content of each subject to achieve an acceptable standard; and the desirability of specifying parameters on the average capacities of teachers and pupils.

The results of the research are discussed at teach-ins with educationists, teachers and investigators.

Organizations Involved. Educational research is carried out by the research workers of the National Institute of Educational Science with the participation of many other institutions including teacher training colleges; educational management organizations in the centres and together localities, and practising teachers.

Research Topics. A number of subjects are to be studied in the next few years :

a) ***Content and Method for all Subjects.*** Implementing the revised curricula; elaborating teaching programmes for certain areas (the making River plains and the mountain areas); working out specific curricula for classes of gifted pupils and for study-and-work schools; studying special educational activities; and studying special educational content, for example environmental protection and population education.

b) ***Specific Studies.*** Production and use of low-cost equipment for physics; the role of metals in the course of organic chemistry at secondary schools; environmental protection in geography; and improvement of the content of electro-magnetism in the physics curricula.

Out-of-school Science Activities and Popularization of Science

Extension Schooling. There are several programmes available to meet the demands of personnel, including workers, peasants and young people who wish to continue their studies at the third level after primary second level general education schools. Third level complementary education conducted mainly through in-service training courses, is available for older cadres and workers (over 40 yeas old). There is a similar programme for young cadres and young people through in-service training or short-term crash courses. This is the most common form of study. Young cadres and excellent young people have the opportunity to follow long-term third level courses at complementary education schools for workers and peasants in various provinces and towns.

The first kind of curriculum aims to broaden general knowledge in natural and social science and improve the capacity of work. The following groups of subjects are compulsory: (a) mathematics, physics, chemistry and biology; and (b) literature, history, geography. Learners may choose which of these two groups to study first for their convenience.

The curriculum provides the learner with basic knowledge chosen from the secondary general education curriculum plus basic knowledge on technology, production and life.

With regard to natural science, the curriculum deals with physics (mechanics—43 periods, molecular physics and heat—25, electricity—43, oscillations and waves—26, nuclear physics—4); chemistry (general chemistry—35, inorganic chemistry—45, organic chemistry—45); biology (cells—3, metabolism—7, human and animal nervous system activities—4, reproduction—3, genetics—18, evolution of living creatures—6); and physical geography (general physical geography—28, Viet Nam's agricultural geography—9, communication and transport geography—3).

The second kind of curriculum aims to provide learners with basic knowledge in mathematics, physics and chemistry. For rural areas, biology and agricultural techniques to improve the learner's logic and scientific style of work and form a scientific world outlook are additional subjects.

The curricula of natural science subjects for in-service training courses in offices and factories consist of physics (mechanics—65 periods, heat—46, electricity—60, oscillations and waves—23, optics—22, nuclear energy—4); chemistry (basic notions and laws of chemistry—11, classification of inorganic compounds—9, group of alkaline metals—4, the halogen group - 6, composition of substances and the periodic system of chemical elements—12, solutions and electrolysis—8, the oxygen—sulphur group—8, the nitrogen-phosphorus group—8, carbon—silicon—6, general properties of metals—8, calcium and its compounds—3, aluminium and its compounds and alloys—5, iron and its compounds and alloys, erosion and antimetallic erosion—8, chemical mathematics exercises—4, oxygenous organic compounds-ethyl alcohol, phenol, formaldehyde, acetic acid, fats, glucose—18, nitrogenous organic compounds—5); biology, following the same content as the first kind of curriculum, with more attention being paid to heredity (material basis of heredity, laws of heredity, human heredity, genetics and the selection of breeds), population education and environmental protection and transformation of nature; and physical geography (knowledge of the universe—4, the earth—5, atmosphere—8, hydrosphere—4, arable lands—7, Viet Nam's industrial geography—6, communication and transport geography—3).

The curricula of science subjects for short-term crash courses are the same as those for in-service training courses. However, more periods are devoted to revision, practical work skills, experiments, chemical, physical and mathematical exercises.

For complementary education classes in the countryside there are additional periods for biology and agricultural techniques (112 periods altogether as compared with 47 periods for biology in the two kinds of schools discussed earlier).

The third kind of curriculum, for excellent cadres and young people in long-term courses at local complementary education schools, consists of all aspects, *i.e.*, ethical, intellectual, aesthetic, labour, physical and military.

The curriculum comprises all the subjects taught at secondary schools, which are mathematics, physics, chemistry, biology, literature, history, geography, foreign languages, politics and industrial and agricultural techniques. After graduation, some of the learners will resume work at their offices or factories and some may sit for selective examinations to enter universities, colleges or intermediate vocational schools.

The curricula of complementary education schools for workers and peasants are divided into natural sciences and social sciences, and the duration of study is 18 months.

Extramural Activities. Apart from the three kinds of schools with curricula described above, the education of young people and adults is also carried out through extramural activities, and through institutions such as farming co-operatives, breeding-farms, fisheries, logging-camps, State-farm factories, workshops and hospitals. Where there are many young people, there is an emulation movement of 'Young people, marching into science and technology'.

Media. The press and news agencies have given much attention to bringing science and technology to readers in general and to young people in particular. Journals are produced by the Vietnamese Institute of Science; the Central Committee of the Ho Chi Minh Communist Youth Union; Viet Nam's General Federation of Labour; the Vietnamese Women's Union; the Ministry of Health and the Vietnamese Medical Association; the Ministry of Education and the Vietnamese Educational Trade Union.

There are also radio talks on science and technology (half an hour to an hour daily) over the Voice of Viet Nam.

Innovations

In the new curricula of science subjects taught at general education schools special attention is given to philosophical viewpoints particularly the dialectical materialist viewpoint.

The theoretical basis of all science subjects has been strengthened. For example, in physics, the theories on molecular kinetics, electronics, laws of indicts and of conservation; in chemistry, the theories of atomic structure and the structure of substances; and in biology, the evolution theory.

The practical nature of curricula is given importance, with links to productive labour.

Science is taught as part of polytechnic education. Knowledge is introduced into the curricula as a basis for understanding the principles of the most important branches of production. For example, simple machines, generators, electrical machinery, the process of producing chemicals, materials in industry, livestock breeding and cultivation are regarded as key topics.

To overcome the shortage of teaching aids, teachers and pupils have been encouraged to make low-cost teaching aids by themselves; 'master' experiment sets such as the 'Mechanics' set and 'Demonstration Electro-Magnetism' set have been produced; and experimental centres for basic general education schools on a neighbourhood basis have been built up.

Aart from ordinary schools, there are also specialized classes in physics, chemistry and biology, aimed at fostering science talents. Every year, national examinations are held to select gifted pupils in mathematics, physics and literature. Many institutes and departments of universities have sponsored specialized classes, particularly for experimental work. Likewise, many farming co-operatives and industrial workshops have sponsored general education schools, with visits and work training.

20

Sri Lanka

The limited resources available to Sri Lanka can provide an acceptable quality of life, only if every able person in the country is afforded the opportunity of gainful employment. The scientific community has also ways felt that this end can be achieved by harnessing the country's resources through the systematic application of science and technology. It is therefore generally accepted that science and technology are fundamental to the country for providing the goods and services which are required to sustain the society.

If the application of modern science is to benefit the people, its development must involve the country's own scientists, in accordance with the needs and the available resources. Any efforts of the scientific community in this direction requires the support of a population which is scientifically literate and is sensitive to the need for change. In recognition of these facts, science and technology have been given greater importance in all sectors of activity, including education.

National Science Policy

In December 1978, the President of the democratic Socialist Republic of Sri Lanka, inaugurating the 34th annual session of the Sri Lanka Association for the Advancement of Science, made the following seven point policy statement on National science and technology objectives which were to :

a) Use science as an integral part of the developmental strategy of the country and to involve scientists in the formulation of policy and in decision-making at the highest levels;

b) Foster scientific activity in all its aspects and in its widest passible scope, and to maintain a vigorous drive towards self-reliance in national scientific and technological capability;

c) Provide equal and adequate opportunities for all to acquire a basic education in science;

d) Ensure that the institutions of education and research produce scientists and technologists of the highest calibre;

e) Provide scientists and technologists with good working conditions, adequate remuneration, due recognition for their efforts and access to scientific knowledge and activity in other parts of the world;

f) Make available as widely as possible within the country the fruits of scientific and technological activity; and

g) Cultivate among people, an appreciation of the value of science and scientific method as an indispensable part of a modern society.

Since then these seven points have become accepted by individual scientists and the scientific institutions of the country, as the national science and technology policy of Sri Lanka.

The National Resources, Energy and Science Authority of Sri Lanka (hereinafter referred to as the 'Science Authority') created by Parliamentary Act in 1981 acts as the implementing and advisory body. The Science Authority has set up several working committees consisting of specialists drawn from the relevant sectors of activity in the country to give expert advice in the different fields of science and technology. The committee that is mainly concerned with science education at school level is the Science Education Committee.

The following four provisions, existing within the system of school education are relevant to the national science policy: (1) Education is free of school fees at all levels (implemented in 1945) (2) School textbooks are issued free to all children at all levels of open access general education (introduced in 1980) (3) A common curriculum was implemented in 1972, with science as an essential component, in all schools up to the end of open access general education; (4) Financial assistance under scholarship schemes is available to those children who qualify for such awards.

The need for concerted efforts towards aducating the out-of-school youth and adults in the relevant aspects of science is also emphasized in the national science policy. A large number of institutions and organizations within the government, corporation and private sectors have stepped into fulfil this need by evolving a wide variety of strategies aimed at popularizing science and disseminating scientific knowledge.

Science Education in Schools

The prescribed minimum age for entering school is 5 years. The school education which spans over 13 years consists of three phases :

Primary level—kindergarten + grades I—V (6 years),
Junior secondary level-grades VI—X (5 years),
Senior secondary level-grades XI—XII (2 years).

Primary Level This is the first phase of open access general education. At this level science is taught as a component part of an integrated 'Environmental Studies' curriculum, within which the learner is offered the opportunity of going through a graded sequence of science experiences.

Junior Secondary Level. This second phase of education is also open to all children. All students follow a common curriculum with separate subjects, one of which is science. The first national examination, the General Certificate of Education, Ordinary Level (GCE 'O' Level) is held at the end of grade X.

Senior Secondary Level. This is the third and the last phase of school education, and is open only to those who reach a minimum level of attainment at the GCE 'O' Level examination. The minimum general requirements for entering senior secondary education are passes in six subjects, including language and mathematics, with at least three of the passes being at credit level. The senior secondary phase of education is divided into three alternative subject streams: the science stream, the arts stream, and the commerce stream. Within each stream a variety of subjects is available out of which a student may choose four. The choice of subjects is regulated by certain requirements. The requirements for entering the science stream are a credit pass in science, or an ordinary pass in science together with a credit pass in mathematics. Students in the science stream offer four of the following subjects : physics, chemistry, botany, zoology, pure mathematics, applied mathematics, agriculture.

The General Certificate of Education Advanced Level (GCE 'A' Level) examination which is held at the end of grade XII has a dual purpose. It is a terminal achievement test with regard to senior secondary education, and it is also the selection instrument for admission to the various universities in the country. The latter function has had a double-edged effect on what actually goes on inside a typical GCE ('A' Level) classroom. As the number of places available at the universities is relatively small in comparison to the numbers sitting the examination, a student has to score very high marks to stand a chance of entry. This encourages both the students and the teachers to work very hard throughout the courses but at the same time it has the effect of making the classroom teaching rather examination-oriented.

In grades XI and XII the choice of subjects by the students in each of the subject streams is greatly influenced by the university regulations prescribing the subject requirements for admission to the various university courses. Within the science stream most students offered chemistry and physics together with botany and zoology or with pure mathematics and applied mathematics. These two subject combinations are enough to enable students to enter the two most coveted university courses, medicine and engineering.

Student Enrolment. The enrolment figures in Table—1, for the year 1981, show the total numbers of students, up to grade X. Science is compulsory up to this level.

Table—1. Students enrolment in the primary and junior secondary levels for 1981

Grade	*No. of students*
Kindergarten	353,730
Grade I	378,443
" II	356,672
" III	360,427
" IV	356,870
" V	299,516
" VI	260,752
" VII	224,172
" VIII	188,373
" IX	146,329
" X (taking GCE 'O' Level for the first time)	104,438
XI (repeating GCE 'O' Level)	138,254
Total	3,167,976

Sources: School census 1981, Statistics Branch, Ministry of Education.

At the senior secondary level, science subjects are taught only in the science stream. Total enrolment figures for the two grades in the senior secondary level and the numbers in the science stream are given in Table—2 below.

Table—2. Student enrolment in grades XI and XII

Grade	*No. of students in all streams*	*No. of students in the science stream*
XI	71,737	19,619
XII (including students repeating the courses)	129,981	41,658
Total	201,718	61,277

Source: School Census 1981

Instructional Time. The time devoted to science teaching in each of the grades VI—XII is indicated in Table—3. Since an integrated curriculum is operative at the primary level, the time devoted for teaching the science component cannot be fixed with certainty. It may vary, depending on the circumstances prevailing in a given school or a given classroom. On the whole, the instructional time for the science component is estimated to be about one hour per week.

Table—3. Instructional time for science in each of the grades VI-XII

Grade	*Subject*	*Number of periods per week*	*Total number of periods for each year*
VI—VIII	Science	6	180
IX—X	Science	7	210
XI—XII	Physics	8	240
	Chemistry	8	240
	Botany	8	240
	Zoology	8	240

Typically a period is 40 or 45 minutes and the total number of periods for a week is 40. To compute the number of periods for a year, the year has been assumed to be the equivalent of 30 working weeks).

Curriculum Aspects. The education system is centrally controlled by the Ministry of Education. The school curriculum, in all its aspects, follows the broad lines set out by the Ministry. Syllabuses are designed by the Curriculum Development Centre of the Ministry, which also prepares detailed teachers' guides and handbooks, and conducts regular in-service training sessions for teachers at all levels. The Educational Publications Department, under the Ministry of Education. Prepares pupil textbooks in all major subject areas. National examinations are conducted by the Department of Examinations, which also functions under the Ministry of Education. Administrative links and co-operation between these separate institutions serve to co-ordinate their activities towards common goals.

Curriculum Changes in the Recent Past. In 1957 a General Science Project for grades VI, VII and VIII was begun by the

Ministry of Education, the outcome of which was the preparation of a syllabus of instruction and schemes of work for teachers. The schemes of work were further supported by short term in-service teacher seminars in different parts of the country.

Spurred on by the success of this project, a major revision of the grades IX and X (GCE 'O' Level) curricula in science subject was undertaken in 1961. Beginning from 1965, certain major changes in science subjects were effected in the GCE 'O' Level examination by the introduction of more valid and reliable techniques of evaluation.

By the time the junior secondary science project* was nearing completion. Curriculum development through the collective effort of groups of educators had gained recognition in the country, as a worthwhile, and in fact essential, activity in the sphere of education. So what began and contained for a decade as *ad hoc* project activities within the Ministry of Education, became formally institutionalized with the establishment of the Curriculum Development Centre of the Ministry of Education.

Curriculum development work in science up to 1972 may be said to have been only of limited benefit to the country, in the sense that until then science was not taught in all schools having junior secondary grades. Prior to 1972, science was taught, as general science in grades VI to VIII, in about 1,000 schools, and as physics, chemistry and biology in grades IX and X in about 600 schools. Even in the schools which taught science at grades IX and X, usually there was a parallel stream of arts students who were denied the opportunity of learning any science beyond grade VIII.

A new educational scheme came into effect in 1972 introducing certain major changes in the educational structure. Under this scheme the junior secondary phase of education was confined to four years (grades VI-IX), and for the first time a common curriculum became operative at the junior secondary level in all schools in the country. Science, presented as one integrated course, was one of the subjects in the common

---

* ROEAP. Bulletin of the UNESCO Regional Office for Education in Asia. *Science education in Asia,* pp. 156—163, Number 18, June 1977.

curriculum. Introducing 'science for all' throughout the open access phase of general education meant that the subject had now to be taught in about 6,000 schools, resulting in a several fold increase in the demand for resources necessary to teach science effectively. To meet this situation a large number of new teachers had to be recruited. They were given an initial brief training before they took to actual classroom teaching. The in-service training programme was intensified to maintain frequent contact with the teachers, especially those newly recruited. The provision of laboratories or science rooms and the necessary science equipment to schools which did not teach science previously was another obstacle which had to be overcome during that period.

As a part of the educational reforms initiated in 1972, the curricula of the primary (grades I—V) and senior secondary levels (grades X and XI, under that scheme) were also subjected to considerable change. A new integrated curriculum was designed for the primary level. It is basically the same curriculum, both in spirit and in substance, which now operates at the primary level.

At the senior secondary level the physics, chemistry, botany and zoology curricula, which up to then had followed the lines of the traditional GCE 'A' Level syllabuses, were replaced by syllabuses which had a distinct national flavour and which were geared to national needs, aims and aspirations. At this time the subjects botany and zoology were replaced by a general biology course and an applied biology course.

With this curriculum reform at the senior secondary level the process of transition from the traditional school curriculum, inherited from the colonial era, to a more functional 'home grown' curriculum was complete. However, it must be emphasized that, although the objectives and content of the new curricula were based primarily on the dictates of national needs, the teaching methodology was greatly influenced by the current thinking within the international arena on the subject of the process of learning.

Further changes in the structure of the education system in 1978 introduced the current era. The duration of the open access phase of general education was extended by two years by the introduction of a kindergarten stage before the primary phase, and designating grade X as the end of the junior secondary phase. Once again new syllabuses, teachers' guides and school textbooks were prepared. The additional year in the junior secondary phase was used to increase the depth of content of the science curriculum, which enabled the content of the senior secondary curriculum too to be upgraded.

Under the 1972 reforms it was decided that biological science at the senior secondary level should be taught as biology (general) and applied biology. This new curriculum became operative in grade X in 1976. Because of the changes in the school structure in 1978, and on the alive of the advisory committee appointed to examine the issue, new botany and zoology curricula were introduced to replace biology.

Once more, far reaching educational reforms are in the offing. Already a white paper, 'Education proposals for reform—general, university and tertiary (technical, vocational and professional'), prepared by the Ministry of Education in Collaboration with the Ministry of High education and the Ministry of Youth Affairs and Employment (1981) has been presented in parliament and has been open to public discussion.

Enactment of new legislation, based on the white paper and the public response evoked by it, would necessarily entail another revision in the school curriculum, including its science component. Preparatory work in this direction has already been initiated within the Ministry of Education.

Curriculum Development—The Mechanism. As indicated earlier, the curriculum development process has been spearheaded by the Ministry of Education. Once policy decisions are made at the national level through legislation, the curriculum development process involves the following essential steps :

a) Curriculum advisory committee are appointed for separate subject areas to translate national policy into general educational aims and provide guidelines for specifying objectives, deciding upon learning experiences and selecting content. Depending on the requirement of particular situations, these committees consist of curriculum development experts, university academics, teacher educators, teachers, and others representing various government and private sector interests.

b) Curriculum committees based at the Curriculum Development Centre are entrusted the tasks of spelling out objectives, considering the learning experiences and outlining the content in the form of a syllabus of instruction. These curriculum committees consist of experienced teachers, officials of the Ministry of Education, who have specialized in curriculum development, and (sometimes) teacher educators. In order to serve in these committees, practising teachers may be invited to work at the Curriculum Development Centre, either on a full-time basis or on a part-time basis for short or extended periods.

(c) The next stage of operation is to produce teachers' guides to help the teacher plan his classroom lessons. This too is carried out by the curriculum committees. At the senior secondary level formal teachers' guides have been provided only for those units where it has been considered necessary. For the other units informal hand-outs, prepared to support in-service teacher education sessions, are considered adequate.

(d) Pupil's texts are written by panels of writers, including at least some members of the original curriculum committee, under the supervision of the Educational Publications Department.

(e) The curriculum development programme merges with the in-service teacher education programme in that the basic planning for face-to-face in-service sessions is done at the Curriculum Development Centre with the participation of those who have had a hand in the previously mentioned stages of operation.

(f) Curriculum development is treated as a continuing process, and once a new school curriculum is under way, the curriculum committees monitor and evaluate the success of the classroom interactions with a view to taking remedial measures. Usually the programmes are monitored through direct observations, through feedback information received via in-service teacher trainers and circuit education officers, and by analysis of results of public examinations.

The curriculum committees also continue to develop new materials to enrich classroom teaching even further. In the recent past, special workshops were found to be a quick and effective way of producing new curriculum materials in situations where the need for such materials began to be urgently felt.

Learning Objectives in Science. Beginning with the early efforts at curriculum development in 1960, learning objectives in science have been derived using several sets of criteria.

One set of criteria relates to the child in the context of the Sri Lankan setting. This is the child (his present attitudes, abilities, knowledge, skills, interests, needs) and society (its hopes and aspirations, opportunities, demands and defects).

Another set of criteria relates to the value of science in education, which is the fundamental character of science as a worthwhile human endeavour, and the contribution that science can make towards improving the quality of life of the individual and the society.

A third set of criteria arising from taxonomic consideration has been proved to be useful in deriving objectives. As scheme that has been frequently used for categorization of objectives is the cognitive domain (knowledge frameworks application and uses of same); the psychomotor domain (skills of specified types); and the affective domain (attitudes and value frameworks).

A further set of criteria relates to the inherent characteristics of learners in general. These are the stages of intellectual development in children, and the process by which children learn.

Such considerations have led to the formulation of somewhat different learning objectives for science, at each level of school education. These objectives are not regarded as immutable and will certainly undergo change in the future in response to the emerging needs of a dynamic society.

Primary Level (Kindergarten to Grade V). The general objectives of the primary level environmental studies curriculum may be summarized as follows. The student should acquire :

a) The ability to see relationships and implications and to draw conclusion from facts rather than learning isolated facts (learning to learn);

b) Critical objective thinking, in place of passive acceptance of others' opinions;

c) Flexibility and adaptability to meet the challenge of rapid change encountered in modern life;

d) Creativity in thought and action; and

(e) Human fellow feeling (co-operation and co-existence).

The specific objectives for science at this level may be broadly stated as developing an enquiring mind and a scientific approach to problems. In this context, the development of the following skills is considered important: (a) observing and reporting/recording data; (b) ordering/classifying and interpreting data: (c) posing questions and devising experiments to find answers; (d) recognizing patterns and relationships; and (e) communicating.

Junior Secondary Level (Grades VI-X). This being the final phase of open access general education, the science curriculum has to provide what is considered the minimum science education that ideally every citizen ought to receive. This function of the curriculum is of utmost importance in that the vast majority of students will receive no further formal education in science beyond the junior secondary level. The greater population of students who complete the junior secondary phase do not enter the senior secondary phase because they are either not inclined to do so or because they fail to reach the qualifying standard at the GCE 'O' Level examination. Of those who proceed to the senior secondary phase, the majority remain outside the science stream.

Learning objectives of the junior secondary science curriculum have been formulated with these factors in mind. They are to :

(a) Understand the methods and the processes used by scientists in solving problems and be able to use the same in appropriate situations;

(b) Acquire skills, attitudes and scientific knowledge relevant to the daily life of individuals engaged in various spheres of national activity;

(c) Develop the creativity needed for scientific inventiveness;

(d) Acquire knowledge, skills and attitudes relevant to the maintenance of personal health;

(e) Appreciate the contribution made by the scientific institutions to national life and be willing to assist their activities;

(f) Understand the problems and perils of technological development and appreciate the need for choosing appropriate technology for Sri Lanka;

(g) Acquire a knowledge of the national resources and the skills necessary for exploiting them judiciously;

(h) Develop the ability of critical evaluation of information disseminated through various media;

(i) Develop an understanding of the major unifying concepts and patterns of science; and

(j) Acquire the academic background necessary for further education in science.

Senior secondary level. At this level, science is taught as four separate subjects : Chemistry, physics, botany and zoology.

The senior secondary science subject curricula have to serve several divergent purpose each of which cannot be delegated to a second place. The curricula have to meet the needs of pupils who will proceed for higher studies in tertiary institutes and contine to study one or more of the above-mentioned science subjects; those who will proceed for higher studies but will not study any science subjects; and those for whom it is a terminal course—for these pupils the importance of a given science subject would lie in its applications to everyday life, and as a vehicle to broaden the mind and improve powers of reasoning.

The objectives of all science subjects are seen, therefore, to have a common ethos with only minor variations among the separate subjects; these minor variations being the outcome of the special attributes of each subject. For a general idea of the objectives of learning science at the senior secondary level, it may suffice to consider here the objectives of one of the science subjects; chemistry.

The student should :

(a) Understand the fundamental concepts of chemistry necessary to comprehend the physical bases of scientific explanations of common phenomena;

(b) Acquire knowledge of the framework of chemistry including major concepts, unifying themes and patterns that would enable the pupil to understand the structure and changes of matter and provide the necessary background to those who wish to pursue chemistry to a higher level;

(c) Show an awareness of the development of chemistry and appreciate past human achievements in the history of chemistry;

(d) Understand the significance, possibilities and limitations of the knowledge acquired in chemistry in relation to technical, social and economic development, show awareness of the impact and influence this knowledge has on society and provide preparation for life in a technological age;

(e) Develop manipulative and experimental skills necessary to be competent and confident in the investigation of materials found in the environment;

(f) Show awareness of the natural resources and understand the physico-chemical bases of problems in the conservation and scientific exploitation of natural resources, with special reference to the situation in Sri Lanka;

(g) Acquire the knowledge and skills necessary for the application of basic concepts in chemistry for technical, social and economic development with special reference to Sri Lanka; and

(h) Show willingness to employ the knowledge and skills gained for the socio-economic development and for conservation and scientific exploitation of natural resources of Sri Lanka.

The Content of the Science Curriculum

Primary Level. The content of Environmental Studies is organized under 11 study areas or themes, which are as follows : Our homes and their inhabitants; What we eat and drink; What we wear; Help for our work; We are different but similar too (unity in diversity); Things around us; Our school and its neighbourhood; People who help us; How we travel and communicate; Our earth and its surroundings; and Things we see and hear.

Compared to the rest of the school curriculum, Environmental Studies shows flexibility of content. The actual content of the classroom lessons depends on the nature of the environment and the resources available in and around the school. Thus in order to develop a given skill, two groups of children in two different schools may engage themselves in widely different types of activities, and the emphasis at this stage is on the process rather than on the product. The syllabus and the teachers' guide (which among other things lists problems under each theme, from which the teacher may select a few to be investigated by his students) the teacher to select relevant content for his classroom.

Junior Secondary Level. At the junior secondary level, science, taught as a single separate subject, assumes a relatively more formal outlook. The teachers at this level possess at least a GCE 'A' Level science background and are more competent at handling formal science. In terms of content the two major attributes of this science curriculum are that as far as possible science is presented as an integrated subject rather than as compartmentalized disciplines; and it is essentially activity based. Both these attributes, though not made patently clear in the syllabus, are amplified in detail in the teachers' guides which make suggestions for integration and detail the activities to be used in the classroom.

Integration is not interpreted solely in the narrow context of establishing links between and among the separate scientific disciplines. The curriculum developers have desisted from creating highly artificial teaching situations by attempting to integrate across disciplines for the mere sake of integration. Instead the science curriculum attempts to integrate pure science in several other dimensions as well. Keeping the objectives of the curriculum in view, attempts have been made to integrate science, (a) across the separate scientific disciplines (e.g. under topics such as 'atmosphere' and 'food'); (b) with other studies such as social sciences, agriculture and health (e.g. under topics such as 'population and food' and 'man and his environment'); (c) through its application to day-to-day life problems (this aspect pervades all topics); and (d) with leisure (e.g. toys that work on 'heat').

Another feature of the junior secondary science curriculum is its spiral nature—that is, different concepts are revisited several times, at increasingly higher levels of sophistication, during the period of five years. This feature serves a dual purpose. First, it is conducive to the mastering of concepts by the children. Second, it exposes the children to a wider range of scientific concepts at the earliest possible age. This is important especially for those children who may leave school before completing the full course of junior secondary education. In this respect, grade VIII is a critical year because that is the point at which those who do not wish to enter the GCE 'O' Level course leave school. For this reason, efforts have been made to include the kind of science, which is most useful in everyday life, in the curriculum of grades VI to VIII. This was one of the factors which contributed to the inclusion of such matters as the functional aspects of transistors and house wiring in the grade VIII syllabus, rather than waiting until the children are more mature.

Senior Secondary Level. At the senior secondary level chemistry, physics, botany, and zoology and taught as four different subjects. In these syllabuses the content is specified as a series of units arranged in a suggested teaching sequence. However, this suggested sequence is not expected to be strictly followed by the teacher. The teacher is free to evolve his own teaching sequence, as long as he takes due care to see that the pre-requisite fundamentals necessary to begin any particular unit have been previously mastered by his students.

Even in the curricula of the four separate science subjects at the senior secondary level a more integrated approach, than was evident in the traditional curricula, has been adopted. The following two features may be noted :

a). In each subject some of the traditional schemes of dividing the content have been abandoned. For example, in botany, instead of studying plant types separately, the morphological aspects of a range of plants are taken up under the theme of 'diversity' and their life cycles under 'reproduction'. In chemistry, instead of dividing the content into inorganic, organic, physical; the entire curriculum has been developed around several major themes such as structure, bonding, energetic and periodicity.

b) The application of each subject to life and its effects on society and environment receives emphasis.

Assessment of Student Performance. Schools conduct their own term, mid-year and end-of-the-year tests. In these the teachers use a variety of assessment techniques such as observation, interviewing, written tests, and continuous assessment. Beyond grade V the written test is the most common form of assessment.

There are two national level public examinations, the GCE 'O' Level at the end of grade X and the GCE 'A' Level at the end of grade XII. Both of these are written examinations. Practical work is not tested separately. However, the theory papers include some questions which test familiarity with practical work. In regard to the 'A' Level examination the students now have to complete a specified minimum amount of practical work at school, in order to become eligible to sit the written examination.

Each of the two public examinations consists of a Paper I containing fixed response multiple choice questions, and a Paper II containing structured and semi-structured free response questions. Some details regarding these question papers are given in Table—4 below.

Table—4. Some details about GCE 'O' Level science and GCE 'A' Level chemistry, physics, botany and zoology question papers

Examination	*Question Paper*	*Number of questions*			*Answering time (hours)*
		Multiple choice fixed response type	*Structured free response type*	*Semi-structured and free essay type*	
GCE 'O' Level	Paper I	40/40	-	-	1
	Paper II	-	8/10	-	3
GCE 'A' Level	Paper I	60/60	-	-	2
	Paper II	-	4/4		3

In each of the cages indicating the number of questions, the denominator refers to the total number of questions given and the numerator refers to the number of questions to be answered by the candidate.

In designing these question papers a table of specifications is used to ensure content validity and objective validity. A modified form of Bloom's classification of the cognitive domain is used to specify the assessment objectives, leading to the categorization of questions into (a) recall of factual information; (b) comprehension; (c) application; and (d) higher abilities (analysis, synthesis, and evaluation).

Science Activities, Laboratory Work and Equipment. Basically, the science curricula at all school levels have been designed to operate on a foundation of practical activities. Although it is not impossible to achieve some of the objectives of the curricula in the absence of practical activities, any one attempting to teach or learn science without giving due regard to the specified component of practical work would fall far short of the intended outcomes. Thus the availability of facilities for practical work as well as the effective utilization of the facilities are indispensable to the success of the school science curricula. The responsibility of supplying the necessary equipment and chemicals lies with the Ministry of Education.

Facilities for Practical Work. The primary level classes do not require a great deal of standard apparatus or equipment for their exploratory and investigatory activities within the subject Environmental Studies. Nor do they require any special laboratory space for it. For the most part they use materials freely available to them in the environment. Where the primary classes form a part of a school with higher forms, they are able to make use of the equipment made available to the upper school. Of those schools, some have received limited financial allocations from the Ministry of Education for purchasing some of the basic equipment, but there are still a considerable number of schools to be provided for in the future.

It has been decided that junior secondary and/or senior secondary science classes should be provided with adequately equipped laboratories. There are two main categories of laboratories among schools: those designed for teaching science in grades VI to X and those designed for teaching the separate science subjects in grades XI and XII.

The former category of laboratory has been designed to accommodate a situation where teaching is done as harmonious blend of theory and practical work, a condition necessary to the successful achievement of objectives of the integrated science curriculum. The same end may be reached, by creating 'science rooms', which are ordinary classrooms converted into a secure place with minimum facilities for science activities and storing equipment.

For teaching chemistry, physics, botany and zoology at senior secondary level a proper laboratory is essential. Out of about 1,900 schools with senior secondary level classes only about 450 schools have a science stream, and these have laboratories designed for teaching the separate science subjects.

Standard lists of equipment and chemicals equipment and chemicals required for junior and senor secondary levels have been prepared by the Ministry of Education with the help of curriculum committees. These lists are subject to revision on the introduction of new curricula. The quantities supplied to each school depend on the student enrolment, the unit for working out quantities being a class of 30 students. An effective system of distributing equipment and chemicals has been set up through the Central Science Store of the Ministry of Education.

A small sum of money is also made available annually to schools to purchase certain specified day-to-day requirements such as soap, zoological specimens for dissection, petrol and so on. The sum received by each school is calculated on the basis of the number of students in each grade.

The Sources of Equipment and Chemicals. The equipment and chemicals are manufactured by the Government Science Equipment Production Unit (holders and stands, insect display boards, ripple tank, vibrators, trolley nits, DNA models); manufactured by local private sector firms and purchased by the Ministry of Education (ammeters, voltmeters, balances); purchased by the government from foreign manufactures (chemicals, microscopes, thermometers, chemical balances, cathode ray apparatus, glassware); received from foreign agencies under aid programmes (e.g. UNICEF); and produced by teachers using local low-cost materials (circuit boards, motors, dynamos).

The total money allocation for purchase of school science equipment and chemicals by the government for the year 1983 was Rs. 16 milliion.* Of this only 4 million was used for purchases from local manufacturers with the balance used to purchase equipment from foreign manufacturers.

Practical Work at the Classroom Level. At the junior secondary level, examinations in practical work have never been held. Yet at this level most teachers are enthusiastic about building up their lessons around practical activities. This may be because they find it extremely difficult, if not impossible, to teach science concepts to children at that particular stage of development without resorting to practical activities.

At the senior secondary level there were practical examinations up to 1970 as part of the GCE 'A' Level examinations. During this era the usual practice was to devote 50 per cent of the teaching time for practical work. In 1970, the practical examination was abolished and was replaced by a

* Approximately Sri Lankan rupees (SRs) 25 = One US dollar

scheme of continuous assessment which was done internally by the school itself. The teacher was expected to grade each student, according to a five-point scale, by observation of the student during normal practical work and by holding a series of practical tests during the course. A grade on the five-point scale had to be awarded for : (i) manipulative skills; (ii) ability to observe and record; (iii) ability to analyse and interpret observations; and (iv) ability to plan and design experiments.

Based on these guardians a final index of performance had to be computed and expressed as a score on a five-point scale. A student had to obtain a minimum score of three to qualify to sit the theory papers. An additional qualifying requirement was that each student had to do a minimum quantity of experimental work (e.g. participation in 50 per cent of the practical work scheduled for the two years in botany and zoology).

This scheme of internal continuous assessment was, by and large, a failure from its very inception, mainly due to lack of an effective programme of supervision. Between 1970 and 1982 practical work in the senior secondary classes was progressively neglected, and untidy, empty laboratories were a common sight in many schools. Lack of interest in practical work began to be reflected in student performance at 'A' Level written examinations, especially in respect of those questions with a practical bias.

Remedial measures to resuscitate practical work in schools were initiated in the last quarter of 1982. A list of experimental work was prescribed for each subject. New regulations were framed to disqualify students who do not complete 60 per cent of the prescribed experimental work, from sitting the 'A' Level examination. An intensive programme of school supervision has been mounted to ensure strict adherence to the above regulations. The supervising teams, led by officers of the Curriculum Development centre, during their visits to schools endeavour to convince the students and the teachers of the value of experimental work in learning science, rather than adapting coercive tactics. With this programme in operation, the year 1983 witnessed a pleasing change within the schools where, once again, experimental work is gradually being restored to its due place within the senior secondary science curriculum.

The schools have been advised to use about 50 per cent of the teaching time of each science subject, for practical activities. The teachers have been advised to build up theory on the basis of practical work rather than perform experiments to demonstrate previously learned theory.

Use of Educational Technology

Educational technology is just beginning to have a significant impact on science teaching. Until quite recently, radio was the only medium used to any considerable extent in the schools, and that too has not developed into a regular practice other than in exceptional instances. Schools are not equipped even with basic items such as slide projectors, film projectors, and overhead projectors. The recently introduced educational television is beginning to make an impact in the schools. A computer education programme is due to begin shortly and work is already in progress to establish a National Media Centre.

Educational Television (ETV). The recently established national television network began transmitting regular educational programmes, especially designed for senior secondary science and mathematics students, in May 1983. At present these programmes are transmitted at the rate of one programme per week in each of chemistry, physics, botany, zoology and mathematics. All programmes are produced in both languages, Sinhala and Tamil. Allowing for school holidays, this works out at 24 programmes per subject per year in each language medium. The present programmes are aimed only at the students of grade XI classes. The number of programmes is scheduled to increase to cover grade XII as well. In the future ETV programmes will be extended to cover other subjects at all levels.

The decision to begin ETV programmes at the senior secondary level was a pragmatic one, based on three main considerations.

(a) It was economically more feasible to only supply television sets and video recorders to the 450 schools with senior secondary science classes;

(b) The majority of the schools with senior secondary classes have access to electricity while such is not the case with the rest of the schools; and

(c) ETV was considered to be a means of reducing the disadvantages suffered by science students in rural areas due to shortages of qualified science teachers.

Of the schools having senior secondary science classes, 420 have access to electricity. Each of these schools has been supplied with one or more 20-inch colour TV receivers. One hundred and thirty-four of the larger schools were also supplied with video-cassette recorders. In those schools without access to mains electricity, solar panels and appropriate models of TV receivers are now being installed.

The ETV programmes are produced as a joint venture of the Ministry of State (production and transmission) and the Ministry of Education (content and methodology).

The Computer Education Programme. The decision to have a computer education programme was made by the Ministry of Education in December, 1982. The two main objectives of the envisaged programme are to enable students in the senior secondary level classes to become acquainted with micro-computers and their simple every day uses (basic computer language and fundamentals of computer programming); and provide an opportunity for school students and out-of-school youth to learn how to operate computers and so take advantage of the rapidly increasing employment opportunities in the computer field.

At the initial stage about 150 of the larger schools with senior secondary science classes will be supplied with micro-computers and audio cassette tape players (for the programs). They already have TV colour monitors for use as visual display units. After the initial phase these facilities will be extended to other schools.

The teachers who will be in charge of the programme in the 150 schools will be trained in six training centres.

The National Media Centre. Work is in progress to establish a National Media Centre at the Curriculum Development Centre. It will produce audio and video tapes, slides, overhead projector transparencies and multi-media packages and make them available to schools. Training teachers in the use of media will be anther vital function of this centre.

It is also expected to undertake surveys and research in regard to the use of media for teaching and learning.

A programme to establish a network of Regional Media Centres, is also envisaged. The work of the regional centres will be co-ordinated by the National Centre and they will service the schools in the various regions of the country. Each regional centre will then adapt the main programme to the special characteristics and needs of its own region.

Teacher Training

At present, except in the case of a few special subjects, the minimum educational qualification required by a person to be recruited as a teacher is three passes in the relevant subjects at the 'A' Level examination. Non-graduates processing this minimum qualification are recruited on the basis of a competitive selection examination. Before 1981, teachers with only 'O' Level were also recruited. The different categories of teachers available for teaching science and mathematics, at junior and senior secondary levels, and their numbers (data for the year 1981) are as follows:

Graduates :	Physical science	916
	Biological science	960
	Mathematics	354
University (under-graduate)		
Diploma holders in science mathematics		205
Trained teachers (trained at Teachers' Colleges)		
	Science	3,654
	Mathematics	3,355
Certificated teachers		124
GCE 'A' Level/'O' Level qualified teachers		4,893

Other than in exceptional circumstances science subjects at the senior secondary level are taught by graduates. Non-graduate science teachers are mostly confined to the junior secondary level. At the primary level, there are no specialized science teachers, and the science component is handled by the teacher of environmental studies. Many of the 62,000 primary teachers are untrained.

Professional Courses in Teacher Education. The universities (under the Ministry of Higher Education) conduct a one-year post-graduate Diploma in Education of the Open University, which is a two-year correspondence course. The Teachers Colleges (under the Ministry of Education) award the Trained Teachers Certificate (two-year course).

All these courses are pre-service in character, although the students for the Diploma in Education, as well as for the teachers' college courses, are selected from teachers who have been teaching for several years. The Diploma in Education courses are open only to graduate teachers. Teachers colleges undertake the training of non-graduate teachers who make up the bulk of the country's teacher population. Teachers colleges provide a variety of course to meet the needs of primary level teachers and those teaching different subject combinations at the junior secondary level.

The Teachers College curriculum consists of : (a) foundation courses in educational psychology and principles of education; (b) general education-first language, English, religion, aesthetics and agriculture; (c) specialization in subject areas such as science, mathematics, English; (d) teaching practice; and (e) school and community activities.

Evaluation for the purposes of awarding the Trained Teachers Certificate is carried out by a terminal external written examination, internal evaluation by continuous assessment and several tests evaluating proficiency in classroom teaching, and a presentation of assigned projects and other professional achievements.

Out of a total of 25 teachers colleges only ten provide science courses. There were 928 trainees admitted into the science courses in 1981. Fourteen teachers colleges offer primary education courses. Admissions for 1981 numbered 645. For these streams the selection of trainees is based on their seniority as teachers.

Owing to a mismatch between teacher recruitment and teacher training in the past, there is now a considerable backlog of untrained teachers, both at the primary and junior secondary school levels.

Distance Education Programme for Training Teachers. A distance education programme has been initiated by the Ministry of Education to train the backlog of teachers while they are in schools and attending to their normal duties as teachers. Initially the course will be open to a limited number of teachers on a pilot basis but will later expand gradually to cover the total population. These courses will comprise : postal communication through printed materials, written assignments; contact sessions with tutors; and direct supervision by tutors.

The minimum period for completing the course and obtaining the Trained Teachers Certificate is two years.

In-service Teacher Education. Training teachers once and for all through one or two year courses has been found to be inadequate to meet the requirements of the changing school curricula. Thus, a systematic and regular in-service teacher education programme has been put into operation by the Curriculum Development Centre. Seminars and workshops are held in all districts for teachers at all school levels.

The basic planning for the in-service seminars is done at the Curriculum Development Centre. Seminars are held with the help of in-service advisers ('master teachers') appointed on a district basis for each of the main subject areas. There are separate regional in-service advisers for primary education, junior secondary science, and each of the senior secondary science subjects. Out of these, only the junior secondary science advisers work full time on in-service education. The advisers of the primary and senior secondary levels are full-time teachers in schools, whose services are used as and when required for in-service advisory work.

The in-service education programme which originally began as a 'maintenance and repair service', has now established itself as a quality improvement programme of vital importance.

Research

A considerable amount of activity involving a research component goes on all the time within the Ministry of Education. When programmes associated with science education are evaluated, practical problems are identified, relating to organizational or curriculum aspects. In either case, effective remedial steps are taken on the basis of studies conducted by officials of the Ministry of Education or by the Regional Departments of Education under the Ministry. But such studies usually remain within the realm of day-to-day office work and are rarely carried on to the level of presentation and publication as formal research papers. For example, the science subject committees of the Curriculum Development Centre are at present taking stock of the extent and nature of practical work being done in the schools in the 'A' Level classes. This is done by studying the situation in selected samples of schools from separate educational districts. Problems encountered by the schools are identified and remedial measures applied as soon as possible. This kind of programme, where corrections are applied through negative feedback loops all along the line, is commoner than long drawn-out research studies, the results of which can be used only at the terminal stage.

Some officials concerned with science education, for example those attached to universities under scholarship schemes to satisfy a requirement for confirmation in their posts, have been able to conduct in-depth studies on problems related to their work and record them in the form of reports and dissertations. Such studies have been of immense use to the Ministry for further planning in relevant areas. Most studies of this nature have been concerned with working out fresh guidelines for developing (a) new curricula in different science subjects; (b) assessment procedures; (c) teacher training strategies; and (d) supervision of science teaching.

The Curriculum Development Centre of the Ministry of Education has applied for membership of the International Project Council to participate in the Second Science Study of the International Association for Evaluation of Educational Achievement (IEA).

Programmes for Out-of-school Youth and Adults and Popularization of Science and Technology

The positive attitude of the Government towards popularization of science and technology may be gathered from its National Science and Technology Policy. The fact that the country has such a policy entitles the various Ministries and other public organizations to devote a portion of the resources available to them for purposes of disseminating scientific knowledge, and developing scientific attitude and skills among the general public. The government also gives due recognition and support to private organizations and agencies that show concern for the popularization of science (*e.g.* The Sri Lanka Association for the Advancement of science).

The Mass Media. The national newspapers, radio and television give wide coverage to scientific topics. They are mostly concerned with the day-to-day problems of individual and family health, agriculture, national development and conservation, as well as a scientific analysis of traditional practices and beliefs. The fact that Sri Lanka has a literacy rate of over 85 per cent, coupled with the fact that a newspaper bought by one individual is often shared and read by many others, makes the newspapers a powerful medium through which scientific information reaches a large proportion of the public. The radio, being a fairly common household item, is also a highly effective medium in this respect. In addition to the school service programmes of the Sri Lanka Broadcasting Corporation, about one tenth of the general broadcasting time is devoted to educational programmes which include a component of science. At present television is available only to a limited audience but programmes of general scientific interest are included among the regular TV transmissions. At present only some of these programmes are locally produced, whilst others are popular progammes obtained from other countries, usually in English.

Adult Education Centres Programme of the Ministry of Education. These centres were established in 1977 to provide information to adults and out-of-school youth about improved agricultural, health, vocational and other practices with a view to improving their conditions and enabling them to participate more effectively in the development programmes of the country.

At the time the programme was established the country was divided into 160 electrorates, and the scheme has been implemented in 140 of them. For this purpose an Adult Education Officer (AEO) was appointed to each division.

The AEO organizes suitable educational programmes for the adults in the area with the participation of many agencies, including public sector institutions, private sector and voluntary organizations. The content of these educational programmes is variable and depends on the needs and problems peculiar to each group. In general, it includes vocational guidance, general information, health, short-term skills training, environmental problems, and effective utilization of traditional knowledge and time tested techniques available in the community.

The Adult Education Centre Programme is the responsibility of the Non-formal Education Branch of the Ministry of Education. Recently, the Ministry has set up a centre for non-formal education research and development, the main functions of which will be development of non-formal education curricula, staff development, documentation and publicity aspects, and adaptation of traditional technology.

The Committee for the Popularization of Science, of the Sri Lanka Association for the Advancement of Science. This is a statutory committee of the association and its main objectives are to disseminate scientific information and promote scientific thinking among school children and the lay population of the country. However most of its activities are directly concerned with school children, for several reasons. In the first place, the school children form an easily accessible and organized target group for implementing systematic programmes of activity. Second, experience has shown that the school children are highly receptive to the ideas and ideals of the scientific community and it is assumed that a scientifically oriented child population would eventually lead to the establishment of a scientifically oriented adult population. Finally, as a strategy for popularizing science within the total community, the school children could be developed into effective agents for carrying the message to the adults.

Some of the current activities of the Popularization of Science Committee are :

'Vidya Viyapthi'. This is the popular science journal of the committee which carries articles written by eminent scientists and scientific writers. Usually, four issues are published each year.

Nature Diaries Programme. The programme is intended to promote the skill of scientific observation and maintaining records among school children. Child volunteers undertake to maintain regular records of selected natural events or phenomena over a period of several months. Awards are given to the school as well as to the student making the best contribution.

Science Day Programme. This is carried out throughout the country (in different areas on different days) with the objective of disseminating scientific knowledge and promoting scientific thinking among students and others. Important components of the programme are popular lectures, discussions by resource persons, demonstrations, science quizzes, film shows, mini-exhibitions and oratorical contests.

Popular Lectures. Under this programme popular science lectures are delivered by scientists in different parts of the country.

Use and Hazards of Agro-chemicals Programme. This programme commenced in 1981 when a group of about 100 school children of upper grades, drawn from different parts of the country, attended a one-day seminar, the theme of which was the Use and Hazards of Agro-chemicals. The purpose of this initial seminar was to sensitize the children to the above problem. Subsequently, 80 children selected from the above group were given training in the safe use of agro-chemicals at the In-Service Training Institute of the Department of Agriculture. Later some of these children conducted seminars for their friends and adults, in their own localities, with the support of relevant expert personnel. This is a concrete example of the strategy of getting the children to act as agents for spreading the message of the scientists among the lay adults.

Environmental Monitoring Programme. A programme has been planned where volunteer groups of senior secondary level students will undertake to monitor environmental parameters in their locality.

Affiliation of Other Science Bodies to the Popularization of Science Committee. Provision exists for any science organization in a school or a locality to seek affiliation to the

Popularization of Science Committee. Such affiliation entitles them to technical support and expertise from the Committee. Specific projects of affiliated bodies may even be backed financially by the Committee.

Current Innovations

Production of Curriculum Materials Through Workshops. Organizing workshops of one to two weeks duration has been found to be a very efficient system of generating high quality curriculum materials within a short period of time. At these workshops groups consisting of research scientists, university teachers, school teachers and curriculum developers jointly discuss and identify learning experiences, select content and develop experimental work for selected topics. Quite a large number of such workshops have been successfully held during the last few years. One such workshop was the UNESCO sponsored National Workshop on the Preparation of Instructional Materials for Teaching certain Non-traditional areas in Chemistry and Zoology. This workshop resulted in the production of three teachers' guides; which are now widely used by teachers of senior secondary classes. They are Natural Resources of Sri Lanka (1979), (related to the chemistry curriculum); Pests of Common Crops in Sri Lanka (1979); and Inland Fisheries in Sri Lanka (1979) (related to the zoology curriculum).

Field Studies Centres Programme. This programme is mainly concerned with utilizing the natural habitat, as the teaching/learning resource for developing environmental concepts in school children. At present there are seven Field Studies Centres located in different parts of the country. Each centre has been developed to provide necessary facilities and easy access to an extensive and ecologically complex natural habitat for environmental study purposes. The habitats, coming within the ambit of this programme include forest reserves, river banks, and a lagoon. There are plans to increase the number of Field Studies Centres, but even with the existing number of Centres a wide variety of natural habitats, where widely different edaphic factors and climatic regimes prevail, have become accessible for study purposes.

Except in the case of the oldest of these Field Studies Centres, which has its own premises with buildings and other facilities, the other Centres have been organized, in the premises of suitably located large schools. Study camps (mostly residential) are held at these centres enabling the students and teachers to conduct studies using the environment as a resource. So far most studies at these camps have been of an ecological nature. But there have been instances where other issues have been considered (e.g. the study camp on the 'Utilization of solar energy' held at one of the Centres in 1981).

Science Education Support Centres Programme. So far three such centres have been established in three widely separated regions of the country to help teachers plan stimulating lessons; handle and improvise apparatus; use the environment as a teaching resources and enrich their knowledge.

21
Thailand

The National Scheme of Education provides for six years of primary education, three years lower secondary and three years of upper secondary education. This new 6:3:3 system was implemented in 1978.

Primary education aims to provide and to maintain literacy and to develop in the individual cognitive ability, numbers manipulation, communication skills and adequate knowledge that may be applicable to future occupational roles. It is also aimed towards personal development and the promotion of attitudes desirable for life in a democratic society. It is compulsory for all Thai children. Secondary education aims to provide appropriate academic and vocational knowledge compatible with the learner's age, needs, interests, skills and aptitudes which will ultimately be beneficial to his chosen career and society. Extensive elective subjects in the academic and vocational areas are offered in the lower secondary level. In the upper secondary level, students are guided to concentrate on areas of specialization needed for their chosen career of occupation. Higher education aims at the full development of human intellectual abilities to facilitate the advancement in knowledge and technology.

Non-formal education is organized outside the regular school system. It may be designed for specific purposes or it may be part of other educational programmes, the objectives of which are to develop ability in problem-solving, or to provide certain

Figure 1. Educational system

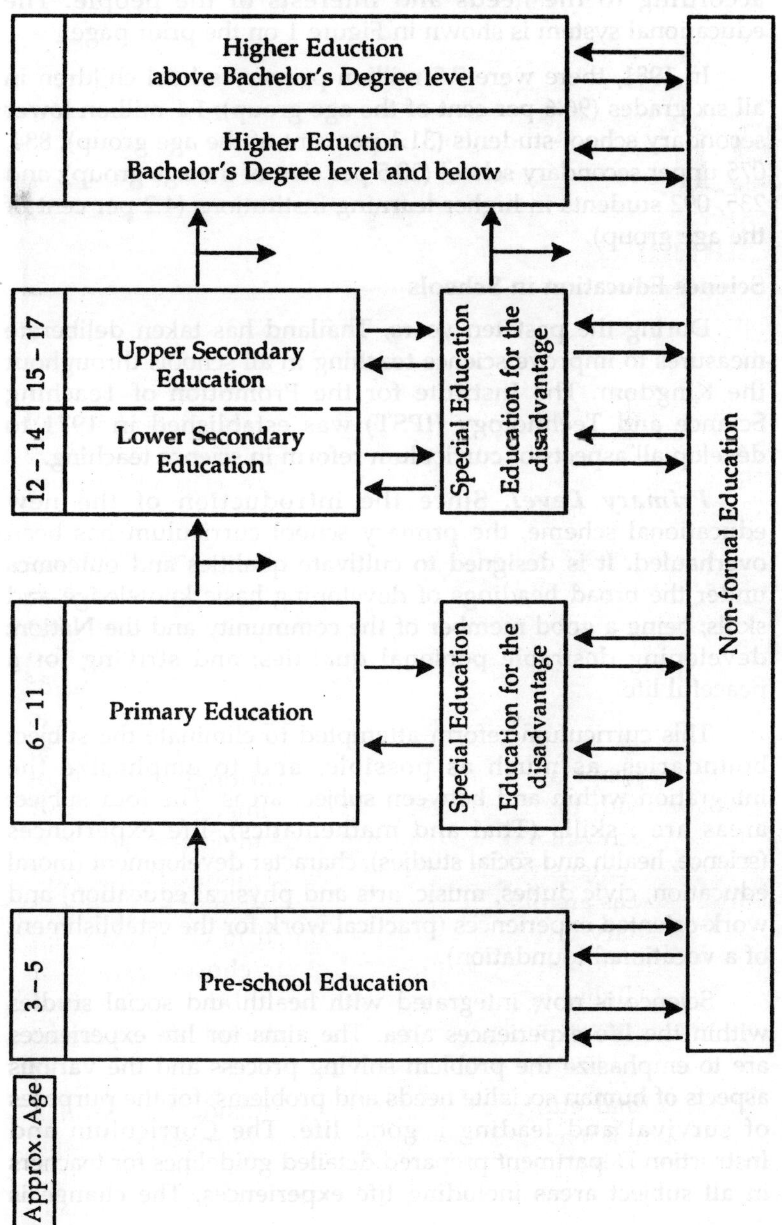

occupational skills or to give specific knowledge and information according to the needs and interests of the people. The educational system is shown in Figure 1 on the prior page.

In 1981, there were 7.5 million primary school children in all six grades (96.6 per cent of the age group); 1.1 million lower secondary school students (31.1 per cent of the age group); 884, 075 upper secondary school (20.5 per cent of the age group); and 235, 092 students in higher learning institutions (4.2 per cent of the age group).

Science Education in Schools

During the past ten years, Thailand has taken deliberate measures to improve science teaching in all schools throughout the Kingdom. The Institute for the Promotion of Teaching Science and Technology (IPST) was established in 1971 to develop all aspects of curriculum reform in science teaching.

Primary Level. Since the introduction of the new educational scheme, the primary school curriculum has been overhauled. It is designed to cultivate qualities and outcomes under the broad headings of developing basic knowledge and skills; being a good member of the community and the Nation; developing desirable personal qualities; and striving for a peaceful life.

This curriculum reform attempted to eliminate the subject boundaries, as much as possible, and to emphasize the integration within and between subject areas. The four subject areas are : skills (Thai and mathematics), life experiences (science, health and social studies), character development (moral education, civic duties, music, arts and physical education) and work-oriented experiences (practical work for the establishment of a vocational foundation).

Science is now integrated with health and social studies within the life experiences area. The aims for life experiences are to emphasize the problem solving process and the various aspects of human socialite needs and problems, for the purposes of survival and leading a good life. The Curriculum and Instruction Department prepared detailed guidelines for teachers in all subject areas including life experiences. The change is rather drastic in the sense that science is no longer taught as a subject but is integrated with health and social studies. Integration has its own merits as well as shortfalls. Most primary school teachers are not familiar with this approach. The in-service training of teachers is not possible owing to the great number of teachers in primary schools. The curriculum guidelines alone are not sufficient to enable teachers to organize the teaching/learning activities to meet the objectives.

In 1979, realizing the urgent need to help teachers to cope with this new innovation, IPST prepared teaching/learning packages for the teaching of science as part of life experiences. These were tried out for grades I and II in 43 schools covering all regions for the country, for grades III and IV in 1980 and for grades V and VI in 1981. Feedback was collected and used for revision. The final version of the teaching materials for grades I to IV have now been completed and those for grades V and VI will be completed soon. The teaching package consists of a detailed teachers' guide, workcards, posters, equipment and other necessary materials. They are put together in kits so that teachers may carry them from one class to another. The kits are so designed that they are low-cost and can be locally made by teachers if they so desire. Since most primary school teachers have a heavy teaching load, the mass production of these kits is essential. The Ministry of Education has made a decision to assign the mass production responsibility to Kurusapa, the commercial arm of the Ministry.

The IPST is still very much concerned with this problem and trying to work out the in-service training of teachers by different approaches, perhaps through school clusters and the Science Teachers Servicing Centres (STSCs).

Science Education at Secondary Level. Science is a required subject for all students in lower secondary schools and is studied for four periods a week. The science course offered at this level is an integrated programme developed by IPST and first implemented in 1977.

At the upper secondary level, students are required to take only four semester courses in science for three periods a week. The students who do not intend to study further in the science related field or those who terminate their study at this level will select the physical and biological science course developed by IPST. The science-oriented students will select all of the three science course—physics, chemistry and biology. These courses were developed by IPST and first implemented in 1976. With the introduction of the new educational scheme, these courses were revised and the second cycle was launched in 1981. Since there are three years in the upper secondary school, these new science courses are designed to cover six semesters for grades X, XI and XII. The study period for biology and chemistry is three periods a week each, and four period a week for physics.

Science Curriculum Development. The movement towards reform of science education in Thailand has been stimulated by the methods being used in the developed countries as well as by the country's own interest to produce good scientists, technologists and technicians.

The IPST was established to :

(a) initiate, execute and promote the study and research of curricula, teaching techniques and evaluation in sciences, mathematics and technology at all educational levels;

(b) promote and execute training programmes for teachers, instructors, lecturers, students and university students on the teaching of sciences, mathematics and technology.

(c) promote and execute research, development and production of science equipment and materials for teaching the sciences, mathematics and technology; and

(d) promote the preparation of texts, exercises, references, supplementary materials and teachers' guides on the sciences, mathematics and technology.

The overall objectives were broad and ambitious, and difficult to fulfil immediately, especially at the early stage of IPST. It was decided initially to focus attention on the development of science curricula at secondary level and mathematics curricula for both primary and secondary levels. The innovation of science and mathematics curricula by IPST was a truly national effort with generous assistance from UNESCO and UNDP.

The projects in the early stage were focused on the development of mathematics for primary schools; mathematics for science students in lower secondary; mathematics for upper secondary; mathematics for non-science students in upper secondary; integrated science for lower secondary; physics, chemistry and biology for science students in upper secondary; and physical science for non-science students in upper secondary schools. A systematic approach to curriculums reform was adopted from the beginning to develop, test and evaluate student's texts and teachers' guides, to develop and guide production of science equipment, teacher training materials, evaluation procedures and instruments. The systems approach served to synchronize and provide adequate preparation for the acceptance of the major outputs and to provide clear insights of the inputs required. This made it easier to see the sequential development tasks as an intricate part of total operation.

In the second phase of the operation, IPST launched eight additional projects which were the development of primary science; basic science for agriculture; basic science for industrial arts; basic science for home economics and arts and crafts; mathematics for agriculture; mathematics for industrial arts; mathematics for economics and arts and crafts; and mathematics for commerce.

The IPST Curriculum Development Model. The major activities in the system used by IPST for the development, implementation and follow-up of the curriculums are shown in Figure 2. Curriculum development is depicted as a continuous process which begins with defining goals and objectives and deciding the themes, content, skills and attitudes to be developed. Criteria for selection of content, activities, attitudes, and skills are established and the curriculum materials are developed; trials are conducted; evaluation data is collected, and the curricula revised and published; teachers are trained; the curricula is implemented and school follow-up established. The second cycle starts with a revision and modification of the goals and objectives after the overall evaluation of the implementation in the schools.

Figure – 2. IPST curriculum development model

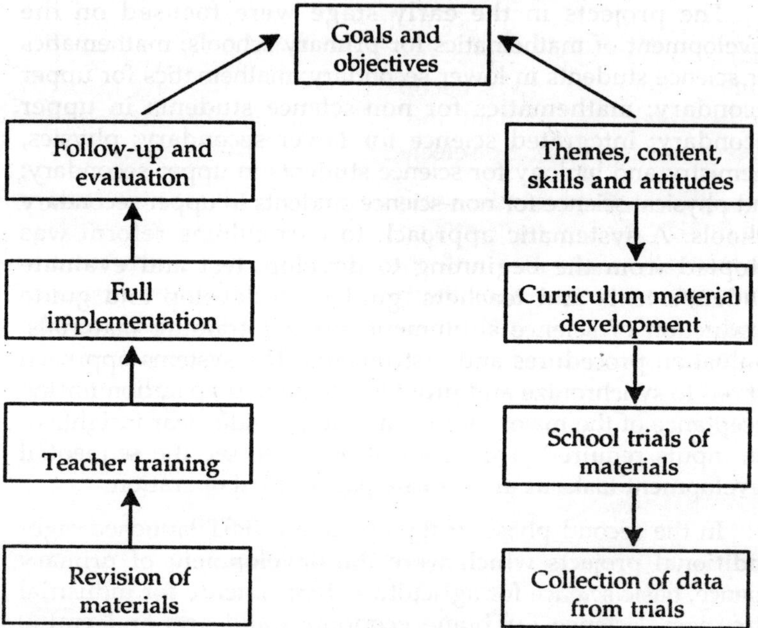

Although each activity shown in Figure 2 follows sequentially, a great deal of concurrent development occurs in the process. In each curriculum, four areas are developed simultaneously, namely, the writing of student's texts and teacher' guides, evaluation, teacher training and the development of science equipment. Writing of the drafts and trial of student's texts and teachers' guides and the revision and completion of the final manuscripts for printing for implementation, set the pace and determine the schedules that the other areas must meet.

The evaluation team first prepares and pretests attitudes, understanding and science process skills through questionnaires and tests. These are administered to a control group and the trial group, before and after the trails. Then when the trials begin in the schools, formative and achievement tests are prepared. At the end of the trials the bank of test items, now pretested in the trial schools, are used to develop diagnostic tests to assist teachers in the early years of implementation.

Teacher training begins within the first year of curriculum development. Teachers are brought to the Institute to try out experiments to assess their suitability, to discuss guidelines and chapter drafts and to test the first designed of science equipment. Some of these teachers become trial teachers, test the trial student's texts, equipment and achievement tests. Some of the in-service instructors are selected from the trial teachers.

The design of science equipment begins also at the time of the first draft of the student's text. The first prototypes are tested by teachers, redesigned and checked before being produced in amounts of up to 300 for the trial schools. After the first trial, equipment is redesigned where necessary and reproduced for the second trial. After completion of the second school trial, the equipment is passed to the industrial design section and then to large scale production.

The development of achievement tests ensure that the examinations are set on the new curricula to assess the achievement of objectives the design team is attempting to reach. The teacher training involves a considerable number of teachers in the development process, and, as a result, they become identified with the new curriculum. Those acting as in-service instructors can draw from their real classroom experience with the curriculum.

Trial and Implementation of the First Cycle Curricula. The first year of school trials for upper secondary school physics, chemistry and biology was completed at the end of February 1973. This involved ten schools, 30 teachers and 720 students. Trials of two upper secondary mathematics curricula, four credit and six credit point courses, the lower secondary general science curricula and the first level of primary mathematics were begun in 1974. In June, 1978 the first graduates from the IPST science curricula entered universities. The trial school programme and the implementation schedules are shown for the science and mathematics curricula in Figures 3 and 4.

School Science Equipment. The development, testing and redesign of equipment followed a similar schedule to that of the student's textbook. The IPST's experience in school science equipment development is considered by many overseas and regional visitors as a forerunner in the application of new dimensions in the design of curriculum projects. Two main reasons for this view have been suggested; firstly, the low-cost equipment is designed and tested as an integral part of curriculum development, and secondly, the large scale production of equipment is the outcome of a cross sectorial venture between a commercial enterprise, Ongkarn Kha, the Ministry of Education, and IPST with UNDP, UNIDO and UNESCO assistance.

Ongkarn Kha is basically a printing and publishing house with its own commercial distribution network for the 73 provinces throughout Thailand. Its potential for success as a school science equipment manufacturer and distributor appears very high. Furthermore, the control of policy by the Ministry of Education gives weight to the arguments in favour of developing the school science equipment within Ongkarn Kha. The real uncertainties lay in the lack of experience in this type of production. However, the Ministry of Education made a decision in 1975 that Ongarn Kha would be given the responsibility of large scale production of science equipment for all schools throughout the Kingdom. IPST then turned over all prototype equipment to Ongkarn Kha immediately the decision was made so that science equipment would be produced in time for the implementation of the new science curricula in 1976.

In-service Teacher Training. The IPST not only trains the staff of instructors but it also organizes all the in-service training programmes. Provides teachers' guides, class equipment, audio-visual equipment, video-tapes and filmstrips as well as supplementary and self-instructional materials for the teachers. It also finances their travel and stipend. More than 25,000 teachers (excluding primary teachers) have been trained from 1975 to the end of 1978 in seven subject areas of IPST science and mathematics curricula. This number represents about 90 per cent of the upper secondary teachers and about 80 per cent of the lower secondary science and mathematics teachers.

Figure 3. **Plan for trial teaching and full implementation for Thailand (first cycle)**

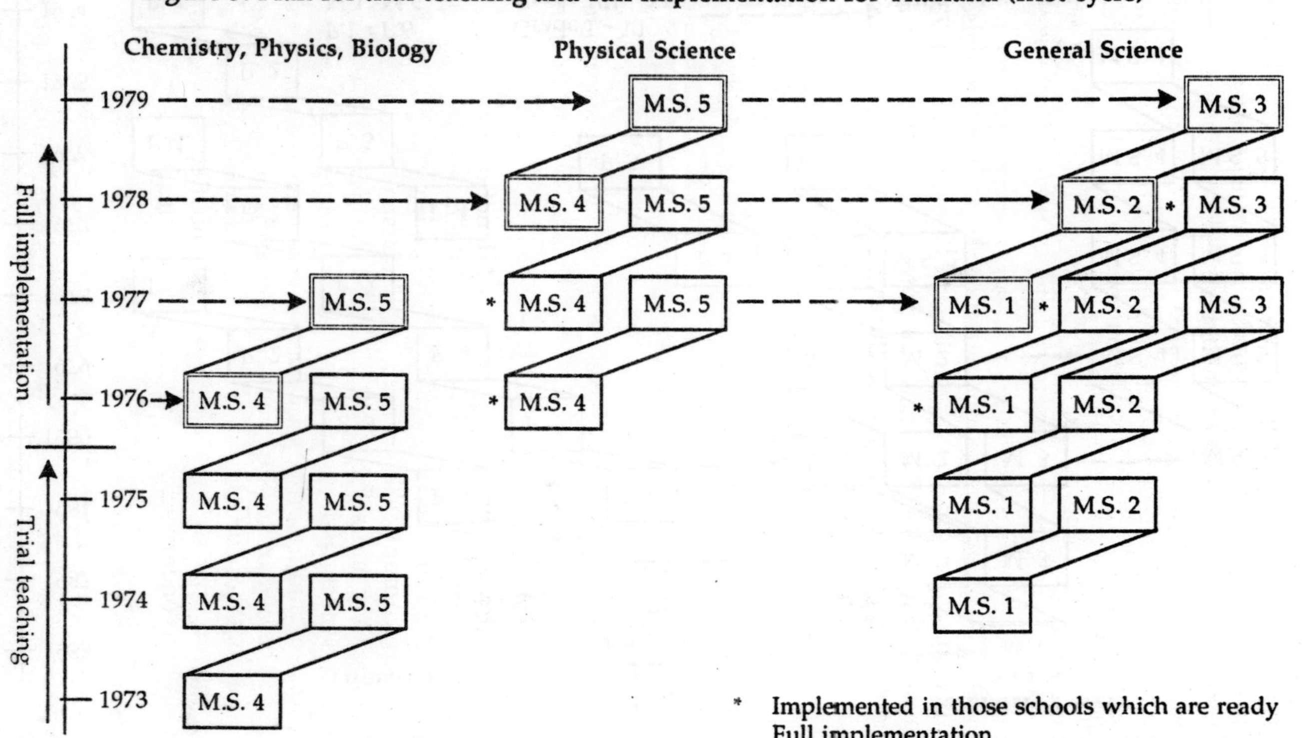

Figure–4. Plan for trial teaching and full implementation for mathematics in Thailand (first sycle)

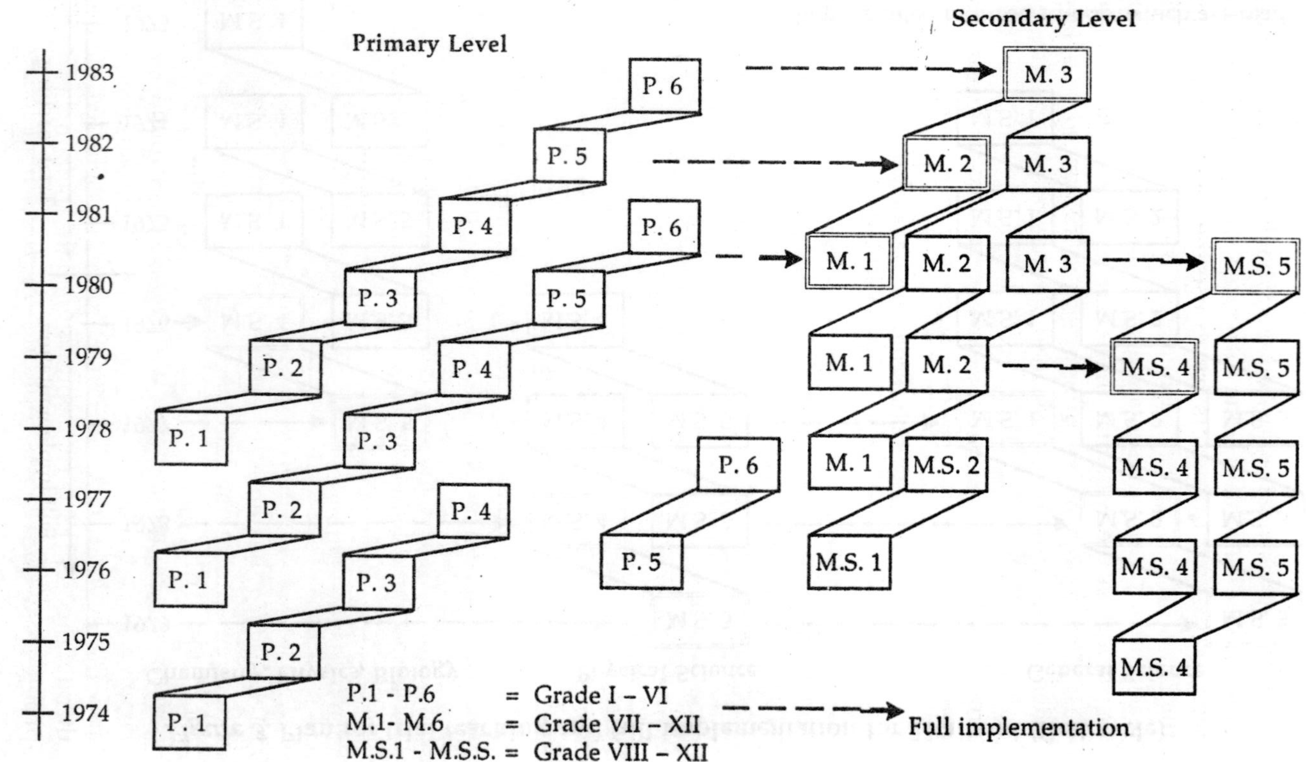

IPST uses an integrated approach to the in-service programme; the content being integrated with methodology and with evaluation. Instructors try to use the methodologies that they would like to see teachers use in the classrooms. The teachers carry to representative experiments arranged by the instructors in the way that they were advocated to do in the class. The design of the programme is influenced to a large extent by the continuing evaluation of teachers' performance and opinions. These evaluations of the IPST teacher training programmes give reasonably clear insights into the nature and needs for continued teacher training.

Development Research. From the beginning, IPST has had a strong commitment to developmental research and evaluation. Right throughout the planning, development and trial of materials, and in the provision of teacher training, information has been carefully collected and analysed. The major purpose of this evaluation has been to assist on-going management and development decisions; to revise on a continual basis, not only the materials being developed but also the UNDP and Government inputs and procedures for development, trial and dissemination. A clear indication of this commitment to continuous evaluation and feedback can be found in IPST publications.

The total evaluation programme is illustrated in Figure—5 for the years 1973 to 1981 on the following page.

The analysis of the results of the students has guided the revisions of trial books, teachers' guides and training materials. Some 50 research papers have been written describing these activities and findings.

School Follow-up. Now that many of the IPST curricula have reached the implementation stage, evaluation research has extended into a stage of school follow-up and continuous renewal. The plans for monitoring the nationwide implementation are indicated by the oval and round circle in Figure 5. a team of seven IPST staff, one from each design team and the evaluation team, visit randomly-selected schools throughout the Kingdom collecting data, tackling teachers' problems in classrooms, holding meetings of teachers and

Figure 5. Evaluation and testing of IPST curricula, 1973-1981

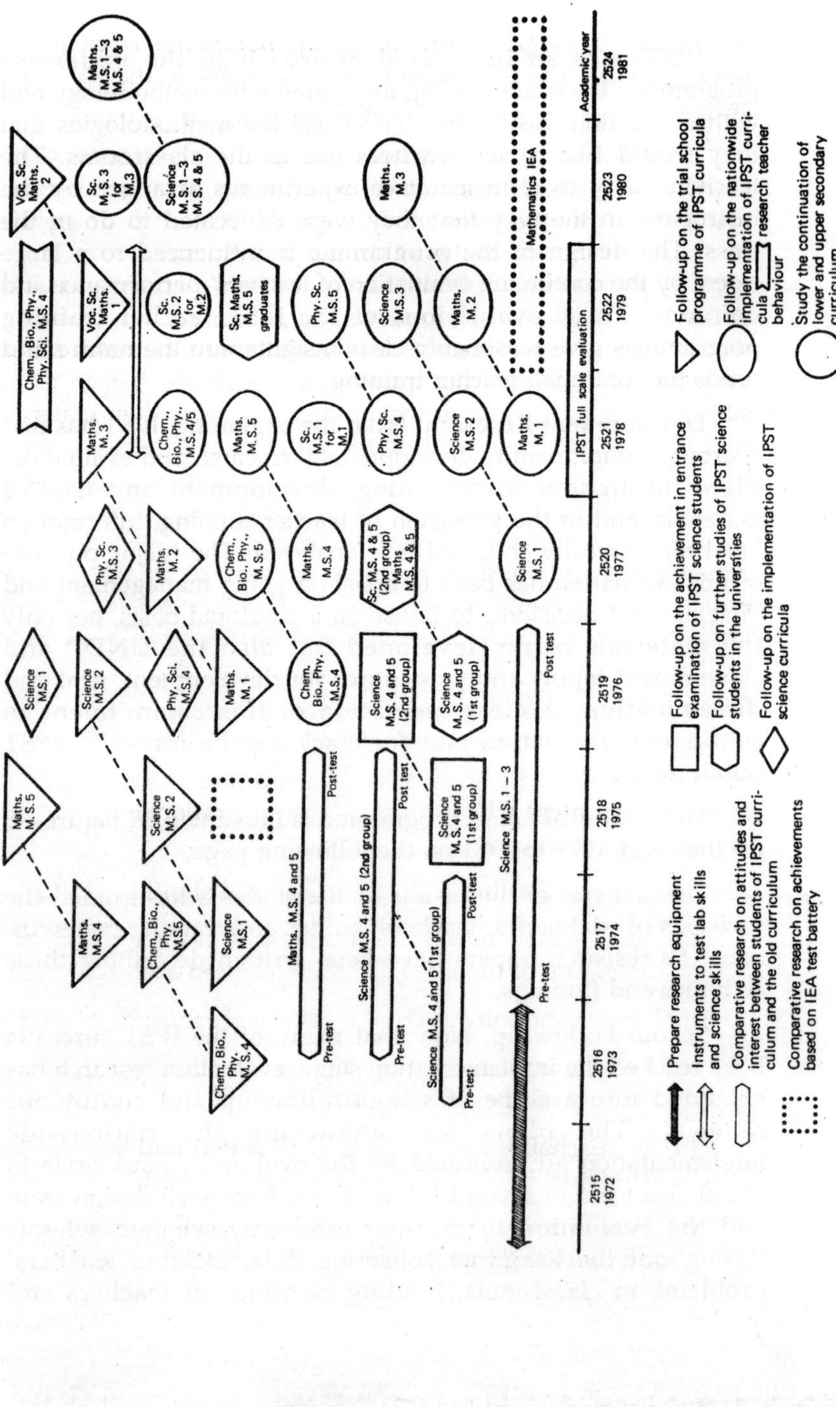

discussing strategies with follow-up personnel from the 20 school groups. The IPST team visited about 300 of the 500 upper secondary schools during 1977 and 1978.

Revision and the Implementation of the Second Cycle Curriculum. The revision and modification of all curriculum materials follow the same model as in the first cycle. All of the findings collected from the follow-up programmes proved to be very useful as guidelines for further improvement. The nationwide implementation served as a large scale trail for the second cycle revision. Reports from direct observations on school visits as well as those from questionnaire gave the design teams sufficient information as to what extent the curriculum materials should be improved. An alternative sequence of concepts might be necessary in some cases; new experiments or new equipment might be more appropriate in others. The applications of science concepts to everyday living were updated to make them more consistent with the advancement of new technology. New editions of all curriculum materials were prepared and implemented for grades X, XI and XII as follows: physical and biological science (1981-1982); and chemistry, physics, biology, mathematics (4 credits), and mathematics (2 credits) (1981-1983).

Criteria for Selection of Content. The IPST curriculum team considered it necessary to formulate criteria for the selection of content which would give some rationale to support the choice of such content.

The criteria are that the content selected should :

(a) lead up to modern science and reflect ideas and structure of the most recently accepted advances;

(b) show continuity and follow a logical conceptual scheme;

(c) have a capacity for unifying and explaining the widest variety of phenomena and data;

(d) be teachable within the time allocated and suitable for students' intellectual maturity and interest;

(e) be within the capability and experience of the teachers and adequacy of racehorses;

(f) contain examples of important applications to technology, agriculture, medicine, industry and social sciences in Thailand;

(g) bring out the relationship to other fields of study, especially to the natural sciences and mathematics:

(h) contribute to the growth and development of the individual as well as society and stimulate the proper utilization of natural resources and the preservation of the environment.

It is obvious that they do not indicate specifically what kind of science content should be included in the science curriculum. Final decisions on the theme and characteristics of the course are ultimately made as a result of the subjective judgement of the curriculum team members.

Science in the Lower Secondary Schools. Science is compulsory for all children at the lower secondary level. The integrated science course is part of the effort to develop new science course by IPST for all schools in Thailand and was first implemented in grade I in 1977. The generalized themes chosen for the six-semester integrated science curriculum are shown in Figure 6, Throughout the curriculum, change, energy and the environment are interrelated and interwoven with the development of skills and science attitudes.

Figure–6. **Themes of integrated science for grades VII-IX.**

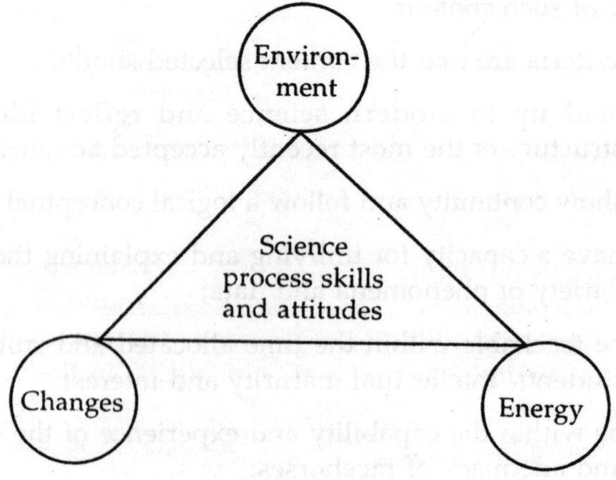

Topic areas grouped around these broad themes and are written as the ideas 'flow'. The topics are organized into chapters and the chapters are grouped into grades VII to IX. A good deal of shifting of ideas and topics from one chapter to another and some regrouping of chapters continue through the expansion stages.

The final grouping of topics around the three major themes and the interrelationship between topics are shown in the conceptual scheme for IPST integrated science in Figure 7 below.

***Figure–7.* Conceptual scheme of integrated science grades VII-IX.**

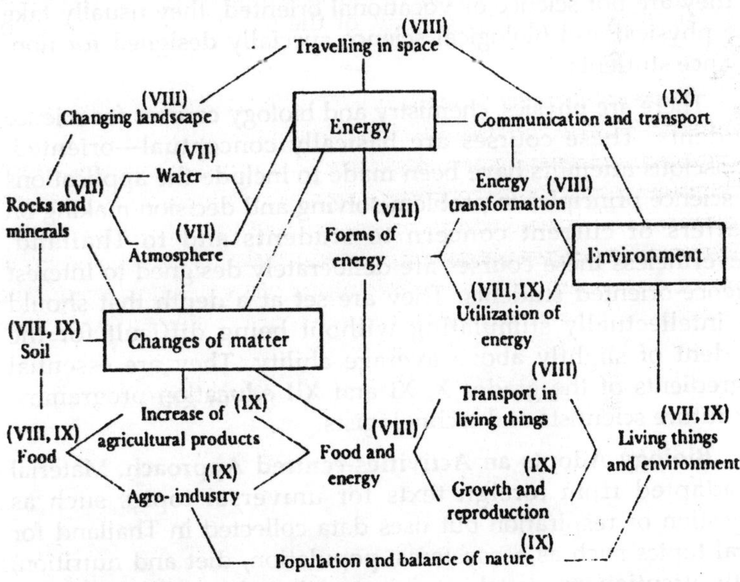

The grade VII topics [labelled (VII) in the figure] are centred around the concept of a 'changing world around us' and make use of many examples of change from the environment. The grade VIII curriculum [topics labelled (VIII) in the diagram] is concerned with energy and changes and the environment. In the grade IX emphasis is placed on the scientific approach, to balancing resources and development. While focused on the environment, the concepts of energy and change are interwoven in the fabric of the content. Decisions are taken continually through this initial development stage. Some basic criteria for selection and style are set as IPST policy; other decisions, more specific to the particular curriculum, are built up as the work progresses.

Science in the Upper Secondary Schools. All science courses at this level are elective. There are three main categories of science courses, (a) for science students; (b) vocational students; and (c) non-science students. Although all courses are elective all students have to select at least 12 periods of science. If they are not science or vocational oriented, they usually take the physical and biological science specially designed for non-science students.

There are physics, chemistry and biology courses for science students. These courses are basically conceptual—oriented. Conscious attempts have been made to include the applications of science principles to problem-solving and decision-making on matters of current concern to students and to Thailand. Nevertheless these courses are deliberately designed to interest science-oriented students. They are set at a depth that should be intellectually stimulating without being difficult for the student of slightly above average ability. They are essential ingredients of the grades X, XI and XII education programme for future scientists and technologists.

Biology Adopts an Activities-centred Approach. Material is adapted from foreign texts for universal topics such as digestion or respiration but uses data collected in Thailand for local topics such as ecosystems, population, diet and nutrition, with attention on developing instruction that will enable the student to examine the biology of his immediate environment.

Physics is presented as a single unified course containing mechanics, heat, light, sound, electricity, magnetism and nuclear physics. The course is experimentally based and requires the development of inexpensive equipment that can be manufactured locally.

Chemistry integrates the laboratory manual with the text in an effort to encourage teachers to teach chemistry as a learner-centred inquiry involving both theory and practice. The experiments can be performed with an inexpensive kit than contains most of the equipment needed. A study of Thai chemical industries and chemical problems relevant to Thai society are introduced.

The student's books contain many activities and experiments around which questions are asked and the students find the answers from observation and from analysis of experimental results. The questions are constructed after analysis of the mental and manual operations required to develop scientific and mathematical concepts.

The questions guide the learning process and place the students in the role of 'discoverers'. The teachers direct the operations, control the pace and provide assistance when a student or group is 'stuck'. Equally important, they also consolidate areas of the subject into formal presentations. The student's books are not texts in the traditional sense but are guides to learning, a new learning in which the learner generalizes and formalizes from the specific and informal, instead of the covers as was the practice in the past.

The teachers' guides complement the student's books. They give the teacher additional background material and information on pacing the programme and on the advance preparation necessary for each experiment. The guides suggest outlines for pre-and post-lab discussions and illustrate how the major concepts in the course might be linked together. The guides also contain many test items that have been tested in the trial schools. They then set out the method of writing items and they encourage the teachers to write their own items for smashing student achievement.

Physical and biological science for non-science students. The four-semester courses are prepared in a modular form including 14 topics of science in an interdisciplinary fashion. The emphasis is on developing science process skills, and the application and social implication of science.

The 1981 requirement is that students have to select five out of nine physical science modules and three out of five biological science modules making up a total number of eight modules in four semesters.

The 14 modules are: Solar energy; Light; Colouring matter; Electrical appliances; Invisible rays; The earth and stars; Synthetic material; Sound in everyday living; Natural resources and industry; Good living; Medicine and life; Our body; Evolution; Heredity and environment.

Science for vocational students. The main purpose for the development of special science courses for vocational students is to develop an understanding of science related to each vocational area. At the same time, science process skills and scientific attitudes are also developed so that students will be able to solve problems in their voction as well as in their everyday life.

Industrial arts students are required to take four semester science courses. There are six major trades, namely, mechanics, welding, metalwork, electronics, electricity and construction. There is a common core in the first semester which covers mainly mechanics. In the second semester, students are divided into two sub-groups according to their different needs. In the third and fourth semesters, as their different needs become grater, a further split is necessary. However, the principle of integration is applied as much as possible. The science courses are mainly experimental and inquiry-oriented, a close link to the vocational subjects is emphasized.

Agricultural students are required to take four one-semester science courses, two of which are mainly biology, one is on chemistry and one on physics applied to agriculture. Home economics students take six modular science courses. They are: colouring-matter, synthetic martial, medicine and life, the world of carbon, food and health and food problems. The nature of the science courses for vocational students differs from those for science students in that the courses are less theoretical but more applicable to vocational interests. Students spend more time doing practical work followed by discussion.

Out-of-school Scientific Activities

Much effort has been spent on curriculum development in the formal school system, since it has a well-organized infrastructure to support. The out-of-school activities are so diverse that they require many different agencies to undertake them. The Science Society of Thailand under the Royal Patronage has always taken the leading role in promoting public awareness of science and technology for national development. The Society is long established, and has, among others, two important divisions, namely, the Science Teachers Section and the Science Club Section. Within its own budget limitations, the Society tries to organize science fairs and exhibitions every year. Through its Science Club Section, competitions of science projects are organized to stimulate enthusiasm and interest in science for youngsters. In addition, the Science Societyals also sponsors science symposia every other year to allow young scientists to present research findings.

In 1982, the Science Society took a further step by proposing to the Government the establishment of a National Science Day. The Thai Government declared 18 August as National Science day, and on this auspicious day, the Science Society also established a Science Award for the best scientist of the year. Hopefully, this incentive will attract promising young persons into science.

The Science Museum under the Department of Non-formal Education, Ministry of Education plays an important role in promoting interest in science and technology for youngsters. Unfortunately, there is only one such museum. It cannot cope with the large number of school children throughout the country. As a measure to solve this problem, the Department established a mobile science museum unit to allow school children in the provinces easier access to science activities.

Some Current Innovation Projects

From the follow-up programmes after the nationwide implementation of all curricula, the IPST has identified many practical problems concerning the teaching and learning of science in schools. Firstly, science equipment is inadequately supplied owing to budget constraints and is of poor quality. Secondly, some teachers have not had the opportunity to attend in-service training, and face difficulties in teaching and handling new experiments and new equipment. New teachers demonstrate that they still require more training which is an indication of inadequate training in many training institutions. Projects are now underway to solve some of these problems.

Innovation in Pre-service Education. While the in-service training of classroom teachers is an approach which has great potential, the time, cost and human resources needed to carry out large scale, long-term programmes are great. In most cases it is only possible to run quality programmes of adequate duration for a small proportion of practising teachers. Improving the quality of teachers through better pre-service education is a slow but more efficient process.

In 1977, after considerable experience and feedback had been gained form the in-service teacher training programmes of IPST, the Ministry of University Affairs initiated the 'Thai-STEP Project' by appointing as project personnel one representative from the faculties of science, one from mathematics and two from the faculties of education from every university in Thailand and from the Teacher Training Department to serve as the project team.

The Thai-STEP group accepted responsibility for identifying the teaching competencies needed for successful implementation of the new secondary school science and mathematics curricula and developing instructional materials to be used in pre-service programmes. To achieve these goals the Thai-STEP project personnel consisting of 60 individuals was divided into four working groups.

Two groups, one in science and one in mathematics accepted the research responsibility. The major activities of the two research groups has involved analysing the new pre-tertiary curricula and the teacher training curricula in Thai institutions of higher education; researching the competencies of science and mathematics teachers; collecting data to set the order, content and proportion of various courses in the teacher training curriculum. Developing guidelines for the preparation of teachers at the pre-service level for submission to the Ministry of University Affairs; and working on the follow-up of in-service teacher training and the implementation of the new science and mathematics curricula.

A number of research instruments have been constructed, tested, revised and used to collect data for formulating guidelines for the Ministry and to provide a research base for the development groups in Thai-STEP. For example, the science research group instruments include tests for surveying the content and concepts of science textbooks and modules in use from grade VII (age 12 approximately) to the second year of university level; science teaching profession competency; the science attitudes of science teachers; and science process skills. There is also a teaching behaviour observation instrument; a science teacher competency questionnaire; and a science teacher curriculum questionnaire. The research group concerned with mathematics teaching has produced a similar set of instruments.

This Thai-STEP science education group has produced 15 instructional packages or modules to be used in the pre-service education of teachers. These are based on 15 different themes related to science teacher competencies. Each module consists of an instructor's guide, background reading for the student, exercise and answers, test items and answers and related audio-visual teaching aids.

The titles of the 15 modules are : The Nature of Science; Concept formation in Science; Science Process Skills; Laboratory Skills; Problem Solving by Scientific Methods; Behavioural Objectives; Introducing a Session; Motivation and Reinforcement in the Classroom; Asking Questions; Teaching Science by Inquiry; Lesson Planning; Laboratory Management; Safety in Laboratories; Science Equipment Maintenance; Measurement and Evaluation in Science. In addition to the 15 modules, the development group has also produced supplementary reading materials on two topics : 'Science curriculums development' and 'Science attitude development'.

The first nine instructional packages were taught on a test basis during 1980 and the final six during 1981. Based on the feedback from the trials, all 15 modules have now been revised. They were presented to the staff of teacher training units, in university departments and teacher training colleges throughout Thailand, at a seminar held at Chiangmai University in December, 1981. At this time, they were accepted by the Ministry of University Affairs and the teacher training staff for implementation throughout Thailand during 1983.

Science Teacher Servicing Centres. The Science Teacher Servicing Centres (STSC) have been established to facilitate the decentralization of certain aspects of IPST's work including the schools follow-up support programme, continuing in-service education and evaluation of the implementation of the new courses. The 36 STSCs now established are within the existing teacher training colleges throughout the country.

The distribution of centres is such that each will serve teachers of two to three adjacent provinces so that all 73 provinces in the Kingdom will be equitably serviced and all schools will be covered. The organization is illustrated in Figure 8 on the following page.

As the figure illustrates, information, instruction and a variety of assistance flows from the IPST to the centres which in turn facilitate the flow to the area teachers. However, the flow of information is a two-way process, since teachers bring problems and ideas to the centres which, if the solution does not exist at the centre, the centre will send to the IPST. The IPST, because of its greater resources, is often able to suggest alternative solutions which may be most appropriate for specific regional application.

A preliminary survey indicated that the assistance most needed by the schools is the production and repair of low-cost science equipment. The next priorities are test item construction, audio-visual services and other specific problems in the teaching of science and mathematics.

Thus, the IPST organized three workshops for STSC personnel on science equipment repair and production; test item construction; and audio-visual equipment maintenance and production techniques.

During 1981-1983, the STSCs have been actively involved in running in-service workshops for teachers in physics, chemistry, biology and physical and biological science for the second cycle implementation of the science curricula for grades X, XI and XII.

Continued involvement of the STSCs with the IPST activities will enable the centre personnel to be familiar with new materials, new methods of teaching and new curricula. This should lead to the improvement of the pre-service teacher education programmes in the long run.

***Figure–8.* IPST and STSC general organization**

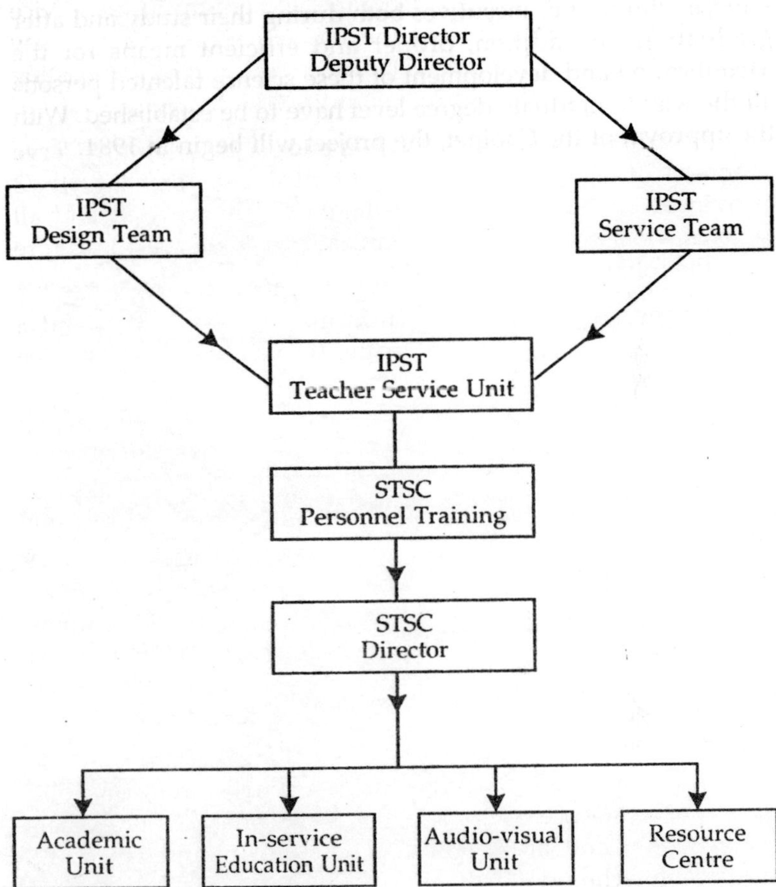

Science Talent Project. At present, there is much concern about the calibre of human resources in science and technology. Medicine attracts high quality students, while engineering is a close second, followed by management science. The Science Talent Project is being set up with the aim of identifying and nurturing young children who posses a high-level to learning abilities and show consistently high academic achievements in science. However, the success of this project requires high level policy and planning. The Ministry of Science, Technology and Energy, the Ministry of Education, the Ministry of University

Affairs and the IPST are now preparing a project document to ensure that young talented persons are encouraged to study science with proper incentives both during their study and after graduation. In addition, proper and efficient means for the identification and development of these science talented persons all the way to graduate degree level have to be established. With the approval of the Cabinet, the project will begin in 1984.

22

Turkey

During the time of the ottoman Empire, Turkey had a religious school system supported by the Ministry of Religious and Social Foundations and some local welfare institutions. Movements to improve the Turkish Educational System began in 1839. In the 1920s a Ministry of Education and a national educational system, similar to the school systems in European countries, containing primary, secondary and higher stages were established and Government took over the officials responsibility for providing at least primary education.

After the proclamation of the Republic on 29 October, 1923, movements were made to modernize in every field, including education. With the passage of the Unification of Education Law in 1926, the duality in the Turkish educational system was eliminated and replaced with a truly Western and secular system.

The foundation of science policy in the Turkish educational system was laid by Ataturk during the years of establishing the Turkish Republic. He emphasized the importance of science and technology in the life and education of the nation in his speeches.

The opinions of Ataturk still influence the education in particular. The National Education Fundamental Law which was passed in 1973, among the Basic Principles of Turkish National Education, states that, 'the curriculum for each level and type of school as well as its educational methods and training aids and materials are continually developed and updated in line with recent scientific and technological developments and adapted to the needs of the environment and country'.

It also prescribes increased productivity in education and its continuous development and renewal based on scientific research and evaluation.

Structure of the Educational System

With small differences, the general structure of the Turkish educational system is similar to that of other Western countries. Organized school education of the Turkish educational system is divided into four stages as shown in Figure 1 on the following page.

Pre-Primary education, which is optional, covers the education of children who have not yet reached the age of compulsory primary education. This education stage prepares children for basic education and helps families in solving their problems related to development and training of children. Although some elementary schools have nursery and kindergarten classes, this stage has not yet been organized uniformly and extended throughout the country.

Basic education covers the education of 6 to 14 years old children. There are two levels of schools at this stage; a five-year primary level and a three-year junior high school level. The first part of basic education is compulsory for all.

Secondary education covers at least a three-year education after the basic education. Secondary education comprises two types of schools. These are three-year general senior high schools, which give general education to prepare students for higher education; and/or four year technical and vocational senior high schools, which help children to gain a vocation or a technical profession or to continue higher education.

Higher education is education which provides further and specialized education. Secondary education comprises two types of schools. These are three-year general senior high schools, which give general education to prepare students for higher education; and/or four year technical and vocational senior high schools, which help children to gain a vocation or a technical profession or to continue higher education.

Higher education is education which provides further and specialized education in various fields for students who have completed secondary education and who have succeeded in the University Entrance Examinations. Most of the departments of the Universities require a four-year education. According to the Higher Education Law, which was passed in 1981, all types of higher educational institutions are now linked to universities, although some of them still keep their former status as two-year vocational high schools. Universities give bachelor's, master's and doctor's degrees in various fields.

Enrolment at Each Stage of Education. The enrolment at each stage of the Turkish Educational System is shown in Table—1.

Science Education in Schools

Soon after the establishment of the new Turkish Republic in 1923, some hasty changes were made in the school curricula in line with the direction of the educational policy of the new government. At that time the most important problem in education was illiteracy, because only 10 per cent of the population know how to read and write. This problem was tackled by the adoption of Latin letters and the opening of a literacy campaign throughout the country in 1928. Then the content and teaching methods of school subjects were revised following the directives given by Ataturk. The revisions emphasized the principles of starting from immediate environment, learning by doing, and gaining useful and practical knowledge and skills instead of memorizing unnecessary information about science.

In 60 years since then, many changes have been made in the school science curricula in order to keep up with changing teaching methods, content and educational technology in Western countries.

Objectives of Science Yeaching. The main aims of teaching science at different stages of the Turkish educational system are expressed in the following behavioural terms.

Figure 1. Structure of Turkish educational system

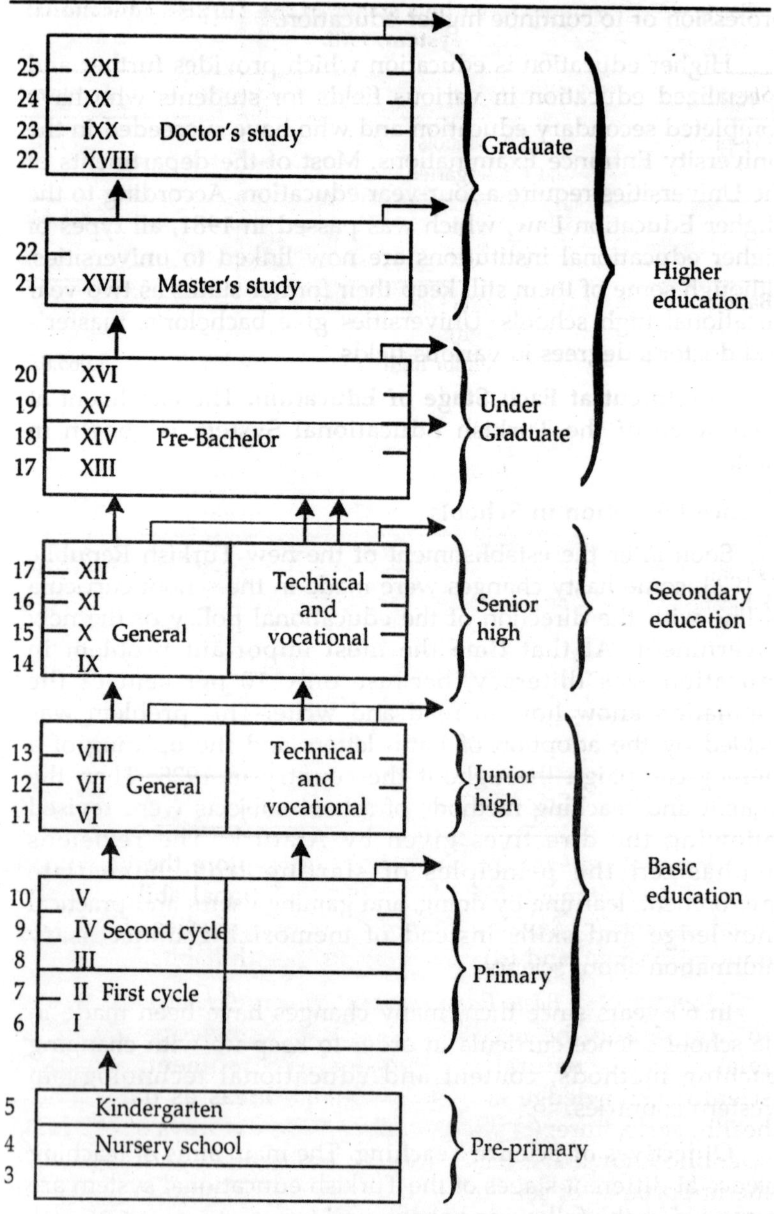

Table – 1. Enrolment at various stages of the Turkish educational system, 1982

Stage	*Kind of school*	*Number of schools*	*Enrolment*
Pre-primary	Nursery schools and kindergarten	2,771	71,703
	First level (Primary)	46,512	5,895,641
Basic education	Second level (Junior high):		
	General junior high	4,281	1,065,878
	Technical and vocational high	610	180,108
	Junior high total	4,891	1,245,986
	Total	51,403	7,141,627
Secondary Education	General senior high	1,181	460,096
	Technical and Vocational High	1,293	366,673
	Total	2,474	826,769
Higher education	Universities	27	235,699
	Grand Total		8,275,798

Pre-Lrimary level. To be able to : (a) explore the immediate natural environment; (b) develop the functional abilities of the sense organs; (c) develop a basic for science studies at the basic education stage; and (d) develop good health habits.

First Level of Basic Education (in Primary Schools). To be able to : (a) obtain the necessary scientific knowledge and skills related to the natural and physical environment; (b) apply scientific knowledge and skills to such areas as daily living, health, agriculture; (c) understand and use the ways of obtaining scientific knowledge and skills; (d) understand and appreciate the importance of scientific and technological studies in the life of human beings; and (e) develop a basis for junior high school science.

Second Level of Basic Education (in Junior High Schools). To be able to : (a) understands the basic principles of science; (b) use scientific thinking and methods in solving daily problems related to science; (c) understand the relationships between science and health, welfare, and technical and industrial development of the society; (d) understand the importance of scientific studies in discovering, using, maintaining, and conserving the natural resources of the country; and (e) develop an adequate basis of knowledge, skills, and attitudes for science education at the senior high school level.

Secondary Education Stage (in Senior High Schools). The common objectives for all types of senior high schools are to be able to : (a) understand scientific facts and principles, as part of general culture, which are necessary for every citizen graduated from high school; (b) develop good health habits; (c) from a basis of scientific knowledge and skills for university education.

Additional objectives for science in senior high schools are to be able to use scientific thinking and methods to obtain and understand scientific knowledge such as facts, generalizations, principles, hypotheses, and theories; and to become aware of the important scientific and technological implications of scientific knowledge and methods following the history of mankind.

Organization of Science Curricula. The current science curricula for different stages of the educational system are organized differently.

(a) At the pre-primary stage science is not a separate subject. It takes place among other activities in the form of both environmental and integrated science activities.

(b) At the basic education stage, in the first three grades of primary, the science curriculum is organized as environmental science integrated with social studies.

In grades IV and V it is organized as general science which covers all the main topics of physical and biological sciences.

In grades VI to VIII all topics of physical and biological sciences are expanded and repeated as general science. In only 33 junior high schools (out of 4,882) is science being taught as integrated science as a trial curriculum.

(c) At the secondary stage all science topics are expanded and repeated again in variously organized forms. In general senior high schools, with traditional science, the science curriculum is organized as the separate subject disciplines of natural science, physics, and chemistry; but if modern science is taught, the science curriculums is organized as physical science (under the name of science), biology, physics, chemistry, and geology.

Out of 2,474 senior high schools, modern science is taught in 435 general high schools and in 552 technical and vocational high schools. In 24 of 'official' general high schools, modern science is taught in either English, French, or German.

In technical senior high schools, the science curriculum may be offered as modern science in which case the science is organized as introductory physical science, physics, and chemistry. If 'conventional' science is taught, it is presented as physical science, physics, and chemistry. Biology is not taught in these schools.

In vocational high schools and conventional science teaching high schools, the science curriculum may again be offered as modern science, with physics, and chemistry as the individual subjects, or as 'conventional' science with natural science, physics, and chemistry.

In two science senior high schools, specifically established for talented students, the curriculum is organized as biology, physics, chemistry, advanced biology, advanced physics, and advanced chemistry. Advanced disciplines are selective subjects, and students have to select one of them. In these courses original projects or scientific problems are studied and there are specific syllabuses.

Time Devoted to Science Teaching. Science is a compulsory subject for all students from pre-primary stage to grade XI.

At the pre-primary stage, science activities take place among the recommended daily activities, and it is estimated that about 20 percent of these activities are related to simple science.

At the basic education stage, 12.4 per cent of the total instructional time at primary level is devoted to science education and 13.3 per cent at the junior high level. Details are given in Table—2.

Table—2. Percentage of time devoted to science teaching at basic education stage

Level	*Grades*	*Total periods per week*	*Science periods per week*	*% of time devoted to science by grades*	*% average of time devoted to science by levels*
First (Primary schools)	I	25	2.5	10	
	II	25	2.5	10	
	III	25	2.5	10	12.4
	IV	25	4	16	
	V	25	4	16	
Second (Junior high schools)	VI	30	4	13.3	
	VII	30	4	13.3	13.3
	VIII	30	4	13.3	

At the secondary education stage, senior high schools are divided into general senior high schools, and technical and vocational senior high schools. The science may be offered as traditional or modern; and the time available will differ. Typical examples are given in Table 3. The greatest proportion of time for science is available in the science high school (29.2 per cent). The general high school with modern science, offers 21.9 per cent of total time for science. The least time for science is in the technical and vocational schools.

Educational System. There is a centralized educational system administered by the Ministry of National Education.

Board of Education. In 1926, in the central body of the Ministry, a Board of Education as established as an advisory

Table—3. Percentage of time devoted to science in various types of senior high schools

Type of school	*Grade*	*Section*	*Total teacher periods per week*	*Science periods per week*	*% of time devoted to science by grade*	*% of time devoted to science by school*
General Senior High School (Teaching conventional science)	IX	—	32	8	25	34.6
	X	Science	32	8	25	
		Literature	32	6	18.8	
	XI	Science	35	7	20	19.5
		Literature	35	3	8.6	
General Senior High School (Teaching modern science)	IX	—	32	4	12.5	
	X	Science	32	7	21.8	21 or 21.9
		Literature	32	6	18.8	
	XI	Maths	33	6	18	
		Nature study	33	12–2 (opt.)	36.3 or 42.4	
		Literature	33	6	18	
Industrial and Vocational Senior High School (Department of Fitting (Teaching modern or conventional science)	IX	—	42	4	9.5	
	X	Maths. and Science	43	4	9.3	
		Vocation	43	2	4.7	75
	XI	Maths. and Science	43	2	4.7	
		Vocation	43	4	9.3	
Technical Senior High School (Teaching modern or conventional science)	IX	—	42	4	9.5	
	X	—	43	2	4.7	
	XI	—	44	6	13.6	9.2
	XII	—	44	4	9	
Science Senior High School (Teaching modern science)	IX	—	36	12	33.3	
	X	—	37	14	37.8	29.2
	XI	—	36	6	16.6	

board to prepare educational policy, laws, principles, rules, and regulations and to develop and evaluate school curricula as well as to undertake educational researches.

This Board has a curriculum department to develop curricula for any subject at any stage of the educational system from pre-primary through senior high school level.

Commission of Curriculum Development. The curriculum department of the Board of Education forms a commission of curriculum development whenever a curriculum development activity is required. This commission comprises, a curriculum developer; an experienced teacher of the subject at the appropriate level; a specialist in the field from a university; an educational psychologist; an educational philosopher (at least at the beginning of the study); an educational sociologist (at least at the beginning of the study); an educational technologist; a specialist in measurement and evaluation.

This commission prepares the curriculum. It is given provisional approval of the Board of Education, and then tried out, developed and evaluated in selected pilot schools. When found to be satisfactory, it is submitted to the Board of Education for final approval.

Changes in the Science Curricula. The frequency with which the curricula are revised is not pre-determined. Various social, economic, technological, natural, and scientific factors may cause the review and consequent change of curricula. For example, the establishment of the new Turkish Republic in 1923, the changing of the alphabet from Arabic to Latin in 1928, the introduction of a multi-party democracy in 1950, the tremendous developments in science and technology in the Western world at the beginning of 1960s, the teaching or modern curriculum development principles and methods at Turkish universities at the end of 1960s, the realization of the importance of educational technology in the instructional processes, and the movement of integrated science in the 1970s, all stimulated changes in science curricula of Turkish schools.

The last revisions and changes in school science curricula were carried out at primary level in 1975, at junior high level in 1977, at senior high level in 1973, and at technical and vocational senior high level in 1980.

Consideration of Real-life Problems. In all the revisions and changes made in the science curricula, real-life problems and social issues have always been considered and reflected. For example, the problems related to 'conservation of energy', 'maintaining and caring for natural resources', 'living and growing in a healthy way', and 'environmental pollution' are considered in the primary and junior high school curricula; the problems related to 'thinking scientifically and solving difficulties by using scientific methods' are considered in primary, junior high, and senior high school curricula; and the problems connected with the 'scientific communication', 'health and genetics', 'population and food', and 'man and the biological and physical community' are considered in the senior high school curriculum.

Evaluation of Student Achievement. The academic year is divided into two terms. The evaluation of student achievement is carried out separately for each term. Student evaluation is based on written examination scores; oral test and classroom discussion scores; homework scores; scores obtained from practical and laboratory work examinations; scores of observed affective behaviour; and the teacher's overall opinion about the student.

The Ministry of National Education recommends that written examinations should be carried out by using objective or at least short answer multi-question tests. (For modern programmes, there are standard objective tests prepared by the Ministry of National Education). In written and oral tests, not only memorization, but comprehension and application should be measured. The practical and laboratory work should be measured in terms of time, technique and quality.

At the primary level of the basic education stage, the teacher combines and evaluates the scores by assigning grades. In all junior and senior high schools, grades begin from zero and go through to ten. The pass grade is five. At all levels and stages, up to higher education, the mean of the grades in the two terms becomes the final grade for the academic year. If it is a fail grade, the student must attend a special two week course and then take a written or oral examination together with a laboratory or practical examination. There are no public final examinations at the end of the primary, junior high, and senior high school levels.

Science Activities, Laboratory Work and Equipment. As in other countries, the quality of science education is determined by the amount and nature of the practical work or laboratory activities.

Time Devoted to Practical Activities. Since 1960, in the subject distribution tables for basic and secondary curriculum, there is no specific separate time devoted to practical work or laboratory activities. Printed materials related to science teaching, published by the Ministry of National Education, do not assign specific periods for practical activities but state that science is a subject which can best be learned by way of first-hand experiences gained through continuous inquiry, discovery, observation, experimenting, problem-solving activities with the help of simple instructional materials. The amount of time required is determined and arranged by the teachers.

Weightage Given to the Practical Activities in examination. Practical or laboratory work may be an examinable subject in the internal assessment process, but, unfortunately, teachers use this type of examination very seldom became the analysis of behaviour and the preparation of a scale of observation are difficult and time consuming tasks. When it is used, the theoretical and practical sides of a science examination are customarily considered to be of equal weight.

The Nature of Practical and/or Laboratory Activities in Science Teaching. At the primary stage, science activities cannot be separated from other daily activities. The guide books published for kindergarten teachers, by the Ministry of National Education, mention science activities which will help children to explore their natural and social environment.

To develop the cognitive, psychomotor, and affective abilities of the children, teachers make use of familiar objects as well as the set of instructional materials for pre-primary schools prepared by the Ministry of National Education.

At the primary school level, science is integrated with social studies in the first three grades. At this level teachers mostly use locally-available simple, low-cost, or free materials for the science-related topics of the programme.

At the second level of the primary school, in grades IV and V, science textbooks have been prepared to help children learn science by doing experiments with free, low-cost, and locally-available simple materials. Each book contains more than a hundred student experiments and some demonstrations to be done with the help of teachers. In addition, the Ministry of National Education has sent at least one set of instructional materials for primary school science to each school. There is no shortage of science teaching materials and equipment at the primary level; all schools are well equipped.

At the junior high school level there are two types of schools according to the organization of the science curriculum. In 33 schools (out of 4,882) science is taught in the form of integrated science as a trial. These schools have been fully supplied with the sets of integrated science materials for junior high schools prepared by the Ministry of National Education. These sets correlate with student guide books.

In the other junior high schools, science is offered as general science. Textbooks, for grades VI to VIII contain more than 250 simple student experiments which can be done by using low-cost or free materials. At the same time, these schools have been equipped with the set of instructional materials for junior high school general science by the Ministry of National Education. Although these sets are not directly correlated with the textbooks, all student experiments and teacher demonstrations can be carried out with the materials in the kit. There is no shortage of science teaching materials and equipment at the junior high school level and all schools are well equipped.

At the secondary stage of the system there are 2,474 senior high schools. In 60 per cent of these schools conventional science is taught, and there are only textbooks and some old types of demonstration equipment available.

At the beginning of the 1960s, under the worldwide influence of revolution in science teaching methods, new science curricula were adapted mainly from United States projects; in biology, the blue version of Biological Science Curriculum Study (BSCS); in physics, Physical Science Curriculum Study (PSCS), and Introductory Physical Sciences (IPS); in chemistry, Chemical

Education Material Study (CHEMS). Textbooks, teachers books, and laboratory guides, were translated and developed to the conditions of the Turkish educational system. All laboratory materials and equipment were made by using locally-available resources.

These changes were designated 'modern science' and today, these so-called modern science programmes are being taught in about 40 per cent of senior high schools. Although all the necessary instructional materials and equipment are being supplied from local resources, the extension of the programmes all over the country is going slowly because of problems with material production and teacher training.

Sixty-two per cent of senior high schools are well equipped with science materials and equipment; 8 per cent poorly equipped, and 16 per cent not equipped at all.

Availability and Production of Science Teaching Materials and Equipment. All science teaching materials and equipment are manufactured locally. There are two big institutions which have been set up by the Ministry of National Education for the design, production, and evaluation of school science materials and equipment.

The Educational Instruments Production Centre was established in 1961. It is the largest enterprise of its kind with more than 700 people in its employ. All types of educational materials and equipment, correlated with school curricula, are designed, produced, and distributed in the form of set or kits for different subject matter areas. This centre is the only institution trying to meet the needs of educational materials and equipment for the science education curricula. In the local manufacture of these kits only 10 per cent of the raw materials are imported from other countries.

The Centre of Education through Film, Radio and Television was established in 1951 to produce educational films, film-strips, and slides. It began to produce educational radio programmes in 1963. After Turkish Television had been set up, it began also to make educational television programmes. It is the only institution which meets the needs of educational films, film-strips, slides, radio and television programmes for science educational curricula.

These two institutions are controlled by the General Directorate of Educational Materials of the Ministry of National Education.

Use of Educational Technology

In addition to the Centre of Education through Film, Radio and Television mentioned above, there is another important organization which connects the central production centres to each other and to the schools. This organization consists of 67 provincial centres of educational materials spread all over the country.

These centres are local institutions having audio-visual equipment and materials to help teachers in their classes whenever required. At the same time, these centres are responsible for the local distribution of science sets and other materials sent by the production centres for the schools.

In these provincial centres, the variety and quantity of the audio-visual materials related to science teaching are inadequate. This is partly due to the fact that the Educational Centre through Film, Radio and Television is not working at full capacity because of financial difficulties. Thus, schools are poorly supplied with audio-visual materials for science teaching. Nevertheless, the Centre of Education through Film, Radio, and Television is producing very good radio programmes, correlated with school science curricula, but they are not being properly used by teachers are not well trained in the use of educational technology.

Teacher Training

Teacher training is the most problematic aspect of the educational system. From the beginning of the Republic until today, there have been many changes in teacher training procedures and the behaviour and qualifications of teachers have also changed significantly.

Minimum qualifications for science teachers. According to the science curricula being used in schools, at whatever level, all science teachers should have gained some common characteristics during their training to enable them to :

a) understand the developmental characteristics and needs of the students at the appropriate level;
b) understand basic science facts, concepts, generalizations, principles, theories, and the relationships between the adequate to the appropriate teaching level;
c) help students develop the scientific attitudes and science process skills necessary to obtain scientific knowledge at the appropriate level;
d) effectively use modern science teaching principles, methods, and techniques appropriate to the level of teaching;
e) obtain select, evaluate, and effectively use the necessary science teaching materials suitable to the teaching level; and science teaching materials suitable to the teaching level; and
f) develop simple science teaching aids with the help of locally obtained, free or low-cost materials.

To develop these behaviour patterns and other necessary characteristics for science teaching the following qualifications are required by the Higher National Education Council.

There are no specially trained science teachers being employed at the pre-primary stage of the educational system, but pre-primary school teachers should be graduates from at least a two-year higher institution based on the senior high school education. During this education 52.1 per cent of the course should be taken from the general culture area; 35.4 per cent from the professional area; and 12.5 per cent from the field of specialization (pre-primary education) and include science and simple science experiments.

All teachers teach all subjects at the primary school level. The minimum qualifications are that a primary school teacher should have at least a two-year higher education based on the senior high school. During this education 33.3 per cent of the courses should be taken from the general culture area; 27.1 per cent of the courses should be from the professional area; and 29.6 per cent of the courses should be from the field of specialization (primary education including a minor area either 'pre-primary education' or 'special education')

A junior high school science teacher should have a three or four year higher education based on the senior high school. During this education 12.5 per cent of the courses should be taken from the general culture area; 25 per cent of the courses should be taken from the professional area; and 62.5 per cent of the courses should be from the field of specialization (science).

A senior high school science teacher should have graduated from a four-year higher education institution based on the senior high school education. During this higher education 10.4 per cent of the courses should be taken from the general culture area; 25 per cent of the course should be taken from the professional area; and 64.6 per cent of the course should be taken from the field of specialization (in this case science).

Meeting the Minimum Qualification. Most pre-primary school teachers are graduates of the child development and education department of two or four-year higher education institutions. About 90 per cent have the minimum qualifications. About 10 per cent are graduates of a vocational senior high school.

Until 1975, primary school teachers were trained in the teacher training senior high schools. In 1975, two-year teachers colleges were established to train prospective primary school teachers. In 1978, the Ministry of National Education began a project to train existing high school graduate teachers to be college graduates within 12 years. Today this project is developing and 52 per cent of the primary school teachers possess the prescribed qualifications.

Before, 1978, junior high school science teachers had been trained in three-year teachers' colleges. These colleges had separate departments for main subject areas. In 1978, the course of instruction was raised to four years. In 1978, the course of instruction was raised to four years. It is estimated that 54 per cent of science teachers have the required qualifications at this level. The Ministry of National Education is trying to improve the qualifications of the remaining 46 per cent through in-service training courses.

Senior high school science teachers have been trained at four-year colleges. It is estimated that 41 per cent of senior high school science teachers possess the qualifications required. The remaining 59 per cent are being trained in the course of the In-service Education Department of the Ministry of National Education.

The General Situation of in-service Training for science teachers. Every year, the In-service Training Department of the Ministry of National Education issues a training plan for the following year. Consideration is given to directives given in the previously prepared long-term plan. New or sudden changes in the curricula made by the Ministry; research and investigations made by the In-service Department related to the needs of schools and teachers; and the requests of the other departments of the Ministry.

In 1983, for example, the following in-service training activities were planned:

a) 200 science teachers involved in the trial of integrated science curriculum;

b) 120 biology, 120 physics, and 120 chemistry teachers to teach at the 'modern science' teaching high schools;

c) 320 science teachers to teach 'introductory physical science' at the senior high school;

d) 150 biology, 150 physics, and 100 chemistry teachers, graduated from three-year colleges, to improve their qualifications;

e) 734 primary school teachers, graduated from two-year colleges, to improve their qualifications; and

f) 155 pre-primary schools teachers to improve their qualifications.

Research

Nature of the Research in the Area of Science. Generally, the research efforts at the Turkish universities cover these and reports prepared mostly for fulfilling the requirements of academic qualifications. Until the 1980s, there were no science education departments at universities. Science education problems and the training of science teachers were among the duties of the Ministry of National Education. In the circumstances research activities in the area of science education have always been very limited.

The problems so far investigated in the area of science education relate to curriculum development and innovation, the achievements of students in science, and the instructional materials and equipment in science.

Types of Research Institutions. There are three types of institutions involved in conducting research in science education. They are :

a) the Scientific and Technical Research Council of Turkey which is an institution established for developing, promoting, organizing and co-ordinating fundamental and applied research in the sciences. It is promoting research activities by providing research grants to universities and other research institutions in the country;

b) the Faculty of Educational Science of Ankara University which has a research centre that takes over some educational research projects from the State sector and other institutions; and

c) the Planning of Programming Department and the Board of Education of the Ministry of Education which undertakes some research and, at the same time, helps researchers by providing documents, data, and statistical information.

Programmes for Out-of-school Rough and Adults and Popularization of Science and Technology.

Formal science and technology education programmes. Formal out-of-school course programmes are administered by the General Directorate of Extended Education of the Ministry of National Education. This general directorate is represented by the provincial directors of adult education in 67 provinces. Attached to them are 631 adult education centres spread all over the country.

These institutions offer hundreds of courses in various fields every year. Some of these courses are designed for giving general knowledge at the primary school level to those who completed the first sage of the literacy courses. These general knowledge courses contain science and health education together with social studies, mathematics, and Turkish language. After 180 hours of training in these courses students may take final examinations and obtain a primary school diploma.

Other science related courses given at these are vocational and industrial courses in photography, home economics, agriculture, animal husbandry, electricity, electronics, iron-work, carpentry, welding, plumbing, motor maintenance and repair, and technical drawings. These courses give knowledge and skills and provide a certificate to perform a job. (In 1981-1982, 7,366 vocational and industrial courses were offered and 177,645 students attended).

Formal radio programmes for science education are the programmes produced by the Centre of Education through Films, Radio, and junior high school students. These programmes are correlated with the formal school curricula and are also useful for the primary and junior high school level science training programmes for adult education.

Informal Science and Technology Programmes. These are radio and television programmes not connected with the school curricula. They are produced by the Turkish Radio and Television Institution an the Centre of Education through Film, Radio, and Television. The programmes deal with health education, nature study; science and technology; home economics; agriculture; communications; innovations in science and technology; innovations in medical sciences.

Science Museums and Exhibitions. The Natural History Museum in Ankara; zoos in Ankara, Istanbul, and Izmir; and the Botanical Grardens in Ankara are interesting cultural centres for all citizens. Science-related exhibitions are held in the large city fairs.

Printed Publications. Specially prepared adult education books, periodicals and encyclopedias containing popularized science, health and technology topics attract many readers.

Current Innovations

The age of entry of the primary school was changed from 7 to 6, beginning from the 1983-1984 academic year; general high schools were changed into comprehensive senior high schools, from the 1983-1984 academic year in a few pilot schools; teacher training colleges and other two-or four-year higher institutions will be linked to universities; a third science senior high school for talented students was opened at the beginning of the 1983-1984 academic year.

A revision and reorganization of the science curricula has turned general senior high schools into comprehensive senior high schools; a revision and reorganization of the science in two- or four-year teacher training schools has converted them into two-year university schools or four-year faculties; and a newly developed integrated science curricula has been organized for the basic education stage. Studies have also been made on the possible establishment of educational technology centres in schools.